ɔël Coward was born in ———————, ————————— on 16 ɔecember 1899. His professional acting career began in 1911 and in 1918 he wrote the first of his plays which was subsequently to be staged. He created a sensation as playwright and actor with *The Vortex* in 1924 and followed through with *Hay Fever* and *Easy Virtue* in 1925 and the operette *Bitter-Sweet* in 1929, for which he wrote book, music and lyrics as well as directing. His *Private Lives* in 1930 launched the stage partnership with Gertrude Lawrence which was renewed later in the thirties with *Tonight at 8.30*. Cavalcade, Design for Living and an autobiography, *Present Indicative*, were the other high-points of this decade. In the early forties *Blithe Spirit* was produced in London and Coward himself toured playing the lead in this and in *Present Laughter* and *This Happy Breed* for six months in 1942/43. He also wrote, acted in, produced and co-directed the film *In Which We Serve*. The forties also saw the films *Blithe Spirit* and *Brief Encounter*. In the fifties Coward began a new career as a cabaret entertainer as well as writing *Relative Values, Quadrille* and *Nude With Violin* and publishing *Future Indefinite*, a second volume of autobiography. He left England and moved first to Bermuda and then to Switzerland. In the sixties he turned novelist with *Pomp and Circumstance* and published his *Collected Short Stories* and a book of verse, *Not Yet the Dodo*. His play *Waiting in the Wings* was produced together with the musicals *Sail Away* and *The Girl Who Came to Supper*. He acted his last stage role in his *Suite in Three Keys* in 1966. He was knighted in 1970 and died in Jamaica on 26 March 1973.

NOËL COWARD

Future Indefinite

with the unfinished

PAST CONDITIONAL

and an introduction by

Sheridan Morley

Methuen

Published by Methuen 2004

1 3 5 7 9 10 8 6 4 2

Future Indefinite first published by William Heinemann Limited 1937
Reissued 1986 in a volume with *Future Indefinite* and *Past Conditional*
by Methuen London Limited; reissued 1992, 1995 by Mandarin Paperbacks;
reissued 1999 by Methuen Publishing Limited

This edition published in 2004 by
Methuen Publishing Ltd
215 Vauxhall Bridge Road
London SW1V 1EJ
www.methuen.co.uk

Present Indicative first published by William Heinemann Limited 1937

Methuen Publishing Limited Reg. No. 3543167

ISBN 0 413 77393 0

A CIP catalogue for this title is available from the British Library.

Typeset by SX Composing DTP, Rayleigh, Essex
Printed and bound in Great Britain
by Cox and Wyman Ltd, Reading, Berkshire

CONTENTS

ILLUSTRATIONS

INTRODUCTION

Future Indefinite, first published in 1954, deals exclusively with the war years of 1939–45 that were the years of *Blithe Spirit* and *Present Laughter* and *In Which We Serve*. But we also now have here the hitherto unpublished opening to what was going to be his third volume of memoirs, *Past Conditional*, written in the mid-1960s and dealing with the 'missing' 1930s that lay between *Present Indicative* and *Future Indefinite*.

Though only the first hundred or so typescript pages of *Past Conditonal* were completed by Noël, they seem to me to contain examples of all that was best in his own autobiographical writing: a travelogue of South America, hilarious Hollywood encounters with moguls and stars of a California world Noël had always managed to avoid, Broadway success in *Design for Living* with his beloved Lunts, diversionary notes on the piano-playing techniques of Jerome Kern and Irving Berlin, and a hauntingly sad passage on the death of a brother most people never knew he had, not to mention the final recollection of a short vicar from Noël's South London childhood whose brains were, in his father's view, far too close to his bottom.

Like Wodehouse, Coward survived to have the last laugh at his own critics; but occasional asides in *Past Conditional* indicate that their hostility especialy in the mid-1950s caused him considerable unhappiness, and certainly *Future Indefinite* was originally received with a lot less critical and public enthusiasm than *Present Indicative*. There were I think several reasons for this, and the first was its timing. Rather than continue with volume two of his memoirs from where *Present Indicative* left off in 1931, which would have been logical enough, Noël had come to believe that his war experiences in Paris and then on various troop and concert tours merited a book to themselves, despite the fact that he had already published in 1944 a *Middle East Diary* which was (as he explains in *Future Indefinite*) to get him into a great deal of Amerian trouble.

But by the time *Future Indefinite* finally appeared in 1954, readers had already had almost a decade of war memoirs and were eager to get on to something new: moveover (as his Diaries now reveal) this was a highly edited and somewhat cautious account of his war, and one inevitably lacking in any of the showbiz glamour with which his public rightly or wrongly now associated the boy wonder of *Present Indicative*. Noël's own feelings about the war and his part in it were often deeply confused, and the result, as the *Economist* reviewer noted, was that 'Coward is here painfully expatriated . . . success faithfully attends him, the eminent appreciate him, Royalty thanks him, audiences applaud him; but he remains somehow not "in", not orientated, uncertain of his proper role; a figure at once more complex and more sympathetic than one would conjecture him to realize'.

If *Present Indicative* was the story of a stagestruck boy becoming a star, then *Future Indefinite* is the story of a middle-aged man trying to come to terms with a world in total disarray. In there somewhere is, I believe, a lot of the truth about the way that the war changed Coward as it did so many men and women of his generation; but his audiences in the 1950s had already proved spectacularly fickle, and they certainly did not either want or expect from him a book that was a serious a documentary as *Future Indefinite*. The diary that he began keeping in 1941 (and that forms the basis for this second complete autobiography) indicates that he started thinking seriously about it in the September of 1947: 'I found myself talking about England so very proudly, though I was talking about England in the war years when her gallantry and common sense were marred by emergency. It is all very confusing. I think I had better get after *Future Indefinite* and get some of my confusion down on paper'.

That process was to take him the next five years, with pauses along the way for such various and different projects as the musical *Ace of Clubs*, the film of *The Astonished Heart* and two rather more successful stage comedies, *Quadrille* and *Relative Values*. But he kept returning to the typescript of *Future Indefinite* as if convinced that in there somewhere, in those logs of tours and troop concerts and the filming of *In Which We Serve* and the writing of *Blithe Spirit*, lay a kind of key to the way that he and his beloved England had been changed by the Second World War. That key proved elusive: by 1952 he was noting, very unusually, the need for some major rewrites ('last part too scurried and not objective enough') and it is clear that he found it a great deal easier to write *Present Indicative* purely from childhood memory than *Future Indefinite* with the help of all his contemporary notes.

Yet what finally emerged in 1954, not to hostility, exactly, but to a politely stifled critical yawn, is important for the altogether different light it throws on Coward as a man. Here we seldom find him backstage, or concerned except tangentially with the problems of his career: instead he is out on the road, doing war work that he sometimes finds either incomprehensible or pointless, but brought up time and again against the question of who he really thinks he is and what he is supposed to be doing with his life at a time when just hanging on to that life was often a full-time occupation.

Through *Future Indefinite* there is no doubt we get to meet an older, wearier, sometimes more confused and cynical man than the youthful achiever of *Present Indicative*: but what seems to me intriguing and important about both these fully-fledged autobiographies is that they are far from the typical or predictable greasepainted cuttings jobs one might have expected. Coward was an avid reader of autobiographies, and he knew a lot about what made the best of them work: he knew that lists of names or places or plays were disastrous, and that in the end the readers wanted to know who he was and where he came from as well as what he had achieved. He constructed these books as carefully as he constructed the best of his plays, and if they are not perhaps as consistently witty or upbeat as those plays then that is simply because he was Noël Coward, not one of his own creations like Elyot Chase or Garry Essendine.

It is of course unfortunate that he never completed *Past Conditional*, because on the evidence here I think that it might have been the most intriguing of all the autobiographies. He was writing it at just the moment when he was about to come back into critical favour after a long geographic and theatrical exile, and

freed from the constraints of the war diaries and his own childhood memories I believe he was beginning to write about himself
in his thirties with a clarity and perception that is not always
evident in the earlier volumes. But, in the words of one of his own
earliest and worst songs, 'ordinary man invariably sighs for the
peach out of reach', and what we have here now can be taken,
along with the Diaries that cover the remaining years of his life, to
represent the most complete picture of Noël that we have ever
been given from his own typewriter.

Sheridan Morley

Future Indefinite

FUTURE INDEFINITE: 1939–1945

WRITTEN: 1947–53
FIRST PUBLISHED: 1954

PART ONE

Present Indicative was the story of my life from birth until the age of thirty-one. It finished just after the production of *Cavalcade* when I embarked on a voyage to South America. The last line of the book was: – 'When we came up on deck there was no England left. Nothing but sea and sky.'

That was November 1931. It is now April 1948 and I am sitting looking out at a blue sea and sky, both far removed from the choppy, grey-green waves of the English Channel. Here there is no shadowy outline of the coast of France appearing out of the mist; there are no sea-gulls flying in thin, watery sunshine; instead there are buzzards; little banana-birds with yellow bodies and pink heads; humming-birds, and strange black creatures with long tails that dive for fish. I can no longer hear the noise of waves tearing away at the shingle, but in the distance there is the more muffled sound of surf breaking on the reef. This is the island of Jamaica and it seems to me to be a good place to start writing a book. When and where the book will be finished there is no knowing, but at the moment anyhow there is enough peace for me to begin it.

It took me four years to write *Present Indicative*, but then I worked on it spasmodically whenever there was enough time. It was something that I could only return to when circumstances allowed and my circumstances during those pre-war years were restless. I was writing plays, acting plays, directing plays, writing lyrics, composing music, making gramophone records, broadcasting and travelling. I was a highly publicised, irritatingly successful figure and much in demand.

Present Indicative was greeted kindly by the critics and was a success both in England and the United States. I read it through the other day and was pleased to find that it was better written than I expected it to be. The style is sometimes convulsive, there are too many qualifying adjectives, it is technically insecure and there are several repetitive passages which slow up the narrative, but on the whole there is little in it that I regret having said: from it there emerges enough of my true character to make it valid within the limits of its intention, which was to record the factual truth about myself in relation to the world I lived in, the people I met and the rewards I worked for and often won. Well, there it is, written and published and done with. For as long as it is in print or obtainable from second-hand book shops there will be people, possibly in diminishing numbers, who will be fascinated or repelled, charmed or unimpressed by the story of an alert little boy who was talented and determined and grew up to attain many of his heart's desires and who, throughout his childhood, youth, adolescence and ten of his adult years, remained consistently fond of his mother. This fact inspired many hundreds of people to write to me in glowing terms. It apparently proved to doubting minds that in spite of success and adulation, and beneath a glittering veneer of wit and vintage playboyishness, I had managed, with extraordinary strength of character, to retain a few normal human instincts. I must admit that I resent the basic assumption that the first gesture of any young man who makes good is to kick his mother in the teeth, but alas it is one of the most annoying disenchantments of success to be praised for the wrong things.

Readers who liked *Present Indicative* and expect this to be a straight sequel to it will, perhaps, be disappointed. For whereas *Present Indicative* covered thirty-one years this book will be concerned only with the years between 1939 and 1945. Not that those pre-war years were lacking in interest and variety. On the contrary they were rich in incident and I enjoyed living them. And I cannot agree with contemporary social commentators that they were so appallingly decadent and degraded. It is true that there was a certain flush discernible on the face of High Society – High Society in the Long Island, Paris, Riviera sense – but on the whole those poor maligned years were not nearly so bad as they are now

2

made out to have been. There were worse things going on in the twenties and thirties than casual amorality in the South of France and ostentatious parties at the Ritz. The Lido contributed less to future chaos than Geneva, and the propaganda of the Comintern throughout the modern world swayed our destinies far more than the perfumes of Chanel.

The temperature and tempo of millions of lives rose and increased in August 1939, but for me the pre-war past died on the day when Mr Neville Chamberlain returned with such gay insouciance from Munich in 1938.

In the December of that year I produced a revue in America called *Set to Music* with Beatrice Lillie as the star. In February 1939 I went to Honolulu with the express purpose of writing a play for myself but wrote some short stories instead. These were later published under the title of *To Step Aside*. In March, feeling that another crisis was imminent, I returned to England. During April and May I stayed in my house in the country and wrote two plays: *Present Laughter* and *This Happy Breed*. I planned to appear in both of these myself in the autumn, acting them on alternate nights with the same company. They both turned out well in spite of the fact that while I was writing them I was aware that they would in all probability never be produced, at least not at the time that I intended them to be. This dismal clairvoyance was ultimately justified. However, bathed, as we all were at that time, in a glow of Governmental optimism and complacency, it would have been churlish to take too gloomy a view of the future and so I persevered, finished them, cast them, presided at our annual Theatrical Garden Party for the Actors' Orphanage, of which I am president, and found myself in the middle of June with six weeks free before I started rehearsals in August. In more ordinary times I would have gone directly to the South of France or Venice or somewhere where I could relax and lie in the sun, but I was oppressed by my own views of the general situation. My mind was uneasy and I had an urge to see for myself a little of what was going on in Europe. I discussed this with Robert Vansittart at the Foreign Office, who was wise and helpful, and a few days later I set forth on a flying trip to Warsaw, Danzig, Moscow, Leningrad, Helsinki, Stockholm, Oslo and Copenhagen.

2

The flight from Heston took about six hours with a brief halt in Berlin. I arrived at Warsaw at six o'clock in the evening, where I was met by Mrs Clifford Norton, the wife of the British Chargé d'Affaires, a representative of the British Council, and several Press reporters and photographers. Mrs Norton drove me in her car with a newspaper man who fired a series of questions at me all the way from the airport to the city. The theatrical ones I answered as concisely as I could; the political ones I evaded. I had always imagined Warsaw, I can't think why, as a grey-stoned, medieval town clambering up a hill; a town of dark alleys and narrow, crowded, twisted streets. And here it was, flat as a pancake, widely spaced, and predominantly yellowish in colour. This last was largely the effect of the evening sunlight and the dust, for it had been a stifling day with no rain to cool the air.

Mrs Norton left me at the Europski Hotel, where I gave a couple more Press interviews, ordered myself a dry martini and looked out of the windows of my room at the city. It appeared calm and secure in the dusk. Immediately before me was a large square, and beyond that the Foreign Office, an impressive white building guarded by sentries. Lights were coming up all over the town and from just below in the hotel terrace café rose the chatter of many voices to the accompaniment of a string orchestra playing a selection from *La Tosca*. There seemed to be a feeling in the air, indescribable really but quite definite, that all this was artifice expertly contrived, an admirable façade behind which the real issues were being decided.

In course of the next few days I explored the city and talked to many people, at least those who could speak either French or English, and most of them could. I met musicians, artists, writers, actors, soldiers, airmen and politicians, in all of whom I detected the same fatalistic conviction that war was not only inevitable but imminent. In none of them did I observe the faintest fear or doubt as to the ultimate outcome. They had complete faith in their Army, their Air Force, their leaders, and their own indomitable

4

spirit of resistance. They were cheered and encouraged by their alliance with Great Britain but the wiser ones doubted that any practical aid we could give them would arrive in time.

There were many gay incidents, adventures and experiences, many pleasant personal contacts and parties and fun in those two weeks. Warsaw had much to give to the casual traveller. It was a light and charming city. The Painted Square is now, I believe, in ruins, but at least I have a memory of its coloured houses, the baroque charm of its florid, faded designs, its twisted porticos and crooked steps. The ageing and ageless sense of the turbulent past brooded over it and gave me the impression that it was hanging there, suspended in time, like an ancient tapestry draped over the shining, clean walls of a modern museum.

Then there was a week-end I spent in the castle of Lancut, the home of Count Alfred Potocki and his mother, Countess Betka. She was a remarkable woman; exquisitely gowned, fluent in several languages, shrewd, efficient, and with the most thorough-going feudal point of view I have ever encountered. The whole atmosphere of Lancut was feudalism rampant. Myriads of servants; a private theatre; a private orchestra composed of about fifty stable boys and grooms, which played the house-party into church on Sunday morning and out again in time for lunch. Before this it gave a few brassy selections in the vast courtyard. On the Sunday morning that I arrived it played 'God Save the King' in my honour and I had to stand to rigid attention, touched by the gesture, but nevertheless in desperate fear that I might burst out laughing, not from any patriotic irreverence, but because one of the trombones was about half a tone off key, and I knew from the bandmaster's expression that he as well as I was painfully aware of it.

After dinner that night the house-party assembled in the theatre to watch a film made up chronologically of some of the famous people who had visited the castle in the past. We saw the Archduke Franz Ferdinand walking very quickly along a garden path only a few weeks before his assassination at Sarajevo; the Kaiser, jerky and jocular, at a shooting party; the Baronne Eugene de Rothschild, then the Countess Schonborn, wearing what appeared to be a white night-gown, and acting with considerable verve in an impromptu mystery drama got up a little too obviously on the spur of the moment during some gay, vanished house-party in the early nineteen-twenties. There were many other famous people and crowned heads and statesmen, driving coaches or having picnics or sipping tea on smooth terraces. There was a certain Family Album nostalgia about the whole film. Those animated, swiftly-moving figures, many of whom were long since dead, making silent jokes, laughing soundlessly, lighting cigarettes, sitting down and getting up, nodding and beckoning and calling noiselessly to each other across the lawns and through the trees, gave me a sense of finality, almost of doom, and yet a doom that seemed to hover perilously near the ridiculous. Whatever sentimental reveries may have been stirring the hearts of my fellow guests, they were sharply interrupted when suddenly the late Queen Marie of Roumania flickered at immense speed across the screen in a barouche, and the Roumanian Ambassadress, who was sitting next to me, burst into tears and had to be led out.

Early the next morning I left with Prince Carol Radziwell to drive to Cracow. He was a charming young man serving in the Polish Air Force, and he drove with an abandon that either betokened nerves of steel or complete lack of imagination. He held strongly developed anti-Semitic views, about which I argued with him whenever we hit a straight piece of road. The country through which we drove for several hours was beautiful, although the small towns and villages seemed dilapidated and poverty-stricken. We certainly did pass a lot of Jews of the biblical sort with dusty caftans and matted black beards, who, although they looked harmless enough to me, if a trifle untidy, were commented upon by my companion with a rising flood of invective in both English and French. I realised quickly that any efforts of mine to convince him that in my experience there were a great many Jews extant who were intelligent, sensitive, generous and kind, and a great many Christians who were the exact opposite, were doomed to failure at the outset, so I gave up the whole thing and led the conversation, whenever possible, to less controversial topics.

Upon arrival in Cracow we explored the sombre, haunted medieval parts of the city for a couple of hours before driving out to the Radziwill castle a few miles away. The sky was overcast and there was a light, thin rain falling. I was aware of a gentle melancholy in the air as we turned into the drive; the trees rustled mournfully and the house seemed to be waiting for us with polite resignation. It was as far removed from Lancut in size, design and atmosphere as the Petit Trianon is from the Kremlin. Carol's father, a handsome, greying man in riding clothes, met us in the hall with several enormous dogs. I was shown into a dim, red-tapestried room on the ground floor with a bathroom adjoining, so that I could have a bath and a rest before dinner, both of which, after that dusty and agitating drive, I badly needed.

That whole evening remains in my memory as charming and strange and unreal as though I had dreamt it. The house was lit by lamps. Everybody was in black because a relative had recently been killed in an air crash. The food at dinner was simple and exquisitely cooked; candlelight flickered over the dining-table, and the conversation, in French, murmured on quietly to the accompaniment of the rain, which by then had developed into a downpour and was beating insistently against the windows. After dinner we went into the drawing-room, where tea was served with little cakes. Inevitably the approaching war was discussed, and again I was aware of that fatalism, that resigned determination to accept whatever was to come, and do the best they could about it. I remember Prince Radziwill saying that it wasn't so much the Germans he feared as the Russians, and looking at him, the typical, high-bred, courteous, urbane and so much hated aristocrat, I sadly saw his point. Later, some time after the fall of Poland, I heard that the Russians had shot him, but in the early months of nineteen-forty Carol appeared in Paris, having escaped from a concentration camp in Roumania, and told me that his father and family were still alive but had been turned out of their house and were living in the servants' lodge on a few roubles a month.

At about eleven o'clock that evening Carol drove me into Cracow to catch the midnight train to Warsaw. He waved cheerfully to me as the train moved out of the station, a dashing figure in his Air Force uniform, and I waved back with equal cheerfulness, but I felt depressed.

On my return to Warsaw I received a message from the Foreign

Office to say that Colonel Beck would receive me at six o'clock on the following evening. Anthony Eden had given me a letter of introduction to him the day before I left London, which had been duly handed, by the Nortons, to one of the Foreign Office secretaries. I had been warned tactfully that it would be much appreciated by His Excellency if the international situation was *not* discussed. This I found damping, as my principle object in wishing to see him was to discover as much as I could of what he thought and felt about the imminence of war. However, I rose above my disappointment and presented myself obediently at the Foreign Office the next evening with a few carefully rehearsed conversational gambits ready in my mind, ranging from the Lunts' performance in *Amphitryon 38* to Eve Curie's biography of her mother. I had been told by Anthony Eden that the Colonel spoke no English at all and that his French, though fluent, was guttural and difficult to understand, and so it was with slight trepidation that I finally arrived in his office. However, within the first few minutes all my fears evaporated. True, his French was guttural and a little hard to understand, but his personal charm was clear. He had a compelling eye, a polished manner, his navy-blue pin-stripe was soigné to the last degree, and he chain-smoked incessantly. Also the gay informality with which he plunged immediately into a detailed discussion of the international situation was extremely interesting. I had no opportunity of heading him off even if I had wished to, and the Lunts' performance in *Amphitryon 38* remained, as far as he was concerned, as though it had never been. He spoke rapidly and nervously; his face, strictly speaking, was ugly and arresting; his figure was taut and spare and he had a habit of twitching the corner of his mouth when he spoke. His attitude was tinged with the same 'Do or Die' bravado that I had noted elsewhere, but with the subtle difference that in him I didn't quite believe it. It was not that there was any lack of conviction in what he said, on the contrary he was more vehement in his assertions of the Polish powers of resistance than anyone I had yet talked to, but all the same I sensed a certain cynical realism behind his words not entirely consistent with what he was saying. It was a most entertaining hour that I spent with him. His humour was

8

infectious, the range of his knowledge and experience widespread, and his manner, even when talking most seriously, was devoid of the smallest trace of ministerial pomposity. He told me that in his opinion Poland would hold out against Germany for at least three months, and that even if by that time Britain had been unable to get sufficient aid to her, her resistance to the brunt of the first German attack would have provided England and France with enough time to prepare a smashing offensive. He went on to say that although in the interim Warsaw and other Polish cities would inevitably be laid waste, the spirit of the people would not fail, and if necessary they would retreat into the vast forests and plains of the hinterland and entrench themselves until the German invasion, however successful it might be at the beginning, fizzled out into inconclusive anti-climax. All this was most cheering, and I left him feeling that perhaps after all I had been over-dramatising my sense of foreboding. In the light of later events I have often recalled that meeting. I have heard sinister rumours of Colonel Beck's hurried retreat into Roumania in the heat of the crisis; reports of treachery, intrigue and cowardice. Whether they are true or not I haven't the faintest idea, but if they are I am very surprised. Possibly after all his French *was* too guttural and hard for me to understand, for he certainly didn't strike me as being a cowardly man. Ruthless and unscrupulous perhaps, but not a renegade. I shall continue to hope that my estimation of him was right.

Before leaving Poland I had one commission to execute, and that was to deliver a private letter to Professor Carl Burckhardt, the High Commissioner of Danzig. This project bristled with difficulties and had a certain E. Phillips Oppenheim tang to it owing to the fact that it *was* a private letter and I was unable to divulge to anyone in authority who it was from. Danzig, ironically designated at that time as a 'Free' City, was difficult to get to. The train service between Warsaw and Gdynia was suspended and the only means of transportation was an aeroplane which sometimes took off to schedule but mostly didn't. I hopefully booked a seat on it and telephoned, with some perseverance, to Professor Burckhardt to say that I was coming on the following Sunday morning to spend the day with him. It was necessary to have a special permit to pass from Gdynia across the line into the 'Free' territory, and this I had not got and was unable to persuade the Polish authorities to give me. As a matter of fact I doubt actually if they could have, as I was not going on official business.

The only hope of evading a possible sojourn in a Nazi jail was that the High Commissioner's car would meet me at the airport and whisk me across the lines in such an aura of officialdom that the sentries would be too impressed to halt and question me. Fortunately this happened. The car did meet me and whirl me swiftly across the frontier, and what is more the sentries smartly saluted me, which flurried me rather, as I had flung my hat on to the floor of the car and had nothing to take off and bow with in response; however, I waved and left them, still at attention, staring after me in some perplexity. Professor Burckhardt was a Swiss. He was a distinguished man and had, among other things, written an excellent life of Cardinal Richelieu. His French was neither guttural nor hard to understand, being pure Parisian without a trace of accent, his position as High Commissioner was obviously no sinecure and was growing rapidly more uncomfortable every day. He was fully aware, he told me, that he might have to duck and run at any moment. After I had delivered the letter, we talked for an hour or so before going for a walk in the town. In the course of talk he told me of three recent interviews he had had with Hitler, at one of which the Fuehrer had really lost control and shrieked the place down. I asked him if he hadn't wanted to laugh. And he said not until afterwards, because at the time it really was too alarming.

We walked through the beautiful old town and he pointed out its architectural and historical splendours to me; he also bought me a bottle of liqueur with flecks of gold floating about in it. It was a Sunday and so the streets were crowded. There were Nazi soldiers and officers stamping about, looking quite insufferably pleased with themselves. The ordinary citizens, I thought, looked less pleased, there was an air of furtiveness and apprehension about them. I had a feeling that if there were a tyre-burst or any other sudden, loud noise they would panic at once and disappear into their houses. We lunched with Burckhardt's family and soon afterwards I had to leave to catch my plane, which left Gdynia at four-thirty. I got across the frontier again without mishap and caught the plane all right, but I have seldom endured such an uncomfortable and frightening flight. We ran into an electric storm immediately after leaving the airport, whereupon the pilot, misguidedly I am sure, decided to fly home at an altitude of about fifty feet. We bumped and banged and rattled, frequently missing the tops of trees by inches, and I descended at Warsaw, bright green in the face, with a splitting headache and reflecting bitterly that if the military pilots of Poland were anything like the civil ones the war was lost before it started.

My last few days in Warsaw were uneventful although sociably agreeable. With the Nortons and others I lunched and dined in open-air restaurants, devoured thousands of red river crayfish, listened to little string orchestras in cafés and under the trees, drank thick, sweet mead made of honey in a dark tavern in the Painted Square, consumed a formidable amount of vodka and generally enjoyed myself immensely. There were other, grander junketings as well, notably a resplendent dinner-party given by Anthony Biddle, the American Ambassador, and his wife. The house was lovely and the garden even more so, and the whole party was a glittering success. I believe that it was the last one they gave before the war crashed into the land and destroyed for ever that house and garden together with so much more that was graceful and charming. Finally, on an airless, sultry night, I was conveyed affectionately to the station by several of my newly-acquired friends and seen into the train for Moscow. Once more I waved with a cheerfulness that I was far from feeling. Once more that sense of valediction and doom descended upon me. The figures of my friends on the platform dwindled into the distance as the train bore me away. I think only one of them is alive today.

3

My train arrived at the Russian frontier at six o'clock in the evening. It was breathlessly hot and the flat countryside was bathed in golden light, but stretching across the sky was a belt of ominous, black storm-clouds.

I had had no time to procure a Russian visa before leaving London, and for the last two weeks the British Embassy in Warsaw had been working hard to get one for me and had, at the last minute, succeeded. There was no possibility of getting a diplomatic stamp or a *laisser-passer* as I was not a member of the diplomatic corps and had no official reason for wishing to enter the country. Nor was I coming in under the aegis of the Intourist agency or the Vox, which is a cultural relations organisation which officially sees to it that any aliens visiting the Soviet Union are shown exactly what the State wishes them to be shown and nothing more. I was making my entrance alone, unheralded, unprotected, and with the added stigma that the destination marked on my entry form was the British Embassy in Moscow. This, although I was unaware of it at the time, was unfortunate. Nobody had told me that not only the British Embassy but all the Foreign embassies in Russia were regarded with the utmost suspicion, and that anyone attached to them, or even visiting them, was, to the simple-minded Russians, inevitably a secret agent. This naif misapprehension caused me a great deal of inconvenience. Luckily, however, I have travelled enough to be immune to the vagaries of Customs men and passport officials. A detached defence mechanism begins to function automatically in me the instant I set foot in a frontier station. I resign myself quite cheerfully to hours of inactivity, to waiting about, being questioned and having my baggage ransacked. I sit down whenever I can, usually with a book; I smoke if I am allowed to; if not, I rise above it, having learned long ago that any display of temperament, any fussing or fuming or resentment, merely makes matters far worse and prolongs the whole tedious business. On entering Russia, however, this philosophic detachment was strained almost to breaking point. For four hours I was questioned, stared at, whispered about and sent ricochetting back and forth from office to office and from official to official. My passport was scrutinised all ends up. My bags were unpacked to the last sock and every garment minutely examined. My dressing-case, which is my own special design and contains enough of the little necessities of travel to last me for a year, is fitted, among other things, with a small medicine chest containing band aid, iodine, aspirin, etc., a hypodermic, various pain-alleviating drugs, castor oil in capsule form, and a small phial of anti-tetanus serum. This outfit, although I have used it comparatively little, has been a great comfort to me on my journeys through tropical jungles and the more out of the way parts of the world. The Russians were so intrigued with it that they forced me to explain slowly, and in detail, the whys and wherefores of every drug and every bottle. This necessitated a lot of expressive pantomime and after a while I began to enjoy myself. I had a fair success with my performance of an anti-tetanus injection, but my great triumph was a graphic impression of the effect of the castor oil capsules. This, to use a theatrical phrase, had them in the aisles! In fact two of my inquisitors laughed until they cried. Finally, after answering all their questions and acceding affably to all their demands, which stopped short only at a request for a specimen of my urine, I was allowed to re-pack my bags, under surveillance, and get into the Moscow express.

The wagon-lit was one of those spacious, old-fashioned models that I could imagine in its heyday conveying the late King Edward the Seventh to Baden-Baden. With the years it had accumulated not only an inconceivable amount of dirt, but a creaking, swaying gait, which gave me the insecure feeling that it might bounce off the tracks at any moment and roll majestically down the embankment. The restaurant car, in which for the first time in my life I was handed a plate with *enough* caviar on it, was of the same Edwardian vintage. The windows were wider and larger than any I have seen in any other train, and the whole coach gave me the impression that I was in a vast glass coffin. Outside, in the black night, the ominous clouds which I had noted earlier had launched themselves into a thunderstorm of demoniac violence, the noise of which, crashing against all those windows, was scarifying. I drank enough vodka to banish the 'Breaking of the Sixth Seal', 'Book of Revelation' sense of doom that had descended upon me, and staggered back to my wagon-lit, where, thinking it wiser not to undress and place myself between those grey, unalluring sheets, I lay down on the creaking bed and, after a while, went to sleep.

Early the next morning the train arrived, to my mind miraculously, in Moscow. Not only did it arrive but it got in only about an hour late, which, someone later informed me, was quite unprecedented. Gordon Vereker, the First Counsellor of the British Embassy, most kindly came to meet me and told me that he had arranged for me to stay in his house because there was a carnival week in progress and all the hotels were full. He was a cheerful, very typical Englishman, wearing a Palm Beach suit and no hat, for the weather was very hot. We piled my suitcases into his car and off we went. My first impression of the city as we drove out of the station was spectacularly unlike what I had imagined it would be. Once more there were wide streets instead of the narrow twisted ones that I had imagined. Again there was strong, hot sunlight, but whereas Warsaw, although dusty, had at least looked cared for, Moscow looked as though the streets hadn't been cleaned for years, which in all probability they hadn't. There were crowds of people drifting along the pavements, doubtless an extra number because it was carnival week. They were poorly clad the men without shirts or ties and the women mostly without stockings. This did not surprise me, for I had hardly expected to find the Russian proletariat parading about in silk hats and morning coats, and black satin and pearls, but what did surprise me was their appearance of aimlessness. Nobody seemed to want to get anywhere. I noticed no giggling, chattering young girls; no flash young men; not one expression on any face that could, by the wildest stretch of imagination, be described as gay. There was not much traffic apart from a few antiquated taxis, trains and bicycles. The surface of the road was bumpy and uneven and spattered with garbage and bits of paper, and the whole effect was depressing. Perhaps I was disgruntled owing to my none too comfortable night in the train. Perhaps my sub-conscious had built up such a wall of preconceived prejudices that I was unable to see over the top of it. Perhaps all these people were happy and vital and having a glorious time, but if they were, prejudice or no prejudice, their way of showing it was unconvincing.

By the time we reached the Red Square and the Kremlin came into view with its photographically familiar minarets and bulbous towers, the scene brightened a little but not enough. There were still fragments of orange peel and cabbage stalks and dirty bits of paper swirling about in the gutters, and there was still that drab, uniform mass of humanity moving along to and fro, quietly and lethargically as though one direction were as good as another, and in any case it couldn't matter less whether they got to where they had originally planned or whether they didn't. I thought of Blackpool or Margate during a carnival week – the bustle and noise; children playing 'tag' up and down the pavements and dodging in and out of the crowds; young men and women arm-in-arm wearing grotesque paper hats and blowing squeakers; bands and barrel organs blaring; ice-cream vendors and sellers of pink 'Rock' yelling their wares; the cheerfulness, the kindly, warm vitality of the English public on parade when it is really out to enjoy itself – and my heart was sad for these poor, bewildered, dreary-looking people drifting through their carnival week at such a slow tempo. Surely in the earlier days, with all their injustices and terrors, even the Russians must have had some lighter moments? Must every now and then have walked gaily through the streets to meet their lovers, or to say their prayers, or to go to a party? The carnival spirit is not and never has been solely the prerogative of capitalists and the aristocracy. On the contrary, in most of the countries I have visited, it is generally the poorer people who seem to have the real capacity for enjoying themselves; the rich are usually too bored and the middle classes too prim. I know it is an accepted theory that the English take their pleasures sadly, but as far as I could see the Soviets didn't take them at all, or perhaps there weren't any to take. At all events I have seldom been conscious of such a mass effect of general lethargy.

Gordon Vereker's house was cool and comfortable, and after we had had some coffee we went along to the Embassy, where I met Sir William Seeds, the Ambassador. He looked frail and strained, for he had recently been ill and also, for a long time, had had the unenviable task of dealing with the complex Russian mentality, and trying to thread his way through a labyrinth of inconclusive, quasi-oriental dialectic to find some indication of what their war policy was likely to be. The view across the river of the Kremlin was dramatic. Somewhere in the fantastic, architecturally tortured building was Stalin, the wily, all powerful, unpredictable enigma who, to date, seemed to have evaded every foreign issue, blocked every diplomatic approach and shown no indication whatever of whether he intended to side with the British or the Nazis, or if indeed he intended to side with either. The general opinion among the diplomatic corps was that he would remain on the fence until the last possible moment, but this was obviously only a guess, for few of them had even clapped eyes on him. At that time, of course, his ironic pact with Hitler was still veiled by the future, and nobody whom I talked to seemed to suspect that such an unpleasant surprise lay in store for us.

In the afternoon Gordon Vereker drove me out to the Stadium to see a football match. We arrived early and for an hour or so we watched a gymnastic display by groups of the Moscow Youth, both male and female. It was very similar to most other gymnastic displays, with the difference that the crowds seemed to be less demonstrative. Perhaps I was spoiled by a visit I had paid to the Stadium in Rome a year before when Mussolini had been present, looking like an over-ripe plum squeezed into a white uniform, and where each twist, turn and gyration of the contestants had been greeted with shrieks of rapturous approbation. There were few shrieks at the Moscow performance, but the general routine was identical except that the Italian Youth had looked a trifle cleaner. Here, row after row of muscular girls in shirts and shorts did handsprings and ran races; young men in singlets and shorter shorts flung themselves over hurdles, threw heavy poles into the air, and drilled, not very tidily, in various formations.

At last the football match began and I was delighted to see that they played with a red ball. The crowd cheered up a bit as the game progressed and it was a distinct relief to see them leaning forward on their benches and actually showing interest in something. Every now and then they applauded and I even heard a few cheers.

It was stiflingly hot and the stone bench on which we were seated was hard, and so after we had watched the match for about three quarters of an hour we decided that we had had enough and got up to go. At this moment a strange man and woman accosted me. They spoke perfect English and were representatives of the Vox Cultural Relations Organisation. They said that they would very much like to take me for a tour of the chief sights of Moscow the next morning. I accepted politely, noticing with interest that they neither looked nor spoke to Gordon Vereker at all. He explained to me later that it was very dangerous for Russians to be seen speaking to foreigners unless they had a specific reason for doing so. The Ogpu spies were everywhere and people who transgressed this rule frequently disappeared, presumably to Siberia, and were seldom seen again. He also told me that all members of the Embassy staff, including himself, were spied on and followed wherever they went, and that undoubtedly I would be too. I asked if the constant feeling of being watched didn't get on his nerves, and he replied airily that he was completely used to it and often handed the spy on guard outside his house a drink through the window.

That evening we drove out into the near country to dine with the Military Attaché and his family. On the way we had to draw into the side of the road and stop twice because a Commissar's car happened to be passing. The house was typically 'Tchekov' and was set in a grove of mournful trees. After dinner we sat on the veranda and talked and smoked cigarettes, and the atmosphere, in the long summer twilight, became even more familiar. The house, before the revolution, had belonged to some well-to-do family long since banished or murdered, and I had the feeling that their ghosts were still wandering among the trees and through the rooms, straightening an ikon on the wall, or pulling a curtain aside to look vaguely out at the lights of the city. It was so perfect a setting for anything Russian that I have ever read or seen that I fully expected Nazimova to appear at any moment in a dark dress and announce that she was absolutely sick of everything.

My hostess was an enthusiastic theatre-goer and she bewailed the fact, as also did I, that I wouldn't have an opportunity of seeing anything of the Russian theatre, as all the companies were on tour during the summer months. This was a bitter disappointment to me. So many people whose judgement I admired and respected had given me glowing accounts of the brilliance and efficiency of Russian acting and production. Lynn and Alfred Lunt had returned, a few years before, from a three weeks' holiday to Moscow, bursting with articulate and technical enthusiasm.

They led me, both talking at once, through every production they had seen. My impressions afterwards were confused, but I gathered beyond a shadow of doubt that as far as lighting, team-work, under-playing, and psychological subtlety were concerned, the Russians had left us a long way behind. In addition to the genuine pleasures they had derived from watching their beloved *Theatre* handled with such taste and imagination, Lynn and Alfred had been entertained by all the leading actors and producers and treated with much honour, as indeed they fully deserved to be. But all that, as I said before, was some years ago, and also they had come to the country respectably and correctly, and not, as I had, crept in inquisitively under the fence. At a cocktail-party given some days later by Gordon Vereker, the Russian correspondent of the *Daily Telegraph* delivered to me some gracious and welcoming messages from some of the principal Muscovite stars, together with the regret that owing to one thing and another they would be unable to receive me. I questioned him about this and he explained that, much as they would have liked to invite me to their houses, in the present circumstances, and without official sanction, it would be exceedingly dangerous for them. This was disappointing, but there was nothing to be done about it beyond reflecting sadly that in a state-controlled workers' heaven the Arts had to toe the line just as much as everything else.

On the morning following my dinner-party in the Tchekov villa, the Vox lady who had accosted me at the football match appeared in a dusty limousine to take me for a good-will tour of Moscow. Gordon Vereker, who had for some reason or other not been working at the Embassy that morning, asked if he might come too, but was politely refused. This put me into a bad temper to start with and I clambered into the limousine scowling. My lady guide, whose manner was sullenly affable, wore – unwisely, I thought – a short cotton dress which was none too clean and exposed, to an alarming degree, her short, hairy legs. She also smelt strongly of stale soup. We drove slowly through the hot streets of the city while she recited what she had been trained to recite, about the glories of the Five Year Plan, and the crèches where working mothers could deposit their tots for the day and collect them in the evening, and how, in so many years, everyone, thanks to the far-seeing and brilliant administration of the Soviet State, would be healthy and wealthy and wise and happy as larks. Every time we passed a scaffolding, which was far too often, she explained in detail just what the building under construction was going to look like and what it was for. Finally, as a sort of *bonne bouche* to finish off a morning of exquisite boredom, she took me for a ride in the Underground railway. Over this she really came to life; her eyes sparkled with enthusiasm, and her conversation lost some of its parrot-like monotony. We ran up and down steps, forced our way into one train, rode through a couple of stations and then forced our way out and into another. She chattered and laughed with all the naive excitement of a young girl being taken on the roller coasters at Coney Island for the first time. The trains were very high and glassy and there were only six stations in all – I think I am right about this, but I may be exaggerating – at all events they were each built in different styles of architecture and decorated with different shades of marble, and the total effect as we whisked through them was of a series of ornate gentlemen's lavatories. Finally we emerged into the sunshine, by which time the limousine had disappeared. I was hot and thirsty and suggested innocently enough that we might have a cooling drink of some sort. She at once assumed an air of stern disapproval and said 'No' with the utmost firmness. We walked along the crowded pavement for a little until mercifully, I spotted a taxi and hailed it. This seemed to shock her even more, but by this time I had the bit between my teeth and was too irritable and sticky to care what she thought. I asked her, without much fervour, if I could drop her anywhere, and again she said 'No,' this time with a furtive look over her shoulder, and I realised, by that one look, that the poor beast was terrified out of her wits. Obviously the limousine having disappeared had disorganised the whole performance, and here she was walking down a crowded street, not marked in the itinerary, with a dangerous foreigner. I also became aware that the taxi man was regarding us both with some suspicion, and so, realising that the longer I stayed talking to her, the nearer it would bring her to the salt mines of Siberia, I wrung her hand warmly, asked her to give the driver my address, jumped in and drove off leaving her standing on the kerb staring after me. She didn't wave.

Nothing of particular interest occurred during the rest of my stay in Moscow. I walked about the city, without official guidance, and tried to visualise it as it had been in the past, but without much success. It was too difficult to imagine Dostoevski and Tolstoy countesses, wrapped in heavy sables, driving in their droshkys through those hot dusty streets – perhaps they never visited Moscow in the summer months anyhow – at all events there was no imprint of their ghosts on the atmosphere, in fact there seemed to be very little atmosphere. The buildings in the Red Square were disfigured by enormous garish posters of various Commissars; there were a number of aggressively modern apartment houses, on every identical floor of which I presumed jolly proletarian families were living in crowded, communal bliss. There were lots of cinemas and advertisement hoardings, and everywhere masses and masses of people moving slowly along the pavements. The shop windows were filled mostly with strictly utilitarian merchandise and there seemed to be a glut of electrical fittings, radio equipment, pots, pans, kettles and brooms. Some of the big stores had made a slight bid for glamour by displaying wax models wearing rather curious underclothes, and in one window I noted an actual evening dress, but the wax model wearing it looked so ashamed that I hurried by with my head averted in order not to embarrass her further.

In all these lonely peregrinations about the city I was fully aware that I was being followed and watched assiduously, and occasionally I amused myself by going into a big store by one door, darting through it and nipping out by another. Also on one occasion I suddenly broke into a brisk trot and cantered up and down several side streets, but it was too hot to do it for long, and nobody seemed to pay the faintest attention anyhow. I only once identified one of my shadowers, an innocuous little man with a green velour hat; I had noticed him several times standing a little way away from me when I was looking in the shop windows. Finally, after I had doubled on my tracks once or twice and made quite sure that he was still near-by, I rushed up to him, shook him enthusiastically by the hand, and said I hadn't seen him for ages and how were Anna and the children? He looked very startled, mumbled something unintelligible, backed away from me, and I never saw him again. Whether or not he spoke English or understood a word I was saying I shall never know.

A few nights later Gordon Vereker saw me into the midnight train for Leningrad and, without regret, I waved good-bye to glorious Moscow.

4

The Leningrad express was a more modern and altogether more comfortable train than the one that had brought me from the frontier to Moscow. My sleeper also seemed to be reasonably clean and I was able, without dismay, to undress and get into bed. I lay awake for an hour or so meditating on the defects in my character that made it so difficult for me to feel enthusiasm and sympathy for this great economic and social experiment that I was seeing, briefly, at first hand. 'Briefly', of course, was the operative word. I was being far too swift and flippant and superficial over the whole business. I should have stayed longer – perhaps taken a small grey flat, and asked many more searching and more intelligent questions. I should have tried to learn a little Russian and plunged into the lives of the people, and gone to live on a collectivist farm for a few weeks before daring to criticise a vital revolutionary movement of which so many intelligent minds in England thought very highly. True, comparatively few of them had been to Russia even for so short a time as I had, but they had obviously read a lot and taken a great deal of trouble and gone into the matter thoroughly. I remembered, some time before, seeing photographs of Lady Astor and George Bernard Shaw in the papers on their return from a brisk tour of the Soviet Union. I forget exactly what they had said to interviewers, but the impression I got was that they were brimming with admiration and enthusiasm. I remembered also talking to Walter Duranty in New York, who spoke glowingly of the charms and Communist-

Social delights of life in the USSR. I have heard that in later years his enthusiasm had cooled somewhat, but this may be merely hearsay. At any rate it was evident that there was something sadly lacking in me, some missing core of human understanding, that debarred me from sharing, with so many intelligent and thoughtful people, the belief that Communism, as practised by the Russians, was progressive and hopeful for the future of mankind. As far as I could see, the Communism propaganded by the Comintern in other countries was widely different from that which existed in Russia itself. Here, in this vast territory through which my train was carrying me, there seemed to be no semblance of freedom for the ordinary citizen. He was spied upon, regimented and punished, frequently without even being aware that he had committed a crime. He was kept arbitrarily in ignorance of what took place in other countries, and risked prison or deportation to Siberia if he spoke freely to any alien visitor who might enlighten him. His working days and his holidays were alike ordered by the State and, cruellest of all, he could have no trust in his heart for his fellow men, any one of whom might be a police spy and betray him for saying a careless word or making a foolish joke at a party.

Personally I have always believed more in quality than quantity, and nothing will convince me that the levelling of class and rank distinctions, and the contemptuous dismissal of breeding as an important factor of life, can lead to anything but a dismal mediocrity. I have frequently seen on the newsreels informatory documentary films about animal life which dealt with the crossbreeding of cattle and showed proud and noble pigs and prize bulls and racehorses being sent abroad, having fetched enormous prices, to compete with lesser alien breeds. I have observed the immense care with which professional greyhounds are weaned and cosseted and trained, great importance being given to who their mothers and fathers were and to the classy, impeccability of their ancestral line, and I cannot help feeling that it is retrogressive rather than progressive to rate the human race at a lower level than their money-making four-footed friends.

I was met on the platform at Leningrad by a lady who seemed to have stepped directly out of the film of *Maedchen in Uniform*.

She wore her hair scragged back behind her ears, a black coat and skirt, and large boots. She fixed me with a compelling eye and I knew immediately that there was no trifling with her. She announced that she represented Vox and that everything had been arranged for me, and, after organising my baggage out of the train and into a waiting car, she drove me briskly to the Astoria Hotel. The Astoria Hotel in past days of lighter social significance had obviously been well run, well furnished and luxurious. Now, however, it appeared to have wilted a bit. A marked divergence of taste was apparent in the decoration and furnishing. Whereas originally the curtains had probably been quiet and unobstrusive and the lamp-shades designed to fit discreetly into the general décor, now all was changed. I suspected that some artistic Commissar's wife had been given the job of re-doing the whole thing and had attacked it with enthusiasm but a defective colour sense. The loose covers and curtains in my dusty suite were so noisy that I almost had to stop up my ears. The wall-paper came under the heading of 'Le Jazz' and had obviously been copied from a railway hotel in Northern France in the early nineteen-twenties. My 'Maedchen in Uniform' left me alone to unpack and I rang for the floor-waiter, feeling that some strong black coffee might alleviate my claustrophobia. Presently he arrived wearing a bottle-green black coat and greyish-white trousers. Fortunately he spoke a little French and so when I had given my order I began to question him casually about life in Leningrad. He immediately became embarrassed and kept on shooting hunted looks at the telephone on the desk and, following his eyes, I observed that the receiver was neatly balanced just off the hook, a trick that I remembered clearly from the 'Nick Carter' detective series that I used to read in the Union Jack library when I was eight years old. Ignoring the poor waiter's pleading expression I sat down at the desk and went on with the conversation, speaking slowly and distinctly. I asked him why everyone in Russia looked so depressed and why the Commissars drove about in large cars while the ordinary people had to fight their way into crowded buses and trams. I asked him if the early days of the glorious revolution had been fun, and whether or not he had got any personal satisfaction from persecuting the hated bourgeosie, or if he had merely stayed quietly at home hoping that the excitement would soon be over. I gave him a glowing account of the Midland Hotel in Manchester and said that, in many ways, it was comparable to this one except that there was a slight shortage of vodka and the décor was brighter. After a little while I realised that the strain was telling on him and so I let him go. As the door closed behind him I lifted the telephone receiver and said: 'That will be all for the moment. Thank you so much,' and hung up. Later, while I was unpacking, I became panic-stricken and wished that I hadn't been so flippant. I was haunted by visions of sinister Ogpu agents appearing suddenly and leading me off to a Russian jail. About an hour later another, much more taciturn, waiter brought my coffee. He had a wary gleam in his eye and looked at me coldly. I suspected that the first one was, at that moment, bumping along in the train on his way to Siberia. Presently, when I had finished unpacking and had my coffee, I decided to shave and have a bath. The bathroom was large and encrusted with marble; the rusty shower refused to work and so I turned on the bath tap marked 'Hot' and was startled to see a tadpole come out of it and vanish down the plughole. Later on, when I had dressed and gone downstairs, I spoke to the manager about it. I explained, as politely as I could, that although he might consider what I was saying to be alien propaganda, in England when we turned on a hot tap, as a general rule, hot water came out of it, whereas if on the other hand we wished for a hot tadpole, we turned on a tap marked 'Hot Tadpole' and, owing to the efficiency of our Capitalist State, a hot tadpole usually appeared. The manager received this gentle reprimand with the utmost courtesy and I walked out into the streets of Leningrad. I hadn't, however, got more than a few yards when my Maedchen in Uniform came up behind me and struck me sharply on the shoulder, which frightened me dreadfully. 'You will be wishing a guide,' she said firmly. I replied with equal firmness that I wasn't wishing any such thing and that I wanted to wander about on my own and gather my impressions of the city without instruction. She looked at me balefully, thought for a moment, and then said: 'There will be a guide for you this afternoon. She is a very fine guide. She will be awaiting you outside the hotel with a car at two-thirty.' With this she turned abruptly and left me. I walked on aimlessly, enjoying the sunshine and the feeling of the city, and wondering idly how many wretched little men in green hats were being hurriedly detailed to follow me. There were mercifully few people about compared with the teeming crowds of Moscow and those that were seemed to be gayer and cleaner and less lethargic. Perhaps the atmosphere had something to do with it, for here the atmosphere was clear and definite. Here it was possible to envisage the romantic past without stubbing your toes too sharply against the aggressive present; here there seemed still to be room for a few ghosts to walk along the pavements without being elbowed off into the gutter. I had never realised how beautiful Leningrad was nor with what exquisite taste it had been ordered and designed. The painted houses along the banks of the Neva, in the old days embassies and legations, were faded now and their light colours were peeling, but they still retained an air, a memory of former dignity. There was spaciousness and charm in the streets and squares, and the superb façade of the Winter Palace stared with grey serenity at the roof-tops and spires of the city. Here all the characters of Russian fiction could come to life easily: the countesses in their sables and droshkys that I had so missed in Moscow; the dashing young cavalry officers in bright uniforms, on their way to assignations with witty mistresses, who would give them scented tea from samovars and discuss the heresies of Anatole France and the latest opera or ballet. Here too the furtive anarchist with the smoking bomb, and the eternally oppressed masses glowering with hate and envy at all the glitter and extravagance. At least, I couldn't help reflecting, then, unlike now, they had something to glower at.

The dining-room of the Astoria Hotel was cool and dim and the tablecloths were filthy. I asked for caviar, which was not on the menu, and got it, doubtless because Vox, having arbitrarily taken my situation in hand, were determined that I should have no cause for criticism. I was glad of this, because it was large and grey and delicious. The chicken that followed it was also large and grey, but less delicious. The waiters who served it were small and grey, and their suits, which had originally set out to be white, were very grey indeed and looked as though they had been slept in. A string orchestra, with a heartless disregard for proletarian feelings, played a selection from *The Dollar Princess.*

After lunch I went into the lobby of the hotel and there was my old Maedchen again waiting for me. With her was a timid, pretty young woman with wide-set blue eyes and a charming smile. This, I realised thankfully, was to be my guide. When she had introduced us, Maedchen issued a series of hissing, last-minute instructions in Russian and escorted us outside to the car. I looked back at her standing rather forlornly on the pavement and suddenly felt sorry for her. Perhaps under that hard, laced-in bosom there beat a romantic heart. Perhaps, when released from the exigencies of her job, she was as merry as a gig and kept her whole family in stitches with her gay stories and bawdy jokes. At any rate I was grateful to her for not assigning to me a hirsute monster like the one in Moscow. My present guide, to whom I will allude from now on as Natasha, that being as Russian and as appropriate a name as any, was palpably nervous at first, but after a while she relaxed a little and even allowed herself to giggle occasionally. She began with the usual routine of carefully rehearsed propaganda and shied away when I said anything not relevant to the subject in hand. Gradually, however, I wore her down and persuaded her to speak about herself, her husband, who worked in a radio factory, and her child, who was eight years old and went to a State school and liked drawing animals. She had a nice voice and a pleasant manner and, when relaxed, seemed to be intelligent. Her English was extraordinarily good and she spoke with hardly any accent. Among other things she pointed out to me the Youssupof Palace where young Prince Felix, a gifted singer with guitar, had lured Rasputin with the promise that he would sing him some of the convulsive Russian gypsy songs that he loved so well. I looked at the house with interest, remembering the graphic account the Grand Duke Dimitri had given me in London several years ago of that macabre and confused episode. It was difficult to imagine a crime of such amiable surrounding. The house looked pleasant and primly aristocratic; there seemed to be no aura of dark horror about it and if there ever were it must have faded many years ago. I fully expected to see an ivory old lady come out of it, followed by her maid carrying a plaid rug, and step into a high electric brougham. I wondered if Rasputin, on arrival, had gone to the front entrance or the back, and whether or not he had the faintest premonition of what was going to happen to him as he stepped across the fatal threshold. I also wondered, still remembering Dimitri's story, how he could possibly have eaten so many cakes crammed with cyanide of potassium without twigging that there was something peculiar about them. In the end, of course, the cakes having proved to be ineffective, they had to shoot him over and over again. They had also had to shoot Dimitri's favourite dog (although what he was doing at the party I shall never know) to provide a reasonable explanation of so much gunfire in the middle of the night. They were then forced to drag the almost dead body of their obstinate guest into a car, drive it to the Neva and throw it over the bridge on to the ice, where it lay accusingly, like a black sprawling shadow in the moonlight.

I asked Natasha if we were allowed to go into the house and see the cellars where the preliminary gambits of the murder had taken place. She said 'No,' disapprovingly, and so we drove on.

During the ensuing days Natasha showed me many of the sights of the city: palaces, factories, boulevards, the inevitable crèches and several churches. When I asked her if it were true, in spite of State-issued instructions and a salutary massacring of the clergy in the early days, that religion still maintained a grip on the hearts of many people, she admitted, under pressure, that it was. I tried to get her to shed further light on this subject, but she began to look scared, and so out of consideration for her feelings I desisted. I tried also to talk to her, without undue emphasis, about our ways of life in the democratic countries as compared with those I had already noted in Soviet Russia. She listened politely enough but made no comment whatsoever, and I gathered from her strained silence that this subject also was taboo; that she had certainly been trained rigorously to barricade her mind against any conversation that smacked even faintly of enemy propaganda. Again for her sake I desisted because she was an intelligent, well-mannered woman and I had no wish to involve her in any trouble, but I had a sudden sensation of despair, of utter hopelessness for the future of the world in which a political experiment of apparently immense significance should, in order to achieve its obscure ends, have to be based primarily upon enforced ignorance; the denial of personal freedom, even of thought; and the organised debarring of an entire race from the slightest contact with any ideas of life other than those arbitrarily imposed upon it by a self-constituted minority.

On the day before I left Russia, vowing never, never to return if I could possibly help it, Natasha drove me out to Tsarskoe-Selo where the famous Palace built by the Great Catherine still stood among its trees and lakes, kept, doubtless, as a reminder to the vast numbers of people who visited it that the dissolute crimes of riches and Royal extravagance did not pay, and that here all that was left of their former tyrants and oppressors was the gaudy shell in which they lived. If pointing this moral was really the idea underlying the State's decision to leave the Caterina Palace more or less as it was in the past, I cannot feel that it was an unqualified success. Walking, with Natasha and several hundred others, through the exquisitely proportioned, sumtuously furnished private apartments, State apartments, dining-halls, ballrooms and galleries, I could not help noticing the rapt, fascinated expressions on the faces of my fellow sight-seers. The impact on them of so much beauty of design, so much colour, such unfamiliar grace and spaciousness, was quite startling. They whispered excitedly among themselves, pointed various *objets d'art* out to each other with little sighs of pleasure, and altogether displayed more mass animation than I had observed since my arrival in Russia. True, they didn't cheer, as the Moscow crowds had at the football match, but they certainly seemed to me to be happier and more alive. The moral implications of the spectacle appeared to be going by the board completely. I think the several professional guides who escorted them must have been aware of this, for their voices became shrill, and they flung themselves into frenzies of invective in a vain effort to lash their audience into the right mood of loathing and contempt. On our way out we passed through the main hall of the Palace and I noticed on one of the walls a large, garishly painted picture. It portrayed, with photographic realism, the terrible disaster that had occurred on the night of the coronation of the late Tsar and Tsarina when the grand stands, erected in a public park for the festivities, had collapsed, resulting in a wild panic and the death of many thousands. I remember reading somewhere that on that stifling summer evening the Tsar and Tsarina had sat in their private apartments, wretched and horror-stricken, listening to the carts, piled high with the bodies of the dead, rumbling by below their windows.

There was a large crowd collected in front of the picture and, haranguing them, a little man with a professionally fanatical expression and untidy hair. Occasionally his voice rose to a scream and he pounded his fist vehemently into the palm of his hand. I asked Natasha what he was saying and she replied, reluctantly, that he was explaining to his gaping listeners that the entire tragic accident had been planned and organised by the Tsar and Tsarina for political reasons! I walked out on to the sunlit terrace and down the steps feeling a little sick and extremely angry. In the car driving home I mastered my rage sufficiently to ask her whether or not she believed such nonsense. She blushed and said in a frightened whisper that frankly she didn't, but that she supposed that sometimes it was necessary to misrepresent facts in order to prove to the people how much better off they were now than they had been before. I restrained the torrent of furious argument that was bubbling up inside me and we drove home to the Astoria Hotel in silence. Maedchen met us in the lobby wearing her usual forbidding and suspicious expression and her black boots. I said good-bye to them both politely but with a certain brusqueness, explaining that I was leaving the next morning and thanking them for having done so much to make my stay in Leningrad pleasant. I then went upstairs, ordered some vodka, and packed my bags with feverish efficiency.

5

The journey from Leningrad to the Finnish frontier takes only an hour, and my relief when the train finally pulled out of the station was considerable. I felt exactly as though I had been let out of prison after serving a long term, and I wouldn't have been in the least surprised if a kindly chaplain had suddenly appeared and given me a change of clothes, five pounds, and a few exhortations to lead a better life in the future.

In 1939 the railway bridge crossing the river that separates Russia from Finland was painted half red and half white. I presume that now it is entirely red. The station on the Russian side was dirty and uncomfortable and swarming with small officials, some in uniform and some not and all inquisitive and suspicious. My luggage was again examined, but less meticulously than before; I was again questioned and cross-questioned, and made to wait about interminably while a yellowish gentleman with a cropped head and a spectacular wart on his chin thumbed through my passport and handed it in turn to several of his colleagues. Finally I was permitted to get back on to the train and sat there for an hour waiting for it to start. It was an unpleasant hour because I was ill at ease and beset with fears. I really had the sensation that I was escaping by the skin of my teeth and might at any moment be hauled out of the train and sent back to Leningrad for further interrogation. I cursed myself for having made foolish jokes; for having complained about the tadpole; for having asked too many questions, and for having, by my manner, made it too obvious that I had been unimpressed by what I had seen of Soviet life and activities. I envisaged gloomily the headlines in the English newspapers if I were detained in the Soviet Union on some trumped-up charge of espionage, and also the inevitable questions that would be asked by Mr Shinwell in the House of Commons. Mr Shinwell had already, on several occasions, displayed a flattering interest in my career, and was for ever popping up and enquiring sarcastically why I was doing this or that, and whether or not his honourable friends were aware that Mr Coward, at infinite cost to the British tax-payer, was being conveyed hither and thither in ships of the Royal Navy. I foresaw with dismal clarity that if the Russians decided to be unpleasant to me Mr Shinwell would have a field day. I looked out on to the platform and noticed a small group of officials in green uniforms, talking excitedly and pointing in my direction, and I was just about to slink along the corridor and lock myself into the lavatory when, at long long last, the train shuddered and grunted and began to move. I lit a cigarette with trembling nonchalance and left the Soviet Union, I hope, for ever.

The Finnish frontier station was most beautiful in my eyes; most beautiful and gay and clean. The officials were smiling and courteous, and one of them even seemed to like my passport photograph. The Customs men, god-like creatures with blond hair and gleaming teeth, marked my baggage without even looking at it, and I was ushered into the buffet, where a waitress, who was a cross between Marlene Dietrich and Lady Diana Cooper, brought me some ambrosial bacon and eggs and a bottle of Lea and Perrin's Worcestershire sauce. My fellow passengers – most of whom were Finns – appeared to be as sensitive to the change of atmosphere as I was. They chattered and laughed and made jokes with the waitresses and there was a holiday feeling in the air. There was a lovely smell too, compounded of roasting coffee, frying bacon, the geraniums in the window-boxes and the heady, intoxicating scent of freedom.

After lunch the train strolled on to Helsinki and I looked out of the window at soft summer hills and the glistening sun.

Sadly enough I have little to say about Finland beyond the fact that I found it enchanting and its people hospitable and kind. I say 'Sadly enough' because it is a dreary comment on human nature that recorded pleasure inevitably makes duller reading than recorded irritation and criticism. I found nothing to criticise in Finland and much to admire. I stayed in a comfortable, well-run hotel. I visited a charming country house belonging to the Baroness Vrede, in which there was some lovely furniture and several large tiled stoves. The food was simple and good and so was the conversation, in fact life itself there seemed to be simple and good and marred by only one discordancy: the threat of Russian invasion. Madame Vrede discussed this, as Prince Radziwill had done, with detached resignation, as though she had steeled herself against what was to come and had prepared her mind to accept the inevitable with fortitude. A year later I saw the opening performance in New York of Robert Sherwood's *There Shall Be No Night*. This moving tragedy, as originally written and played, dealt with the conquest of Finland by the Nazis. Later, when the Lunts performed it in London, the locale was changed to Greece, for by then the drama of Finland was over and done with, and its sad destiny no longer of dramatic interest; also it had not been invaded by the wicked Nazis but by the friendly and efficient Russians, a fact which at that time would have limited considerably the play's popular appeal. However, on opening night in New York as I watched Lynn Fontanne grimly and quietly loading a gun, and explaining as she did so exactly what she proposed to do when the invaders approached the house, my mind went back for a moment to Madame Vrede talking to me in the twilight of a summer evening only a short year ago. I remembered her gently ironic smile when I said, admittedly not with much conviction, that perhaps after all a Russian invasion might not be quite so bad as a German invasion. I remembered her sitting there on the terrace with her hands folded patiently in her lap and her eyes looking out over the wooded valley, and saying: 'They will come. We have no means of preventing them. And when they do, it will be all over.'

During my stay in Helsinki someone suggested that I should pay a call on Sibelius, who, although he lived a life of the utmost quiet and seclusion, would, I was assured, be more than delighted to receive me. This, later, proved to be an overstatement. However, encouraged by the mental picture of the great Master being practically unable to contain himself at the thought of meeting face to face the man who had composed 'A Room with a View' and 'Mad Dogs and Englishmen', I drove out graciously to call upon him. His house was a few miles away in the country and my guide-interpreter and I arrived there about noon. We were received by a startled, bald-headed gentleman whom I took to be an aged family retainer. He led us, without any marked signs of enthusiasm, on to a small, trellis-enclosed veranda, and left us alone. We conversed in low, reverent voices and offered each other cigarettes and waited with rising nervous tension for the Master to appear. I remembered regretting bitterly my casual approach to classical music and trying frantically in my mind to disentangle the works of Sibelius from those of Delius. After about a quarter of an hour the bald-headed man reappeared carrying a tray upon which was a decanter of wine and a plate of biscuits. He put this on the table and then, to my surprise, sat down and looked at us. The silence became almost unbearable, and my friend muttered something in Finnish to which the bald-headed gentleman replied with an exasperated nod. It then dawned upon me that this was the great man himself, and furthermore that he hadn't the faintest idea who I was, who my escort was, or what we were doing there at all. Feeling embarrassed and extremely silly I smiled vacuously and offered him a cigarette, which he refused. My friend then rose, I thought a trifle officiously, and poured out three glasses of wine. We then proceeded to toast each other politely but in the same oppressive silence. I asked my friend if Mr Sibelius could speak English or French and he said 'No'. I then asked him to explain to him how very much I admired his music and what an honour it was for me to meet him personally. This was translated, upon which Sibelius rose abruptly to his feet and offered me a biscuit. I accepted it with rather overdone gratitude, and then down came the silence again, and I looked forlornly past Sibelius's head through a gap in the trellis at the road. Finally, realising that unless I did something decisive we should probably stay there until sundown, I got up and asked my friend – whom I could willingly have garrotted – to thank Mr Sibelius for receiving me and to explain once again how honoured I was to meet him, and that I hoped he would forgive us for leaving so soon but we had an appointment at the hotel for lunch. Upon this being communicated to him, Sibelius smiled for the first time and we shook hands with enthusiasm. He escorted us to the gate and waved happily as we drove away. My friend, whose name I am not withholding for any secret reasons but merely because I cannot remember it, seemed oblivious of the fact that the interview had not been a glittering success. Perhaps, being a rising journalist, he had already achieved immunity to the subtler nuances of social embarrassment. At all events he dismissed my reproaches quite airily. Mr Sibelius, he said, was well known to be both shy and unapproachable. I replied bitterly that in that case it had been most inconsiderate to all parties concerned to have arranged the interview in the first place, for although I was neither shy nor unapproachable, I was acutely sensitive to atmosphere and resented being placed in a false position possibly as much as Mr Sibelius did. We wrangled on in this strain until we reached the hotel, where we parted with a certain frigidity. Later, troubled by conscience, I wrote a brief note of apology to Sibelius, who, despite the fact that his seclusion had been invaded and the peace of his morning disrupted, had at least received me with courtesy and given me a biscuit.

There were several other, less constricted, social occasions during the remainder of the time I spent in Finland that I enjoyed immensely. The people I met were uneffusive and genuine; they took me sailing along the coast, and we picnicked in the small bays and inlets and swam in cool, clear water. There was a little night life too, but nothing spectacular. I remembered a cabaret where a lady sang 'Deep Purple' in French and a gentleman gave a spirited rendition of 'I'll See You Again' on a xylophone. Altogether it was a gay holiday and only very occasionally, for a few brief moments, the shadow of the future lay across the conversation, and I was allowed to feel, as I had felt in Poland, the imminence of change and dissolution.

6

Stockholm in July 1939 had not only changed its clothes for the summer but had changed its atmosphere too. Perhaps my view of it was jaundiced by my growing conviction that the whole of Europe was headed for imminent catastrophe, and my imagination prejudiced by the sinister portents I had observed in Poland, Russia and Finland. There seemed to me to be a leaden wariness in the air. The people I met and talked to were outwardly friendly and hospitable as usual, but I sensed a hidden uneasiness in their attitude to me as a visiting Englishman, as though my presence among them, while not being immediately embarrassing, might through some incident, some change of circumstance, prove to be very embarrassing indeed. There were of course many Germans in the city, more, it seemed to me, than there had been when I was there before. There was a group of them at the next table to me in the dining-room of the Grand Hotel. They might have been high-ranking military strategists in civilian clothes, travelling salesmen, minor officials attached to the German Legation, or merely ordinary tourists. Whatever they were, I was convinced that they were all secret agents. I looked at them with cold eyes and an expression of superior aloofness that I hoped would convince them that I knew accurately and to the last detail all there was to know about their subversive activities. This apparently was a failure, as one of them winked affably at me, which forced me to turn my head away and look grandly out of the window at nothing.

The British Minister, knowing that I was going on to Norway, asked me if I would mind taking the 'Bag' with me on the night train to Oslo, and so, imbued with a sense of political importance, and carrying a courier's passport covered with imposing red seals, I boarded the train and locked myself into my sleeper. The early hours of the night were disturbed for me by visions of masked spies with skeleton keys forcing their way in, wresting the secret documents from my defenceless grasp, and leaving me weltering in a pool of blood. However, nothing happened at all and I delivered the 'Bag' to a vague gentleman in a bowler hat on the platform at Oslo the next morning. I spent only a few days in Norway because by this time I was becoming bored with darting from capital to capital when I might have been lying in the warm Mediterranean sunshine, probably for the last time for many years. The curiosity that had prompted me to embark on these journeys in the first place had been abundantly satisfied. There were no longer any doubts in my mind about the imminence of war and chaos and destruction. The atmosphere of every place I had visited was heavy with it. At home in the House of Commons Mr Chamberlain, goaded to exasperation by some of the younger members suggesting that in the face of growing European tension it might be a good idea to forgo the usual summer recess, had petulantly moved for a vote of confidence in the Government. This political curl-tossing had won the day and our Parliament was on holiday. The Prime Minister himself, I suspected, was probably at this very moment fishing in some quiet English stream, wearing a curious tweed hat, and dreaming happily of his inevitable niche in posterity. The man of peace who had saved the world. I remembered gloomily a witticism attributed to the late Lord Birkenhead: 'The most we can hope for from dear Neville is that he should be a good Lord Mayor of Birmingham in a lean year.' This was a lean year all right and showed every indication of becoming a great deal leaner. Mr Chamberlain however was not Lord Mayor of Birmingham, but the Prime Minister of England.

In Copenhagen, in spite of warm Danish hospitality and the charms of the Tivoli Gardens in summer, my nostalgic yearning for the South of France crystallised into a firm resolve to have just one more look at it, even if only for a week, and so I got myself on to a plane and flew, via Paris and Marseilles, to Cannes. I arrived in the evening, in time to look out of the window of my suite in the Carlton Hotel at the lights coming up along the Croisette. From the balcony of my suite I could see the whole sweep of the coast, far away to the right the Estoril mountains, smoky-grey in the moonlight, and to the left, over the glittering lights of the Palm Beach casino on the point, the dark shape of Cap d'Antibes crouching in the sea. Conflicting strains of music rose from the little bars along the Croisette, and below me, from the terrace of the hotel, came the steady buzz of voices broken occasionally by sudden laughter and the clinking of ice in glasses. The air was cool and gentle after the heat of the day and the sense of leaden foreboding that had oppressed me for the last few weeks evaporated. I felt that it would be somehow discourteous to tarnish the tinsel enchantment of that familiar playground with premonitions of death and destruction. It would be like a fortune-teller at a gay party announcing to a young woman flushed with happiness and vitality that she was to die of cancer within the year. Perhaps, after all, the imminent madness, cruelty and futility of war were not as inevitable as I thought. Perhaps there was still time for some miracle to happen; for some superman with strength and courage and common sense to cut through the vacillations of frightened politicians and stand up to the loud-mouthed braggarts who were bent on plunging the world into chaos. Perhaps even they, the Dictators, would suddenly, at the last moment have a change of heart; realise in a blinding flash of revelation that war was no solution, that it never had been, and never could be, and that the course they had set themselves must, in the long run, only lead them to ignominy and death. Then, with sudden desolation, I knew that there were no perhapses; that the destiny of the human race was shaped by neither politicians nor dictators, but by its own inadequacy, superstition, avarice, envy, cruelty, and silliness, and that it had no right whatever to demand and expect peace on earth until it had proved itself to be deserving of it. Saddened but not defeated by this reflection, I went down to dinner.

The preliminary tour of *This Happy Breed* and *Present Laughter* was scheduled to begin in Manchester on September the 11th and so I had only a week to bask in the irresponsible sunshine before rehearsals started. The sets and dresses were under way, and the cast all engaged and straining at the leash, so there was nothing but the destruction of civilisation to worry about. Leonora Corbett and Joyce Carey, my two leading ladies, were staying at Antibes, covered in Elizabeth Arden sun-tan oil and anxiously studying their scripts. Gladys was nearby on a private yacht. Somerset Maugham was in his villa on Cap Ferrat; Arthur Macrae, Marlene Dietrich, Alan Webb, Charlotte Boisselvain, Barry Dirks, Eric Sawyer, and countless other friends were available to lunch with, dine with, drink with, and swim with, and there were picnics on the islands with *langoustes* cooked in garlic, and crisp French bread and vin rosé; motor trips to Nice and Monte Carlo and San Tropez; occasional dressy evenings in the Casino enlivened by elaborate gambling systems, which usually resulted in anxious whispered calculations followed by quick dashes to the 'caisse' to change more traveller's cheques. There was also a very fast speed-boat which I hired recklessly at a fabulous price, feeling that at that particular moment any extravagance was justified. On the evening before I left for London I went off in the boat to say good-bye to Maxine Elliott in her lovely villa, the Chateau de l'Horizon. I landed at her little private jetty below the swimming pool and walked up the twisting path, shaded by oleanders, to the house. There was no house-party because Maxine was very ill, and the terrace and the pool, in the past invariably thronged with people, wore an air of sadness. Maxine

Elliott was wise and kind and good; her supreme selfishness, of which she frequently accused herself, lay in the indulgence of her own generosity. She entertained lavishly and with exquisite taste, and to stay in that house, which she had designed and built so lovingly, was a special pleasure.

I went upstairs into Maxine's bedroom. She was in bed, bitterly against her will, and looking more beautiful than I had ever seen her. She joked about her illness and said that she was a cat with nine lives, eight of which had been lived to the full; the next attack, she said in her charming deep voice, would be the grand finale. She grumbled a good deal about being forced to stay in bed, and railed against the doctor and Fanny, her beloved maid, for refusing to allow her to get up and walk about and play games and go for drives. I stayed gossiping with her for about an hour, and then, noticing a tired look in her eyes, I kissed her and went away. I stepped into my speed-boat at the jetty and it started, as usual, with a roar. When it was a little way from the shore I turned and looked back at the house, and there was Maxine, leaning against one of the supports of her balcony and waving a white handkerchief. Her white hair, her white night-gown, and the handkerchief were tinged with pink from the setting sun. I waved back and then the lovely picture became blurred, because I knew, in that moment, that I should never see her again, and my eyes were filled with tears.

The next morning Gladys and I flew back to England.

7

The next three weeks were devoted to rehearsing morning, noon and night. The cast was quick and enthusiastic and learned their lines; the plays began to take shape; there were no quarrels and no hitches; the sets arrived in the theatre ahead of time and were put up and everyone concerned seemed to be making an extra effort; to be inspired with a special urgency; like people in a tropical country who, hearing the wind rising, close and bolt the shutters and busy themselves assiduously with household tasks, hoping against hope that it may not after all be the dreaded hurricane.

The dreaded hurricane, however, was drawing nearer and nearer with horrible swiftness. All over the country hope was dying. Young men began to appear on the streets in uniform, looking proud and a little self-conscious. There was the usual crop of people in the know; people whose friends' friends had husbands working for the Government and who knew, on impeccable authority, that Hitler was bluffing; that the Germans were even less prepared for war than we were; that London was going to be destroyed completely on the coming Tuesday; that Mr Chamberlain was going to pop off in still another aeroplane and persuade everybody to kiss and be friends; and that Hitler had cancer of the throat and couldn't possibly live through the winter. So many people knew so much and the words and phrases and rumours with which they tried to comfort their listeners and themselves were so often belied by the growing fear in their eyes.

On the Sunday morning following the first week of rehearsals I was sitting in the garden of Goldenhurst with Jack and Natasha Wilson and Joyce. We had driven down the night before, elated with the progress of the plays, and trying to keep at bay the growing suspicions in all our minds that the war would come before we could open. It was a lovely morning bathed in peace and security. There was a heat haze on the marsh and the sun glinted on the sea in the distance. Joyce, I remember, was engrossed in the *Sunday Times* Crossword and we were all shooting facetious suggestions at her, when Cole came out of the house and said that Sir Campbell Stuart wished to speak to me on the telephone. As, I regret to say, I had never heard of Sir Campbell Stuart, I told Cole to say that I was out. He returned a little later to say that Sir Campbell would ring up again in an hour's time and that it was urgent. Upon being questioned he admitted that Sir Campbell had a peculiar voice and that the whole thing sounded rather fishy. Just before lunch Sir Campbell rang up again and I answered the telephone myself, and that was the beginning of one of the most violent detours my life has ever made. He certainly had a peculiar voice, but what he said was more peculiar still. He began by announcing abruptly that he could only speak to me for three minutes as he had to rush off to 10 Downing Street; that he had a matter of extreme urgency to discuss with me and wished to see me that night. I replied that that was impossible as this was my only day in the country and that I should not be driving up to London until very late. This didn't discourage him in the least, and he said that he would come to my studio in Gerald Road at midnight precisely, and did I like Paris? Slightly bewildered by this apparent irrelevance I said, with remote dignity, that I was devoted to Paris but it would really be more convenient if we could meet at some other time. 'It's very important,' he said. 'To-night at midnight,' and rang off. Irritated by this peremptoriness I rejoined the others, and when Robert Boothby arrived for lunch I asked him if he could shed any light on this strange character who had telephoned me out of the blue. He roared with laughter and explained that Sir Campbell Stuart was a director of *The Times;* that he had been a protégé of the late Lord Northcliffe and had worked successfully on propaganda in the last war. He added that he was an unusual man, not enormously popular in political circles, but that he had power and a great deal of drive. I would like to say here that the question of what exactly I was going to do in the event of war had been perplexing me for some time. Owing to my affiliation with the Navy through the Royal Naval Film Corporation which Lord Louis Mountbatten had organised in 1937, I knew that it was tacitly assumed by the Admiralty that I would be willing to work as a sort of welfare officer and organise entertainments for the troops both in shore establishments and at sea whenever possible. This, of course, would have been an easy solution of my problem, so easy indeed that I distrusted it. For many years past I had been privileged to be a guest of the Royal Navy in all parts of the world, and in every type of ship, ranging from the battlewagons to submarines. This will always be to me a subtle and most important honour. I am primarily a writer and a man of the theatre, and the major portion of my working life has naturally lain in capital cities. Realising a long while ago that, for a writer particularly, too much urbanity is limiting, I determined to travel as much and as far as I could, and mix with all sorts and kinds of people whose ways of living and views of life were as far removed from mine as possible. This was a deliberate policy and I had pursued it, whenever opportunity offered, since I was twenty. The slogan 'Join the Navy and See the World' had for me a special significance. I joined the Navy for the first time in Shanghai in 1930 when I was invited to take passage in H.M.S. *Suffolk* to Hong Kong. Since then I had joined the Navy and seen the world whenever I could possibly wangle an invitation.

Thus it was fairly obvious that if war came the simplest course for me would be to join the Navy again, in whatever capacity that was suggested, do what I was told as efficiently as I could and be done with further argument. I should be living and working among people whom I trusted and liked in an atmosphere with which I was pleasantly familiar. The state of war would of course change it to a certain degree, but the essentials would remain the same. Everything, including my personal inclinations, seemed to point in the same direction but for one formidable obstacle, which was my conscience. Perhaps, on looking back, it was nothing after all but my ego and not my conscience at all, but I felt at the time, and I still feel that I was right, that my mental attributes and my creative talent would be of more service to my country than any theatrical experience in organising entertainments. I know a number of people who could do this as well as, if not better than, I. I also felt, arrogantly perhaps that for me to spend the duration of the war sitting in offices in various shore establishments, dressed as a Lieutenant-Commander R.N.V.R. and arranging which artists should precede which, would be a waste both of my time and my capacities.

It was obvious that Sir Campbell Stuart was going to offer me a job connected in some way with intelligence or propaganda. It was also obvious, as he had asked me so pointedly if I liked Paris, that it would have some contact with France and the French. This fact prejudiced me in favour of the idea even before I knew specifically what it was. I have always liked France and the French people, and I spoke the French language with reasonable fluency, although with only a bowing acquaintance with its grammar. However, with a little concentration that could soon be remedied. Bob Boothby, who was driving up to London in the afternoon and dining at Chartwell, en route, with Winston Churchill, suggested that I should go with him and get Mr Churchill's advice before taking steps in any direction. This seemed to me to be a wise plan and so we telephoned, I was duly invited, and off we went. I had known Winston Churchill for several years but never very well. We had met from time to time, with Anthony and Beatrice Eden, with Diana and Duff Cooper, at Maxine's villa in the South of France, and I had been once or twice to Chartwell, where he had lectured me firmly but kindly about painting in oils instead of dabbing away at water-colours. He had always been courteous and agreeable to me, although I had a gnawing suspicion that there was something about me that he didn't like. This of course worried me, because the thought of there being anything about me that anybody doesn't like invariably worries me, and, naturally, the possible disapproval of Winston Churchill, whom I so admired and respected, ceased to be a mere worry and inflated itself into a major disaster. However, I determined not to allow these hypothetical doubts to impair my natural poise and make me uneasy in his presence. After dinner I played and sang to him some of my lighter songs which he has always liked, 'Mad Dogs and Englishmen' being his favourite with 'Don't Put Your Daughter on the Stage, Mrs Worthington' as a close runner-up. Altogether the evening might have been written off as an unqualified success but for the fact that the purpose of my visit was lurking in the shadows, and my instincts told me that whatever questions I wanted to ask him about my proposed war service should have been asked before dinner, and not afterwards, when the atmosphere was gay and relaxed.

However, time was passing and I had to get to London by midnight for my mysterious assignation with Sir Campbell Stuart, so I finally rose reluctantly from the piano and asked Mr Churchill if he would give me ten minutes of his time, as I was in a state of indecision and in need of his considered advice. He led me into another room and we sat down with a whisky and soda each, and I proceeded to explain, as concisely as I could, my situation with regard to the Navy; the problematical offer from Sir Campbell, and my own feelings as to the best service I could give to the country if it came to the point of war. It was, on the whole, an unsuccessful little interview. I was aware throughout that he was misunderstanding my motives and had got it firmly into his mind that I wished to be a glamorous secret service agent. I tried vainly to disabuse him of this by assuring him that nothing was further from my thoughts, and that even if my heart were set on such a course, the very fact of my celebrity value would prove an insuperable obstacle. I emphasised repeatedly my firm conviction that my brain and creative intelligence could be of more service to the Government than my theatrical ability. I think the word 'intelligence' must have been the monkey wrench, because at the mere mention of it he said irascibly, 'You'd be no good in the intelligence service.' I endeavoured, with growing inward irritation, to explain that I didn't mean 'The Intelligence' in inverted commas, but my own personal intelligence, which was not in inverted commas. He would have none of it, however, and went off at a great tangent about the Navy (which in any event was preaching to the already converted). Finally, warming to his subject, he waved his hand with a bravura gesture and said dramatically: 'Get into a warship and see some action! Go and sing to them when the guns are firing – that's your job!' With, I think, commendable restraint, I bit back the retort that if the morale of the Royal Navy was at such low ebb that the troops were unable to go into action without my singing 'Mad Dogs and Englishmen' to them, we were in trouble at the outset and that, although theoretically 'Singing when the guns are firing' sounds extremely gallant, it is, in reality, impracticable, because during a naval battle all ship's companies are at action stations, and the only place for me to sing would be in the ward-room by myself. At last, realising that little had been gained, and a great deal of my hard-won popularity at the piano lost, I thanked him for his advice and went sadly away. On the drive up to London I re-enacted the whole interview in my mind and came to several conclusions, one of which was that my facility for light entertaining, although I am grateful for it, can on occasions be a serious disadvantage. I saw Mr Churchill's point clearly. In his view I was primarily an entertainer, a singer of gay songs, and that, come rain or shine, peace or war, victory, defeat or bloody chaos, that was what I should remain. I knew also that his admiration for me in this capacity was wholehearted and sincere. But what he failed to realise was that I didn't sing and play nearly as well as he thought I did, and that I could do one or two things a good deal better.

There would obviously be countless opportunities in the coming years for me to sing to troops, and I was resolved to do it gladly whenever the circumstances demanded, but I could not and would not take a palpable line of least resistance when I knew in my innermost heart that if I were intelligently used by the Government, preferably in the field of propaganda, where my creative ability, experience of broadcasting and knowledge of people could be employed, I could probably do something really constructive instead of wasting the Government's time and my own energy in some set, time-serving routine. I do not think that my conviction over this was either extravagant or conceited, but even if it was, the motive underlying it was sincere. I was thirty-nine years old, and in the last war, when I was yanked into the Army at the age of eighteen, I had distinguished myself by falling on my head; resenting bitterly the Army, the war and everything to do with it; and finally ending my inglorious career as a soldier in an advanced state of neurasthenia in the Colchester Military Hospital. Psycho-analysts, after reading my account of this period of my life in *Present Indicative*, have advanced the theory that this neurasthenia was self-engendered and the outward manifestation of inner conflict; that the concussion and coma resulting from my fall on returning from musketry drill was in reality a form of hysteria induced by a subconscious escapism, a compelling urge to break away from the rigours of unfamiliar Army routine. This theory is probably correct except in one detail. My longing to escape was far from being subconscious. I would have done anything in my power to escape from the routine and regimentation which crushed me down to a level of despair that I had never experienced before and have never experienced since. The fall on my head was motivated by an unsubconscious wooden slat which tripped me up. The ensuing concussion and coma which lasted for three days I cannot vouch for, as I have no recollection of it. I only know that when ultimately I was discharged from His Majesty's service (with, I hasten to add, a small pension, which proves that someone must have blundered) it was the happiest day of my life. All that was in October 1918, and now, in August, 1939, I could look back over the intervening years and reflect gratefully that Fate had been prodigiously kind. With all their ups and downs and victories and defeats, they had been wonderful years and lived to the full. I had worked and played all over the world; achieved many of my ambitions and, above all, acquired a few friendships that could never die, and which would uphold me in whatever circumstances I might find myself, regardless of wars and changing worlds, until the end of my life. Now was the moment of all moments to think clearly and unemotionally, and to face facts honestly. If I bungled this moment, and by doing so betrayed my own code of morals, I should never be comfortable with myself again and, what is more, whatever books or plays I lived to write in the future would be inevitably and irrevocably tainted by the fact that I had allowed to slip through my fingers the opportunity to prove my own integrity to myself. That was how I felt in 1939. That was how I reasoned with myself, and that was what I sincerely believed.

The first step therefore was to decide what I wanted to do and then go ahead and do it. I arrived home on that fairly fateful evening just before midnight, and at twelve o'clock precisely Sir Campbell Stuart appeared. The ensuing interview lasted for about three hours and was highly enjoyable. The keynote of it was professional charm. We both worked hard and succeeded in charming each other to a standstill. Oddly enough, although it was such a set piece, that mutual charm session formed a very pleasant basis which has remained firm through many vicissitudes. Sir Campbell's appearance surprised me considerably because, having been told by Bob Boothby that he was a Canadian, I expected him to be broad-shouldered, breezy and rather tough. Instead, however, I was confronted by a tall, very thin gentleman with a ragged moustache, slightly projecting teeth and kindly, grey eyes. He wore a dark suit and, like my Maedchen in Uniform in Leningrad, large black boots. Unlike her, however, he had an irrepressible sense of humour and proceeded, in the first few minutes, to flatter me so outrageously that if it had not been for the twinkle in his eye I think I would have asked him to leave. He said, among other extravagances, that the reason he wished me to represent him in Paris was that he knew, on excellent authority, that I was revered and adored by the French nation; that my brilliance and wit was a byword from one end of France to the other; that Monsieur Jean Giraudoux, who at the moment was about to become the French Minister of Information, would take it as a personal compliment if I agreed to work on propaganda in Paris, and that my appointment as representative of Sir Campbell Stuart would do much to consolidate the 'Entente Cordiale'.

Fascinated by this news of my, hitherto unsuspected, importance to the French nation and relieved that Sir Campbell had not suggested that I should go immediately to the Maginot Line and sing a translation of 'Mad Dogs and Englishmen' to bolster up the morale of the *poilus*, I relaxed in a warm glow of self-satisfaction, and allowed further cascades of comforting flattery to wash over me. Presently, when the softening process had obviously begun to take effect, and Sir Campbell realised that I was about ready for the kill, he became suddenly practical and outlined clearly and articulately exactly what he wanted me to do. This was to go to Paris immediately on the declaration of war and set up, in his name, a Bureau of Propaganda in friendly cooperation with the French Commissariat d'Information. The propaganda was to be directed exclusively into Germany and Sir Campbell, from his secret headquarters in the English country, would supply me with directives and ideas, which I, in turn, would be required to discuss with the French. He informed me that as far as the English side of the business was concerned the whole organisation was complete and ready to operate immediately. He also told me that he would give me a Chief of Staff and whatever secretaries I needed, and that the Chief of Staff in question would be David Strathallan, the son of Lord Perth. He added that Strathallan, being a Viscount, would also impress the French very favourably. I remember remarking that if the French were so Debrett-minded, it would be better to get a marquis or even a young duke if there were any available. Sir Campbell rose above this with an indulgent laugh and continued to paint, in increasingly glowing colours, the picture of myself in the French capital, suave and brilliant, conducting the propaganda bureau with matchless efficiency and, by so doing, making an important personal contribution to ultimate victory. All this was gratifying, but I wasn't entirely convinced. To begin with, I felt that to deal with propaganda exclusively directed into Germany while other organisations were handling the neutral countries might lead to overlapping and confusion. It seemed to me that all propaganda should be under one head. Sir Campbell gaily agreed but said that unfortunately it wasn't feasible. We talked on and on and I told him of my tacit commitment to the Admiralty. This he also rose above with nonchalance. A great friend of his, he said, was a certain Admiral who, being the head of the Secret Service, could wield unearthly powers and could whip me out of my commitment without any hard feelings in any direction. He then told me that, if I agreed to work for him, I would receive no salary but that all my expenses would be paid; that I should have to start being briefed right away, which, in view of the fact that I was rehearsing during the day, would mean a couple of hours' concentration every night, and that the whole business would have to be conducted with the utmost secrecy. I was to tell nobody, not even my closest friends, and that if the Press should get an inkling of what I was up to it would be disastrous. I remember thinking at the time that this was perhaps a little excessive, but I did not realise then, although I certainly realised it later, that Sir Campbell had a romantic passion for secrecy. I think really that this was an amiable form of self-dramatisation. Whatever it was, it was destined to cause me a great deal of inconvenience in the future. At all events when he left at about 4 a.m. and got into his car, with a controlled furtiveness that the late Sir Henry Irving would have envied, I retired to bed in a state of considerable confusion. Sleep was out of the question for a long while and I lay in the dark trying to sort things out. In the main the idea seemed a good one, stripped of Sir Campbell's rococo compliments and viewed with a practical eye. It was a job that with hard work and concentration I might be able to do well. It would at least give me an opportunity to use my mind and my imagination, And it would also be utilising my position as a writer, for the French, unlike the English, had a wholesome respect for literary talent and actually considered artists to be people of importance. Balanced against these obvious advantages were many doubts that tormented my mind. I was not sure of Sir Campbell Stuart. I had never clapped eyes on him before in my life, and although he had been most courteous to me

I was in no way certain as to how far he could be trusted. For all I knew he might not have been Sir Campbell Stuart at all and the whole thing turn out to be an elaborate hoax. And yet as he had put it to me it had seemed sensible enough. I was a well-known British Writer. I was fairly popular in France. Propaganda was, or should be, primarily a writer's job. I finally went to sleep worried and undecided and dreamt that I was appearing as a clown in the Cirque Medrano and that Winston Churchill was in a box applauding vociferously.

The next morning I missed rehearsal and went to see Robert Vansittart at the Foreign Office. As a man whose wisdom and knowledge I respected and whose friendship I valued he seemed to me the most likely source of impartial information regarding Sir Campbell Stuart. I explained my situation to him and the offer that had been made to me and, rather to my surprise, he seemed to think it would be a good idea for me to accept it. He said, as Bob Boothby had said, that although Sir Campbell Stuart had many enemies in political circles, he also had many influential friends and was a man of energy and considerable ability. He added that if, after a month or so, I found that I was unhappy in the job, it would always be possible to resign from it and try something else. Fortified by this advice I went across to the Admiralty to see the Second Sea Lord, Admiral Pridham-Wippell. He received me with a pleasant but rather rueful smile and the first thing he said was: 'I hear you have been whisked away from us!' This, I must admit, startled me; it also impressed me with the fact that Sir Campbell was certainly not one to let the grass grow under his black boots. I told the Admiral, with the utmost sincerity, how sorry I was in one way not to be working for the Navy, but that in the face of the offer I had had I really felt that I ought to accept it. He agreed without rancour and wished me the best of luck. I left him, feeling rather miserable but at the same time relieved that I had anyhow made a definite decision.

The next two weeks were strenuous. I rehearsed the plays in the mornings, afternoons and evenings, finishing as a rule about ten-thirty, and went home to my studio. Then, sometime between eleven o'clock and midnight, Campbell Stuart himself would arrive or Colonel Dallas Brooks, Royal Marines, his second-in-command. Together or separately they briefed me on the details of what was expected of me and explained the intricacies of the organisation in England, all of which, I need hardly say, were of the utmost secrecy. The headquarters of Sir Campbell and his merry men lay sequestered in the depths of the English country-side, where I should have thought it would have been fairly easy to find by any German agent with the faintest enterprise. However there it was, secret as the grave and buzzing with hidden activities. Colonel Brooks was as charming as Campbell Stuart but in an entirely different way. He was large and good-looking and impeccably dressed in a blue pin-stripe suit. He had won a D.S.O. for conspicuous gallantry at Zeebrugge in the last war, and was a typical Royal Marine officer, which means that he was efficient, sentimental and had perfect manners. His delivery was measured and he seemed to have as great a passion for secrecy as Sir Campbell. Whenever I asked him any question which seemed to him to verge on the indiscreet, he would assume a veiled, quizzical expression and tap his nose with his forefinger. I liked him at once and he taught me a secret code which I was to use in moments of supreme urgency. It was a naïve little code and consisted mainly of calling people by different names. These names he wrote down on bits of paper and when I asked him if, after learning them by heart, I should chew them up and swallow them, he smiled dimly and said that that would not be necessary.

On August the 30th and 31st we had rough dress-rehearsals of *This Happy Breed* and *Present Laughter*, and both plays went through with remarkable smoothness considering that we were still over a week away from production. On Friday September the 1st the Germans invaded Poland and it was obvious that it would only be a question of days, or perhaps hours, before we were at war. It was a miserable company that assembled that morning on the stage of the Phoenix Theatre. They had all known, of course, that if war came we should not be able to open, but, like everybody else, they had been hoping all along for a miracle to happen. Now it was too late for any further hoping and we all said good-bye to each other and made cheerfully false prophecies for the future. Everyone behaved beautifully and there were only a few tears. Joyce and Gladys and Jack and I lunched at The Ivy as usual, and we were over-bright and jocular and made little jokes to tide us over.

On Sunday morning David Strathallan arrived at my studio, for we were to drive down to the Hush-Hush headquarters for our final briefing. Together we listened to Mr Chamberlain's lachrymose announcement that a state of war had been declared between England and Germany. Then we got into my car and drove off. David was intelligent and gentle, and I suspected that his obvious integrity would soon override French disappointment at his being a mere viscount. At any rate it was a great relief to me, knowing that we were to work together in the closest co-operation, to discover that he had humour and was not the type to be easily flurried by anything or anybody. We got as far as Lord's cricket ground when the air-raid sirens started wailing. It was a curious sensation, because although we had heard that particularly dismal sound before when the sirens had been tried out for practice purposes, now it was the real thing and for the first time I experienced that sudden coldness in the heart, that automatic tensing of the muscles that later on was to become so habitual that one hardly noticed it. A zealous A.R.P. warden appeared from nowhere and waved us to take cover immediately. We were ushered into a large apartment building and led down into the basement, which was rapidly becoming overcrowded. Everyone was calm, but one lady carrying a baby was in tears. I remember wondering whether this was going to be a real knock-out blow, a carefully prepared surprise attack by Hitler within the first hour of war being declared. It was an unpleasant thought and well within the bounds of possibility. More and more people came hurrying down, and I decided that if I had to die I would rather die in the open and not suffocate slowly with a lot of strangers at the bottom of a lift shaft. I hissed this to David, who agreed, and so we forced our way up the stairs and into the hall. Here, to my surprise, we found Morris Angel, the famous theatrical costumier, who said, ignoring the disapproval of the A.R.P. gentleman who was trying to force him down the stairs: 'I think this calls for a bottle of Bubbly!' He then led us up to his flat on the third floor, introduced us to his wife, who was very cross because the electricity had been cut off and her Sunday joint was ruined, and opened a bottle of excellent champagne. With this we toasted the King, each other, and a speedy victory for the Allies.

Hush-Hush headquarters was in Bedfordshire. Some kindly villagers in their Sunday best directed us to it, seemingly unaware that they were indulging in careless talk of the most dangerous kind. One man even offered to come with us on the footboard in case we missed a turning in the lane. We finally arrived at a gate festooned with barbed wire from which some very young sentries sprang at us with loud cries. We pacified them by showing passes and went on through an impressive park to the next line of defences, where the same process was repeated. At last, after we had been passed through an office, questioned, cross-questioned and, I think, finger-printed, we were escorted to Sir Campbell's private establishment, which was a mock Tudor villa some way away from the main buildings. It had an air of suburban peace about it, which was very soothing after the perils of the latter part of our journey, and we relaxed gratefully and had an excellent lunch. When this was finished Campbell took us on a personally conducted tour of the whole outfit, and most impressive it was. We were introduced to various heads of departments and a great many intricate operations were explained to us, very few of which I grasped. David, being more serious-minded than I, nodded his head wisely, made appropriate clucking noises, and gave every indication that he understood perfectly. I was much comforted by this, for it gave me an opportunity to study Campbell's technique in dealing with his staff. It really was an admirable performance. He was jocose, serious, gay and shrewd in turn; his personal approach to each individual was perfectly attuned to his psychological knowledge of them. He over-decorated occasionally, and was perhaps a little too ebullient, but the whole business was a superb exhibition of personality and kindly egocentricity. I could see clearly why he had good friends as well as powerful enemies. I could also see why he might very easily be distrusted in political circles. There was a childishness about him, his phraseology was too extravagant, and he seemed too eager to impress. In spite of and because of all this, however, my heart warmed to him and has remained warm to him ever since.

David and I, crammed with secret and confusing information,

drove back through the summer twilight to London. We were to leave on the following Thursday for Paris. David was going by train and boat with the luggage. I was to be flown across in a special plane with 'The Papers'. It all sounded very dashing and a trifle alarming. I dined quietly and went to bed early; and thus ended, for me, the first day of the war.

8

On the morning of September 7th I flew to France in a Vega Gull. There was only room in the plane for the pilot, the observer and myself. I wore a dark suit and a bowler hat and carried a gas mask in addition to various contrivances that had been hooked on to me: a parachute and a sort of inflatable belt for keeping me afloat in the Channel. I also carried a brief-case containing 'The Papers', most of which were marked 'Secret', and all of which were dull. It was a clear, lovely morning; the light was strong and the countryside, as it slipped away beneath us, had a shiny, model look as though it were not real at all but had been accurately reproduced in coloured papier mâché. The roofs of the houses were too red and the pine trees too green, and I felt that the traffic on the roads and the trains running along their lines might all suddenly stop dead if someone pulled a switch. The sky was a light, sharp blue with exactly the right amount of woolly clouds, and the whole idea of war, and the fact that my life was so violently altering its course, seemed quite inconceivable.

Apart from a couple of camouflaged planes that came up to have a look at us there was no sign anywhere that everything wasn't perfectly normal. A flight to Paris in a private plane; lunch on arrival, probably at Larue's or somewhere in the Bois, an afternoon of shopping or just wandering about, then dinner and a theatre. I had known many such gay, unsignificant arrivals in the past. I had always enjoyed arriving in Paris more than any other city in the world from the very early days when I had little money and used to go via Newhaven and Dieppe, first class on the boat, second class on the trains, sitting up with my head wobbling against the harsh lace antimacassars, and occasionally pulling aside the blind to peer out at the brightly-lit stations. Then later the ineffable pleasure of walking out of the smoky station into early morning; driving through the empty streets in a taxi; watching chairs being unstacked outside the cafés, and smelling that indefinable, pungent smell that belongs to no other city. This arrival would certainly be unlike all the others. The lightness in the air would be less, perhaps there would be none left at all. War had come again, and not only Paris but the whole world was changing, and there was no time to be wasted in irrelevant nostalgia. The snows of yesteryear had better melt as quickly as possible even from one's memory. We flew out over the Channel. The sea was flat calm and utterly deserted; it wasn't until we had almost reached the French coast that I noticed one self-conscious-looking freighter, which must have been going very slowly for there was hardly any wake at all. I looked back at England, still clear in the distance, and wondered dispassionately whether or not I should ever see it again. At that moment it seemed quite possible that I shouldn't. Paris was even less prepared for defence against air attack than London, and it was conceivable that the Germans might decide to start the war with a bang and bomb it to hell. I had been through all this before in my mind of course. I had spent many hours trying, not always successfully, to get myself into the right attitude of mind, but there had been difficult moments. A great deal had happened in the last few weeks and far too quickly. And now here I was, embarking on a new phase of life which was certain to be utterly different from anything I had known before. I would have to be painstaking and efficient, and force myself to tolerate routine and dullness, for I wasn't naif enough to imagine that running an 'Enemy Propaganda Office' in Paris was going to be breathlessly exciting. I hoped, however, for a few interesting and dramatic moments, and these hopes, I am glad to say, were not entirely unrewarded.

As the plane approached Tréport the pilot looked ruefully over his shoulder at me and said that he had to fire off a gun with coloured rockets; that there was a different identifying colour for each day of the week, and he had forgotten which was today's. He added cheerfully that the French might quite possibly shoot us down. I suggested that he fire off all the colours at once and see what happened. He did so and the effect was very pretty. Presently two planes came up and forced us to land. Then there ensued a lot of light-hearted explanation, the burden of which fell on me as neither the pilot nor the observer could speak French. Finally we were allowed to take to the air again and set out on the last lap to Paris. We plodded along at an altitude of a thousand feet without further incident. It wasn't very bumpy, so I was able to doze a little and go back in my mind over the last few days. They had been difficult days and I was glad they were over and that I was finally away. The worst had been a horrid drive down to Goldenhurst in the black-out to say good-bye to Mother and Jack and Natasha, who were waiting there until they could get a passage home to America. Joyce Carey came with me for company and Gladys Calthrop drove on ahead in her own car because she was taking some things down to her Mill. We caught up with her at the point just before Ashford where she turns off, stopped both cars, lit cigarettes and had a little light conversation. We were rather high and full of jokes about driving in the blackout, which was then, of course, new to us. I remembered Gladys flicking her cigarette into the ditch, making a cloud of sparks, which I pointed out was a direct invitation to the German Air Force to drop everything they had on to us. Joyce and I drove on. Ashford was dark and the streets were crowded, so we had to go slowly. There were no signs of life at Goldenhurst from the outside. When we got out of the car there was a lot of scuffling, and Jack appeared with a carefully shielded torch and led us proudly into the big room to show us his handiwork, which I must say was shattering. He had been very conscientious indeed. There were blue bulbs in most of the lamps; two bicycles leaning against the bookshelves, the windows were thickly veiled in black material; all very right and proper and indescribably depressing. The library was better because the curtains were naturally thick, and there were no blue bulbs. We hurriedly had a drink and became more cheerful. Natasha, looking lovely and business-like in dark blue trousers and a white shirt, was knitting a most extraordinary boot. She had christened it 'Horsey', and to this day I don't believe it ever had a companion.

I went up and talked to Mother in her room. She inveighed spiritedly against Jack's zeal in making the house look so dreadful. 'A lot of nonsense,' she said, 'I can't see my hand before my face, I nearly fell down the stairs, and the whole thing's idiotic!' We had food in the dining room, which was deeply shrouded, with only candles on the table. There was an unreal, nightmare atmosphere which was funny in a way, but our hearts were heavy. A little later all the good-byes were said and, with Joyce by my side dutifully prepared to light cigarettes for me, I drove away along the drive, up the hill to Aldington past The Walnut Tree; along the twisting bit of road to Smeeth station and the main road. On arrival at the corner where I had so often waited in the Ford luggage wagon to meet friends who had driven from London and guide them home, I remember wondering, not too sentimentally, but with a remote, affectionate detachment, if I should ever see Goldenhurst again. It had been important in my life for many years and I had done a great deal of work there. I had also done a great deal of work in other places. Goldenhurst was not essential by any means, nevertheless I should certainly miss its comfort. I should miss the early breakfasts downstairs in the library before a blazing wood fire; working all the morning staring out over the marshes to the sea; the evening drives to Gladys's mill with perhaps a complete act to read to her and Patience Erskine, and then driving back along the winding marsh roads in the late dusk with the headlights making patterns on the hedgerows. I should miss finally arriving home, leaving the car in the garage and walking across to the house, sometimes along the straight bit of drive from which I could see the light flashing at Dungeness, and sometimes by the crazy-paving path between the pond and the tennis court. I should miss the welcoming fire in the big room, and popping up to say good-night to Mother, if it wasn't too late, and then perhaps playing the piano for a little or sitting down with a whisky and soda and planning tomorrow's work. Happy days all right. Happy and productive and good. Then, driving away with Joyce through the black-out, it was part of the past already, but now, suspended between the French countryside and the sky, a different life, a different world. 'To remember with tears'? Perhaps. To remember anyhow with gratitude.

PART TWO

I

Paris, during the first weeks of September 1939, was dusty and deserted. Most of the main shops, restaurants, hotels, theatres and cinemas were closed; the streets, compared with normal times, were virtually empty and there was an arid mournfulness enveloping the whole city. Criss-crosses of paper disfigured many of the windows; the boulevards were lined with acres of vacant chairs and tables; the few people who were about looked furtive and worried, and there was no lightness in the air; in fact there seemed to be very little air, for the heat was oppressive and lay over the abandoned quais, squares and avenues like an absorbent grey blanket sucking up all moisture and leaving the atmosphere stale and devitalised. The Ritz, gallant to the last, was open – at least the Place Vendôme side was; the Rue Cambon side, however, had thrown up the sponge and lay shuttered and dark at the end of its long passage lined with empty showcases. One of the few relics of pre-war light-heartedness that remained open was Maxim's, and it was there that I dined on the night of my arrival with Captain 'Hookie' Holland, the Naval Attaché, who had left a note at the Ritz to greet me, bidding me to dine, and offering to help me with my job, whatever it might be, in any way he could. David Strathallan, who arrived in due course with our luggage, came too, and we ate caviar and *filet Mignon* and drank pink champagne just as though life in Paris was as gay and care-free as it so often had been. Albert, the *maître d'hôtel*, hovered and smiled and bowed as he had hovered and smiled and bowed for many years. Had we but known it, he was destined to continue to do so throughout the Occupation, for Air Marshal Goering later adopted Maxim's as his favourite restaurant. On this evening, however, such a far-fetched contingency naturally didn't occur to us; the degrading fate that France was to suffer during the next five years was still in the dark future, and the question of defeat and enemy occupation was beyond the bounds of possibility. Some difficult times might lie ahead perhaps; there might be a few air raids and discomforts and anxieties, but on the other hand no war lasted for ever, and there was after all and above all the Maginot Line.

Hookie, apart from his office in the Embassy and a secret hideout in the country where he hobnobbed with various French Naval executives, had the use of an office in the Ministère de La Marine just across the road. This, he explained, I could use whenever I wanted to make an urgent telephone call to England, for it had a direct line to the Admiralty from which I could be connected to Dallas Brooks at Electra House. Both David and I were delighted, for at that time apparently the only direct telephone line to London was from the Embassy and that, in our as yet ambiguous position, we obviously would not be permitted to use. To have achieved, through Hookie's kind co-operation, telephonic communication with our Chiefs on our very first night in Paris seemed to us a fabulous piece of luck and would, we hoped, be regarded as a striking proof of our speed and efficiency. True, Hookie told us that we should have to be careful what we said on the line because it was tapped continually, but, remembering my secret code, I was able to reassure him: 'That will be all right,' I said with a suave smile.

Our initial efforts to establish a smooth-running propaganda organisation in close and friendly co-operation with our French allies were not remarkably successful. The day after we arrived we called, as we had been told to do, upon a Captain of Marines who, Dallas had explained, had a shrewd, capable mind and, despite a somewhat unprepossessing appearance, was smart as a whip and thoroughly *au courant* with everything that was going on. We finally ran him to earth in the Hotel Danou, where he was sitting up in bed sipping milk and bismuth because he was suffering from stomach ulcers. He seemed depressed and not quite as brilliantly *au courant* with everything that was going on as we had been led to expect. We suggested that our first step must obviously be to contact Jean Giraudoux, who was the Minister of Information, and Andre Maurois, who, I had been informed, was his right, hand. The Captain gave a small, defeated belch and shaking his head gloomily said that he didn't think it would be possible to see Giraudoux or Maurois just yet, and that we had better look round a bit first and get our bearings; he added that in any event he didn't know either of them. He then expatiated at some length on the perfidy and folly of the French as a race, and spoke bitterly of some abortive interviews he had had with certain officials in the Commissariat d'Information. From the way he pronounced their names I gained the impression that his knowledge of the French language was still in the preliminary stage. Finally we persuaded him to rise from his bed of pain and take us to see an elderly Admiral at the Invalides, who apparently was the only Frenchmen to date who had evinced any interest whatsoever in the Campbell Stuart Propaganda Bureau.

Admiral Fernet, to our immense relief, was intelligent and helpful. He was also short and stocky, had twinkling grey eyes and had known Proust quite well. Our interview with him was at least agreeable and we left the Invalides feeling a little more hopeful.

In the afternoon I telephoned to Jean Giraudoux and was immediately invited to dine with him that night.

The dinner with the Giraudouxs was delightful. I picked them up at their *appartement* on the Quai d'Orsay and we all piled into a car – there were several other guests – and went to a 'Bistro' in Montparnasse where the food was delicious. Madame Giraudoux was charming. Jean-Pierre Giraudoux, her son, was charming, and Jean Giraudoux himself was charming as always. The other guests were gay and vivacious. We discussed the French Theatre, the English Theatre and the American Theatre; we talked of Jouvet, the Lunts, Helen Hayes, John Gielgud, Edith Evans, Yvonne Printemps, and Pierre Fresnay, who it appeared, had plunged Yvonne into despair by suddenly becoming a *zouave* and retiring into the secret fastness of the Maginot Line. We also discussed, naturally enough, Jean Giraudoux, Noël Coward, Henri Bernstein, Marcel Achard, Edouard Bourdet and the Comédie Française, which Bourdet had reorganised entirely, some said brilliantly, some said indifferently. A subject, however, that was not mentioned at all was Propaganda into enemy territory. I tried once or twice to get the conversation round to it, but each time I was frustrated and so I finally desisted and gave myself up to the pleasure of the evening.

A few nights later I dined with André Maurois, who, Campbell Stuart had told me, was to occupy the position of my 'Opposite Number'. André Maurois in his exquisite house in Neuilly seemed unaware of this peculiar distinction. We discussed French literature, English literature and American literature. We also discussed mutual friends and reminisced cheerfully about the various occasions on which we had met in the past, when there was no war or even threat of war and the glittering decadence of the 'twenties and the 'thirties was at its height. There was no one else present beside André and his wife, and so after dinner I thought it was time to get down to business. I took the plunge and told them firmly about Campbell Stuart and my position as his representative; I emphasised the importance of establishing, as soon as possible, a clear liaison with the Commissariat d'Information so that we might pool our mutual ideas about Propaganda-into-Germany, and tabulate concisely for our mutual benefit the directive policies of our respective Governments. Maurois laughed pleasantly, although I thought a trifle cynically, and said that it all sounded very easy and effective as I had put it but that he feared it might not be quite so simple to organise as I had hoped. He also said, what I had felt from the first, that propaganda into enemy territory as a separate operation was liable to overlap propaganda into neutral countries, thereby causing a great deal of confusion and waste of time. He explained various political intricacies concerning the Commissariat d'Information and Giraudoux's rather invidious appointment as Minister. He obviously thought highly of Giraudoux as an artist and a playwright but seemed sceptical of his administrative capacities. As far as he himself was concerned he was vague. Officially he was attached to Giraudoux, but the exact scope of his activities had not yet been defined. He implied fairly firmly that he did not think he would remain in this equivocal position for very long because, being bi-lingual, he felt that he would be more useful as a Military Liaison officer. He concluded by assuring me that he would do everything in his power to help me, and that if I was in the slightest doubt about anything I was to telephone him immediately. As at that moment I was in the gravest doubt about almost everything, it was as much as I could do to restrain myself from asking him the way to the nearest call-box. Realising, however, that such a display of flippancy might be undiplomatic I switched the conversation to lighter topics and, a little while later, warmed by his kindness, but chilled by the foggy indefiniteness of the whole situation, I drove back to the hotel, where I had a brief, discouraged talk with David, and went to bed.

By the end of our first week in Paris we had achieved a little, but not so much as we should have liked. After some telephonic bullying by me, Jean Giraudoux arranged for us to meet Professor Tonnelat, Monsieur Vermeil and a tiny, rather cross Colonel called Schul in the Commissariat d'Information, which, in gayer days, had been the Hotel Continental. All three of these gentlemen had been connected with propaganda during the 1914–1918 war. Professor Tonnelat was harassed but kindly, Monsieur Vermeil was less harassed but equally well disposed, and Colonel Schul was crochety from the outset. I gathered that he had little affection for 'Perfide Albion' and viewed David and me with considerable suspicion, in which I had to admit I saw his point. David, who for secret purposes of State had been created a bogus Captain of an unspecified regiment, looked exceedingly nice in his uniform but lacked military deportment. I was impeccably dressed in morning clothes and looked as if I might be on my way either to the Foreign Office or the Theatrical Garden Party. We were staying at the Ritz, which was undoubtedly a frivolous address, and no one in the Commissariat d'Information had ever heard of Sir Campbell Stuart. However, we pressed on and arranged to have meetings twice a week to discuss 'Directives'. As far as I knew, the 'Directive' of His Majesty's Government propaganda policy at that period was the drafting and dropping of leaflets in tens of thousands on to Germany. The R.A.F. unenthusiastically did the dropping, and the leaflets were closely printed admonishments translated from speeches by Mr Chamberlain and Lord Halifax. Their subject matter was concerned mainly with the fact that war was wicked and peace was good and that the Nazis had better beware because the Allies were very strong indeed and prepared to fight to the death to defend the democratic way of life. All of which was admirable, though a trifle inaccurate and more than a trifle verbose. Some time later I wrote in a memorandum that if the policy of His Majesty's Government was to bore the Germans to death I didn't think we had enough time. For this I was reprimanded. The Germans meanwhile were flooding France with lurid and most effective cartoons depicting carnal British officers raping French ladies in looted châteaux; and baths of blood into which grinning English Tommies were pushing French *poilus*. We had no way of knowing what teasing leaflets our own Government was having dropped over neutral countries, but we suspected gloomily that they were long-winded, moral and ineffective.

I went to the British Embassy to call on Sir Eric Phipps, whom I had known for several years, taking with me a letter from Sir Campbell Stuart. The letter was in an envelope marked 'Very Secret', which was enclosed in a larger envelope marked 'Secret and Confidential'. The Ambassador opened it with a quizzical expression, which turned out to be fully justified, for it was merely a letter of introduction explaining in general terms how charming I was, and how Sir Campbell hoped that Sir Eric would receive me with kindness and give me every consideration. Perhaps galvanised by this, Sir Eric gave me a dry martini and a very good dinner, during which he tried with wily diplomatic suavity to coax my secrets from me. I think he said 'What the hell are you up to?' but I may be misquoting him. At all events I was forced to admit that I hadn't the remotest idea. However, he kindly said that either David or I or both of us could attend the daily Ministry of Information meetings, which took place from twelve to one in a gilded room on the ground floor, and that if we wanted any help in any way the Embassy was always at our disposal. I was touched by this and also soothed, because I was beginning to feel fairly silly.

Perhaps here I had better warn the reader against condemning too hastily my flippancy in describing many of these incidents. Actually it is only now, over ten years later, that I can see those months in Paris in their proper perspective and laugh at them and at myself without bitterness. I am proud to say that even at the time my sense of humour did not entirely desert me, but I was deeply in earnest, and although I could not avoid realising quite early on that the job I had undertaken was neither so serious nor so important as I had been led to believe, I still felt that it had potentialities, and I was utterly determined to make a success of it within or without its limitations. David was equally determined and never for a moment allowed absurdities and discouragements to deflect him. My gratitude to him was then, and is still, profound. At all events we persevered doggedly and managed, after two weeks of cajoling, coaxing, writing and telephoning to Chefs-du-Cabinet, and insisting on interviews with any officials whom we considered might be useful to us, to get at least some idea of the obstacles we would have to overcome and the varying degrees of *laisser-faire* we would have to override before we could rent an office, set up shop and really start work.

During those two hectic and exasperating weeks I decided to avail myself of Hookie Holland's kind offer, and telephone to Dallas Brooks from the Ministère de la Marine to report progress. Feeling suitably mysterious, but without any noticeable disguise, I arrived at the Ministère after seven o'clock in the evening as Hookie had told me to do. No suspicious sentries challenged me and the whole operation was a good deal simpler than going into the Galeries Lafayette. There was a French P.O. in the outer office, to whom I said *'Bon soir'* graciously; he replied with a grunt and made no attempt to prevent me from going into the inner office. I gave the special number to the telephone operator, upon which I heard a shrill scream of laughter and, to my intense surprise, was put through to the British Admiralty immediately. Whether or not the operator was laughing at my accent or at a book she was reading I shall never know. I was put through in a few seconds to Electra House, where Dallas Brooks answered the telephone himself. I at once embarked laboriously on the code he had given me. 'This is Diplomat speaking,' I said. (Diplomat was my code name.) To this he replied rather irascibly, 'Who?' 'Diplomat,' I said again slowly and clearly, and then went on with a rush to explain that I had interviewed 'Lion' (Sir Eric) and established successful contact with 'Glory' (Giraudoux), but had not yet been able to get in touch with

'Triumph' (Daladier), although I had had a charming interview with his Chef-du-Cabinet, whose name I was unable to divulge as we hadn't got a code word for it— He interrupted me at this point by saying: 'What the bloody hell are you talking about?' Repressing my rising irritation I started from the beginning again, articulating very, very slowly as though I were talking to an idiot child. There was a pause and he said wearily: 'It's no good, old boy, I can't understand a word.' At this I really lost patience and explained to him the code, word for word. This foolhardy betrayal of an important secret must have shocked him immeasurably, because there was a moment of silence and then he hung up. I returned fuming to the hotel, where I typed out the whole thing in a letter which I marked 'Secret, Confidential and Dull'.

He explained some weeks later verbally that he had been asleep when I rang up and thought I was Reggie! An unsatisfactory explanation if ever I heard one. However, he tried to atone for his obtuseness by teaching me another code which really was a code. I think he must have known I should never be able to master it in a thousand years. It consisted entirely of numbers which had to be subtracted and added and multiplied, and as I was then, and still am, incapable of adding up a bezique score, no good ever came of it, and if ever I had been captured by the Gestapo they would certainly have had a tough time getting me to betray it. At the end of the first week of oppressive heat and anti-climax I decided to fly back to England, to explain verbally to Sir Campbell and Dallas Brooks our various difficulties, and to offer a few suggestions for surmounting them.

A number of planes flew to and fro daily, and, provided one had the slightest claim to officialdom, it was easy to get a passage.

David came to Le Bourget with me and saluted self-consciously as the plane took off. The heatwave was over; the weather was sharp and clear and, apart from the strange emptiness of the Channel, the outward aspects of the flight seemed to be much the same as usual; inside the plane of course the atmosphere was different from pre-war days: there were no women wearing mink coats and carrying jewel cases and hat-boxes, no stewards or stewardesses, and no clamorous children. Most of my fellow passengers were in uniform, and the few who were not looked inscrutable and, like me, carried brief-cases and gas-masks.

We landed at Hendon, where I managed to find an Admiralty car which drove me and two others to our destinations.

Upon arrival at Gerald Road I was greeted by Lorn (my secretary) with the gratifying enthusiasm usually accorded to a warrior returning home after several months in the trenches. Jack and Natasha were in London and, having at last succeeded in procuring a passage to America, were due to sail in a few days' time.

After telephoning to Mother at Goldenhurst to let her know that I was so far unscathed, I rushed off to Electra House, where Dallas Brooks and Campbell Stuart were waiting, without any visible signs of impatience, for hot news from the Propaganda Front. I fear that, as usual, my articulateness overrode my discretion; I talked a great deal and very quickly, outlining the frustrations, obstructions and general apathy that David and I had been grappling with, and pleading earnestly that our position in Paris should be clarified, not only to the French, but to the British Embassy and all concerned. I explained, with some bitterness, that the air of mystery and secrecy surrounding our endeavours was making us appear both pretentious and silly, and was also quite unnecessary because, in actual fact, nothing we were preparing to do was either mysterious or secret. I suggested that a Bureau of Propaganda was a normal institution in wartime and that although later on, when firmly established, it might conceivably be utilised as a cover for less open activities, at the moment of its inception it must be and could be nothing but what it was: an organisation for the dissemination of propaganda into enemy territory. They listened to my tirade indulgently and took me out to dinner at the Carlton Grill.

During the week-end I was invited out to 'Hush-Hush' head-quarters and treated by Sir Campbell, as usual, with the utmost charm.

On the Monday I flew back to Paris, having extracted from him a promise to come over himself as soon as possible and assess the various difficulties of the situation at first hand.

A week or so later he kept his promise and arrived, radiating vitality, accompanied by Major Tony Gishford, his secretary, and Dallas Brooks. David and I met them at Le Bourget with a hired car and whirled them in state to the Crillon. During the few days they spent in Paris I watched with interest Campbell's dynamic personality working at full blast. It was a remarkable performance. He flew from office to office and minister to minister; names were scattered through the air like confetti; projects of far-reaching magnitude were discussed, blown up like gas balloons, and exploded painlessly. Bewildered French officials were invited to lunches and dinners, charmed and flattered by his inadequate French but more than adequate persuasiveness, and although, at the end of it, both they and I were still hazy as to what it was all about, the immediate effect was impressive.

On the third day of the visit the same hired car drove us all to Arras to lunch with Colonel Mason-Macfarlane, the Director of Military Intelligence. The luncheon took place in the Hotel de l'Univers. The D.M.I., tall, grey-haired and a trifle bent, had a twinkle in his eye; he had also an individual, almost pedantic way of speaking, and a passion for light verse. I liked him at once and, later on in the war, when he was Governor of Gibraltar, I stayed with him frequently. His second-in-command, Major Gerald Templer, had a swift mind and was extremely nice, but I felt instinctively at the outset that they both viewed Campbell with suspicion. Under their polite, cold gaze, his lively affability seemed to wilt a little; his flattering implications splintered against their flinty disapproval, and even his personal charm took on a rococo quality. I was reminded suddenly of a comedian I had seen many years before giving an audition to a group of unsmiling managers and agents: in the face of their dreadful unresponsiveness his jokes fell flat, his antics became increasingly strained, and his whole performance, bereft of the laughter which alone could give it life, died coldly on the bare stage. Whether or not Campbell was aware that he was not being quite so easily victorious as usual, I don't know, but I suspect that he sensed the nip in the air.

Dallas remained bland and amiable throughout the meal; David looked slightly uneasy, and I, spurred on by an over-developed social conscience, wore myself out.

After lunch we all assembled in Mason-Macfarlane's office to discuss the intricacies of front-line propaganda and if, when, and how it could be coordinated with our less specialised, more general policies. It was finally decided that either David or I should visit the D.M.I. once a fortnight in order to exchange ideas and, by working together in happy liaison, eliminate, as much as possible, the prevailing confusion.

During the four-hour drive back to Paris Campbell was in the highest spirits. We had, he assured us, in an incredibly short space of time, formed a basis of solidarity between the front line and our organisation which, in the ordinary course of events, might have taken weeks or even months to achieve. 'There is nothing so essential in matters of this kind,' he added enthusiastically, 'as the Personal Approach.'

From then on things began to move. David and I were empowered to rent an office as soon as possible, and engage a carefully vetted, tri-lingual secretary. It was also suggested that I find a flat in a conveniently central position in which to entertain not only Mason-Macfarlane when he came to Paris but any other eminent gentlemen, either military or civil, who might be useful to us. Before leaving Le Bourget in a flurry of white snow and black boots, Campbell assured me with the most winning sincerity that not only was he pleased with my work, but absolutely astounded by the swiftness with which I had acquired a complete grip of the whole situation. 'You are doing,' he said firmly as he stepped into the plane, 'a more vital and important job for your country than either you or anyone else realise.'

Reflecting that only the last part of his sentence was accurate, I waved him away into the grey sky and drove back into Paris with David.

2

By the end of October quite a lot had happened. In the first place, Paris, having recovered from the initial scare of being bombed, had begun to come to life again: theatres, cinemas and restaurants opened timidly at staggered hours and staggered days of the week; more people and traffic appeared in the streets; the war clouds receded and banked themselves on the far side of the Maginot Line, and the autumn sun shone with all its might.

David and I obediently rented an office at Number 18 Place de La Madeleine, in which we installed some office furniture and a newly-found secretary, Miss Cameron. Miss Cameron was, from first to last, our greatest asset: she had a dry, Scottish sense of humour, her secretarial efficiency was beyond criticism, she could speak German, French and Spanish fluently, and her political morals, carefully vetted by the Deuxième Bureau, were impeccable. A tall Dutchman with a Scottish title, Lord Reay, was added to our staff. He was most agreeable and ploughed through the reams of secret 'bumph', which was sent to us daily, with a sort of sleepy diligence. Cole, my personal servant, was despatched to me from England by Dallas Brooks, and settled down at once to learn French, which he contrived to speak and read with surprising fluency in a very short space of time. Cole had come to me originally as cook-valet when I was playing *Tonight at Eight-Thirty*, in 1936; since then he had become an integral member of the household, and, after many years and many vicissitudes, he still is. The quality of his mind evinced itself early and Lorn and I soon realised that he was far better read than either of us. At the present moment of writing he has moved up to being my secretary, while Lorn has become my 'representative', a state of affairs that bewilders everybody but us.

With the aid of an old friend of mine whom I had originally met in Rio de Janeiro in 1931, Madame Guinle, I found a flat in the Place Vendôme. It was not large but it was light and gay and very convenient, being in the centre of Paris, and only a short walk from my office. In due course Cole and I moved into it, having bought some fairly expensive furniture at the Samaritaine de Luxe, and taken over the services of the *femme de ménage* Yvonne, who had worked for the previous owners. She was a voluble Lyonnaise, she saturated everything with garlic, and was very good for Cole's French.

About this time it was borne home to me that, although I could speak it fairly fluently, my own knowledge of the French language left a lot to be desired; I decided therefore to take lessons in grammar, and proceeded to look around for someone suitable to give them to me. Subsequently, on the the advice of Louis Jouvet, I interviewed a lady named Blanche Prenez, who agreed to come, either to the flat or to the office, on three afternoons a week, and try to force into my brain the intricacies of French syntax. I warned her in advance that this would be a difficult task, for she would almost certainly discover that she had to teach me English grammar at the same time. She light-heartedly accepted the challenge, and the lessons began then and there and continued until I left Paris finally in April, 1940. Blanche Prenez, apart from being an experienced teacher, was a most endearing character. Her age was somewhere in the late forties; she was dumpy, with twinkling blue eyes and hair that had been dyed several different shades on several different occasions and had at last achieved a variegated permanence. She was fiercely patriotic; she adored the Theatre and her criticisms both of acting and playwriting were shrewd and frequently witty. In addition to all this she contrived, by alternately bullying and cajoling, to instil into me a great deal more grammatical knowledge in a few months than anyone else would have been able to do in so many years. She kept after me remorselessly; she forced me to write pages of subjunctives, one of which was; *'Il faut que vous ne me guillotinassiez pas!'* She made me tell her long stories, during which she corrected me and interrupted me on every line until I could have throttled her; she made me read aloud *David Copperfield*, and translate it into French as I went along and, worst of all, she insisted that, in between lessons, I did homework. I fought like a steer against this but she overruled me, and I was compelled to spend miserable hours in bed, wrestling with the damned subjunctives, declining hideously irregular verbs, and composing bright, informative little essays about the events of the day, which she would gleefully tear to pieces the next time she appeared. Just before I left France I arranged for her to translate my book of short stories, *To Step Aside*, and, I am thankful to say, paid her for the whole job in advance; I have hoped ever since that the money was of some comfort to her, for I never saw her again. In England, in 1944, I received an anonymous message which said she had died of tuberculosis in Nantes; later on I heard rumours that, some while before her death, she had been arrested and tortured by the Gestapo. I have no proof of this, but, knowing her vituperative hatred of the Germans and her fanatical love of her own country, I have a dreadful suspicion that it may be true. I owe so much to her patience, her firmness, and her deep affection, and I should have been so proud if she could have seen me acting in Paris, in French with a French company, in 1948. I can only hope that she would have been proud too, but I rather doubt it. It is strange to recall that, during those gay lessons, we had a recurrent joke which concerned an English lady who spoke French so affectedly that she pronounced 'Dunquerke' 'Doonque-querker!' – an ominous, tragic word on which to base a joke.

Shortly after we had established ourselves in the Place de La Madeleine, I discovered a pleasant-looking, bogus Squadron Leader loitering in the annexe of the British Embassy. His bogusness lay in the fact that he had never been in an aeroplane in his life; the explanation of his uniform was that he was a radio expert and spoke French perfectly; and he was loitering in the Embassy annexe because he required an office to work in and there wasn't one available. Upon learning this I offered him accommodation in our office, which he accepted with grateful alacrity, and moved in immediately. Once installed, he proceeded to wreck, for all time, our one and only radio in the short space of half an hour. From then on he was known affectionately as the Squadron Wrecker. His name was Bill Wilson; he was tall and thin and had a French wife, and a slightly professorial manner which was entirely misleading. He led his own life in our office, where he had technical conferences from time to time with curious gentlemen from the B.B.C., and occasionally disappeared abruptly into the hinterlands of France, from which he assaulted us with highly-coloured postcards in verse.

Another addition to our personnel was Paul Willert, who was large, articulate and ready to argue heatedly on any given subject. He had a knowledgeable and bitter contempt for international politics; he spoke German and French, and lived with his wife Brenda and a small white poodle in the Place Dauphine. Their apartment was enchanting, and I often lunched or dined there, while the Seine flowed gently by under the windows and we discussed, frequently with considerable violence, the incompetence, negligence and stupidity of those in authority over us. Paul's gift for invective was highly developed and although he occasionally betrayed a certain facile intellectual defeatism slightly tainted with Bloomsbury, and was often madly irritating, I never had a dull moment in his company. In our office he represented the, by then, more furtive side of our activities. His function was to establish private liaison between us (Sir Campbell Inc.) and various reputable and disreputable refugees with whom it might have been indiscreet for the office to have direct contact. Often he would vanish for a while and reappear later wearing an expression of sinister prescience that was hard to bear.

Our staff was now complete except for Peter Milward, an irreverent and cheerful friend of Edward Molyneux's, who volunteered his services and was subsequently installed as a Press Scavenger. His job consisted of wading doggedly through all the French daily newspapers, from which he picked out anything equivocal, subversive or informative, and, having translated it and commented upon it, placed it on my desk. With this expanding *état-majeur* it was not surprising that we became rather cramped and were forced to move to a larger suite of offices on a higher floor.

By November the social life of Paris was in full swing again. Lady Mendl entertained in her famous Villa Trianon in Versailles; the Duke and Duchess of Windsor entertained in their house on the Boulevard Suchet; there were lunch-parties, supper-parties, dinner-parties, cocktail-parties, private views, opening nights; in fact all the clamorous paraphernalia of peace-time existence, with the one difference that we were at war. This embarrassing actuality brooded lightly over the festivities and was seldom obtrusive: the fact of its existence, however, inevitably affected some of the superficial aspects of society. It was considered 'chic', for instance, not to wear evening dress, except in the presence of the Duke of Windsor, who had announced in no uncertain terms that he liked *le smoking*; fortunately there were only a very few mutterings of rebellion against this edict and a soigné time was had by all. There also appeared on the face of *la vie Parisienne* an unpleasant rash of functions and entertainments in aid of war charities. As yet, of course, there had been scarcely enough war to justify them, but they provided a form of occupational therapy for those of Le Gratin whose nerves had been cruelly jolted by the events of the last eighteen months. However, behind this gaily-painted social drop-curtain there was naturally a great deal going on. Droves of cabinet ministers and high-ranking staff officers flew back and forth between London and Paris, and were photographed, singly and in groups, looking appropriately grave. Conferences of far-reaching significance took place daily in the War Office, the Invalides, the Commissariat d'Information, the Quai d'Orsay, the Ministère de La Marine, and Maxim's.

My conferences, on a lower scale, were held twice a week, alternately in my office and in Professor Tonnelat's office in the Hotel Continental. They were, on the whole, fairly dreary. Occasionally Mason-Macfarlane with Ewan Butler or Gerald Templer appeared and enlivened proceedings a bit, but even so I cannot believe that much was achieved beyond the exchange of a few ideas which were seldom put into execution.

On January 1st, 1940, I began, for the first time in my life, to keep a day-to-day diary and, although it is neither detailed nor comprehensive and consists usually of little more than a small page of scribbled telegraphic sentences recording the events of the day, it has been of value to me in writing this book. To any reader other than myself I fear that it would appear fatuous to the point of idiocy. Few memorable aphorisms adorn its pages, and as it is written the last thing at night when I am tired and sleepy, it is slapdash, repetitious, and frequently illegible. Nevertheless, it serves its purpose as an aid to memory, and despite the fact that it has less literary value than a railway time-table, for me, and for me alone, it is evocative and, every now and then, curiously touching. So often when I open it at random I come upon a phrase, written in the long vanished heat of the moment, that sends my mind hurtling back to stare in dismay at the picture of myself sitting up in some strange bed in some strange hotel or tent or ship, writing down the day's frustrations with an indelible pencil and a desolate heart. The Paris entries in this journal are, however, less poignant than some that came later on in the war, and I find, on re-reading them, that the deepest emotion they arouse is irritation. It was certainly a period of anti-climax, and although there was a tremulousness in the air, a sense of unease, it was too vague to weigh heavily on people's spirits; in fact it is questionable whether or not the large majority was even conscious of it. I believe, or rather I like to believe, that I was, but I am not sure. It is so easy, when reconstructing the past, to endow oneself with superior foresight. Of course I should like to feel that, however blind and obtuse others may have been, I was one of the few who really sensed impending disaster. It seems incredible now, in the lurid glare of later events, that I lived through those months without a twinge of premonition, but perhaps I did; perhaps, with so many of the people I knew, I averted my gaze from the sinister horizon and assumed that somehow or other everything was going to be all right. My diary, I am bound to admit, records no specific flashes of clairvoyance: it records annoyances; books read; lunches and dinners eaten; occasional diatribes against the incompetence of officialdom; convivial evenings with the D.M.I.; quiet evenings with Edward Molyneux. It also records the hectic arrivals and departures of Campbell Stuart and his entourage; some fairly acrid descriptions of 'Policy' conferences, and a few sidelights on characters and personalities; but nowhere in its pages can I find, alas, a nice meaty example of true prophetic instinct. I have searched through it meticulously hoping against hope to discover some illuminating phrase such as: 'Saw Daladier today – He says definitely, that France will be invaded, defeated and occupied in the early summer – Oh dear!' But no, the numbered days are void of prescience.

3

Gallantly determined to overcome my inherent detestation of fixed routine, I arrived resolutely at the office every morning between nine and nine-thirty and sat, swathed in supreme authority, at my desk. Miss Cameron bashed away at the typewriter in the next room, from which I gathered that she must have an extensive circle of acquaintances; large trays of papers were brought to me daily – the papers were mostly mimeographed copies of the B.B.C. Monitoring Service, which was efficient but verbose, and they were marked 'Secret', although any interesting information they contained had usually appeared in the Continental *Daily Mail* three days before. During our first weeks in the Place de La Madeleine, buoyed up by a grinding sense of duty, I read them through page by page, marking with a red pencil any items that might be of interest to our organisation, and passed them on to David, who marked what he thought might be useful to us with a green pencil. After this, as far as I can recall, they were never seen again. By noon the office was generally a hive of activity. Peter would appear brandishing a scurrilous attack on somebody or other in one of the French 'dailies'; Paul would put his head round the door and say, in a voice choked with sinister implication: 'I've got to meet someone at Weber's – I may be quite a long time!' – and disappear; David would burst in, white with rage over a letter from London H.Q. which had completely disregarded an urgent question he had written a week previously. Reay, who shared David's office, typed laboriously and interminably, although to this day I have not the faintest idea what he could have been typing. Occasionally odd people would come to see me; among them a madwoman who arrived one morning in a red hat, and announced that her husband had been killed in the 1914–1918 war and that because of this she had nourished ever since an undying hatred for the Germans. I nodded sympathetically and said that I saw her point. She then said, with a certain peremptoriness, that she wished me to arrange for her to be sent immediately to Frankfurt, that her cousin had married a metallurgical engineer there in 1932 and that this fact would provide good cover for her. I explained gently that the dispatching of secret agents to Germany was not my department, and suggested that she go to the Deuxième Bureau, where they specialised in that sort of thing. She asked me whom she should interview there, which flummoxed me for a moment, but I rallied quickly and said: 'General Poincingy-Duclos, and say that I sent you.' With this I asked David, who was purple in the face, to show her out.

Our big moment in the office occurred two or three times a week: this was the arrival of 'The Bag' from London. 'The Bag' was heavily sealed and contained, in addition to the inevitable wads of B.B.C. monitoring papers, our personal letters. It was always opened with ritualistic solemnity, and occasionally I spoke a brief incantation over it before the seals were broken. When we had all grabbed our private mail the intensive business of the office subsided until we had read them. My own letters were usually from Mother, Lorn, Joyce or Gladys, and occasionally a verse from Winifred (Clemence Dane). I found it nostalgic, immured in my Parisian vacuum to read titbits of gossip and news from my other life, which, it seemed, was going on very nicely without me: plays were opening and closing; so-and-so had fallen down in the black-out and bruised her knee; there had been a blazing row at the Actors' Orphanage between the matron and the headmaster; The Ivy was more crowded than ever at lunch-time; James Agate had said something disagreeable to Lilian Braithwaite, who had retaliated; the clock still stood at ten to three and there was honey still for tea. Frequently when too oppressed by these echoes from dear green England, I was compelled to leave the office abruptly and have a very good lunch. Of course I flew home to dear green England whenever opportunity offered, and this occurred on an average about once a month. I usually managed to arrive on a Friday, discuss whatever had to be discussed with Campbell or Dallas, and spend the rest of the weekend with my loved ones. They were happy interludes and I looked forward to them eagerly.

My first evening in London was almost always spent in Clemence Dane's rickety little house in Tavistock Street, Covent Garden. There we all foregathered: Gladys, Lorn, Joyce, Dick Addinsell, Olwen (Winifred's secretary), Winifred herself, and Ben (her neurotic fox terrier). Winifred is large in every way, and her capacity for friendship is without limits; apart from her recognised fame as a writer she is a brilliant sculptress and painter, and her vitality is inexhaustible. From 1930 onwards, whenever I have returned from abroad, or even from the wilds of Manchester, I have always winged my way, like a homing pigeon, to that cosy, friendly, long-suffering room on the first floor overlooking the market. I say 'long suffering' because the poor place has to put up with a great deal: its pictures are changed constantly; it is often flecked with paint and spattered with clay; it has been deafened for years by discussions, play-readings, piano-playing and film conferences; it has been barked in, sung in, shouted in, eaten in, and, occasionally, slept in; it has had to endure sudden, unpredictable onslaughts of tidying, which ill become it, and its walls are sodden with argument. It has also had to stand firm, not only against enemy bombing, but against the impact of violent personalities both alive and dead: Queen Elizabeth, Nelson and Shakespeare are constant habitués, together with Sybil Thorndike, Alexander Korda, Alfred Lunt, Lynn Fontanne, Katharine Cornell, Mary Martin, etc., etc., not to mention Winifred herself. If its walls have ears, I can only hope that they had the sense to plug them with cotton-wool many years ago.

Back in Paris after these brief excursions, life continued its routine course. It would be unfair to emphasise too heavily its monotony because there was always something going on to agitate us mildly and keep us on our toes, but, on the whole, I felt then, and I feel now, that our work was sadly lacking in importance. This was neither Campbell's fault nor ours; we did our best with the material at our disposal, and he did his best to encourage and help us in every way possible, but I suspect, although I have no actual proof of it, that he was considerably more ham-strung by bureaucratic intrigue than he cared to admit.

That there was an overlapping of policies and directives there can be no doubt, both in France and England. There was no supreme head of Propaganda appointed in either country. Had there been, the various groups and organisations which were all working away so industriously and so separately might have been successfully co-ordinated; as it was, everything seemed to be in a tangle, and there was nobody with enough power and authority to unravel it. Certainly, in my opinion, there was far too much importance attached to secrecy. Hardly a missive arrived in our office that was not stamped either 'Secret' or 'Confidential', and in nine cases out of ten anything contained in them could have been read aloud in the Reichstag without menacing Allied security in the least.

Naturally enough the words, 'Secret Service' and 'Intelligence' have a melodramatic ring about them: there is always a certain fascination, not only for the thriller-trained layman, but for many of those actually engaged in Intelligence work, in the fact of knowing something that many other people don't know; in being privy to information which, if it leaked out, might seriously effect the trend of great events. This is understandable and perfectly valid when the information concerned genuinely is secret, but when nearly all official papers, regardless of their contents are religiously stamped 'Secret and Confidential' it becomes both tedious and confusing. I came to the conclusion early on in the war that there were far too many adult, sometimes elderly, men in official positions who had never outgrown their schooldays; a great number of them still retained a perennial 'boyishness' which was particularly noticable in intelligence matters. In some of my later contacts with such men I remember often feeling surprised that they didn't suggest that we crouch down under the desk and play Indians.

The Secret Service virus was epidemic in Paris in 1940. Everybody was up to something, especially, of course, those who were up to nothing. The most unexpected people would arrive suddenly from London, wrapped in mystery and wearing strange, secretive smiles; indeed one young man whom I had known slightly for years came out into the open and announced to me firmly, with his habitual stammer: 'I am h-h-here on a t-t-t-terribly s-s-s-secret m-m-m-m-mission!' To many of my acquaintances, both in Paris and London, it was a foregone conclusion that I was involved in espionage up to the eyebrows, and it was quite useless for me to protest against their implications, because whenever I did so they merely smiled knowingly and ostentatiously changed the subject. Finally I was forced to give up the struggle and look as mysterious as everybody else.

Shortly after Squadron-Wrecker Wilson joined us in the Place de La Madeleine I asked him to explain to me, as simply as possible, the technicalities of radio, warning him at the same time that my obtuseness in such matters was appalling. I have tried at various times of my life to grasp the rudiments of inventions such as the telephone, the camera, the wireless telegraphy, and even the ordinary motorcar, but without success. My mind, when faced with such, to me, miraculous phenomena, becomes a blank, and I am ashamed to admit that a ten-year-old boy of average intelligence has a far clearer conception of the marvels among which we live than I could ever hope to achieve.

I have driven cars of all shapes and sizes efficiently for thirty years, but if any piece of their mechanism happens to require the simplest adjustment I am utterly confounded and have to walk to the nearest garage. I have even flown an aeroplane without disgracing either myself or my instructor, but no one has yet been able to make me understand why or how it takes off, flies through the air, and comes down again. Television, of course, and Radar and Atomic Energy are so far beyond my comprehension that my brain shudders at the very idea of them and scurries for cover like a primitive tribesman confronted for the first time with a Dunhill cigarette-lighter.

When depressed by these vast fissures in my intelligence I comfort myself, defiantly, with the reflection that as there are quite a number of important things that I do know about, I had better content myself with these and waste neither my time nor my energy endeavouring to acquire knowledge which my brain resolutely refuses to accept. In 1940, however, I was still foolhardy enough to hope that, if I really concentrated, really willed my mind into a state of receptiveness, I could learn at least some of the basic principles of White Man's Magic, and by doing so increase my efficiency in my job. Bill Wilson persevered and after a while I could talk fairly glibly, although without profound conviction, about 'Alternating wave-lengths', 'Cross-bearings', 'Jamming', etc. This stubbornly learned but, alas, ephemeral knowledge nevertheless stayed long enough in my mind to enable me to accomplish at least one job of relative importance, actually the only achievement during the whole of my time in Paris upon which I can look back with real pride; a pride that is in no way lessened by the fact that the entire affair was quite outside my province and none of my business.

It had been agreed between the French and the English in August 1939, that in the event of hostilities all radio activities in France should be centralised, all transmissions controlled and

77

restricted to certain wave-lengths, and all independent, commercial and unofficial stations shut down immediately. One morning towards the end of October, Bill, pale with anger, burst into my office with the announcement that although 'Radio Normandie' had obediently closed down according to decree, a small commercial station at Fécamp, only a few kilometres distant from it, was blasting away merrily by night and by day. It was obvious, even to me, that this station, situated where it was, could provide cross-bearings for enemy aircraft on their way down the Channel to bomb Portsmouth, Southampton, and other towns on the south coast of England. From that moment, egged on by Bill Wilson, Douglas Colyer, the Air Attaché, and later by other R.A.F. officers, I started a determined campaign to get Fécamp closed down, and finally, on January the 4th, two months later, it was.

During those two months, however, I learned a lot. I learnt, for instance, that men of apparent integrity, occupying positions of considerable responsibility can when financial interests are involved, behave with shoddy evasiveness. I learnt that graft, corruption and petty intrigue, far from diminishing in time of national emergency, seemed to gain from it an added impetus; all of which of course I should have known before, but at that time, on the threshold of middle age, I was still naif enough to be shocked. It is to this day a matter of surprise to me that I worked myself into such a state over that damned radio station, and although, as things ultimately turned out, I am glad that I did, I am still faintly puzzled that I should have fought so doggedly over it and minded so much. I can only assume that, at the moment when Bill first mentioned it to me, I must have been going through one of my periods of frustrated zeal.

First of all I flew to London and explained the situation to Campbell Stuart and Dallas Brooks, both of whom expressed appropriate concern and, having agreed that it was a disgraceful breach of security, presumably wiped it from their minds. Next I tackled Lord Chatfield, the Minister for Co-ordination of Defence, who, being an old friend, saw me immediately and listened carefully and seriously to what I had to say. When I had finished my story he told me not to worry any more, because a minute had been signed by the War Cabinet two weeks previously ordering the Fécamp radio station to shut down at once. I received this reassurance with scepticism and asked him if he had a radio handy; he replied that he had, and led me to it, whereupon, with a beating heart, I fiddled inexpertly with the controls for a few moments until suddenly, to my mixed fury and relief, there it was: 'Radio Fécamp broadcasting a programme of recorded dance music.' Lord Chatfield was genuinely astonished and very angry indeed, and, after thanking me for bringing it to his notice, ushered me out.

I returned to Paris glowing with the consciousness that I had been instrumental in getting a dangerous wrong righted, and feeling that at least I had made a small but bona-fide contribution to the war effort. However, my glow faded swiftly a few weeks later when I discovered that not only was Fécamp still operating as usual but that it had never closed down for a split second.

By this time my blood was up and I proceeded to unearth a number of disturbing facts. One of these was that fairly eminent French politicians were financially concerned in the enterprise.

At about this time Winston Churchill was making one of his periodic visits to Paris and so, nothing daunted, I telephoned Duncan Sandys, his son-in-law, who was accompanying him, and asked if Mr Churchill could see me for ten minutes as I had something of considerable urgency to bring to his notice. I was not in the least surprised when Duncan replied that an interview with Mr Churchill was out of the question as he was occupied every moment of the day; however, he went on to say that if I cared to pop round to the Ritz and explain to him what my urgent business was, he would pass it on to his father-in-law if an opportunity presented itself.

After a quick check-up with Bill on the technical aspects of the situation, and praying that I should be able to explain briefly and concisely the one all-important fact that danger threatened our south coastal towns from any transmitting station in the Normandy area, I hurried off to the Ritz, where Duncan Sandys was waiting for me in the foyer.

We sat down in two heavily brocaded chairs and I proceeded, as intelligibly as I could, to put the facts before him. Perhaps I was over-eager, too emphatic; perhaps my sense of drama over-coloured and over-weighted my argument, because I felt, while I talked, that my words were falling on stony ground. He was polite and attentive and listened indulgently, but there was something in his manner that gave me the impression that he was humouring me, like a benevolent uncle who nods understandingly when his small nephew announces shrilly that he has just seen three full-blooded pirates in the back garden. After the interview, when I rose to go, he smiled charmingly and said what a good idea it would be if only I could write a gay, morale-lifting war song, something on the lines of 'Mad Dogs and Englishmen'. I knew then how dismally I had failed, and with a sad heart left him, reflecting on my way back to the office that the Churchill family's passion for 'Mad Dogs and Englishmen' verged on the pathological.

A few days later, by which time my determination had become almost fanatical, I called upon one of the eminent French politicians who was interested financially in Radio Fécamp. The E.F.P. received me graciously and spent about twenty minutes explaining how passionately devoted he was to the Arts, and that all he had ever really wanted to do in his life was either to write or paint or compose music. I gathered from his conversation that his admiration for me was unbounded, and that if he only had one tenth of my glorious talent he would have renounced the drab world of politics years ago and been a far happier man. I listened to all this with becoming modesty and waited for the pay-off. This came when presumably he considered that I was sufficiently soaked with flattery to accept it.

Abruptly, and with a marked change of manner, he said that he had heard that I had been concerning myself with the question of whether or not a certain radio station at Fécamp should continue to operate. I smiled ingenuously and admitted that I had heard the subject discussed at various times, but that as my knowledge of such matters was virtually non-existent I was not really qualified to give an opinion either way. I here interpolated a self-deprecatory giggle, as one artist to another, implying that he could speak freely without there being much danger of my being able to understand more than the simplest aspects of the situation. The giggle must have reassured him, for he launched forth immediately into a lengthy refutation of all the arguments against Fécamp and explained, with slightly overdone emphasis, that the whole matter had been gone into by experts, and that although there were certain scaremongers who feared that transmissions from that area might provide enemy aircraft with cross-bearings on their target, such fears were unfounded and nonsensical, for the simple reason that all radio stations shut down automatically the moment an Alert was sounded.

I listened to this rationalisation with what I hoped was the right degree of puzzled attentiveness, and had the sense not to remind him that the crux of the whole argument lay in the fact that Fécamp could provide guidance for enemy aircraft long *before* they were identified and the Alert sounded. Encouraged by my docile acceptance of his explanation, he produced a typewritten brochure setting forth all the arguments in detail. I looked at it wistfully, wondering what possible wiles I could employ to induce him to let me take it away with me. I knew that if only I could get it to my office, have it translated into English, and give copies to the various air authorities concerned, it might be possible to get any specious statements it contained officially refuted. I glanced at it casually while he stared at me and drummed his fingers on the desk, then I handed it back to him with a light laugh and a shrug of the shoulders saying that it was far too long and involved to be taken in at a sitting, I would take his word for it. This indication that my interest in the affair was obviously superficial seemed to relieve his mind and, after a moment's thought, he handed it back to me again and said that he would hate me to have any misapprehensions about the situation and that I could take it home with me and study it, on the strict understanding that I show it to no one else and would promise to return it to him by special messenger the following morning. Still protesting that I probably wouldn't be able to understand a word of it, I placed it in my pocket and switched the conversation back to Art. He was an urbane and affable man and we parted in a shimmering haze of mutual compliments.

The next morning I had the brochure returned to him by special messenger, having had it copied, translated and sent to the Air Attaché. After that nothing happened for a while, until one morning Air-Marshal Barratt called me up from Rouen and said that Fécamp was still functioning in spite of all orders to the contrary, and that the moment had come for pressure to be brought to bear on Monsieur Daladier and General Gamelin. I protested that I knew neither Daladier nor Gamelin personally and that, although I fully realised the seriousness of the situation and was willing to do anything in my power to help, actually it was none of my business, and should be handled by the British Ambassador. The conversation ended with him urging me, in the event of non-co-operation from the Ambassador, to do the best I could. Startled, and of course flattered, by his confidence in my powers, I contacted Douglas Colyer, the Air Attaché, immediately, and we went to the Embassy to call on Sir Ronald Campbell, who had only recently replaced Sir Eric Phipps. Sir Ronald listened to what we had to say and agreed that something should be done, but I could sense from his manner that he felt it to be more a Service problem than a diplomatic one and, I suspected, was understandably wary of involving himself in what might turn out to be an unpleasant and complex imbroglio. At all events he said that he would make enquiries and do what he could.

A day or two later, as nothing had transpired, I embarked on a course of action which was slightly dishonest but, on the whole, enjoyable. I went to call on Jean Giraudoux wearing an expression of dreadful urgency, and told him, in the strictest confidence, that I had heard, on impeccable authority, that a scandal of horrifying dimensions was about to burst regarding Radio Fécamp. I told him that the Press were all standing by ready, and that the resulting repercussions would not only cause grave inter-Allied disunity, but would almost certainly unseat the Government. He appeared to be considerably disturbed by this information, particularly as he himself, quite unwittingly, had authorised a message of Christmas cheer over Radio Fécamp only a week or so previously. He was a dear man and I felt a twinge of conscience at upsetting him, but I also felt that the end might justify the means. I insisted that he procure for me an interview with Daladier's

Chef-du-Cabinet immediately so that I could place the whole matter before him myself. He agreed to this and rang up then and there for an appointment.

About a quarter of an hour later Monsieur Genebrier received me, and I went through my whole act again, implying a close personal liaison with both the English and French Press which was entirely imaginary. Monsieur Genebrier, looking as startled as poor Giraudoux, assured me that he would approach the Prime Minister that afternoon and telephone me the result at five o'clock. I said firmly that on no account was he to do any such thing; that my connection with the matter was unofficial and my warning confidential. I then left him with the assurance that I would communicate privately with the Air Attaché, who would be awaiting his telephone call punctually at five o'clock.

At five thirty that afternoon Douglas Colyer called me up triumphantly to say that he had received a notification that Fécamp would be shut down finally at midnight. As a matter of actual fact it wasn't shut down until forty-eight hours later, but the battle was won, and I felt quite light-headed with relief and extremely pleased with myself. The whole affair had been an obsession with me for weeks, and whether or not my conviction of its importance was exaggerated, it seemed to me then, as it does now, that for financial interests to be permitted to override security measures in time of war was both sinister and disgraceful.

Perhaps I made a cracking fool of myself. Perhaps my dramatic sense over-egged the pudding and inflated it out of all proportion to its actual significance. Certainly, by poking my nose into what was officially none of my business, I made a few powerful enemies. At all events it was done; the piddling little radio station was closed down, and Bill Wilson, Douglas Colyer and I celebrated the occasion by giving ourselves an excellent dinner and then going on to hear Edith Piaf sing in her night-club.

As far as I was concerned the affair had one very agreeable repercussion. At the beginning of April I was invited by Air Marshal Playtair, who was the Air Officer Commanding in France, to visit him at his headquarters in Rheims. I took a long week-end off from Paris and duly arrived on the morning of April the 6th. I was met by a cheerful Squadron Leader called Hamilton whom I had known before, and for three days, either in a camouflaged car or in a small reconnaissance plane, I was driven and flown to our Advanced Striking Force stations, and discovered many old friends that I had known at Lympne and Singapore and other parts of the globe before the war. Back in Rheims I was wined and dined and made much of. It was a gay and exciting interlude and I shall always be grateful for it.

4

From the beginning to the end of my time in Paris I was victimised, even more than usual, by my own publicity value. Certain sections of the English Press were irritated, I suppose naturally enough, because they had been given no information about the job I was doing. As a matter of fact it would have been perfectly simple to have issued a statement at the outset explaining that I was working for the Government as the official representative of Sir Campbell Stuart, but this was not done and as I had been told by both Campbell and Dallas that on no account was I to give any newspaper interviews, nor discuss my activities with anyone beyond those who already knew, my status was never clearly defined, and I had to press on in exasperated silence against a rising tide of absurd mis-statements and far-fetched rumours, one of which, at least, caused me much personal annoyance and, I suspect, a certain amount of public harm.

Sometime in early 1940 a paragraph appeared in the 'Peterborough' column of the *Daily Telegraph*, announcing that I had been seen 'sauntering along the Rue Royale in naval uniform'. Hookie Holland was temporarily in London, and I immediately got through to him at the Admiralty and asked him to have the statement officially denied. I know that he did his best, but whether he succeeded I never discovered. In any case it was too late; the damage was done, and a short while afterwards the *Sunday Pictorial* came out with a two-page attack on me, shrilly demanding, on behalf of the British Public, why a well-known theatrical 'Playboy' should be allowed to don, at will, the uniform of one of the Fighting Services. This sanctimonious article, written in the usual oleaginous journalese, brought forth a flood of letters from strangers, some anonymous, some signed; some insulting or downright abusive, and some merely sorrowful or contemptuous. I found this hard to bear, but what annoyed me most was the thought that such shameless and bland inaccuracy should be read, believed and commented on by many thousands of my countrymen whose affection and respect I had striven to gain through all my professional years.

Actually, of course, it wouldn't have mattered so very much if it had been true. Many men of unquestioned integrity accepted honorary rank in the Services during the war when the exigencies of their jobs, or the area in which they worked, made it more convenient. Indeed the question of whether or not I should wear some sort of uniform had been discussed by Campbell and Dallas and me in the early days of my appointment. They both seemed to think it a good idea as a means of facilitating any journeys I might have to make through military zones. I held out against it on the grounds that I thought I could be more effective as an independent civilian; the same argument I had used in 1939 when I had been offered the honorary rank of Lieutenant-Commander R.N.V.R. after my participation with Lord Louis Mountbatten in the forming of the Royal Naval Film Corporation. I hated having to refuse the honour because for me it would have been a most gratifying accolade, but I sincerely felt that considering many of my naval friends were commanders and captains – indeed some of them were admirals and commanders-in-chief – it might be embarrassing for them to see me come bouncing on board their ships, glittering with unearned gold braid, and compelled to salute them whenever they spoke to me.

I believe, had it been really necessary to my job in 1939, that Their Lordships of the Admiralty might have been induced to renew their offer, but it was not really necessary.

And I felt strongly that my name, my reputation, and my friends would get me wherever I wanted to go within reason, an assumption which I am proud to say was abundantly justified during the later years of the war.

Another, more light-hearted, Press episode occurred in early December. Douglas Colyer, who was then still a Group Captain, telephoned me one morning in great glee to say that he had been made an Air Commodore and had a very fetching brass hat. I told him to come round at once and show it to us. This he did and the staff saluted and curtseyed with proper deference. We had nothing to celebrate with except some not very good sherry and a glass jar of boiled sweets from Boissier's which we couldn't open. When we had drunk some of the sherry I presented him officially with the sweets, and he promised that he would get one of his minions to open the jar and would send some back to us in an envelope marked 'Secret'. A few minutes later when I was in the lobby seeing him out, I said, in a sharp, peremptory tone, 'Please see about that Boissier business as soon as possible.' Assuming an air of meek subservience, he said: 'Aye, aye, Sir,' saluted, and disappeared into the lift.

It was then I noticed a strange young man who had evidently secreted himself behind the door when I opened it. Realising that further concealment was impossible he stepped forward and said that he had been sent by the *Daily Express* and would I give him an interview? I replied that I was very sorry but my orders were to give no Press interviews in any circumstances. Unrebuffed, he advanced closer to me and peered inquisitively past me through the open door into my office. 'My Editor wishes to know,' he said, 'just exactly what war work you are engaged in.' Aware that it would be impolitic to lose my temper I explained to him gently that I perfectly saw both his and his Editor's point, and that although I was not at liberty to discuss my work, I could at least assure him that it was a routine job; that there was nothing mysterious about it, and that I would be sincerely grateful if he would take my word for this and do me the honour of regarding me, for the duration of the war, as an ordinary civilian and not as a theatrical celebrity. I then rang for the lift, ushered him into it, and away he went.

The next morning I was called up by the censorship department of the British Embassy. 'We have just had to censor a startling article about you,' said a voice with a slight giggle in it. 'It states, among other things, that "Mr Noël Coward, in impeccable civilian attire, sits all day behind a vast desk in a luxury office in the Place de La Madeleine, issuing orders to officers of the highest rank"!'

That was one of the few occasions in my life when I have been profoundly grateful for censorship.

In November I was asked by the Military Attaché to appear at an Anglo-French troop concert in the theatre at Arras, and to persuade Maurice Chevalier to appear too. Maurice, after a little coaxing, agreed, and in due course we set off along that interminable road on a bitterly cold Saturday afternoon. There were to be two performances on Sunday and Monday evenings respectively, and a full dress-rehearsal on the Sunday afternoon.

The first performance was attended by the Duke of Gloucester, Anthony Eden and a group of Dominions V.I.P.s who were making an official tour of the area. Among these was a good-looking Australian of middle height with a forceful personality and rather bushy eyebrows. His name was Richard Casey, and on the Monday morning, just before he left with the others for Paris, we had a drink and a brief discussion of the shape of things to come, in course of which he told me firmly, for there was nothing equivocal either in his speech or his manner, that I owed it to myself to visit Australia. He spoke lovingly and with humour of his own land, and I liked him so much that I found myself agreeing that, whenever opportunity offered, I would fly straight to the Antipodes. The significance of that encounter was not apparent at the time and we parted as casually as we had met.

By March, 1940, I began to get restless. My initial patriotic fervour had evaporated in a haze of anti-climax and, apart from my gratuitous interference over Radio Fécamp, it seemed to me that I had achieved very little. My position remained ambiguous officially, and although both Campbell Stuart and Dallas Brooks assured me that I was doing a useful job, I was becoming increasingly aware that actually I was doing nothing at all beyond presiding at meetings, at which much was discussed but little achieved; giving diplomatic dinners and lunches occasionally to various Big Shots passing through Paris; and generally providing a pleasantly social façade, behind which a great deal should be happening, whereas in point of fact nothing was.

When Campbell and Dallas and entourage descended on us for brief visits the tempo increased and the temperature rose. We gave two large lunch-parties in a private room at Larue's for Campbell to meet certain eminent members of the French Governmental hierarchy with whom we were supposed to be in constant and breathless contact. The first one was more or less work-a-day, with the dear professors and others from the Commissariat d'Information, interspersed with prominent journalists such as de Kerillis, 'Pertinax', Buré, etc. The second one, however, was sensational and included among others our own British Minister, Oliver Harvey, all three Service Attachés, Hookie Holland, Douglas Colyer and Willie Collier, and, as a political *bonne bouche*, Paul Reynaud and Georges Mandel, whom I placed on either side of Campbell with myself opposite so that I could keep one ear cocked and be ready to intervene in the event of any lingual emergencies. Campbell behaved beautifully until the end, when he inadvertently lost a good deal of the ground his charm had gained by announcing that he had to leave immediately for an appointment with General Gamelin. Before I could stop him he had risen, shaken hands briskly with Reynaud and Mandel, and vanished like a dancing dervish. Whether or not he actually had an appointment with General Gamelin was beside the point. What really mattered was that even supposing he had an appointment with the King, Churchill or the Dalai Lama, he had commited a grievous offence against the laws of protocol by leaving before two eminent French Ministers. I watched Paul turn scarlet and David turn pale, and the three of us launched ourselves upon the rapidly stiffening guests of honour with such a spate of gay, flattering conversation that they had no time to take more than inward umbrage. Finally they left, mollified I hope, if a trifle confused.

An air of misty indecision enveloped our propaganda activities. Every now and then, during our conferences, somebody would give birth to a fairly good idea and for a while we would all enlarge upon it eagerly, but by the time it had been referred to the High-Ups in the Commissariat d'Information and to our own headquarters in England, and various modifications had been suggested and argued about, whatever effectiveness the original idea might have had was dissipated and it disappeared into the limbo never to be heard of again. Personally I contributed one sound suggestion, but nothing came of that either. The Germans at that time were boasting that the R.A.F. had never flown over Germany. As we knew perfectly well that night flights were frequently made over Berlin in order to drop the usual turgid pamphlets, which were immediately collected by the police and disposed of before dawn, I recommended that, instead of dropping leaflets which were of a size easily discernible on the darkest night, we should deluge the city with specially made sticky confetti, each scrap of which should have the Union Jack on one side and the Tricolor on the other. I contended that if bags of this were scattered from a great height, the confetti would stick to the roofs and pavements and window-sills, thereby convincing the sceptical Berliners that the R.A.F. could reach their town easily, and have the added attraction of driving the police agents mad. This idea was ultimately turned down on the grounds that it was too frivolous. Under such cutting criticism my creative impulse withered and I settled back to listen politely to other, less provocative and more seemly suggestions.

The office was running smoothly. There were Cabinet crises and reshufflings. The days and weeks went by.

On looking back now on those strange, frustrating months, I find it difficult to believe that I ever lived them at all. They seem in my memory to be, not exactly vague, but irrelevant, almost as though I had dreamed them.

PART THREE

I

On the evening of Thursday, April the 18th, I left Paris. David, Paul, Peter, Bill and Cole saw me off at the Gare de Lyon. The station was dimly lit owing to the 'blue-out', but apart from this the departure seemed to be much the same as usual; grey women in overalls were wheeling trolleys festooned with pillows, trolleys with magazines and papers, and trolleys with ham rolls, chocolate, fruit, biscuits, and bottles of wine. There was the usual smoky, railway-station smell and the usual din. I leaned out of the window of my sleeper talking and laughing with my see-ers-off as I had done so often in the past; the familiarity of the scene was intoxicating and nostalgic at the same time. I might have been off on a holiday to St Moritz, Cannes or Venice: the hour was the same, the place was the same, even the train looked almost the same although perhaps a little less clean than it used to be. I shouted parting instructions, drank everyone's health from a small, flat bottle of cognac that Bill had given me, and implored them all to press on valiantly, to be good and noble and true and, above all, to see to it that Number 18 Place de La Madeleine upheld its world-wide reputation of being the most efficiently organised, smoothly run and vital weapon of political warfare in existence. The train began to move, they laughed and waved, and Paris slid away from me for five years.

I settled back on the hard, dusty, blue upholstery, took another swig of cognac and relaxed. I felt light-hearted, more so than I had felt for months: I was off on my travels again and although I was bound neither for St Moritz, Cannes nor Venice, it was even so, in many respects, a holiday. Six weeks would pass quickly, but in their passing they would let a lot of fresh air into me, and the monotony of office routine and all those depressing meetings would perhaps feel less oppressive when I returned in June. The wagon-lits attendant in familiar brown uniform came in to collect my ticket and passport; the usual urgent little man passed along the corridor ringing a bell and shouting 'Première Service'; the train, gathering speed, rattled and swayed through echoing suburban stations until presently the rhythm became steady and set and there was nothing to be seen from the window but my own reflection mirrored in blackness.

Early in March, during one of my flying visits to London, I had dined with Campbell and explained that I was becoming oppressed and irritated by the Paris routine and by the growing conviction, despite his encouraging assurances to the contrary, that I was achieving very little. In the early days when we were establishing the office, forming liaisons and seeking contacts, my celebrity value, allied to my theatre training in organisation, had been useful, but now, when everything was running smoothly and all necessary contacts had long since been consolidated, I sincerely felt that I was becoming increasingly stale and ineffective; David ran the office far more efficiently than I ever could; everything was under control, there was no longer any need for improvisation, bluff or show-off, no further necessity for making snap decisions and cutting through bureaucratic pomposities and red tape; there were no longer any crises, excitements and sudden urgencies, and no more hurdles to jump. I am sure that Campbell, who was no mean psychologist, recognised in all this, plausible as my arguments were, that the real truth lay deeper. It was, in fact, my same old trouble: the gnawing, irrepressible restlessness, the longing for change, the stubborn resistance to routine that had conditioned all my years in the Theatre and out of it.

Campbell, whose swift ear discerned, behind my arguments and explanations, the frenzied beating of wings, looked at me with a quizzical twinkle in his eye and said that I could take six weeks' leave in April. Later on, the matter was further discussed and both he and Dallas decided that if I took my six weeks in the United States, which was what I wanted to do, it might turn out to be very useful from several angles. They said, with truth, that I could, at least, travel about a bit, listen to what was being said, talk to leading newspaper owners and editors, etc., and obtain a certain amount of first-hand information on the general attitude of mind. I asked Dallas if he would like me to send him a weekly resumé of my observations in a code to be selected by him, but he shuddered and said 'No.'

I dispatched a cable to Jack, hinting that he might expect to see me in April, and settled down impatiently for the time to pass. I arranged to sail on the S.S. *Washington* from Genoa on April the 20th, although both Campbell and Dallas seemed to think, taking into account my Press reputation as an international naval spy, that it might be risky for me to travel alone and unprotected through Italy. I don't believe that they seriously envisaged any actual danger, but they did point out that if by any chance any trouble should occur, it would be difficult to extricate me from a neutral country.

If anyone had told me at that time that I was high up on the Nazi black list, I should have laughed and told him not to talk nonsense. In this, however, I should have been wrong, for, as it ultimately transpired, I was. In 1945, when the Nazi list of people marked down for immediate liquidation was unearthed and published in the Press, there was my name. I remember that Rebecca West, who was one of the many who shared this honour with me, sent me a telegram which read: – 'My dear – the people we should have been seen dead with.'

When the Germans invaded Norway and Denmark, the atmosphere in Paris changed completely overnight: to say that it lightened would be inaccurate, but it certainly became more alive. The moribund lassitude of the last few months vanished, there was a nervous excitement in the air and I felt, walking down the Boulevard des Italiens, as though the voices of everyone had been raised a full tone. It was of course the same, irrational, 'Something is going to happen at last' sense of relief that I had felt in England when, after so much dread and anticipation, war was finally declared. The Commissariat d'Information was full of unaccustomed bustle and fuss and tremulous with surmise. Our own office reacted differently but definitely. David became paler than ever and looked grave; Paul wandered in and out with an 'I told you so' expression on his face; Bill looked resigned and tried repeatedly to get through to the B.B.C. Peter kept on appearing and re-appearing with news bulletins from the Press; only Lord Reay and Miss Cameron remained apparently unmoved and continued to type. I too was infected by the 'Something is going to happen at last' contagion, but the realisation that this would almost certainly cancel my trip to America depressed me. A little later, after the first excitement had died down, and after Mr Chamberlain had announced roguishly that Hitler had 'missed the bus', I flew to London to see Campbell.

To my surprise he said that in the present circumstances he thought it was even more important that I should go to the States than it had been before. The reaction of the Americans to the sudden break-up of what they themselves had christened the 'Phoney War' would be interesting to observe at close quarters, and any personal reports I sent back to him on the subject might be extremely useful. This was a relief in one way, but I felt reluctant to leave the office and the staff and the job just as things were beginning to be exciting. At all events it was finally decided beyond further equivocation that I was to leave Paris as arranged on April the 18th, get myself on board the ship the moment I arrived in Genoa and remain locked in my cabin until it sailed. On looking back, this over-cautiousness appears to be fairly idiotic, but I suppose, at the time, it was quite sensible. In any case I was forced to disregard it, for upon reaching Genoa in the afternoon of the 19th I discovered that, even if it were possible for me to get on board the ship twenty-four hours before sailing time, which was doubtful, I should not be able to take my luggage with me and could expect neither food nor service.

Not fancying the idea of spending the night locked in a stuffy cabin with neither pyjamas, tooth-brush, food nor drink, I gallantly snapped my fingers at peril and went to the best hotel, where I engaged a comfortable room with bath. Later on, further emboldened by an excellent dinner and a half-bottle of Chianti, I walked recklessly out into the crowded streets without even pulling my hat over my eyes. I wandered about through the arcades, sat outside various cafés, sipped Drambuie, watched the people, and bought a large packet of nougat. Just before midnight I arrived back at the hotel unmolested and went peacefully to bed, reflecting that either the great Gestapo scheme for luring me into Germany and extracting from me, on the rack, the secrets of Number 18 Place de La Madeleine had gone badly awry, or that the Nazis just didn't care.

I got myself and my luggage on board the *Washington* the next day without incident. The sun was shining, the dock was crowded, and people were screaming and yelling and throwing paper streamers as though there were no war anywhere and nothing but gaiety, cheerfulness and good fellowship from one end of the world to the other.

The Captain invited me to sit at his table and also to have a drink with him in his cabin. His name was Harry Manning, and he was typically American in the best sense: tough, humorous, and easy-going. He was an ex-flyer and had flown a great deal with Amelia Earhart. In course of conversation I remember asking him whether or not, in the event of a German submarine stopping the ship in mid-Atlantic and demanding my body, he would hand me over. 'Sure,' he said. 'Why the hell shouldn't I?' I took an immediate liking to him.

The voyage was without incident. I relaxed and read and slept and prepared my mind for the inevitable impact of New York, an impact which had always, even in times of peace, been strong and over-stimulating and which, in present circumstances, might put a severe strain on my self-control. The American attitude to the European war during the period of apparent anti-climax between September, 1939, and April, 1940, had been growing more and more irritating to those immediately concerned with it. The Isolationists' – 'Let 'em get on with it – it's none of our business' – viewpoint had been clearly expressed in various American newspapers and magazines and I had noted, in several of the correspondents and other visitors from the States, a determination to regard the existing stalemate as a comforting proof that nothing further was going to happen. There was also the line, taken by many, that America, having once pulled England's chestnuts out of the fire and won the last war for her, was not going to be so easily fooled a second time, and even supposing that the war flared up into a conflagration that destroyed the whole of Europe, she, America, would remain neutral and unscathed, swish aside her skirts from the dust of conflict, rise above the entire abortive situation and, by so doing, fulfil her rightful destiny as the one inviolable sanctuary of Democracy in Western Civilisation.

Even my experienced and loving affection for America suffered a slight setback in the face of such naïve and shrill whistling in the dark. Admittedly, what small knowledge of international affairs I had was very recently acquired, but, even so, it seemed to me that for adult citizens of a great country so blatantly to pull the wool over their eyes was a frightening proof of the human capacity for self-deception.

Having for many years regarded America as my second home, I was naturally more concerned by all this than many of my countrymen who, less fortunate than I, had never enjoyed American hospitality, never experienced that welcoming, ardent kindliness and had no personal ties and memories and affections over the water.

Crossing the ocean again in an American ship, my mind was troubled with apprehensions. I was longing to see New York once more, to see my friends, to go to theatres, to look from high windows at the lights of that fabulous city. I looked forward also to American trains, to sandwiches in drugstores, to weekends in Connecticut with Jack and Natasha, and the view from my little bedroom on the top floor, across the sound to Long Island. There was so much of America that I knew well and loved and respected, and now, owing to war, and heightened temperatures and fears released, it might be difficult, less welcoming, it might indeed be infuriating.

2

My determined efforts to steel myself against the impact of arrival turned out to be a waste of nervous energy, for this instance proved to be in no way different from countless other arrivals. The Press reporters and photographers came on board at Quarantine and were as friendly to me as they had always been in the past;

nobody snarled any virulent isolationism in my face; there were no tasteless witticisms about the 'sit-down war'. There was the usual queuing up for the Immigration authorities; the usual rushing about and noise and chaos, while the city of New York glided by in the morning mist, the ferry boats hooted, and the small, stocky tugs nuzzled and shoved the ship alongside the dock. Jack and Natasha were waiting at the foot of the gangway.

Not having much luggage I got through the Customs swiftly and was soon driving across town to the St Regis. When the first spate of *non-sequitur* and mutual gossip had exhausted itself and we had had cocktails and lunch at Twenty One, Paris, England and the war had receded so far that I wouldn't have been surprised if Jack had suddenly informed me that rehearsals started on Monday, and that the opening date had been changed from Wilmington on the 23rd to New Haven on the 27th.

The air was quivering with theatrical tension because Lynn and Alfred were opening that very night in the new Robert Sherwood play, *There Shall Be No Night*. After lunch we went along to the theatre, where we found Alfred in the throes of last-minute lighting. After a little while Lynn appeared, having been leaving flowers for me at the St Regis, and we sat in the empty theatre all talking at once while the stage lights went up and down and on and off. Then, for a sudden moment, surrounded by my old friends, I was stricken with a dreadful homesickness for the past, a sickening longing to be part of it all again instead of just a visitor from another world on six weeks' leave.

At six-thirty, Neysa McMein, another of my very dear ones, appeared at the hotel and we talked while I finished dressing. Neysa was one of the rare people in the world whose genius for friendship could pierce through all façades, surmount all defences and find its way immediately and unerringly to the secret heart. This exquisite sensitivity she preserved untarnished until the day of her death in 1949. Never, in all the years I knew and loved her, did I see her foolish or flurried or mistaken. The quality of her own truth was so wise and sure and so rich in humour that it gave grace to everyone who knew her, which was a prodigal output, for her friendship embraced all sorts and kinds and classes of people. In case I should be accused of over-idealisation, of praising her too highly, of allowing my own affection for her to blind me utterly to her defects, I will add that her clothes were erratic, her political views frequently unsound, her spelling appalling, and her luck at games of chance maddening. At all events, when she arrived at the St Regis that evening, her instinct told her at once that beneath my joy at seeing her and in spite of the fun and excitement of being in New York again, there was a core of uneasiness, an area of discontent somewhere that had to be dealt with. While I was dashing in and out of the bathroom, putting cufflinks into my shirt and grappling with my tie, she proceeded to deal with it so thoroughly and so effectively that by the time we had joined Jack and Natasha for dinner my fears had vanished and I was in such a mood of wise, kindly, international tolerance that if anyone had rushed up to me brandishing the Stars and Stripes and screamed, 'England is done for and the British Empire stinks!', I should merely have smiled sweetly and said, 'God bless you.'

The first few days passed in a whirl as the first few days in New York invariably do. It always takes me at least a week to become acclimatised, to be able to put myself down, to be able to sleep for more than five hours a night. Reunions with old friends, theatres, suppers, Press interviews: all, or nearly all, pleasurable and stimulating, and all, or nearly all, cheerfully insignificant. Jack and Natasha were deeply involved in the organisation of a Gargantuan Allied Relief Ball which was to be held at the Hotel Astor on May the 10th. Jack was running a cabaret in a private room, and so I immediately became involved too, and spent a great deal of time rushing from theatre to theatre and dressing-room to dressing-room persuading glamorous stars to promise to appear.

On the Saturday afternoon I drove out to Jack's house in Fairfield, Conn., with Hope Williams. We purred along the wide interminable boulevards of the Bronx; past the familiar rash of lunch-counters, gas-stations, vacant lots and immense blocks of apartment buildings in course of construction. Further on, in the hinterland of Connecticut, where there are small hills and valleys, orchards and twisting roads, it is possible for a fleeting moment, every now and then, to imagine that you are in England, Buckinghamshire perhaps, somewhere between Fulmer and Gerrards Cross, or Kent, on the road from Canterbury to

Maidstone before it joins the main by-pass; but the illusion is transient, for the quality of the land is different, less trodden down by the centuries, less secure, and far less gentle. I always feel that in America the land itself, however smooth and well cultivated it may be outwardly, has no inward acquiescence; it is as though it were not yet quite broken in, still half-tamed and a bit skittish; as though it still had hopes of winning in the long run. On the main highways, of course, it is so tame that it sits up and begs; shackled by intersected parkways, made foolish by hoardings, drive-ins, road-houses and hamburger heavens, it knows it is beaten and can only retaliate mildly by effacing itself to such an extent that it has no resemblance to country at all. I often feel when driving along the Merit Parkway, for instance, that I might just as well be indoors.

Hope Williams another of the enduring bonds that bind me to America, I had first known in the 'twenties in the full flush of her brilliant but disappointingly brief stage career. A curious shyness, a certain detached spiritual independence prevented her from enjoying completely her success in the theatre. She had a charming speaking voice and delivered lines in a special way of her own, with a sort of beguiling tonelessness. She always looked well-groomed and her clothes were as much a part of her personality as her cropped blond hair and quizzical blue eyes. She was slangy without being vulgar, modern without being brash, and her gaucheries of movement had a peculiar grace. Her popularity was considerable; her name flared up in lights for a little, and then, suddenly, it wasn't there any more. Her nervousness and diffidence and lack of ego lured her away to gentler pleasures and, ever since, she has lived contentedly for a large part of each year on a ranch in Wyoming. She, like Neysa, had her own brand of quiet wisdom and, driving along in the car that day, not having seen her for at least two years, there was no need to explain anything; I could just talk at random, generally or intimately, without the faintest likelihood of being misunderstood.

Jack's house stands on a ridge overlooking a golf course and the Sound. At night a lighthouse flashes, and in day-time in the summer white-sailed yachts form a little corps de ballet in the distant harbour. None of it had changed since I had last seen it in

1938. In the spring of 1940 it felt enviably peaceful. I looked out of the window at the view while I was changing for dinner. Dusk had fallen, the lighthouse was already on the job, there were no ominous undertones, no fears nor dreads nearer than three thousand miles; serenity lay over the scene, indeed, I felt it lay over the whole continent of America, like a cellophane wrapping, keeping out all the dangerous germs and viruses of war and disruption, preserving every vitamin intact. I tried to envisage a squadron of Messerschmitts flying in low over the darkening water, the bombs curvetting down and tearing ragged craters on the golf course, ripping through the wooden frame houses, leaving flame and smoke curling up into the sky. I listened with my mind's ear to the harsh staccato splutter of machine-gun fire, to the wail of sirens; but I could neither see nor hear any of it, it was too far-fetched, too absurdly beyond the bounds of possiblity.

Alfred and Lynn came down on the Sunday and we discussed the play and the notices, and the war and me and Paris, and the invasion of Norway and the play and the notices.

The next morning I flew to Washington. I felt, having promised Campbell a report on my personal observations of the general situation, that Washington would be the best place to start observing. Paul Willert, who was an old friend of Mrs Roosevelt's, had given me a letter of introduction to her, and so, when I had settled myself in the Carlton Hotel, I sent it round to the White House by special messenger. This done, I went to lunch at the British Embassy, where I sat next to the wife of the Australian Minister, who told me that her husband, Richard Casey, had met me in France and very much wanted to see me again. This was a pleasant piece of luck, and we agreed to get together at Walter Lippmann's on the following evening and make a date. She was gay and intelligent and there obviously was no nonsense about her, and one more link was forged in the chain that was to lead me across the world.

In the evening I dined with Joe Alsop. The evening was hot, so we dined in the garden and no word of the conversation, which was largely political, could have rasped the nerves of the most vulnerable Englishman. The dinner-party was select and consisted of Felix Frankfurter, Senator Murphy and Senator Byrnes. They talked sensibly; their opinions seemed to me to be the result of careful consideration and were neither swayed by bias nor tainted by wishful thinking. I also felt instinctively that, courteous and pleasant as they were, they were none of them likely to soft-pedal their views merely because there was an English visitor present. They appeared to accept as inevitable America's ultimate participation in the war, and to face a truth which so many Americans were reluctant to admit: that the present conflict, although still confined to Europe, was not merely a squabble between far-away decaying nationalisms, that could safely be allowed to burn itself out in a splutter of remote gunfire, but was a world issue far transcending the predatory, racial wars of the past, on the outcome of which depended the survival of Western Civilisation. The conversation, however, was not exclusively devoted to such grave matters. There were jokes as well and lightness of touch and delicious food and wine. Altogether it was a well-mannered, adult evening, and I returned to my hotel a great deal the better for it.

The next day a note arrived from Mrs Roosevelt inviting me to dine that night. This flung me into a slight dilemma, for I had already arranged to dine with Walter and Helen Lippmann, but I rang them up and explained truthfully how anxious I was to meet the President and Mrs Roosevelt and that probably such an opportunity would not occur again, whereupon they gracefully forgave me and I promised to join them at eleven-thirty.

Upon arrival at the White House I was led, much to my surprise, directly to the President's study, where he received me alone and we talked, uninterrupted, for quite a while. So much has been written about Franklin D. Roosevelt, so much love, hate, praise, blame, vilification, prejudice, abuse and hero worship have been poured over his memory, that one more personal impression of him cannot matter either way. I never knew him well although we met subsequently on two occasions. I knew nothing of his alleged perfidies, his political treacheries, his reckless expenditures, his double-faced diplomatic betrayals and his unscrupulous egomania. I know nothing of them now. All I knew of him then and later was that he had kindness, courage and humour. Even discounting his personal charm, which was impressive, these qualities seemed to me to be perfectly clear in him. Perhaps his immediate friendliness to me, his utter lack of pomposity, his apparently effortless manner of putting me at my ease, blinded and flattered me to such an extent that my critical perceptions atrophied. Perhaps it was all a professional trick; perhaps such facile conquests were second nature to him and the whole performance was a habitual façade behind which he was regarding me with cynical contempt. If this were so I can only say that he went to a lot of trouble to deceive me, and for motives which must remain for ever unexplained.

His study was typical of him, I think. It was furnished unpretentiously and in quiet taste: there were a number of personal knick-knacks and books and models of ships; his desk was solid and business-like, although at the moment it had banished affairs of state for the day and given itself up to frivolity, for it was littered with an elaborate paraphernalia of cocktail implements. There were bottles, glasses of different sizes for short and long drinks, dishes of olives and nuts and cheese straws, also an ice bucket, a plate of lemons with a squeezer, a bowl of brown sugar, two kinds of Bitters and an imposing silver shaker. Among all these the President's hands moved swiftly and surely; they were flexible hands and never erred, whether he happened to be looking at what he was doing or not. He was evidently proud of his prowess as a barman, as indeed he had every reason to be, for the whisky-sour he finally handed me was perfect.

Throughout the whole operation he talked incessantly. He commented guardedly on Neville Chamberlain, glowingly on Winston Churchill and casually on international affairs. He jumped lightly from subject to subject, occasionally firing a question at me and suspending cocktail-mixing for a moment while he waited for my reply. He even told me a few funny stories, at which my heart sank, for as a rule I resent and despise funny stories, but he told them briefly and well.

Presently Mrs Roosevelt came in with Miss le Hand and Mr and Mrs Henry Morgenthau. The President proceeded to mix a fresh brew of whisky-sours and the conversation became general. The first thing that struck me about Mrs Roosevelt was her grace of movement; the second, that she was as warm and approachable as her husband. Never having seen her before I was surprised to observe how discourteous cameras had always been to her: they had shown merely a heavy face with a too large mouth; their inaccurate lenses had transformed her wide friendly smile into a grin and ignored the expression of her eyes, which was gentle and slyly humorous; they had also ignored her quality of distinction, which, in its essence, was curiously Victorian; I could imagine her driving through the nineteenth-century English countryside to take tea with Mrs Gaskell.

When dinner was announced she ushered us all out of the room first and the President remained behind. When we were settled in the dining-room he was wheeled in by his valet, who transferred him from his invalid chair to his ordinary chair at the head of the table. This operation was effected smoothly, without fuss, and without the faintest suggestion of spurious gallantry. This good-looking man, bursting with energy and vitality, bearing so lightly the heavy responsibilities of his position, just happened to be paralysed from the waist down and that was that; it seemed to be the most natural thing in the world and cried for no pity.

It is an established rule that no liquor may be served in the White House and so, fortified by the illicit Presidential whisky-sours, we settled down to pleasant food and delicious iced water.

After dinner I obliged with a few songs at the piano, and noted with a pang of dismay the President's marked partiality for 'Mad Dogs and Englishmen', which he made me sing twice. It could now only be a matter of time, I thought, before I received an official request from him to go to Norfolk, Virginia, and sing it to the naval cadets. Happily, however, this idea didn't occur to him, and after a little while the party broke up and he asked me back to his study for a night-cap. This time he talked specifically about the war and America's, as yet, confused attitude towards it. He explained, candidly and without prejudice, the point of view of the Isolationists and the various political, emotional and religious elements underlying it. He had, I felt, a personal admiration and affection for England, but he, rightly, seemed to consider that it was unnecessary to stress this and spoke of our problems and policies and statesmanship realistically rather than sentimentally. When finally I rose to go he asked me to come and see him again before I returned to Europe, and I left the White House with the conviction that it was fortunate, not only for Great Britain, but for all the democratic peoples of the world, that the man in command of the vast resources, potentialities and power of the United States of America possessed both vision and common sense.

By the time I arrived at the Lippmanns' house most of the party had left, but Richard Casey and his wife were still there and we sat out on the porch where it was cooler and talked about Australia, or rather they did. As I had noticed when I first met him in Arras, Casey's whole personality lit up when he talked of his native land; Maie, his wife, shared his enthusiasm, and when finally I had left them and retired to bed in the Carlton, my mind was so stimulated that I couldn't close my eyes, and I lay in the darkness while a procession of Koala bears, kangaroos, sheep and wallabies, occasionally shepherded by Marie Burke, whirled through my brain together with a series of confused visions of stately eucalyptus trees, mountains, valleys, deserts and limitless sandy beaches. I ultimately fell into a deep sleep troubled by regret that Mother and Father had not had the sense to emigrate with me in 1905, instead of merely moving to Lenham Road, Sutton, Surrey.

The next day I flew back to New York and spent the afternoon listening to Moss Hart read me his new musical play, which was to be called *Lady in the Dark*, and was destined for Gertrude Lawrence. Although I had not heard the score, the book seemed to have the authentic ring of success. Gertie, as usual, was undecided, she wouldn't say 'Yes', she wouldn't say 'No'; Moss, treading for the first time this well-worn path of anxiety and frustration, implored me, almost tearfully, to reason with her. He seemed to be so agitated, so obviously heading for a nervous breakdown, that I agreed to coax her, or failing this, bash her into definite acceptance. Consequently, a few days later, I took her out to lunch and wagged an authoritative finger in her face as I had so often done in the past. She shilly-shallied a bit, took refuge in irrelevancies, giggled and finally gave in. All things considered, it was a profitable little lecture, for *Lady in the Dark* proved to be one of the greatest triumphs of her career.

Many months later, in March 1941, when I was passing through New York on my way back from New Zealand, I saw her in it and watched, spell-bound, the brilliant assurance with which she wove her way through the intricacies of that varied and difficult part. The play had not then been running very long and her performance was still fresh and exciting. Gertrude Lawrence, of all the actresses I know, could, when she was playing true, give me the most pleasure. Having worked with her a great deal and known her all my theatrical life, it was doubly fascinating to sit in a crowded theatre and observe what she did with words and music that had not been written by me; with scenes that I had not directed or even seen rehearsed. I remember her on the opening nights of *Oh Kay* and *Nymph Errant* sweeping, with her rich talent, the whole audience into frenzies of applause. Watching her in *Lady in the Dark* with a loving but critical eye, I saw her do it again. Except for two scenes in the psycho-analyst's office when she over-dramatised, her performance was magnificent, no one else could have done it, I, who knew by heart every trick, mannerism, intonation and turn of her head, was as completely enslaved as if I were an enthusiastic layman seeing her for the first time. Later on, I believe, she slipped a bit and began to embroider and overemphasise, but this I never saw. All I saw was Gertrude Lawrence at her very best, which, to me, means a great artiste.

On the evening of May 9th, 1940, the night before the great Allied Relief Ball, I went over to Werba's Theatre in Brooklyn to see Katharine Cornell play *No Time for Comedy*. After the performance Neysa and I went back with her, Guthrie McClintic, Gert Macey and Margalo Gilmore to supper in Beekman Place. Every evening I have ever spent in that quiet house, overlooking the East River, has had its own special enchantment.

It was late when I left and I walked back across town to the St Regis through the nearly empty streets, reflecting happily how much I was enjoying myself and how comforting it was to be back again for a little in my own 'world', which, although esoteric and generally deaf to the clamour of international affairs, can give much to those who really belong to it. I had no regrets, beyond a little superficial nostalgia, about leaving it temporarily, because I knew that when the war was over I should be back in it, casting, arguing, rehearsing, slapping on the Max Factor, exhorting some people not to over-act, imploring others to put more into it;

thanking and blessing audiences for their wonderful receptiveness; cursing them under my breath for being a lot of wooden-headed clods. I should know again all the stresses and strains, the fussings and fumings; the gloomy conferences and inedible meals in provincial hotels, the awful final dress-rehearsals in provincial cities; above all, the feverish concentration, the elimination of the outside world and all that was going on in it, when a new scene had to be written or one of the cast fired and replaced. All this I missed sorely and when I compared it in my mind with the Paris office, the policy meetings, the lunches and dinners clanking with axes to grind, I shuddered and my heart sank. It sank still further a few minutes later when the elevator boy at the St Regis told me with dramatic glee that Germany had invaded Holland. I let myself in to my suite, sat down and lit a cigarette: sleep was out of the question, and there didn't seem to be anything else to do.

The next day was horrible, horrible and interminable. Headlines screamed from all the papers; radio programmes were interupted constantly by 'Flash' announcements; there was a note of hysteria in the voices of the announcers: some were vibrant with melodramatic implication, some heavy with doom. I was surprised to find that I definitely missed the maddening suavity of the dear B.B.C. boys. I went round to Jack's flat early and we crouched over the radio, Natasha in tears and me with lead in the pit of my stomach. Jack was quiet, miserable and exasperated. I think his exasperation was due to a subconscious awareness that the fact of his being an American separated him from Natasha and me. To a certain superficial extent this was true. Natasha, as usual in times of stress, spoke mostly in French: we were both so ineradicably European and this was, all too obviously, the beginning of the end for Europe. It was worse for Natasha than for me. Being an Englishman, I was more insular, a little more detached than she. I had then, and preserved all through the grim years to come, a strange, deep-rooted conviction that, whatever happened on the other side of the Channel, my own country would somehow survive. She, although Russian-born, was, to all intents and purposes, French. Most of her youth, and all her adult life until she married Jack in 1937, had been spent in France. France was the home of her loves and memories and allegiance.

Here in New York, married to an American, she still felt herself to be an alien and I knew, much as she loved Jack, that she was suddenly lonely with that bleak, desolate loneliness which only foreigners in strange lands can ever really experience. Naturally, on that bright spring morning in New York, neither she nor I could foresee with what appalling swiftness the French 'débacle' was approaching: there was still room for hope; still reason for believing, with the British Expeditionary Force intact on French soil, that combined Allied resistance might succeed in beating the Germans back. There was still indeed the Maginot Line.

Added to our sick feeling of dread was the minor but unpleasant realisation that we had the Allied Relief Ball to get through. Obviously, postponement was out of the question and the only thing to do was to put on bright faces and endure it as best we could. The very idea of dressing up, being gay, dancing and singing songs, seemed, in that beastly moment, to be macabre. However, it had to be faced and so we pulled ourselves together and concentrated for the rest of the day on dealing with last-minute details. I had immediately sent cables to Campbell, Dallas and David saying that I wished to return, but I couldn't hope for a reply until the following day.

The Ball that evening was a great success and our private cabaret a triumph, in spite of the fact that there were far too many people, and there was the usual clamour of all the stars wanting to go on at the same moment. Gertie Lawrence was tireless and no trouble at all: she merely looked lovely, did everything she was asked to do, and worked unflaggingly.

At seven o'clock in the morning, Jack, Natasha, Joe Moon, my accompanist, and I had breakfast in Child's Restaurant on Broadway, blinking in the light of day and far too exhausted to feel any emotion at all. The headlines in the morning papers screamed louder than ever, but we shut our eyes and ears to them and went wearily home to bed.

A cable in reply to mine arrived from Campbell Stuart, also one from David in Paris. The tenor of them both was the same: they both stressed the point that although the war situation had taken a grave turn for the worse, everything was under control as far as our organisation was concerned, and my return would not affect matters either way. Campbell's indeed told me specifically to stay where I was until I heard from him. Accepting this as a veiled reminder that I had agreed to utilise at least a part of my leave in making out a private report for him on what I had heard and observed, I decided, without much enthusiasm, to carry on with my plans as arranged. These included visits to Chicago, Los Angeles, San Francisco, Salt Lake City, Omaha, Cincinnati and Cleveland. On Monday the 13th, therefore, I boarded the train for Chicago.

It is difficult to recapture now, so many years later, my feverish discontent during these few weeks in the States. All the amenities, the material comforts, of American life that I had so much looked forward to were there to be enjoyed, but somehow, somewhere there was a catch in it. The over-luxurious journey from New York to Chicago in the 'Twentieth Century'; the red carpet laid across the platform; the obsequious coloured porters in their white coats; the deep armchair in the club car; the superlatively dry dry martini before dinner; the dinner itself, perfectly served and of such infinite variety, so far removed from the sullen table d'hôtes of our own dear Southern Railway; the wide commodious bed stacked with pillows, the efficient, hygienic private lavatory; the celestial iced water with which I could slake nocturnal thirst by merely turning on a special tap. All these unspiritual but positive delights were there in abundance as usual, but my sybaritic pleasure in them had evaporated; the fearful winds of war and change and disruption had blown it away. Instead of soothing me, pouring balm on my exacerbated nerves, these triumphant symbols of man's progress from the straw pallet, the ox cart and the outside privy merely irritated me: I felt perversely and, I am sure, wrongly that I should have welcomed the ox cart and the outside privy and slept more tranquilly on a straw pallet after a dinner of herbs and a nice glass of mead.

My dry martini was spoiled for me by the conversation of two commercial gentlemen sitting opposite me: they both wore garish neck-ties and were abusing, at the top of their lungs, President Roosevelt, Mrs Roosevelt and everything they either of them said or did. The edge was taken off my appetite at dinner by a repellent small boy at the next table across the aisle, who was accompanied by a stout, doughy-looking woman, presumably his mother. The boy, in the intervals of shovelling food into his mouth, was explaining, in a monotonous nasal whine, the abysmal inanities of some comic strip he had been reading. The din he made was abominable, but nobody made the faintest effort to control him, indeed several of the other diners clucked and smiled indulgently, which, of course, encouraged the horrid little extrovert to further transports of exhibitionism. The peace of my wide, luxurious bed was destroyed for me by an article I read in one of the magazines I had bought at the station. The article, purporting to be written by an authority on international affairs, was unsigned, and so charged with hysteria, pseudo-religious pacifism and anti-British bias that it flung me into a passion, and I spent wakeful hours tossing and turning and planning in my mind crushing replies to it. None of them were ever written or even thought of again, but the composing of them lulled me eventually to sleep.

Chicago was stimulating theatrically but politically unrewarding. I was there too briefly to have time to contact strangers, and the town was full of old friends. Clifton Webb was playing *The Man Who Came to Dinner* at the Selwyn: Tallulah Bankhead was in *The Little Foxes* at the Sam Harris next door, and Katie Hepburn was drifting huskily and enchantingly through *The Philadelphia Story* at the Blackstone. We had supper-parties at the Ambassador East, during which arguments about the world situation flared up with histrionic ferocity. Tallulah was garrulous and frequently sound in her opinions, although the violence with which she stated them proved them to be based on emotion rather than 'high reason and the love of good and ill'. Katie's comments were sensible, to the point, and generally designed to curb the ebullience of Van Heflin, her leading man, who, either from genuine conviction or from a mischievous pleasure in taking the opposite side, repeatedly threw pinkish monkey wrenches into the works, thereby drawing explosions of Southern wrath from Tallulah, acid reproofs from me and a few scandalised ejaculations from Clifton.

Present on the first of these occasions was a Chicago lawyer named Tom Underwood. I watched him sitting quietly with a Scotch highball in his hand and a twinkle in his eye while the spate of words frothed and foamed around him. He seldom gave an opinion on any of the world-shaking issues under discussion, unless directly appealed to, but when he did, he spoke with such authority and was so evidently well informed that I resolved to talk to him alone. On my second morning in Chicago I therefore called him up, and we had a quiet lunch, during which he confirmed the impression I had gathered the night before: that he was well informed, that he spoke with authority because he knew what he was talking about, and that his was one more name to write down on my private list of Americans who, in spite of being so far removed geographically from the war, refused to allow their minds to be deflected by Isolationist propaganda and realised, without panic or prejudice, the full implications of what was taking place. These implications we discussed at lunch and his understanding and acceptance of them reassured me on several counts, the most important of which was the fact that despite many indications to the contrary, such as the magazine gurglings of muddled sentimentalists, the scared fulminations of ill-informed senators and the flagrant anti-British diatribes in the Hearst Press, there were, in every major city of the United States, a number of men at least who were capable of independent thought and who, in the dangerous times ahead, could be relied upon to preserve their integrity and stand firm on the most essential premise of all, which was that England and America should stick together in sickness or in health, in peace or war, profit or loss, for ever and ever, Amen. It is incredible to me that any adult of reasonable intelligence could deny this obvious truth for a moment, but many doubted it then and many doubt it still. Today, with the wind rising again and the skies darkening, the asses are still braying, the saboteurs are still busy, not only the paid ones, the professional trouble makers whose appointed job it is to reduce civilisation to anarchy, but the silly men, the little men, the bigots, the fanatics and the fools. It is a desolate spectacle, as depressing now as it was then. Tom Underwood, if he should ever read this book, will doubtless be surprised that he made so lasting an impression on me. I have never seen him since and he could never have guessed, on such a fleeting acquaintance, how eagerly and gratefully I welcomed that, on the whole, unremarkable conversation.

I left Chicago on the night plane for Los Angeles, seen off, in a blinding rainstorm, at one o'clock in the morning, by Clifton, Katie and Tallulah. It was an elaborate plane with every modern convenience; I had a bunk to sleep in and, happily, no magazines to read.

Cary Grant met me at the airport and drove me to his small house by the sea in Santa Monica. He was friendly and cheerful as usual; the house was comfortable; he gave me a car and chauffeur and a valet of my own so that I should be in no way dependent on his comings and goings and could drive about, elegantly pressed and groomed, to visit the studios and call upon my friends. He and Randolph Scott shared the house, which was on the beach, and we lay in the sun, swam in the redundant pool, with the Pacific pounding away a few yards from us, relaxed and gossiped and, for a little, the war turned away and allowed me to have a good time. Hollywood is lavish to its visitors, particularly if the visitors have any claim to celebrity. In my case I had it both ways. Leaving aside the harassing but flattering attentions of Press photographers, radio agents, newspaper columnists, etc., I had a number of friends, some of long standing, whom I was eager to see. In the course of those very few days it seemed to me that I saw them all, and more. There was hardly a dull moment, or even time for introspection, except on the rare occasions when I found myself alone in my car driving from somebody's house to somebody else's house. There were cocktail-parties, dinner-parties, studio luncheons, interludes in projection rooms looking at unfinished movies, and longer interludes looking at completely finished ones. There was also an impressive banquet given by Darryl Zanuck for Winthrop Aldrich, the Head of the Red Cross. The keynote of the occasion was patriotism and a number of English actors present made moving speeches. I sat gripping Madeleine Carroll's hand under the table and feeling rather out of it.

Meanwhile the war news got worse and worse. I had a small radio in my bedroom to which I listened each morning while I was having breakfast. Outside, the ocean glittered and the famous Californian sunshine gave monotonously the best performance of its career; the mountains stood about idly like benevolent Nannies keeping a protective eye on their infant charges playing in the park. Behind and beyond them were two thousand miles of deserts and plains and flourishing, populous cities reaching to the Eastern Seaboard; beyond this were a further three thousand miles of grey sea stretching to the shores of Europe, breaking on the edge of that cruelly darkling plain 'where ignorant armies clashed by night'. They clashed by night and they clashed by day: along the once peaceful roads German tanks were advancing relentlessly; German aeroplanes were filling the once quiet air with hideous sound and scattering the earth with death. The British Expeditionary Force was trapped. It was unlikely that more than a few thousand English soliders would be able to escape. England was waiting, calmly of course, but with the dreadful, controlled calm of someone who knows that catastrophe is imminent and is yet powerless to avert it. Englishwomen were running their houses, queuing up for their groceries, serving in canteens, driving cars, working in factories, offices, theatres, cinemas, hospitals and ministries, with, all the time, the growing realisation that hope was fading, that only a miracle could save their sons and husbands and brothers and lovers from annihilation. The minor miracle that did occur – the fabulous victorious defeat of Dunkirk – was still nearly a week away.

I, eating scrambled eggs and crisp Beechnut bacon in a bedroom overlooking the Pacific, was five thousand miles away, and I suddenly knew that I couldn't bear it and that I must leave at once. I telephoned and got a reservation and then drove out to Fritzi Massary's house to lunch. Fritzi was sitting on the terrace when I arrived; by her was a radio, and the tears were running down her face. Liesl and Bruno Franck, her daughter and son-in-law, were sitting together in a hammock-seat staring at the bright garden while the announcer's voice stabbed out the latest bulletins. Fritzi switched off the radio when I appeared and flung her arms round me; Ella, her maid, flew out of the house and embraced me too, and after a while, with the radio silenced and with the aid of a strong bourbon and ginger-ale the atmosphere became less tremulous and I relaxed and we laughed and talked of other things.

Later on that day, after I had packed, and after a hurriedly organised farewell cocktail-party at Cary's, Marlene Dietrich drove me away in her car. It had been an understood thing between us for years that she should always see me off at airports and stations and docks whenever she happened to be in the vicinity, and here we were again bowling along in her black Packard as we had done so often before. We didn't talk much, beyond a few local Hollywood superficialities, but she knew that I was feeling low and I knew that she knew and it wasn't necessary to go on about it.

Afterwards I reflected how curious it was that, in a moment of intense patriotic unhappiness, the people who had comforted me most were, by birth and breeding, completely Teutonic.

Upon arriving in New York I found cables from Campbell Stuart and Dallas Brooks explaining that under the new National Government Duff Cooper had been appointed Minister of Information and that he was taking over our organisation. Knowing that Winston Churchill had never been a fervent admirer of Campbell Stuart, I gathered, rightly, that he was out of a job, for the time being at any rate. I had no way of knowing to what extent this would affect our Paris office and whether it would continue to function as it was or be reorganised or disbanded; I therefore cabled to Duff Cooper suggesting that I return at once either to Paris or London, whichever he thought best. On the following day I received an ambiguous reply from him saying that he thought I could be of more use in America, but that I must use my own judgment as to whether I returned or not. Although I had no illusions about my importance to the Paris office, where I had been little more than a figure-head for several months, I did feel strongly, having founded it and weaned and nursed it into health and strength, that if it were to be disbanded, I should be back in time for the finale. Also the suggestion that I could be of more use in America, although possibly true, was too vague to be accepted without further definition and discussion. Maybe I could indeed be of considerable value in America if I were appointed to some specific job, but, without official backing, without being attached either to the Embassy, the British Information Service, or any other British organisation sanctioned by the Government, I would be in an invidious position and unable to achieve anything at all.

Realising that Duff, of whose friendship I was assured and whom I had known well for many years, was probably too engrossed in the arduous business of taking over the Ministry to give much time to my affairs for the moment, I excused his courteous vagueness, restrained the impulse to send back a caustic reply and merely cabled him that I *had* used my own judgement and was flying to London as soon as I could get a reservation. This was a good deal easier said than done and the next few days were maddeningly frustrating. There was apparently no possibility of getting on to a plane for Europe for at least a month. However, finally by argument, persuasion and string-pulling, I managed to procure a reservation on the Clipper scheduled to leave on June the 8th. There was no ship sailing that would have got me home any sooner and so I resigned myself to waiting as patiently as I could. During those interminable ten days, with the news growing steadily worse and the emotional tension in New York rising, I tried really hard to keep outwardly calm and not to allow the prevailing hysteria of the Press and radio to get me down. I also tried repeatedly to analyse my emotions coldly and clearly; to still my anxieties by segregating them, by separating the sheep from the goats. How much, for instance, of this general desolation I felt was really true? How much of it was based on facile sentimentalism? I remember looking up the word 'patriot' in the Oxford Dictionary: 'Patriot. One who defends or is zealous for his country's freedom or rights. Hence, Patriotic, adjective; Patriotically, adverb; and Patriotism, noun'. It was accurate enough as far as it went and there was almost comfort in its flat brevity. I wondered how truly zealous I was for my country's freedom or rights, or if whatever zeal I had was merely superficial; the result of middle-class upbringing, naval influence, and having read Kipling and written *Cavalcade*. True, I had not intended *Cavalcade* to be so Jingoistic, so True Blue Conservative in tone as many people imagined, nor, as many people also imagined, had I dashed it off with cunning political foresight to coincide with the fall of the Labour Government. I had merely decided to write an episodic play depicting thirty years of English life, and it had emerged as my instincts and talent had dictated. However, there it was; in essence definitely patriotic (adjective); a fairly durable proof of my own personal patriotism (noun); and here was I, nine years later, beleaguered in a neutral country at a time of infinite peril to England, weeping patriotically (adverb).

I found it difficult to prove to myself that this patriotic sentimentalism was merely a veneer, superimposed on my real mind by circumstances, by people I had met, by a too easy acceptance of values and traditions that I had not taken the trouble to analyse. Surely, fundamentally, I was too sensible and also too egocentric to permit such outmoded nonsense to sway me? My fears for my personal friends, the people I loved, were easy to understand; also my irrational, but quite natural, desire to be with them in time of trouble rather than comfortably ensconced on the other side of the Atlantic. But England itself? That damp, weather-sodden little island from which for many years I had escaped at the first opportunity? How could I, face to face with myself, admit solemnly and truthfully that I minded so much? By straining thus to coax myself into a mood of cynical detachment, to apply to my quivering nerves a little cool, intellectual balm, I actually wasted a great deal of time, because all that emerged finally from it was the realisation that I was entirely incapable of an intellectual approach to anything; that I had no cynical detachment where my emotions were concerned, and that I was a flagrant, unabashed sentimentalist and likely to remain so until the end of my days. I did love England and all it stood for. I loved its follies and apathies and curious streaks of genius; I loved standing to attention for 'God Save the King'; I loved British courage, British humour, and British understatement; I loved the justice, efficiency and even the dullness of British Colonial Administration. I loved the people – the ordinary, the extraordinary, the good, the bad, the indifferent, and what is more I belonged to that exasperating, weather-sodden little island with its uninspired cooking, its muddled thinking and its unregenerate pride, and it belonged to me whether it liked it or not. There was no escape, no getting round it, that was my personal truth and in facing up to it, once and for all, I experienced a strong relief. From that moment onwards, 2 a.m., in my bedroom at the St Regis Hotel in New York, on Thursday the 30th of May, 1940, one part of my mind at least remained at peace until the end of the war.

I was fortunate that I was able so firmly to consolidate my feelings about my country so early in the war, because in the months and years to come it handed me a few unpleasant surprises.

A few days after this soul-searching took place I was invited again to the White House, and I arrived at Washington in the full blaze of a June afternoon. A car from the White House met me at the airport and conveyed me, sweating profoundly, through the airless streets. There is something unique about Washington in the grip of a heatwave; I know nothing to compare with it excepting perhaps Calcutta just before the monsoons, and there, at least, the heat is expected and familiar, so everyone is prepared for it. Summer always seems to catch Washington unawares, to break over it like an awesome seventh wave, flooding it with sudden, sweltering discomfort. There is air-conditioning, of course, and there are iced drinks and sun-blinds and electric fans, but even those fail to dispel, for me at any rate, a feeling that such breathless oppressiveness must herald a cosmic disaster, that some feckless star has changed its course and we are all about to frizzle, curl up and die.

The President received me in his private office. He was sitting at his desk in his shirt-sleeves, mopping his face with a handkerchief and looking utterly exhausted. He wearily motioned me to a chair and asked his secretary to bring two large Coca-Colas with lots of ice. We talked for about an hour, solemnly this time and without jokes. The evacuation of Dunkirk evidently had moved him profoundly and he spoke of it at length, enlarging, without sentimentality, on the epic quality of the whole operation; this quality, he said, lay deep in the British character and was compounded of diverse ingredients: stubbornness, gallantry, refusal to envisage the possibility of failure, lack of imagination, vision and an inherent genius for improvisation. None but the British, he said with a faint smile, could transform a full-scale military defeat into a shining spiritual victory. Later on he asked me if I thought there was a possibility of the Germans successfully invading England. I replied 'No' immediately, and he said gently that although my vehemence did me credit he wondered how much of it was based on logical reasoning and how much on blind faith. I then explained as clearly as I could that my absolute conviction that England would never be conquered was based neither on logical reasoning nor on blindness, and that its strength lay in the fact that it was shared unquestioningly by well over forty million of my fellow countrymen. All of us, I said, were aware that our defences were inadequate, that our Air Force was outnumbered and that we were in for a very bad time; and all, or nearly all, of us realised that the situation was grim in the extreme, but even so, even in the face of every glaring indication to the contrary, we knew, beyond all logic and reason, that England would not be beaten. 'If that isn't blind faith,' said the President dryly, 'I should like to know what is.'

Later on I wondered, a little irritably, if I had appeared foolish in Roosevelt's eyes: if my bland assertion of faith in England's survival had sounded naive, silly, or even spurious. I felt uneasy and almost ashamed, as though I had drunk too much at a party and wakened the next morning with the vague awareness that I had been showing off, talking out of turn, making an ass of myself. However, by the time I had finished dressing I had arrived at the comforting conclusion that, whatever he thought of me, I had only said what I believed to be true, and although he might consider me ill-informed and possibly hysterical, he was too astute not to recognise my sincerity. When I joined him in his study for a cocktail I was relieved to see that there was no apparent change in his manner towards me; he offered me a dry martini without contempt.

After dinner the President disappeared and, discovering that Mrs Roosevelt had to make an appearance at an Agricultural Students' dance at the Mayflower Hotel, I offered to accompany her. My admiration for her increased when I observed how simply and how kindly she handled the affair. First of all there was the official reception, which took place in the lobby of the hotel. A red-faced gentleman in a white dinner-jacket made a speech of welcome and a young girl dashed forward in a startled manner and handed her a bouquet. Then we were ushered into the ballroom, where the agricultural students were assembled in a vast semi-circle. Mrs Roosevelt, followed sheepishly and anonymously by me, started off from the left and worked her way doggedly to the right shaking hands and saying something appropriate to each one. I shook hands firmly too, and when they mumbled their names at me I mumbled mine back without any sign of mutual recognition; some of the handshakes were so agricultural that I winced, and everyone looked very hot. When this was over we were escorted to a raised dais, where we sat down, were offered a drink and invited to watch a square dance. I had only seen a square dance once before, years ago, in Genesee Depot, Wisconsin, with Lynn and Alfred. Then everybody had arrived muffled to the ears and there was deep snow outside and an atmosphere of country frowstiness inside. This occasion was more elaborate and, although equally noisy, more formal. It was fascinating to see the fierce concentration of all those moist, healthy young faces; they 'dipped for the oyster' and 'dug for the clam' as though their lives depended on it. The setting, of course, was entirely incongruous, but my mind's eye dismissed the modern hotel décor, the immaculate dance band, the careful evening dresses and the chandeliers, and substituted for them paper decorations, oil lamps, wooden benches round the walls, gingham and organdies and a fiddle and an upright cottage piano; then the whole thing fell into place and became genuinely gay and touching and accurate.

When it finished Mrs Roosevelt made a brief speech and we were led back through the lobby by the reception committee and tucked into the car. On the way back to the White House Mrs Roosevelt said that she would like to show me the Lincoln Memorial by moonlight, and so we made a slight detour and presently drew up before that austerely beautiful monument reflected in the water. The air had cooled a little and the dark sky was without a cloud. There was the muted noise of an aeroplane revving up on the airfield in the distance and, further away still, the plaintive whistle of a train; that typical, for ever American sound that always, when I hear it in movies, fills me with nostalgia; a sort of second home-sickness. Our own English trains have a shriller, more purposeful note; they always seem to be whistling for a very good reason, either because they are approaching a level-crossing, or going into a tunnel, or coming out of a tunnel, or whirling round a curve. The American whistle is less definite and has a more mournful quality; it conjures up higher mountains, deeper valleys and vaster distances; its implications are more timeless and strangely devoid of urgency.

President Lincoln looked out quietly at the glittering lights of the spread-out city that he had known so well in its younger, smaller days; at the flashing Coca-Cola signs, at the illuminated names of movie stars scurrying along the marquees or cinemas; at the Capitol, rising like a dignified, flood-lit blanc-mange; and perhaps at Mrs Roosevelt and me sitting in a shiny black car drawn into the side of the wide parkway. I wondered how he would have reacted to the present dangerous, misunderstood world situation: 'I intend no modification of my oft expressed personal wish that all men everywhere could be free' '– and that government of the people, by the people and for the people, shall not perish from the earth.'

3

On Sunday, June the 9th, I drove out to La Guardia airfield with Jack and Natasha. The Clipper, which according to schedule should have left the day before, was sitting complacently on the quiet water like a large prehistoric bird. The airport was buzzing with the usual rumours: there would be three hours delay, there would be six hours delay, there was engine trouble, the plane was not going to take off at all. We stood about and sat about talking brightly. Natasha's manner was tremendously gay and I knew that she was near to tears. Several people had come to see me off: Lynn and Alfred, Ruth Chatterton, Constance Collier, Eleonora von Mendelssohn, Neysa, Tallulah and Clifton. Madeleine Carroll and Simon Elwes were to be my travelling companions and there was a great deal of Press photography, and the atmosphere, beneath the thin veneer of cheerful behaviour, was sad. My own spirits were fairly low; it seemed more than probable that I should not see Jack, Natasha, Alfred and Lynn nor any of my other American friends again for a long time, perhaps never. The large prehistoric bird was about to take Madeleine, Simon and me, together with nine depressed-looking gentlemen of mixed nationalities, away from peace, security, abundant food and bright lights, and plump us down in a world where there were bombs, black-outs, food rationing and many fears; a shadowed world, ennobled perhaps by suffering, redeemed by fortitude and courage, but quite definitely damned uncomfortable.

At long last the final good-byes were said and we were herded into a launch which conveyed us to the Clipper. As I climbed on board I turned and waved, but my friends were already too far away to be distinguishable.

The flight, from the material point of view, was the acme of comfort. We had cocktails and a good dinner; the weather was clear and our passage through the upper air was so smooth that there was no sensation of moving at all; we might just as well have been sitting in a well-appointed bus that had become somehow embedded in the sky. There were several Frenchmen on board who sat staring straight in front of them with misery in their eyes; occasionally they spoke to each other and they cheered up a bit after a couple of cocktails, but they were profoundly unhappy men and I felt very sorry for them. Presently, even before the cocktails, the poignancy of the last good-byes faded in my mind and was replaced by a detached sense of excitement. Madeleine and Simon, I think, felt this too and we became extremely cheerful, perhaps irritatingly so from the point of view of our fellow passengers. Simon was returning to England. Madeleine was determined to get, via Lisbon, to the South of France, where her fiancé and her family were. I had my train reservations for Paris on the Sud-Express which left Lisbon on the morning after we were due to arrive. Lisbon was our point of departure. From there we would all three shoot off in our separate directions and deal with our own separate private problems; meanwhile here we were whirling through space with nothing to do but to enjoy the situation and get the best we could from each other. In this I must say we succeeded triumphantly. None of the three of us knew each other well. We had met on and off over a number of years, but only casually, without significance and, strangely enough, we have only met casually since. But that journey established an intimacy between us which, as far as I am concerned, will always remain. We talked without ceasing and laughed immoderately; the uncertainty into which we were flying at such high speed, combined with the fact that we were the only British passengers on the plane, set us apart in our own company, gave wings to our conversation and brought us closer than we could ever possibly have been in less specialised circumstances.

The next day, when we were somewhere between the Azores and Lisbon, the pilot sent word back that Italy had entered the war. This galvanised our fellow passengers into a state of frantic volubility and for a while the noise was considerable. We arrived at Lisbon at 7.30 p.m.

Early the next morning I was rung up from the Embassy and told that the Ambassador wished to see me and would I come at once and have breakfast with him. I hurriedly packed my overnight bag so as to be ready to catch the train, which left at twelve-thirty, and drove in a taxi to the Embassy. The Ambassador, Sir Walford Selby, whom I had never met before, received me kindly and proceeded, unknown to him and to me, to save my life. The upshot of his conversation was that he felt it his duty to forbid me to go to France, as the Embassy had been unable to establish any communications with Paris for the last ten days and the situation was growing steadily worse. I explained that my reservations were made and that I was anxious to get to Paris as soon as possible if only to help in evacuating my office staff. He then told me to cancel my reservations and that he would guarantee me priority on a plane direct to England within the next few days. From there, he added, I could fly across to Paris in a couple of hours if circumstances permitted it, but that if I persisted in travelling overland as arranged he would have to put it on record that it was entirely against his official advice. Impressed by the urgency of his tone and the common sense of his words, I agreed, and we sat down to breakfast. The Sud-Express left that morning without me and arrived, presumably, in Paris on the morning of the 13th, twenty-four hours before Hitler. Had I been on it I should have only discovered my flat empty and the office evacuated and abandoned; I should also have discovered that every avenue of escape was closed and, in due course, been arrested, imprisoned, and possibly shot. I owe indeed a great debt of gratitude to Sir Walford Selby.

The few days I spent in Lisbon were strained but uneventful. Madeleine managed, by the expenditure of a great deal of personal charm, and determination, to get herself flown to Madrid, whence she intended to make her way to Hendaye and over the border into France.

Simon was due to leave on the 14th, in the same plane with me. The Ambassador asked me to speak at the British Club the day before I left, which filled me with inward dismay because I loathe making impromptu speeches and there was no time to prepare one. However, he had been more than kind to me and the least I could do was consent. It was a stag luncheon and consisted of about seventy-five club members and a few journalists. As usual on such occasions, I was nervous and picked at the food without enthusiasm, wishing myself anywhere else in the world but where I was. However, once the secretary had introduced me and I was on my feet I felt better. I started by reading them a fine piece of writing from the *New York Times* on Dunkirk, then I spoke firmly about Anglo-American relations, reiterated my conviction that in spite of all alarms and portents England would survive, and finished up, rather theatrically, with the Toast from *Cavalcade*. They were a receptive audience and my nerves vanished when I began speaking. It was no moment to indulge in personal nervous flurries, anyhow. They were all British except two of the journalists; I was a transient British visitor, our home was in danger and we were far away. I, luckier than they, was going back. Even if I had muffed every word and made a stammering fool of myself they would have understood and been sympathetic and would, I think, rather have listened to me than not. As it was, I didn't do badly and I hope that at least I cheered them a little.

The flight from Lisbon to London was smooth. The plane left at nine o'clock in the morning of June the 14th. There were only a few passengers, among them the Portuguese Ambassador, who sat opposite to Simon and me and talked incessantly: words poured from him in an endless stream punctuated by staccato barks of mirthless laughter. This interminable, agitated monologue combined with the rhythmical roaring of the engine had such a soporific effect on me that my eyes ached and I had to bite my lips and dig my nails into the palms of my hands to prevent myself from falling into a deep sleep. Fortunately, just as I was about to give up the struggle and sink into a coma, the hypnotic spell was broken by the plane landing at Bordeaux. Simon and I staggered out into the sunshine and went straight to the airport café, where we revived ourselves with black coffee heavily laced with cognac. The place was crammed with people; the noise was deafening and the atmosphere quivered with hysteria. News had come through that the Germans had entered Paris that morning. We sat squashed against the wall at a corner table and watched the crowd milling about. Many people, both men and women, were in tears. Others looked grey, defeated and without hope. I felt rather sick and after a while we went outside.

Our plane was standing on the runway with a cordon of gendarmes round it to prevent refugees from attempting to stow away on board. I think, but I am not sure, that it was the last civilian aircraft to touch down in France for five years. I remember feeling a sudden, irrational urge to jump into a taxi, drive to the station and get into the first train for Paris: nothing could be easier of course, because the trains would be empty. I longed to see what was happening; whether the city was shuttered up and deserted, or whether there was fighting in the streets, and whether or not Cole and David and the office had got away in time. With a pang I conjured up a picture of my light, cheerful flat in the Place Vendôme; the cool quiet of the entrance hall after the bright heat of the Place; the rickety little *ascenseur* with its flapping glass-panelled doors and open top, creaking slowly up to the fifth floor on its oily steel pole; the familiar unforgettable smell of floor polish, dusty stair carpets and other people's cooking which, quite inoffensively, permeated the whole rambling building. My flat had its own particular smell; there was cooking mixed up with this too, but it was not predominant; what was predominant was wood-smoke: even if we had not lit the fire in the salon for days the acrid, smoky odour of it still lingered. I wondered if Yvonne had stayed on in the flat and was at this moment sitting in the kitchen, or if she had packed up as much as she could and abandoned it to its fate. I wondered also about my French friends;

which of them had managed to escape and which of them had remained: Blanche Prenex in her tiny flat in the Avenue Victoire, sitting behind bolted doors, seething with anti-German fury; Yvonne Printemps in her sunny house at Neuilly; Jean Cocteau, Maurice Chevalier, Genevieve Tabouis, Denise and Edouard Bourdet, Henri Bernstein, Eve Curie, Bébé Bérard, Marie-Louise Bousquet etc., etc., and again etc. There were so many that I knew and liked and had fun with, more than I had realised, now, suddenly, with appalling swiftness, quarantined in defeat, out of my reach perhaps for years, possibly for ever. The thought of the Nazis swaggering through the streets of Paris, as, only a year before, I had watched them swaggering through the streets of Danzig, was unbearable. I discovered, standing there on the airfield at Bordeaux, that my affection for Paris was deeper and stronger than I knew; that its fall and surrender affected me personally much more than I imagined it could, almost as though I belonged to it. Simon, noticing, I think, that I was looking miserable, suggested that we expend the francs we had over on some champagne, a couple of bottles for the pilot and his assistant and one for ourselves. I agreed to this with the proviso that we gave it to them after we landed at Hendon. We just managed to get the three bottles in time before we were ordered back to the aircraft. Upon boarding it we noted, to our relief, that the voluble Ambassador had found some friends and moved to the forward end of the plane. Every seat was now occupied. In the two places on the other side of the aisle from us were a youngish man and woman; she was polishing her nails violently with a chamois leather buffer that she had taken from her bag; he had his head down and was staring at a book on his lap; I noticed two tears splash on to the open pages. In the two seats opposite us, one of which had been vacated by the Ambassador, were two nuns. They sat quietly with their hands folded, wearing expressions of complete blankness. Remembering that Simon was an ardent Catholic I restrained the impulse to hiss at him that two nuns travelling together were well known to be terribly unlucky in planes, trains or ships, and that we were practically bound to crash on the take-off. Presently the aircraft gave a shudder as though it shared my superstition and began to lumber uneasily along the runway. One of the nuns crossed herself with a quick surreptitiousness that endeared her to me; the plane came to a halt, turned slowly into the wind, revved up its engines with such violence that our cheeks wobbled like jellies, and it finally took off. I pressed my forehead against the small glass window and watched France sink away into the summer haze. A little later we managed, with the help of the steward, to open our bottle of champagne, and when we had drunk most of it out of plastic mugs, we felt cheerful again.

The plane flew low over the Channel Islands, we could see fishing boats rocking in the harbours and children playing on the beaches, and then, lower still, we flew across the Hampshire coast and on towards London. The countryside was bathed in golden, late afternoon sunlight; trees and telegraph-poles made black shadows across the roads and fields and we could distinguish cattle standing about in the lush meadows. The impression of calm and peace, of remoteness from war, was extraordinary. There it lay, the English land, waiting gently for the dusk that follows a long summer day.

PART FOUR

On Sunday, July 21st, I sailed from Liverpool for New York on the *Britannic*. The ship, crammed to the gunwales, had been lying in the Mersey for twenty-four hours with several other large vessels until the convoy escort was ready to usher it on to the bosom of the Atlantic. Many of the passengers lived in their lifebelts and we queued up for everything; meals were staggered because there were too many of us to be served at one sitting. We queued up not only for lunch and dinner but for baths, lavatories and even lifeboat drill. The ship was overrun by children ranging from babies a few months old to cheerful little boys of twelve and thirteen who wore neat grey flannel suits, scampered up and down the decks chattering to each other in clear, treble English voices, and treated the whole voyage as high adventure, which indeed it might have been. There were several play-pens put up on the promenade deck in which anxious mothers could deposit their younger offspring and snatch a few hours of comparative peace. Fortunately the weather was calm, so there was no seasickness to contend with. However, from dawn to dusk the noise was earsplitting. Only after dinner in the smoking-room, when the young had been stowed away in their bunks, was it possible to be quiet and make believe for a little that it was an ordinary voyage without urgency and the underlying dread of sudden disaster. I spent a good deal of time in my cabin trying to review the last five weeks as objectively as possible.

My day-to-day diary offered me little but a series of flat statements, occasionally enlivened by a sudden outburst of frustrated rage. I seemed to have been tied into a strait-jacket of Frustration since the moment I had set foot on English ground in June. I found it difficult to believe that that hopeful, happy landing was only five weeks ago; it seemed years away, years of decisions, counter-decisions, plans, hopes, disappointments and interviews. Above all, interviews. My friends in high places had been amiable, understanding and patient, they had also been very, very busy. I had telephoned them, waylaid them, written to them, forced my way into their offices and homes and nagged at them to give me a job that I considered worth while. This, of course, was the stumbling-block, because what I considered worth while differed radically from what they considered worth while. I could have obtained some minor position in the Ministry of Information; I could have organised entertainments at shore establishments anywhere from John o' Groats to Land's End in spite of the fact that hundreds of other people were doing exactly that, both in uniform and out of it. I could have become, with a little string-pulling, a Welfare Officer in the R.N.V.R., which would have been an excellent solution of my problem within its limits, but it seemed to me then, as indeed it had seemed before, that the limits would have been too limiting. One clear fact only emerged from all the blather, and that was my conviction that wherever I went and whatever I did my celebrity value should be utilised to its fullest extent. This obviously was sound sense, and after much discussion with influential friends, non-influential friends, loved ones and casual acquaintances, I finally decided to follow the advice Duff Cooper had given me at the outset, which was to go back to the United States, where, he assured me, I could be far more useful than in England. So here I was setting forth on my travels again with a Ministry of Information ticket and a private letter from Duff Cooper to Lord Lothian in Washington. I had, of course, a fairly clear idea of the recommendations contained in the letter, but I had not actually read it. My feelings were mixed, because I had so recently spent six weeks in America and had no wish to return so soon; the mission I was embarking upon was hazy and unspecified and one that the British Ambassador might be unwilling to recognise. Also I was leaving behind a great many people I was fond of and a great many things that mattered to me. In addition to frustrations, irritations and perplexities, there had been an intricate problem to deal with during those five weeks. This was the question of whether or not we should evacuate the children of the Actors' Orphanage to

Canada or America for the duration of the war. My committee and I were much concerned about this and the discussions of it were long and many, and complicated by the fact that all of us, being actors and highly articulate, talked at once. Finally it had been decided that all the children under the age of fifteen should be transferred to America. A Hollywood committee of British actors and actresses was hurriedly formed under the aegis of Dame May Whitty and it was ultimately arranged, thanks to the generosity of the Gould Foundation in the Bronx, that our orphans should be taken in, educated and cared for. The whole business was further complicated by the fact that only a few of them were actually orphans; many had one parent living and in some cases both. This entailed, of course, getting permission from the various parents and relatives concerned. When I sailed on the *Britannic* this was still under discussion; the Hollywood committee was arguing with itself and, by cable, with us whether the children should be settled in California among the oranges and sunshine where there wasn't anywhere for them to live, or in New York without the oranges and sunshine where there was. All this I had guaranteed to deal with on arrival in New York.

Meanwhile the grey ships of the convoy steamed on across the Atlantic with alert little destroyers rounding them up and barking at their heels. Happily no submarines appeared and the voyage was uneventful. Upon arrival in New York I was met by a hot and flustered gentleman from the British Information Service, who implored me breathlessly to tell the Press that I was arriving unofficially on my own theatrical business. This irritated me and I explained to him that the Press, as usual, had met me at Quarantine, but that he need not worry for I had been the soul of discretion. New York was hotter than hell and Washington even hotter, and I rocketed back and forth between the two cities, interviewing, persuading, arguing and cajoling, all without the faintest effect. Lord Lothian was sceptical about the Duff Cooper plan, but assured me that I could be of considerable service if I travelled about the States for a while and talked to key citizens, notably news editors and tycoons in the various cities, about England and the British war effort, so off I went by train and plane and talked at every possible opportunity. In each city I visited the hospitality was, as always, unfailing. People I had never met in my life gave dinner-parties, cocktail-parties, lunches, week-end parties; during which I made speeches, sang songs and generally tried to make myself as attractive as possible. I received much genuine kindness and, naturally enough, a good deal of 'lionising'. Only occasionally I ran into trouble and had to bare my teeth in a snarl; once when a purple-faced business magnate, at a dinner in Salt Lake City, announced with fatuous conviction that Britain was done for and that I could be god-damn sure that America, having won the 1914–18 war, was not going to be played for a sucker a second time. This of course was routine Isolationist stuff and I dealt with it accordingly. It was not a notable victory, because after I had withered and insulted him well beyond the bounds of social behaviour, he seemed to forget entirely what the argument was about, and, placing a pudgy beringed hand on my shoulder, asked me if I played golf. Another maddening occasion was a brief interview with ex-President Hoover in Palo Alto, California. He delivered a tirade against England and the perfidies of the British Government which went on for about a quarter of an hour, during which I sat with Paul Smith, the editor of the *San Francisco Chronicle*, smoking a cigarette and watching Mr Hoover's small eyes suffusing in his large, square face. On this occasion I refrained from any comment whatsoever, because he seemed so dangerously cross that even the lightest verbal pin-prick might have given him a stroke. I discovered later that the reason of his outburst was that he had been prevented by the British from going over to occupied Belgium and France and delivering food to the starving populations. Similar excursions apparently had earned him spectacular acclaim in the last war; and although it had been explained to him that any food taken by him to occupied countries would immediately be appropriated by the Nazis, and therefore be of no assistance to anyone but the enemy, the craze to do publicised good had obviously driven common sense from his mind, and there he stood, a humanitarian *manqué*, and hopping mad into the bargain. There were, in addition to these, a few minor tussles, but on the whole my self-imposed Odyssey was rewarded by much more sympathetic understanding than I had anticipated. It also cost me a great deal of money, for I was travelling unofficially and paying my own expenses out of my private bank account in New York. The fact that by doing this I was breaking the law and making myself liable to heavy fines and imprisonment had been tactfully withheld from me both by the Minister of Information and the British Ambassador. I pressed on therefore in cheerful ignorance, upheld by the thought that I was at least spending my own hard-earned money in my country's cause. The total amount expended was, in English currency, approximately £11,000.

I returned to New York. I returned to Washington. I reported what I had heard and observed and what, if anything, I had deduced from it. Lord Lothian was flattering and grateful, but President Roosevelt and Harry Hopkins were definitely more interested. In the meantime the orphans arrived from England; and were installed in the Gould Foundation, where they were welcomed enthusiastically and made a great deal more comfortable than they had ever been in their lives. They splashed about in a swimming pool; learned baseball; were wrapped in hygiene and psychiatry and surfeited with the Grade A milk of human kindness. The generosity of the American welfare officials, indeed the generosity of everybody concerned, officials or not, was so heart-warming and so unstinting that it could never be adequately repaid and, I hope, never forgotten. The fact that when the children ultimately returned to England many of them were exceedingly difficult to manage was nobody's fault. The immediate amenities of living in modern America are greatly in advance of those of war-scarred England and it was tricky trying to persuade the adolescents, particularly the girls, that life was real, life was earnest, and that lipsticks, motor rides, summer camping and chocolate Malteds were *not* the goal. Some of them settled down all right and a few, with praiseworthy determination, returned to the States when they were old enough and married. The smaller ones, of course, missed their luxury cots only briefly and accepted their greyer surroundings without lasting regrets.

2

During my voyage across the Atlantic in the *Britannic* I met a man whom I had known slightly before called Ingram Fraser. He was nice-looking, suave, spoke impeccable French and was, to me, quite palpably involved in some form of cloak and dagger business. It was difficult then, as indeed it still is, to distinguish between those who were genuinely engaged in some branch of the Intelligence services and those who were merely shooting a line and pretending to be. There was a saying, much quoted in the war years, that if an Englishman told you he was a secret agent it was a lie, and that if an American told you the same thing it was true. Ingram, however, was English, or rather Scottish, and we walked round each other warily for days. Finally, on the last night of the trip, we sneaked out of the smoking-room with our whiskies and sodas and went into the ladies' writing-room, which was not used in the evenings and was unlighted because of the black-out. Here, in the eerie darkness lit only by the glow of our cigarettes, we exchanged mutual confidences. No desperate secrets inimical to the security of our troops on land or sea emerged from the conversation, but a few small kittens were let out of a few small bags and were allowed to frolic for a little before we popped them back and returned to the smoking-room. The upshot of it was that shortly after my arrival in New York Ingram took me to visit a man who was to have a considerable influence on the next few years of my life. His name was William (now Sir William) Stephenson, and he was known colloquially as Little Bill. Little Bill received me in a chintz-covered room in the Hampshire House. He was small, quietly affable and talked very little. He gave me two strong 'Cuba Libres' one after the other, and waited politely for me to talk a great deal. I obliged, up to a point, and was asked to return a few evenings later. He did not make the psychological mistake of swearing me to secrecy. He never mentioned secrecy at all. That impressed me, because by that time I was of course perfectly aware that whatever his exact occupation was, it was very secret indeed. It is not my business here to discuss his activities except when those activities impinged upon my own life, which from time to time they did. This, for me, momentous meeting took place at the end of July, 1940, and from then until the end of the war the realisation that Little Bill completely trusted my integrity, had faith in my discretion and understanding of my motives, was a great comfort to me. That suite in the Hampshire House with the outside chintz flowers crawling over the walls became pleasantly familiar to me, and in later years, when he moved into equally luxurious but more aesthetically austere surroundings, I mourned it.

Another casual acquaintanceship that had begun in the Hotel de l'Univers at Arras in November, 1939, and been renewed in May, now became significant. During one of my frequent visits to Washington, Richard Casey, the Australian Minister, invited me to lunch and asked me if I would like to go out to the Antipodes as a guest of the Australian Government to make broadcasts about the British war effort and give concerts for troops in training and for the Australian Red Cross. He showed me cables he had received from Robert Menzies, the Prime Minister, and Sir Keith Murdoch, the Minister of Information, assuring me of a wonderful welcome. This, being the first concrete offer I had had to do anything constructive since Campbell Stuart had asked me to go to Paris in August 1939, cheered me up considerably. I went to ask Lord Lothian's advice, which was definite and, I thought, almost over-enthusiastic. I suspected from the glint of incredulous relief in his eye that the possibility of my being removed to the other side of the world was the best news he had heard since Science and Health. Not that he betrayed this in any undiplomatic manner; he merely slapped me on the back and asked me to stay lunch, after which he graciously ushered me out and, a trifle prematurely, wished me 'Bon Voyage'. Poor Lord Lothian. He was a kindly man and I fear my constant re-appearance in his Embassy must have irritated him exceedingly. He promised to wire his approval of the Australian visit to Duff Cooper. I also cabled to Duff, and then returned to New York to discuss the project with Little Bill, who thought it a good idea provided I got back in the following March, when, he said, he would have something of great importance to discuss with me. Encouraged by these two approvals and without waiting for Duff's reply (which was just as well, for neither he nor anyone in the M. of I. even acknowledged my cable), I wired to Robert Menzies in Canberra accepting his invitation and received a confirmatory cable by return. After a series of detailed advices, recommendations and projected itineraries had flown between Washington and Canberra, it was decided that I should leave by ship, rather than by plane, to give myself time to prepare a dozen broadcasts and read up as much information about Australian history as I could cram into my brain. Finally, on October the 16th, I sailed from San Pedro, California.

3

The *Monterey*, one of the ships of the Matson Line, was comfortable and half-empty. The voyage lasted for three weeks. We stopped for a day in Honolulu, where the ukeleles played 'Aloha', leis were hung round my neck and the well-remembered harbour obligingly produced all its familiar glamour. The native boys dived for nickels and dimes while the music came wafting over the blue water as we drew alongside. Diamond Head rose, plum-coloured, in the sunlight, and if there was a war being waged anywhere one felt that it couldn't even be so near as the other side of the world; that it must be on another star.

Later on in the war, when my journeys were by air and less relaxed, I often looked back on the curious, detached peace of that voyage to Australia, while the *Monterey* steamed across the, as yet, un-blooded Pacific. Soon after we left Honolulu we were told that our course would be deflected, because orders had come through to the Captain that instead of calling at Fiji and Pago-Pago, and arriving ultimately in Fremantle, we would go via Japan and the China Sea and arrive in Sydney. There was a good deal of anxious surmise and discussion among the passengers. As far as I was concerned, I didn't mind one way or the other. The detour would give me a few more days to work on my broadcasts and prepare myself for my impact on Australia and Australia's impact on me. Also I was delighted at the idea of visiting Yokohama and Tokyo again, and also Shanghai, where, in the February of 1930, I had written *Private Lives*.

The ten days and nights separating Honolulu from Yokohama followed each other demurely and without incident. As we neared the Japanese coast the weather became colder and there were no more flying fish. At last, one windy, rainy morning, I looked out at the bay of Yokohama, at the miniature hills and cliffs, bright green under a heavy sky. We were approaching the docks and so I spruced myself up to go ashore. However, I needn't have troubled, because none of the few English passengers were given permission to land. I asked the Japanese Immigration Officer for an explanation of this, but he merely looked at me with an expression of cold dislike and turned his back on me. I controlled an overwhelming urge to kick him across the smoking-room and went to see the Captain, who said that nothing could be done, so I resigned myself to a day of irritated solitude in an empty ship and retired to my cabin with a book.

To be confined to a ship in harbour was dismally frustrating. There, lying just near, was the alien town with its shops, streets and cafés to be explored. Here was I, having planned to drive to Tokyo, do some shopping, have a drink at the Imperial Hotel and a Sukiyaki dinner in some recherché Japanese restaurant, imprisoned either in my cabin or the smoking-room, or leaning on the deck rail looking wistfully at the activities of the port. By dinner-time I had worked myself into a rage. I asked my table steward if he was going ashore. He said 'Yes', with a slight leer, and added that about a dozen of the crew always made up a party when the ship was in Yokohama, where the night-life was even gayer than in Tokyo. This later proved to be a gross over-statement; however, I bribed him to wangle me a crew pass and spent the next hours disguising myself as a tough American seaman. My bedroom steward entered into the spirit of the thing and produced a cap and a duffle coat. I emptied my pockets of anything that might identify me and also left behind my watch and identity bracelet. In due course I was conducted below and introduced to 'the boys', and off we went. We were lightly searched by an official at the harbour gate, during which I gave a performance of slightly drunken resentment which delighted 'the boys'. After this initial excitement, I regret to say the evening was rather dull. We went from bar to bar and brothel to brothel; a few tattered-looking geishas appeared from time to time and led some of 'the boys' away for a little while. They returned to us later, looking, I thought, far from refreshed. By 2 a.m. some of us were drunk, some of us were irritable and all of us were sleepy. Actually the only thing that interested me in our progress from bar to bar was the preponderance of Germans. In every place we visited there were numbers of them, drinking gallons of musty beer and occasionally heiling Hitler. One of them, a second officer on an oil tanker, came and sat next to me. His English was fairly good but not nearly as good as my American. Our conversation was fatuous to the point of imbecility but it convulsed 'the boys'. At long last my table steward and I rounded up as many of our companions as we could find and reeled back to the ship. The evening fortunately had passed without incident and there were no repercussions, although I reproached myself afterwards for my silliness, for had I by chance been caught I might have found myself in serious trouble. There might even have been more questions asked about me in the House of Commons.

A few days later we sailed up the Whang-Po river and slid alongside the Shanghai Bund. The city looked unchanged, and, except for a few observation posts drooped with barbed wire at the corners of certain streets, there was no outward indication of war. The traffic and noise and general hubbub of the waterfront was the same as before, bicycles and rickshaws weaved in and out between the larger vehicles and 'Coolie' blue was, as usual, the predominant colour. It is a wonderful blue and was the first thing to attract my eye, when, years before, I arrived in Shanghai for the first time.

The *Monterey* stayed in Shanghai for two whole days, so I packed a suitcase and went to the Cathay Hotel, where I was received with enthusiasm and given a large suite filled with managerial flowers. Although there was no actual plaque announcing that I had written *Private Lives* there, the management, despite the rigours of war and occupation, had obviously remembered the fact with pride, which touched me. I enjoyed those two days; it was a relief to be on land again and there were several old friends to visit and much to remember. I was determined to call on Madame Birt (Mamita) although advised on all sides not to because both her daughters, Tita and Margot, were married to Italians and her husband, Dr Birt, was apparently an ardent Nazi. This, though disconcerting, I decided to ignore. Mamita had been hospitable to me in the past; she was a remarkable old lady and I was fond of her, and so, with some difficulty, because she had changed her address, I ran her to earth in a small, dark flat in an apartment building. She received me with surprise, and then, after some strained, formal conversation, burst into tears. After that the tension lessened and we talked of old days and vanished pleasures in a less tormented world. It was, on the whole, a sad little reunion, but I was glad I went, for I think my visit cheered her. In addition to this I did a broadcast, defiantly anti-Japanese in tone; visited another old friend, Oke Hartman, in a lacquered Chinese house where I ate a delicious but interminable Chinese dinner; bought two vast tins of caviar and several bottles of vodka from a Russian restaurant proprietor, and finally returned to the ship.

Between Shanghai and Manila the weather changed and became tropical again; the flying fish reappeared and broke the oily surface of the sea in vast shoals, skittering along until the hot sun dried their wings and they plopped back into the water. I spent most of each day either reading or banging away at my typewriter. The broadcasts were not easy to write, as I had no idea of what the Australian public would or wouldn't like. I persevered, however, on the assumption that lack of pomposity and simplicity of style were the two key rules to follow when writing for any public. I tried to inject a little humour into them here and there whenever an opportunity offered, and hoped for the best. When finished they were innocuous and, I fear, a trifle dull. However, when I eventually spoke them into the microphone they apparently satisfied the listeners, for I received many letters from people in out-of-the way places, saying how comforting it had been to hear news of home at first hand. These broadcasts were later published in booklet form in aid of the

Australian Red Cross, and, later still, Heinemann's published them in England.

The ship paused in Manila for one night. I gave a Press interview, made a short impromptu broadcast and then dined with the American High Commissioner. The news had just come through that Roosevelt had been re-elected, and I remembered the last time I had seen him, sitting up in bed in the White House having his breakfast. He was in a very cheerful mood because he had at last managed to get Congress to agree to allow Great Britain to have the fifty destroyers about which there had been such a hullabaloo. When I asked him point-blank what he thought his chances were of winning the election, he said briefly, with a twinkle in his eye, 'Willkie will talk and I won't.'

From Manila to Sydney the *Monterey* was crammed with American service wives and children. The pandemonium was deafening, the dining-saloon like Bedlam, and the stewards run ragged. I emerged from my cabin very seldom, generally at dead of night when the decks were deserted. There were a number of cocktail-parties given daily in different cabins; these often ended in tears and, on one occasion, in a rousing, hair-pulling, face-slapping free-for-all, which assumed such serious proportions that the Captain had to be sent for. Judging from the eye-witness account given me by my bedroom steward it had been a remarkable spectacle involving, all told, about twenty people. The origin of the fracas remained obscure, but apparently it began with a slight argument between two naval wives about their respective children. Mother love, particularly in America, is a highly-respected and much-publicised emotion and, when exacerbated by gin and bourbon, it can become extremely formidable. On this occasion it burst all bounds and the ship rocked with the repercussions for several days.

Meanwhile the islands of the East Indies slipped by; there was a series of spectacular dawns and sunsets and at night the stars grew larger and larger. At home the blitzes had lessened, and England, grim but undismayed after its first baptism of fire, was settling down to the rigours of the first real war-time winter.

I had lots of time to think during those long sweltering days and nights. Now, looking back across so many years, I find it difficult to recapture the curious, over-comfortable, nightmare quality of that voyage. Perhaps nightmare is too dramatic a word to use; it was only really nightmarish at moments when imagined horrors took advantage of a few hours' imsomnia and pounced on to my nerves. Most of the time I managed, as far as I can remember, to be fairly detached and to concentrate on my forthcoming tour of Australia.

Now, in the early 1950s, those alarms and despondencies and desperate moments are over and done with, endured and dealt with more than ten years ago. Even then, in November, 1940, in my cabin in the *Monterey*, the agitations of a few weeks back had faded and lost their reality. If only one could train oneself to remember in moments of crisis or despair how swiftly the passage of time, even a comparatively little time, can relax tension and deaden pain. Gay episodes I find easier to recall. I can enjoy retrospective laughter again and again, but retrospective tears never. The eyes remain dry.

4

The *Monterey* arrived in Sydney harbour at mid-day on November the 16th. The rain and mist that had enveloped us all the morning cleared by the time the ship drew alongside, and I was able to get a bird's-eye view from the upper deck rail of my reception committee. There seemed to be a great many of them and I was shattered for a few seconds by an attack of 'First Night' nerves. I felt panic-stricken, under-rehearsed and desperately unsure of my lines. My heart sank still further when I saw a radio van and newsreel cameras. I am not very good at making impromptu speeches, although in later years I have improved. I was entirely alone with no supporting cast and not even an assistant stage-manager to cue me. My brain felt woolly and clogged with fear and I knew with dreadful certainty that when the microphone was shoved under my nose I should make a complete fool of myself.

Fortunately by the time the Press men had come on board and photographed me and fired questions at me, my nervousness had diminished enough to enable me to step ashore with outward certainty at least. I was greeted by a bewildering number of officials, who rushed me immediately to the dreaded microphone; the news cameras clicked; flash-bulbs blinded me and I managed to stammer out a few stereotyped phrases without utterly disgracing myself. However, I was unable to prevent my mind's eye envisaging thousands of disgruntled Australians, in faraway townships and sheep farms, crouching eagerly over their radios in expectation of a gay flood of Mayfair witticisms, only to be fobbed off with a strangulated, disembodied voice, saying 'Hullo, Australia – I am very happy to be here.' When this unimpressive performance was over there were more introductions and hand-shakings and I was hustled into a car and driven to the Australia Hotel. People in the streets waved as I passed, and I waved back and smiled until my face muscles ached. Upon arrival at the hotel I was plumped straight into a Press reception. Now to me there is nothing in the world so nerve racking as a Press reception. It isn't that newspaper men and women individually are so very different from anyone else; it isn't that they are universally malign and ill-disposed and determined to strip their shivering victims of every shred of dignity and charm. On the contrary, most of them, with a few exceptions, are human, kindly and interested. *En masse*, however, the atmosphere they create is uneasy and sticky with prejudice. This prejudice is, I am sure, quite unintentional in most cases and, on the whole, understandable. Newspaper reporting, either of events or people, depends for its effectiveness on superficial observation and snap judgments; speed and brevity are essential and there is rarely time for subtle analysis or true assessment of character. Usually, in the case of a celebrity, the label has been fixed and the clichés set for years. Sometime in the past, when they stepped into contemporary fame for the first time, some reporter coined a phrase, some interviewer emphasised a peculiarity, some incident occurred that stamped their per-sonalities indelibly on to the journalistic mind. From then on they are typed once and for all and the prejudice is formed. In my particular case the die was cast in 1924, when *The Vortex* was produced in London and I was rocketed overnight into a blaze of publicity. *The Vortex* was a social drama of the 1920s, satirising a small group of wealthy, decadent people. I played the part of a neurotic misfit who took drugs, made sharp, witty remarks and was desolately unhappy. There was my label, ready to hand and glaringly printed. Nicky Lancaster was twenty-four, well groomed, witty and decadent. Noël Coward, who played him, also was twenty-four and presumably well groomed, witty and decadent. Whether or not he was a drug addict was never accurately proved, although it was frequently suspected; his underlying desolate unhappiness, although suspected, was never proved either, but none of that was important. All that was important for monotonous future reference was the created image – the talented, neurotic sophisticated playboy. In later years this imaginary, rather tiresome figure, suffered occasional eclipses but they were of short duration. *Cavalcade, Bitter Sweet, This Happy Breed, Brief Encounter* and *In Which We Serve* scratched a little gloss off the legend, but not enough to damage it irreparably. It still exists today in 1952, with the slight modification that I am now an ageing playboy, still witty, still brittle and still sophisticated, although the sophistication is, alas, no longer up-to-date, no longer valid. It is a depressing thought, to be a shrill relic at the age of fifty-two, but there is still a little time left, and I may yet snap out of it. 1940, however, was twelve years ago and the journalistic synthesis of me, owing to continual repetition, was flourishing like a green bay tree. For instance, apropos of the fracas in the House of Commons about my American trip, the *Sunday Express* had stated: 'In any event, Mr Coward is not the man for the job. His flippant England – Cocktails, Countesses, Caviare – has gone. A man of the people more in tune with the new mood of Britain would be a better proposition for America.' The *Daily Mirror*, not to be outdone, made the following pronouncement: – 'Mister Coward, with his stilted mannerisms, his clipped accents and his vast experience of the useless froth of society, may be making contacts with the American equivalents . . . but as a representative for democracy he's like a plate of caviar in a carmen's pull-up.' These sinister references to caviar – once with an E and once without – struck at my conscience like a dagger when I remembered the two large tins I had bought in Shanghai, also there were my stilted mannerisms and my clipped accents, to say nothing of those legions of countesses I had left behind, presumably in a series of Mayfair luxury-flats.

It was not to be wondered at that this publicised sybarite, this mannered exotic, flicking the useless froth of society from his blue pin-stripe, was a trifle apprehensive. There was a great deal of prejudice to be overcome when I walked into that crowded room in the Australia Hotel, Sydney, and I was definitely aware of it even if they themselves were not. The effort to be friendly was not difficult. I am prepared to be friendly if people are friendly to me, and the atmosphere, although charged with alert expectation, was in no way unkind. The strain, however, lay in resisting the temptation to play up to their pre-conceived notion of me and give the performance they were subconsciously demanding. A few irreverent flippancies and witticisms and the serious implications of my visit would be undermined. I had no exaggerated idea of the importance of my mission and no illusions that my visit to Australia was fraught with any particular significance. All I wanted to do was to let the Australians know a little about what was happening in England, help to raise money for their Red Cross and sing to as many of their soldiers, sailors and airmen in training camps as wished to listen to me. This initial meeting with the Press obviously was of immense importance to the whole enterprise. The impression I made on them would immediately be relayed over the length and breadth of the continent, and I was determined that that impression should be of my genuine character and not of my superficial legend. After the first quarter of an hour or so I felt the tension relax and my own nervousness relax with it. There were some anxious moments; a few yawning abysses opened at my feet; there were one or two important and malicious questions fired at me, notably from those reporters whose papers were in opposition to Robert Menzies and the Government whose guest I was; but, taken all in all, disaster was avoided and I was led to my suite for ten minutes breathing space before making another broadcast.

When this was over I was hurried off to a reception given for me by Mr P. C. Spender, the War Minister. The reception was a large one and I shook hands with several hundred people. I had no time to say anything particular to anyone beyond the usual 'How do you do' and 'How happy I am to be here', but I was conscious of much warmth and kindliness.

At six o'clock I rushed off to pay my official call on Lord Gowrie, the Governor-General. He was a tall, handsome man with white hair and twinkling blue eyes; there was something in his manner, an emanation of kindness and common sense, that put me at ease, and he assured me that he would support me in any way he could during my tour but warned me, as Richard Casey had done, that it would be arduous.

After this I had just time to get back to the hotel, bathe and change and get to Prue Dickson's house for dinner. Prue Dickson was the daughter of Violet Vanbrugh and Arthur Bourchier, and we had first met in *Peter Pan* in 1914, when she played Curly, and I, Slightly. The dinner-party was mercifully small and I ate Sydney oysters for the first time. I think I ate two and a half dozen. The dinner-party, however, was but a brief prelude to the Red Cross Ball given in my honour at the Town Hall. This was a concert as well as a ball, and several famous Australian artists had consented to appear and sing my music. It was my first public appearance and the crowds in the streets and in the Town Hall itself were enormous. I heard afterwards that owing to the high price of admission the attendance was not quite as great as had been hoped. If this was so I can only say that I was very thankful. To me there seemed to be quite enough. When I drove up in the car with Prue there was a guard of honour of V.A.s (Voluntary Aids) and W.A.N.S. (Women's Australian Nursing Society), each about a hundred strong, waiting for me on the steps. I was received by the Lord Mayor and Lady Mayoress. I walked up and down the rows of attractive, uniformed Australian girls, shaking hands with each one. Inside the hall I stood with my host and hostess while people filed by and were introduced to me one by one, all of which took a long time. At last the concert began and I was able to sit down and enjoy myself. The orchestra was good and Marie Bremner sang 'I'll See You Again' and 'I'll Follow My Secret Heart' beautifully. Inevitably I had to climb on to the stage and make a speech. Whether or not I sang any songs I forget, but I believe I dashed off 'Marvellous Party' and 'Mad Dogs and Englishmen' in sheer desperation. This function ended just before midnight and I made a tour of various nightclubs until 2 a.m. Not, I hasten to say, for pleasure but because I had to find a good accompanist for my troop concerts.

I can sing certain songs to my own accompaniment, but I am far happier and more at ease when there is someone to play for me. I find that I can command more authority over my audience when I am standing up; also, when chained to the piano, half my attention is devoted to my playing with the result that the projection of the lyrics is more difficult and often less effective.

My search, that first night in Sydney, was finally rewarded at Romano's, where I found an excellent pianist who agreed to come and rehearse with me early the next morning, and play for me in the afternoon at my first troop concert at Ingleburn Camp, which was about seventy miles away.

At two-thirty I went to bed, took three aspirin and went to sleep. That was the end of my first day, or rather half day, in Australia and those that followed were exhaustingly similar.

My tour lasted seven weeks and was, to me, both strenuous and rewarding. The Red Cross made a profit of approximately twelve thousand pounds from my appearances in different cities. My broadcasts, judging by the letters I received, gave pleasure to many people in out-of-the-way places who were unable to come to any of my performances. The newspapers and magazines, with only two exceptions, helped me enormously by publicising me with courtesy and kindness.

The two exceptions were *Smith's Weekly* and *Truth*, both of which were in opposition to the Government. These gleefully reprinted anything derogatory they could find in the English Press, which offered them a wide, though not varied, choice. When they couldn't quote they invented and on the whole, wasted a vast amount of energy and printer's ink with little effect. Only on one occasion did they achieve a brief triumph when I was faced at a training camp outside Melbourne with an audience of 'Diggers', who proceeded to shout me down before I had even started to sing to them. This unexpected hostility startled me for a moment and horrified my poor accompanist, Sefton Daly, who was not so inured to the vagaries of troop audiences as I was. I let them get on with their whistling and catcalls for a little and then announced, with some firmness, through the microphone, that I intended to sing steadily for three quarters of an hour whether they liked it or not. This dreadful threat silenced them for a moment and gave me a chance to bawl out, 'Don't Put Your Daughter on the Stage, Mrs Worthington', which drew from them a few grudging titters, after which I was allowed to get on with the rest of my programme. At the end they applauded and cheered vociferously, and carried me out of the hut on their shoulders, which was uncomfortable but gratifying. A half an hour later I gave another show in the same hut, which was not quite big enough to accommodate the whole camp. The word must have got round that I was more 'dinkum' than had been anticipated, because this time, although they were rather slow in the uptake, there was no overt hostility.

When both these curious performances were over and I was having a cup of tea with the Commanding Officer, he explained that *Smith's Weekly* and *Truth* were the only papers his chaps ever read and that they had been, naturally enough, prejudiced against me. I asked him why he hadn't warned me about this before I went on, to which he replied that he didn't want to upset me. Bewildered by this reasoning I asked him if, in warfare, he would prefer to be warned of an enemy ambush awaiting for him just around the corner, or would rather be left in happy ignorance and allowed to walk straight into it. At this he laughed superciliously and said it wasn't quite the same thing, was it! After that the subject was dropped.

To offset this disconcerting episode, all the other troops concerts went smoothly from start to finish. The public performances were all successful and the audiences wonderful.

Dick Casey, in a note he wrote to me just before I sailed, said: 'If I were you I'd tell the people who are in charge of you that (A) you'll work like a black for five days a week, but (B) you can't make any appointment before 1 a.m. and (C) you have to have two days a week without any appointments at all. If you don't make some such stipulation they'll run the legs off you. However, if you want to break these rules yourself to meet people you like the look

of – well, you have only yourself to blame.' Well, I had only myself
to blame, I suppose, because I made no stipulations at all and
cursed myself later for having been so sure of my own endurance.
The itinerary handed to me was certainly formidable, but not
unmanageable. If, at the outset, I had begun cancelling engagements and saying I couldn't do this or that, it would have caused
disappointment, given rise to a number of complications and
created a bad impression. The Government had appointed me an
A.D.C. called Monte Lake, an efficient secretary, Mavis Gully and
Jim Wilcox, a fair, tough young man, who was excellent company
and my Press representative. For the first few weeks an amiable
man called Mackenna was the sort of major-domo of my
entourage; later, however, he was withdrawn from the band-
wagon and Myles Cox took over. Myles had a saturnine
appearance and a most unsaturnine temperament. He kept me in
order with infinite tact. We were a gay little troop and on the few
occasions when we could all get together and relax we had a very
good time. Such occasions were rare, and after the first couple of
weeks Mavis had to be supplied with an assistant.

The routine was as follows. Myles supervised all arrangements
and organised transport and plane tickets, time sheets, etc.; Monte
appeared in the morning and briefed me on the day's doings, and
Mavis appeared for an hour or so every day and stood over me
while I autographed photographs, letters and books. Jim looked
after the newspaper men, photographers and interviewers and
nipped them into my presence whenever there were a few minutes
available. Monte accompanied me everywhere and whisked me in
and out of functions; he also had to get me in and out of cars,
which was sometimes more complicated. The police were cheerfully co-operative and supplied me with a bodyguard for those
occasions when we feared the crowds might get out of hand. The
pianist I found at Romano's played for me once at my first troop
concert at Inglebourne. Actually he played only three songs, was
taken ill and staggered from the stage, whereupon I had to take off
my jacket and fend for myself. Finally, after a series of auditions
and much trial and error, Marie Burke sent me Sefton Daly, a
young New Zealander, who had played for her frequently. He was
a good pianist and a fine natural musician, but he couldn't read at

sight. This was a serious defect, but I so very much preferred his playing to those I had heard who could read from sight that I engaged him and set him to learn the whole of my repertoire, song by song. Luckily there was a good deal of time every day when I was going over factories, visiting airfields, opening and closing bazaars and making interminable speeches, when I had no need of music. During these excursions he sat at home in the hotel slogging away until, in a remarkably short while, he had really mastered most of my principal numbers and was starting on the more obscure ones. Those early concerts must have been nerve-racking for him, but he never betrayed it and never let me down by so much as a B flat. He was also, later, when he had time, a great addition to our travelling circus and enlivened many a civic reception by giggling at the wrong moment.

Sydney, Melbourne, Adelaide, Perth, Fremantle, Canberra, Brisbane, Launceston, Hobart. Back and forth and up and down I went until I was dizzy. By the time I reached Brisbane I had, most reluctantly, to cancel my projected visit to Cairns and Darwin because I was so exhausted that I could hardly speak. But after three days in a small hotel on the Queensland coast I returned to the attack, if not bursting with energy, at least refreshed.

Wherever I went I was received with heart-warming friend-liness. I had been warned beforehand that Australians were inclined to be touchy and quick to take offence. If they are, I can only say that I didn't notice it. I found them cheerful, unpretentious and without guile. The only touchiness I observed every now and then lay in their intense, perhaps over-intense, civic pride. Each city I visited was quite obviously convinced that it was better in every way than any of the other cities. This exaggerated spirit of internecine rivalry only occasionally exceeded the bounds of courtesy – once when I was attacked in Sydney because I happened to say something in praise of Melbourne and once in Melbourne when I happened to say something in praise of Sydney.

Apart from this inter-state rivalry I found little to criticise in Australia and much to admire. I would have liked, had time permitted it, to visit a sheep farm and see some of the real country at close quarters rather than from several thousand feet in the air.

I would have liked to have driven through the hinterland of Victoria, New South Wales and Queensland and had the leisure to observe Australian life away from the big cities. Perhaps some day I will. At all events, the places I did see and the people I did meet made me anxious to return quietly one day without publicity and without an official itinerary.

My farewell performance in Sydney, which closed my tour, was a special matinée given in aid of the bombed-out victims of the London blitzes. Lord Gowrie drove in a hundred miles from the country to support it and all the leading artists of Australia appeared willingly and gladly as theatre people always do. It was a tremendous success and, with the help of generous donations, a total of two thousand pounds was raised. I presume that this was sent to the Lord Mayor of London, but I do not know for certain for I never received any acknowledgement.

I spent Christmas with Lord and Lady Gowrie at Canberra, endured an unpleasant bout of colitis, and then spent a week by myself in a lovely little house on an estuary belonging to an old gentleman called Mr Allen. This kind man, having heard that I needed a few days' rest, put his house and housekeeper at my disposal. We had never met until he drove me out to install me in it. I shall always be grateful to him because, although I spent only a few days there, the peace of it ironed me out and gave me a little time to review the last few weeks and conserve energy with which to face the next few weeks.

On December the 31st there was no sun until the evening at about five-thirty, when it suddenly emerged and seemed to set the estuary on fire. I went down and swam in the pool which was netted to keep out the sharks, and then settled myself with my back to a rock, with a packet of cigarettes by me, and looked out across the silver-grey water and yellow sandbanks to the farther shore. There was a fishing-boat a little way off and the chugging of its Diesel engine and the squalling of seagulls were the only sounds in the stillness. I looked back over the year that was just ending; at its ups and downs, its hopes, disappointments, excitements and despairs, and wondered rather bleakly if 1941 was going to be so supercharged with emotions and frustrations and so overcrowded with events and people.

1940, in immediate retrospect, seemed to me to be the most difficult, complicated year I had ever lived, so many adjustments and re-adjustments and changing circumstances. The first months of the year in Paris; the office routine, the propaganda conferences, the agitations over Radio Fécamp, the flights back and forth between Paris and London in snow and sleet, the inter-office pollcy discussions and arguments; then the six weeks' visit to America and the Clipper flight home. The return to America to still more irritations and frustrations. The emigration of the Orphanage; the endless train and plane journeys across the States. The voyage across the Pacific; Honolulu, Japan, China; the arrival in Australia. The handshakes, Press interviews, rehearsals, performances, bazaars, Rotary lunches, troop concerts, broadcasts, civic receptions and speeches of thanks. Above all, the people, the innumerable thousands of people. Individual faces flickered across my memory like a montage sequence in a movie: Blanche Prenez, my French teacher, convulsed with laughter at my misuse of the subjunctive; the nun crossing herself as the plane took off from Bordeaux; the sneering little Japanese officials refusing to let me land in Yokohama; Madame Birt weeping for lost years in Shanghai; Dick Casey describing Australia to me, his eyes alight with enthusiasm; ex-President Hoover abusing England to me, his eyes beady with anger; Marlene seeing me off at Pasadena; Robert Menzies welcoming me in Canberra. Kind faces, suspicious faces, famous faces, unknown faces; rows and rows of quite expressionless faces staring at me like plates; my own face leering at me from Press photographs, grinning, smirking, performing – the routine smile, so simple, so human, 'so unspoiled by his great success'; the camera angles so unpredictable, the results so often nauseating. How invaluable it would be, I reflected, if just once, just for a brief spell, I could see myself clearly from the outside, as others saw me. How helpful it would be, moving so continually across the public vision, to know what that vision really observed, to note objectively what it was in my personality that moved some people to like and applaud me and aroused in others such irritation and resentment. How salutary it would be to watch the whole performance through from the front of the house, to see to what extent the mannerisms were effective and note when and where they should be cut down. I know, as all public performers know, that it is impossible to please everyone, but it would be a comfort to know for certain, just once, that I was at least pleasing myself. I tried, lying there in the fading light, to put myself in the place of an ordinary Australian Digger, a true product of the wide open spaces, suddenly asked to sit on a hard bench in a stuffy Nissen hut and enjoy the restrained antics of a forty-year-old Englishman with no voice and a red carnation in his buttonhole. What, in the songs I sang, in the allusions I made, could possibly be entertaining to him? He obviously would have preferred a really fine singer or a saucy blonde in a décolletée evening gown, or an experienced low comedian who could convulse him with slapstick and funny stories. I was always aware of this every time I stepped on to the stage, always conscious of my inability to give my audience what it really wanted. The public performances in theatres and cinemas and Town Halls were, of course, quite different. On these occasions the audiences were urban and mixed and my stardom was an asset rather than a defect, but those poor Diggers were the ones who really commanded my sympathy and my gratitude. That I was able to keep them quiet for an hour was certainly a great tribute to my personality, but a still greater tribute to their natural courtesy and good-humour. Had I known at that moment how much those anxious misgivings were destined to torment me during the next four years I think I should have plunged into the water outside the shark net and prayed for the worst. As it was, the interminable troop concerts of the future were mercifully veiled from me. I knew I had a certain amount of them to get through in New Zealand, but that would only be for a month, after which I could relax for a bit and go home.

The last light went from the sky, the stars came out and, girding my towel round me, I walked up to the quiet house. That night, after dinner, I wrote out the final draft of my farewell broadcast, which was scheduled for the evening before I sailed, and went to bed. When the year 1940 actually came to end with its toast-drinkings and handshakings and bell ringings I was fast asleep in blissful, peaceful solitude.

5

My ship, the *Mariposa*, arrived at Auckland on Monday, January 13th, at seven-thirty in the morning. The anchor was dropped about a mile from the dock and so I had a leisurely breakfast and proceeded to bath and shave in good order. While I was shaving there was a knock on the door and thinking it was the steward I called 'Come in'. After a moment I emerged from the bathroom stark naked and came face to face with a completely strange man clutching a Homburg hat and looking, naturally enough, rather startled. I apologised lightly for my casual appearance, put on my dressing-gown and offered him a cigarette. He then told me that his name was Stevens and that he had been accredited to me as a sort of A.D.C. by Mr Fraser, the Prime Minister, from whom he brought cordial greetings. He had also brought the Mayor of Auckland (Sir Ernest Davis) and three Press gentlemen, who were waiting on deck. I hurried into my clothes as quickly as I could while Stevens gave me a rough outline of my itinerary for the next few days. He was an affable young man and inclined to be perky.

The itinerary sounded reasonable enough, a good deal less strenuous than my Australian programme, and my spirits lightened considerably. By the time I had met the Mayor and been photographed on gangways waving archly to imaginary crowds the ship had drawn alongside the harbour. We drove sedately to the hotel and I was both relieved and a little dunched to observe that my arrival in New Zealand had apparently caused little stir among the population. Sefton Daly had arrived before me, delighted to be visiting his homeland under my glittering auspices, and was waiting for me in my suite with a young man called Jack Maclean who was to be my secretary. We ordered coffee immediately and settled down to study the order of the day. Lunch with Lord Galway, the Governor-General, a civic reception in the Town Hall, then my first broadcast at seven o'clock, and that was all. I could hardly believe my eyes. Sefton giggled sympathetically at my astonishment and reminded me that New Zealand was less dashing and go-ahead than Australia and that I must be prepared for a slower tempo.

I questioned Stevens about the civic reception, whereupon he looked rather glum and said he hoped it would be all right. I gathered from his manner, that however much he hoped, he was fairly certain that it would be far from all right. I then asked how the tickets were selling for my first public concert in two days' time, and he said 'So-so'. This was altogether too much for Sefton, who retired hurriedly to the bathroom. Later, when Stevens and Jack Maclean had gone, we had some coffee and looked the situation squarely in the eye. Evidently someone had blundered. Either there hadn't been enough advance publicity or the people of Auckland just weren't interested. In any case it seemed probable that we were in for a flop. God knows I wasn't exactly yearning for a repetition of the non-stop run-around I had been given in Australia, but a happy mean would have been acceptable. This felt like the doldrums. Envisaging a quarterful Town Hall and an almost empty theatre I started to laugh, and by the time the waiter came to fetch the tray we were both scarlet in the face.

My lunch with the Governor-General was pleasant enough. He was agreeable but seemed a little vague when I questioned him about New Zealand. Perhaps he was sick of it.

The civic reception, contrary to expectations, was a triumph. The Town Hall was packed to the ceiling and I was given an enthusiastic welcome. Not only this, but the streets were lined with people to see me drive away, which astounded Stevens almost as much as it astounded me. It also cheered me a great deal. There is nothing so damping to a publicised visitor, keyed up to expect a hullabaloo, as to be faced with no hullabaloo at all. I drove smugly back to the hotel to run through my broadcast.

From that first bleak morning onwards everything was fine. My first two troop concerts the next day were highly successful, and my public concert on the Wednesday evening was a riot. The first part of the programme consisted of Heddle Nash, a tenor, and Mary Pratt, a fine contralto. Both of them were great favourites and sang beautifully. The last half as usual I had to myself and sang for an hour. There were three thousand people in the house, and Sefton and I debated whether or not we should have to give Stevens first aid.

The Prime Minister and the Government had really taken

trouble to make my visit as pleasant as possible. Sight-seeing trips had been arranged and sometimes two or three days had been left free of engagements, for which I was grateful. The whole New Zealand trip, as Sefton had predicted, was taken at a much slower tempo. In the principal towns there was, of course, a great deal to be got through – the usual public lunches and dinners and speechmaking, but in between times I was allowed to rest and enjoy the glorious scenery of both islands. In Rotorua I was given a Maori welcome. This was very special and took place in a church hall. I was met at the door by a painted warrior who capered round me for some minutes and finally made me pick up two sticks from the floor. After I had achieved this not impossible feat a great uproar broke out and I was presented to the chiefs and the local belles, with whom I rubbed noses; this was damp but convivial. Then came the entertainment, which consisted of native songs and dances, slightly spoilt for me by the fact that the male dancers wore ordinary grey flannel trousers under their straw skirts, which, I thought, vitiated the primitive barbarity of the occasion. The younger Maori maidens obliged with some modern Tin-Pan alley tunes which they sang with more enthusiasm than accuracy. The old guard, however, when the party got really going, sang some of the vintage Maori songs, which were entrancing. At the end of all this I sang a few numbers myself, which were listened to with polite bewilderment, and was presented with a carved wooden box and an ink-stand.

Rotorua is famous for its geysers, hot springs and thermal baths. I was taken through a Maori village where they cook, work and bathe in pools of different temperatures provided considerately by the Great Redeemer. Ocassionally the Great Redeemer goes too far and a bit of ground caves in and someone gets scalded to death. Personally I felt that to be able to boil an egg in a puddle outside your front door, although undoubtedly labour-saving, was not really enough compensation for having to live immediately on top of the earth's hidden fires.

Stevens accompanied us everywhere. He was really a nice young man, but desperately jocular. He invariably greeted me every morning with 'Good morrow, kind sir. How are we this merry morn?' He alluded to any hotel proprietor as Mine Host and referred to any female, regardless of age or size, as Girlie.

We were driven through rich green country; we visited the Waitomo caves and saw millions of glow-worms glittering on the rocks overhead like stars; we picnicked, on our journeys between airfields and training camps, among vast ferns. 'Down with the jolly old rug,' Stevens would say with a merry laugh, and down went the jolly old rug.

The South Island is more spectacularly beautiful than the North Island because of its vivid snow capped mountains. Christchurch is a lovely town, gently reminiscent of an English cathedral city. This is Sefton's birthplace and he played two of his own compositions at my concert, which were, rightly, received enthusiastically. The high spot of the whole tour for me was a troop concert in the Town Hall at Dunedin. The audience of several thousand men had marched from surrounding camps, some of which were as far as fifty miles away. They marched through the town with bands playing about an hour before the concert was due to begin. This, although a thrilling spectacle, filled me with dread, for I had no symphony orchestra and no other artists to help me through the evening. All those gallant men were going to get was just me and Sefton's two compositions. They were quick-witted and wonderful; one of the most receptive all-male audiences I have ever performed to. I sang for an hour and forty minutes and then, as they still seemed eager for me, went on for a further quarter of an hour. At the end I felt so exhilarated that I could cheerfully have given another performance then and there.

Wellington was hectic and crowded and there was a fuss about my public concert being broadcast because it had been hinted that some of my lyrics might not be quite proper enough to be blown out over the ether. As I detest aggressive puritanism, or indeed any kind of puritanism, this flung me into a rage and I said firmly that either the concert must be broadcast in its entirety as arranged or not broadcast at all. The battle raged for several hours and I was ultimately victorious. The concert was a success and there was a reception afterwards in the Mayor's parlour, during which I had a slight set-to with the Mayoress. She was, I am sure, an excellent Mayoress, but seemed to me to suffer from delusions of grandeur, or perhaps she was a prey to agonising shyness and, like many such unfortunate people, sought to conceal it beneath an over-forthright manner. At all events, whatever subconscious motives prompted her behaviour, the result was gratuitously rude. She said to me in ringing tones that I was never to dare to sing 'The Stately Homes of England' again as it was an insult to the homeland and that neither she nor anybody else liked it. I replied coldly that for many years it had been one of my greatest successes, whereupon she announced triumphantly to everyone within earshot: 'You see – he can't take criticism!' Irritated beyond endurance I replied that I was perfectly prepared to take intelligent criticism at any time, but I was not prepared to tolerate bad manners. With this I bowed austerely and left the party.

Afterwards when my rage evaporated, I regretted having been so quick to take offence. It is the duty of a visitor to remain unmoved in such situations and, on the whole, I think I have succeeded pretty well in restraining my feelings in public. Every now and then, however, some little incident happens, some particular inanity flicks my nerves, snaps my control and, to my dismay, sends me stamping down into the arena. A sudden, unprovoked attack is always startling, especially when one is on show and 'observing the niceties'. Apparently for certain individuals men and women in the public eye are regarded as fair game. There they stand, the admired and the envied, smirking and bowing, surrounded with gushing sycophants: why shouldn't they be knocked off their balance occasionally, taken down a peg or two, made to look foolish? It does not occur to such mutinous observers that the poor beasts may be a great deal more vulnerable than they appear to be. A central figure at a social function isn't always as happy as he looks: he is seldom permitted to talk for more than a few minutes with anyone he wants to talk to, and very often is bogged down, for what seems like hours, with someone whom he doesn't. Then there is his own degree of natural poise to be considered. Is he really as much at ease as appears on the surface? Is that attentive smile, that charming assurance, really genuine? Or is it perhaps masking an inward shyness, a desolate boredom, a frustrated longing to spit in the face of cackling pleasantries and rush screaming from the room? In Hollywood and other parts of the United States husbands and wives obtain divorces every day of the week on the grounds of mental cruelty. I have often thought of founding a society for the 'Prevention of Mental Cruelty to Celebrities'. To me the worst offenders are those women whose self-righteous egocentricity makes them wish to impress the celebrity rather than be impressed by him. These crusaders cherish the belief that forthright criticism, preferably in public, is more admirable than conventional politeness. They feel, I am sure, by saying what they think, straight-from-the-shoulder-and-no-nonsense, that their devastating honesty provides a refreshing breeze in a stuffy atmosphere, and that they will be gratefully remembered for it. 'Who was that attractive little woman in the mauve hat? She actually told me that she loathed my plays and that I over-acted! I should like to see *her* again.' In this belief they are, alas, misguided. They will be remembered certainly, but not quite in the way they would have wished. They will be remembered for having made the task of the guest of honour just a little harder than it need have been. They will be remembered for having placed him in a position of acute embarrassment. They will also be remembered, not for their moral courage, but for their lack of social grace.

Happily my progress through the years has been fairly untroubled by such idiots, but they crop up every now and then. Usually a sort of conditioned reflex, a personal radar, warns me of their approach and I am able to mow them down before they can get far. Occasionally, however, they take me completely by surprise and there I am with a brawl on my hands.

The official part of my New Zealand tour finished in Wellington, and I flew back to Auckland to wait for a day or two for the Clipper to take me to Canton Island, where I had arranged to stop off for a week to catch my breath and get some sun. I occupied the few days by writing some long-delayed letters home; luxuriating in the knowledge that I had no more speeches to make and no more songs to sing, and that I could stay in bed late in the morning and return to it early at night with enough vitality left over to enjoy reading a book. Stevens and Sefton were still with me and we went to a jolly old movie or two. At one of these the manager, in a fit of misguided enthusiasm, flashed on the screen an announcement that I was present in the cinema. This produced gratifying applause and finally resulted in a free-for-all in the lobby at the end of the performance. It was a Saturday night and the theatre was full, and it took us about twenty minutes to get out on to the pavement and into the car. Once in it there was near tragedy. A mother, obviously in the grip of mass hysteria, handed me her baby through the window, screaming: 'Kiss my little girlie, go on, kiss her!' At this moment the car started to move and I was caught with the little girlie's head while the mother hung on to its legs. With commendable presence of mind I struck the mother sharply on the head with my left hand and yanked the child into the car with me before its back was broken. There was a great deal of shrieking, the car stopped, and I handed back girlie unhurt and unkissed. She had, however, utilised her brief moment of perilous reflected glory by wetting me to the skin.

6

My Clipper left Auckland at 7.30 a.m. on February 3rd and arrived at New Caledonia in the afternoon, where the passengers were allowed to go ashore, drive about, bathe, and dine aboard the Pan-American yacht *Southern Seas*. There was no point in going to bed because we had to leave again at three-thirty in the morning, so I spent the hours enjoying a light drinking bout with the Captain, a homesick North Countryman called Beardsall, Crowther, a pilot who had flown me from Batavia to Singapore in 1936, and a couple of others. It was a pleasant interlude, romantic too in its own way because it had a quality familiar to all travellers – an evanescence, a 'here today and gone tomorrow' friendliness enhanced by tropical stars, lights glimmering in the distant town and the small waves of the lagoon slapping gently against the side of the ship.

The plane was due to arrive at Canton Island at 7 p.m. the following evening, but owing to head-winds there was a delay of three hours; there was also a feeling of tension because there were no other islands within hundreds of miles and the passengers (perhaps the crew as well) were beginning to wonder how much longer the fuel would hold out. At last, however, there was a gleeful shout from the forward end of the plane and we all pressed our foreheads against the tiny circular windows and stared down into the blackness where, thousands of feet below us, was a small cluster of winking lights looking like a Cartier bracelet flung on to black velvet. Canton Island is a coral reef, one degree south of the equator, twenty-nine miles round and no wider than a few hundred yards at any point. It enclosed a lagoon into which there is only one narrow entrance from the open sea, not wide enough to give passage to anything larger than a launch. The Clipper made a perfect landing, the doors were opened and the warm tropical night air came swirling in. The passengers walked along a little wooden jetty and straight into the lounge of a typical American luxury hotel. The effect was startling. I had settled in my mind for a ramshackle bamboo guest-house with wide tumble-down verandas and inadequate plumbing, and was prepared to endure all manner of creature discomforts for the sake of rest and sun. I had certainly not bargained for private showers, luxurious beds, shining Fifth Avenue chintzes and a chromium cocktail bar. The Clipper took off again at noon the following day, leaving me behind in the empty hotel with seven clear days in which to swim and read and enjoy myself.

The island, although scenically disappointing, for there was no scenery beyond a few palms was exactly what I wanted. A glorious lagoon a few feet away full of vivid tropical fish, pounding surf a few yards away to supply a permanent lullaby, a tennis court, a small sailing-boat belonging to Dick Danner, the island entomologist, and, above all, time to spare.

The hotel was run by a young American couple called Jack and Lordee Bramham. In addition to them there was a sprinkling of men concerned with the running of the airport, and the ground staff for servicing the planes. A hundred yards or so away from the hotel was the British Residency and a radio station. The official British residents were a Mr and Mrs Fleming. Frank Fleming had built the house, aided by some Chamarro boys, virtually with his own hands. He ran the radio office, raised the Union Jack solemnly every morning and lowered it every night. They were two very nice people. My note about them in my diary reads as follows: 'Called on Flemings after dinner and had a drink with them. Typically English in the best possible sense, simple, unpretentious and getting on with the job. They came here alone, before Pan American, from Fiji, or rather he did. He built the house they live in and she joined him later. They have relatives in London and Sussex and suffer occasionally from bad bouts of homesickness coupled with a certain irritation at the Americans, who have so much luxury such a little way away. They have no official photograph of the King and Queen, only a framed reproduction from the *Illustrated London News* which has buckled because the rain-water got into the frame during the last cyclone. Promised to report this when I get home. Feel there is a story in them.'

A few months after my return to London I had the opportunity of telling the Queen about the buckled reproduction, and a few days later received a letter from her lady-in-waiting informing me that a photograph of Their Majesties had been sent to Mr and Mrs Fleming. Later still, in 1949, I made an approximation of their characters and situation the basis of a story called 'Mr and Mrs Edgehill' *(Star Quality:* Heinemann). I sent it to them the moment it was published, but I don't know if they ever received it.

There were other story possibilities on Canton Island – there always are in small isolated communities. Local conflicts and dramas and comedies swell to terrific proportions when there is nothing but surf and sky, the elements surrounding you and no escape, not even for a week-end. Even during the short time I spent on Canton Island there were several excitements. One was the arrival, three weeks late, of the supply ship. This was a great moment; we had lived on fish for days and were right out of cigarettes. The ship was sighted in the early afternoon. Everyone cheered. There was, as usual, a heavy sea running. The launch put out through the narrow channel and managed to reach the ship safely, but on the way back, loaded to the gunwales with much-needed stores, it capsized in the surf and sank like a stone. Fortunately no one was drowned, although some of the crew were badly battered by the reefs. The cigarettes, thank God, floated ashore in their tin containers.

There was also the episode of the cyclone. The New Zealand-bound Clipper was due one evening at 8 p.m., but owing to a cyclone blowing up between it and Canton Island, it was delayed for several hours, too far from Honolulu to be able to turn back and too far from any other possible landing place. The evident drama of the situation was made even more poignant on the island because the wife of Hal Graves, the airport manager, was on board the plane with their newly-born child. From eight until one in the morning we all sat about, either in the hotel or the airport office, waiting for news. Radio messages occasionally got through, but the weather was so appalling that they were mostly unintelligible. Then came the news which we both hoped for and dreaded – the Clipper was coming in to land. Hal Graves, white and shaking but in perfect control, rushed out to the launch followed by me and Jack Bramham. I was wearing bathing trunks and a mackintosh because the rain was torrential and there was no sense in wearing anything else. The launch, with its revolving circular light, chugged up and down the lagoon in the blackness. We on the deck were straining our eyes to try and spot the plane through the mist and the rain. Suddenly there it was immediately above our heads; it zoomed low over the hotel, missing the roof by inches, disappeared completely and then, a few seconds later, reappeared and dropped gently down on to the water. I remember yelling violently with relief. Mrs Graves and the baby emerged unscathed and so did the rest of the passengers. They looked shaken I thought, but cheered up after some whisky and hot soup.

The same prowling cyclone that had provided us with this drama kept everyone weatherbound in the hotel for four days. The America-bound Clipper which was to take me away managed to land two days later, but was unable to take off again, and so there we were, two full passenger loads and two crews all milling about, and all, in varying degrees, frustrated, uncomfortable and cross. Lordee and Jack kept their heads; extra beds were made up in odd places, the meals were staggered and general chaos reigned until the morning of the fifth day, when the weather lifted enough for the New Zealand-bound Clipper to take off. With relief we waved it up into the clouds. The relief, however, was short-lived, for the plane was back again in two hours with engine trouble.

Early the next morning, after several hours of conflicting rumours, my Clipper finally took off. As it taxied along the lagoon I looked out through the spray at the dawn coming up. The plane circled round once and headed back to the world. The week's holiday I had planned had lasted sixteen days, but seemed somehow much longer than that. I felt that I had been living on that coral strip for months. Australia and New Zealand had dropped into the far past. I craned my head to look back just before we flew into a cloudbank. There it lay, that tiny coral circlet in the blue water; the jetty, the lagoon, the coloured fish, the little white terns so tame that they perched on your hand, Lordee and Jack, Hal Graves's baby screaming its lungs out and Frank Fleming, wearing an old pair of khaki shorts, hauling up the flag.

6A

The cyclone which had been causing everyone such inconvenience had either gone off in another direction or blown itself out of existence, for after only an hour or so in cloud the plane was droning along through clear sky with the sea far below glittering in the sunlight. I read and dozed fitfully, reflecting how agreeable air travel can be when the weather is good and how excessively disagreeable when it isn't. We were due to arrive in Honolulu in the late afternoon, where I hoped to spend a few hours with the Dillinghams before taking off again at midnight for Los Angeles. This hope was more than gratified, for I was forced, owing to weather conditions, to spend four days with them. However, on that bright morning, poised between infinity and the sea, there seemed to be no cloud in the universe, until a distinguished-looking gentleman with a beard came over and sat next to me. He introduced himself as Professor Fischel and explained that he was the nephew of King Feisal. We had, he said, a great mutual friend in the late Lord Lloyd. I stared at him in astonishment and said: 'Why late?' He then went on to tell me that George Lloyd had died a few days previously in London. The bitter surprise of this made me speechless for a moment, and seeing from my expression how upset I was, he apologised for giving me bad news so abruptly and left me to myself. I was grateful to him for this consideration and lay back with my eyes closed trying to adjust my mind to the shock. I have been told that when the body suffers a sharp blow the entire organism reacts immediately; all gland secretions are affected, first-aid units are automatically sent scurrying through ducts and channels to the scene of the trouble and the blood-stream itself changes its consistency. In fact a 'Calling all cars' state of emergency is declared and a combined therapeutic operation is set in motion in a split second. When the mind suffers a sharp blow I presume that something of the same kind occurs; a general rally is sounded, an immediate anaesthesia administered, either in the form of a fainting fit or temporary incredulity, or just merciful numbness. Very few civilised people give way to transports of noisy grief on the receipt of bad news. It is later that the heart aches and the eyes fill with tears.

Up until 1941 Fate had been considerate to me. I had suffered no sudden bereavements, lost no really close friends since the death of John Ekins in 1916. People I had known and liked had died from time to time, causing me momentary regrets but touching me with only the shadow of real sadness. The death of George Lloyd was a horrible shock to me. He was a great man in many ways. He had dynamic vitality, humour, tremendous executive ability and, to me, always a kind and generous heart. He was an Imperialist, in the best sense because his passionate love of England and his unshakable belief in the British Empire were based on common sense. He taught me much in the fortunate years that I knew him, and I was aware then, in the trans-Pacific Clipper, faced with the fact of his sudden death, that if ever I did anything in my life to change his good opinion of me I should be very ashamed.

7

Three weeks later I was in another Clipper heading across the Atlantic to England via Bermuda, the Azores and Lisbon. The ceiling was low but my spirits were high. I was bearing a pouch with some letters for the Foreign Office and a courier's passport, which gave me a sense of mysterious importance. Little Bill had offered me a job which, in his opinion and in mine, would be of real value to the war effort, and would utilise not only my celebrity value but my intelligence as well. I had had some intensive briefing in New York and Washington and was now in a state of, alas, premature exaltation. It is not my intention in this book to give an account of the work for which I was being groomed, because the whole enterprise was nipped in the bud by High Authority in London before my plane had reached Bermuda. There the crushing news was broken to me in a cable from Little Bill. He gave no explanations, merely a brief message announcing that the whole thing was off, but I gathered from the very terseness of the message that 'A greater power than we could contradict had thwarted our intents'. It was a horrid disappointment and cost me some black hours, but there was obviously nothing to do but rise above it, figuratively and literally, and fly on home as soon as possible. On looking back over those difficult, enraging moments in 1940 and 1941 it is curious to reflect that, in the long run, fate always proved to be on my side. If the Duff Cooper American scheme had come off I should never have had the rewarding experience of Australia and New Zealand. If Little Bill's job had materialised I should never have written *Blithe Spirit*, *In Which We Serve* or *London Pride*. When I received that devastating message in Bermuda, however, all these were in the future and I returned to England with my spirits lower than they had been when I started.

On arrival at Bristol I was met by Gladys, looking very smart in her M.T.C. uniform, and when the Immigration and Customs officials had finished with me we drove up to London. During that two hours' drive all inner anxieties and disappointments were elbowed out of my mind by the sheer pleasure of being home again. My studio in Gerald Road was still occupied by Dallas Brooks, who had been living in it while I was away, so we drove to Claridge's, where Lorn was waiting for me in an elaborate suite. So vast and imposing was it that I decided there and then to give it up the following morning and return to my own spare room at the studio. On that first night home, however, after a gay reunion party at Clemence Dane's, I retired to bed slightly fried, blissfully happy and in excessive luxury.

The next day the Press had been invited to meet me at Gerald Road. All the little men who had been busy vilifying me when I was at the other side of the world – I had been looking forward to meeting them face to face and telling them exactly what I thought of them for months, but, of course, when they actually arrived nothing happened at all. I found, when confronted with them on my own ground, that the whole occasion was utterly without importance. Instead of the white-heat of self-righteous indignation with which I had intended to sear them there was nothing in my heart but boredom. They were all polite and most of them seemed to be quite amiably disposed. When they had all been given drinks they sat about expectantly, and so I told them, rather dully I fear, the accurate story of my activities since September 1939. I explained, mildly, that I had *not* run away from the perils of war; that I had *not* worn a uniform to which I was not entitled; that I *had* been officially appointed as Sir Campbell's representative in Paris; that I *had* been sent to America by the Minister of Information and that my visit to Australia and New Zealand had been at the express invitation of the Governments of those Dominions. I then went on to remind them, without heat, that whereas it was perfectly within their rights as newspaper men to comment as unfavourably as they wished on my talents, either creative or interpretative, they had no right whatsoever, without incontrovertible proof, to impugn my private character or my personal integrity. They listened attentively to all this, and when I had finished one or two of them asked some uninspired questions, which I managed to answer without any undue strain on my temper, after which they each had another drink and went away.

The reports in the newspapers the next day were quite civil, although only one of them was an accurate statement of what I had said. This account was written by the only woman reporter present. I suspected when I read it that she would either go far in her profession or get the sack immediately. I have never discovered if either of these surmises were correct.

In due course I moved back into the studio. Dallas was no trouble as a tenant-guest, and as he was out most of the time that I was in, and vice versa, we got along very happily for a few days until the Luftwaffe intervened and blew our agreeable little ménage to pieces. This occurred on the evening of April the 16th. When the raid started I was dining at the Hungaria. The restaurant was underground and all we could hear at first was a series of distant thumps. Presently the manager came to our table and said that the raid was becoming serious and that we had better stay where we were. This advice was immediately disregarded, our party dispersed and I walked down towards the Admiralty with Robert Neville, who at that time was Deputy Director of Naval Intelligence. There had been a few minor raids since my return six days before, but this one was obviously on a much bigger scale. Having left Robert Neville at the Admiralty I hailed a taxi in Trafalgar Square and drove off along the Mall. The sky above Carlton House Terrace was red with the reflected glow of fires, presumably in the Piccadilly district, and the rooftops and chimney-pots were etched black against it. There was a lot of noise and gunfire and, every so often, a shattering explosion. My taxi-driver drove hell for leather, keeping up a breathless running commentary as he did so. I was interested to note, this being my first experience of a blitz, that I was not frightened at all. This surprised me, because physical courage has never been one of my strong points. I can only suppose that I was so inured to the terrors of air raids by listening to the over-dramatic accounts of them on the American radio, that the actual experience was an anti-climax. This curious detachment under bombardment remained with me throughout the war, and I have never been able to understand it. I do hope that, to the reader, this does not appear to be retrospective smugness, because it is actually true. I have been far more frightened flying in the ordinary aeroplane between London and

Paris than I ever was in an air raid. To me the feeling of inevitability, the knowledge that there was nothing I could possibly do about it, numbed any fears I might have had and induced a form of objective fatalism. I wish I could achieve this same immunity from sickening fright when I am in a car with a dangerous driver. I was badly frightened on several occasions during the war, but those occasions had nothing to do with anything so impersonally lethal as bombs and landmines and doodle-bugs.

As my taxi rattled along Ebury Street I saw ahead of me the four corners by South Eaton Place blazing to the skies. This I realised was too near the studio for comfort. The taxi deposited me at my door in Gerald Road. I invited the driver in for a drink, but he refused and drove away, leaving me to scramble over rubble and broken glass in the alleyway to get to my front door. Fortunately my electric torch was new and bright and its beam saved me the trouble of fumbling for my latchkey by disclosing that only a little of the front door was there. The stairs inside were a shambles because the skylight had fallen in. I crackled up them and into the studio, where I found Dallas Brooks, also with a torch, wearing a grey dressing-gown and rubbing a slight bump on his forehead where the bedroom chandelier had struck him. Before he had had time to register my arrival a bomb fell near-by and the whole house shook. 'The buggers,' he said laconically and went to the whisky decanter. After we had each had a quick drink I told him I had some morphine capsules in my pocket, that I was going out to see if I could help the wounded, and that he'd better dress and come too. He replied with some grandeur that he would with pleasure, but that he had lost his glasses. While we were both groping about looking for them there was another louder explosion which brought down the main skylight, shattered the high windows and sent two oak doors skittering past us like ballet dancers. This was followed by a slower, more ominous noise from the direction of the Mews. 'That,' I said, 'sounds like the office.' I stumbled down the three steps leading to the Mews side of the house, where there is a sliding door. This stuck fast, but I managed to move it enough to peer with my torch into the darkness and verify my suspicions. It was indeed the office. The whole ceiling had fallen in and was lying on the floor. I went back through the studio and out of the house, calling to Dallas to follow me as soon as he could. I raced round the corner into South Eaton Place gripping my box of morphine capsules in the pocket of my coat. The spectacle at the corner of Ebury Street was horrifying. Houses were blazing, the road was a mass of rubble: some fire-fighters were standing quite silently with a hose directing streams of water on to the flames. There was a momentary lull in the raid and the sudden cessation of noise was eerie. I asked an A.R.P. warden if I could be of any help with the injured and he said all who could be got out had been taken away an hour ago. At this moment I noticed, coming towards me rather mincingly across the rubble, two smartly-dressed young girls in high-heeled shoes. As they passed close by me I heard one say to the other: 'You know, dear, the trouble with all this is you could rick your ankle.' This example of British understatement so enchanted me that I laughed out loud. The warden looked sharply at me, obviously suspecting hysteria, and said hadn't I better get indoors. I explained gently that at the moment there was very little indoors to get into, then we exchanged cigarettes and a little light conversation until Dallas joined us wearing full Marine regalia and a tin hat.

Later on, after we had got a couple of gallant old girls out of a tobacconist's and led them into the house next door to my studio, where they were wrapped in blankets and given some whisky, we made our way to Gladys Calthrop's house in Spenser Street, I on a bicycle and Dallas on foot. She received us with relief and we sat drinking hot tea while the raid started up again. Presently I dropped off to sleep on the sofa and was awakened by the All Clear.

The next morning Gladys and I went round to Gerald Road to see by daylight the real extent of the damage. Lorn, to whom I had telephoned, met us there with Ann, my housekeeper, who made us some coffee. We sat gingerly in the studio itself, on the edge of a soot-covered sofa, and shook our heads like mandarins. The skylights were all down; the main windows, which were enormous, had shattered inside their heavy curtains, so that the curtains were bulging out over the two grand pianos. In my bedroom, where Dallas had been sleeping, the chandelier was down, also a lot of plaster. Lorn's office was in the worst mess. The ceiling was on the floor and up out of it was rearing a tall filing cabinet on which stood an uncracked photograph of Jack and Natasha, smiling. The spare room, which I was occupying until Dallas moved out, was undamaged. The bed was neatly turned down with my pyjamas laid out on it, but everything, bed and furniture and pyjamas, were so thick with soot that they looked like black velvet. On the whole the damage was much less than I feared, but the place obviously couldn't be lived in even if we could get the windows boarded up, so I telephoned to the Savoy and reserved a room for that night, and we all trooped out to look at the wreck of the streets. The houses on the corner were still smouldering and groups of people were standing about staring aimlessly, their faces looking wan and papery in the cold morning light. There was a hopeless, beastly smell in the air. I suddenly felt miserable and most profoundly angry.

8

The day-to-day account in my diary of those weeks immediately following my homecoming is inadequate to say the least of it – nothing but a telegraphic jumble of people's names, half-formed impressions, visits to the movies with Joyce, discussions with Lorn, lunches, teas and dinners with so-and-so and such-and-such, and hardly any indication whatsoever of what was really going on in my mind. A stranger reading it in the hope of finding some clue to my character would, after the first few pages, dismiss me for ever as illiterate, incoherent and trivial to the point of idiocy. Even my own efforts to recapture from it, for the purposes of this book, a gleam of genuine significance, a hint of what I really felt, have resulted in bewildered exasperation. 'Discussion with Lorn' – what about? 'Long talk with Duff, very satisfactory' – why? 'Lunched with Joyce and Arthur, laughed hilariously' – what at? 'Bought bicycle at Fortnum's and ordered tin hat at shop in Victoria Street.' 'Tea with the Cranbornes; what a dear she is!' – what did she murmur to me over tea that so endeared her? 'Drinks at the Berkeley with Eric and Bob' – Eric and Bob who? 'Fell off bicycle' – where? After grim concentration and a great deal of brain-racking I have managed to fish out of this irrelevant welter an occasional clue, a slight spur to memory, but the overall picture is blurred and confused and gives me very little to go on. I can remember clearly two genuine emotions that illuminated that particular period. One was my relief at being home again and among my friends, and the other was a completely new appreciation of the charm and quality of London. London as a city had in the past never attracted me much. It was my home, of course, and I knew it intimately, perhaps too intimately. In my early days I had known its seamy side and later on more of its graces, but it had always seemed to me a little dull and smug compared with the romantic gaiety of Paris and the sharp vitality of New York. Now suddenly, in my early forties, I saw it for the first time as somewhere where I belonged. This sentimental revelation was made clearer to me by the fact that I was staying in a London hotel for the first time in my life. It was a strange sensation to step out of the comfortable impersonality of the Savoy into the personal, familiar streets of my childhood. I felt a sudden urge to visit the Tower and the Abbey and Madame Tussaud's and go to the Zoo. The move from Gerald Road to the Strand had transformed me overnight into a tourist in my own home, and as such it seemed more attractive to me and more genuinely gay than it had ever been before. I am not sure that that particular quality of gaiety survived the war. The rigours of peace and post-war party politics have done much to dim its glow, but in 1941, the real lights of London shone through the blackout with a steady brilliance that I shall never forget.

Three days after I had moved into the Savoy, Gladys and Bill Taylor and I were dining in the Grill, which was crowded. The usual Alert had sounded and we were half-way through dinner when two bombs dropped near-by, the second of which blew in one of the doors of the restaurant. There was dead silence for a split second after the crash and then everyone started talking again. With gallantry, tinged, I suspect, with a strong urge to show off, I sprang on to the orchestra platform where Carroll Gibbons was playing the piano, and sang several songs before anyone could stop me. The startled diners had little chance, anyhow, because Carroll was on my side and I had the microphone. Faced with the limited choice of staying where they were or rushing out into the blitz, the majority resigned themselves to the inevitable and we had quite a little party. Judy Campbell joined me on the platform and sang 'A Nightingale in Berkeley Square', and a group of slightly drunk but charmingly vocal Scotch-Canadians in kilts obliged with 'Shenandoah' and 'Billy Boy' in loose harmony. The whole occasion was a great success and there was a lot of cheering.

A day or two later the management of the Savoy courteously offered me a 'River Suite' at the same rate that I was paying for my single room. I suspected Carroll's wily hand in this, but I accepted gratefully without quibbling. It was a nice suite and I lived in it happily for several months.

During the next two weeks I see in my diary (one of its rare moments of coherence) that I spent a week-end with Gladys at her Mill near Ashford. The weather was nippy and the house, as usual, freezing, for Gladys is famous for her imperviousness to temperature. However, I grabbed two hot-water bottles and slept blissfully, sniffing up the fresh Kentish air. We drove over to Goldenhurst, a melancholy experience. All my furniture was in store at Whitstable and the house looked pathetic and derelict with only trestle tables and camp beds. On the whole it had been well cared for and the Commanding Officer, with whom we had tea, couldn't have been nicer, but I left with a feeling of nostalgia. My diary reports as follows: 'Visited G. Garden in fine condition but house oppressed by ghosts. Captain M. nice. Tea in what used to be Mother's sitting-room. Poor old Goldenhurst, I wonder if I shall ever see it again – have a strong feeling that I shall not. It seems that that is all over.'

On Friday, May the 2nd, Joyce Carey and I caught a morning train from Paddington, bound for Port Meirion in North Wales. For some time past an idea for a light comedy had been rattling at the door of my mind and I thought the time had come to let it in and show it a little courtesy. Joyce was engaged in writing a play about Keats, so here we were, 'Hurrah for the Holidays', without buckets and spades but with typewriters, paper, carbons, bathing-suits, sun-tan oil and bezique cards. We arrived on a golden evening, sighed with pleasure at the mountains and the sea in the late sunlight, and settled ourselves into a pink guest-house. The next morning we sat on the beach with our backs against the sea wall and discussed my idea exclusively for several hours. Keats, I regret to say, was not referred to. By lunch-time the title had emerged together with the names of the characters, and a rough, very rough, outline of the plot. At seven-thirty the next morning I sat, with the usual nervous palpitations, at my typewriter. Joyce was upstairs in her room wrestling with Fanny Brawne. There was a pile of virgin paper on my left and a box of carbons on my right. The table wobbled and I had to put a wedge under one of its legs. I smoked several cigarettes in rapid succession, staring gloomily out of the window at the tide running out. I fixed the paper into the machine and started: *Blithe Spirit.* A Light Comedy in Three Acts.

For six days I worked from eight to one each morning and from two to seven each afternoon. On Friday evening, May the 9th, the play was finished and, disdaining archness and false modesty, I will admit that I knew it was witty, I knew it was well constructed and I also knew that it would be a success. My gift for comedy dialogue, which I feared might have atrophied from disuse, had obviously profited from its period of inactivity. Beyond a few typographical errors I made no corrections, and only two lines of the original script were ultimately cut. I take pride in these assertions, but it is a detached pride, natural enough in the circumstances and not to be confused with boastfulness. I was not attempting to break any records, to prove how quickly I could write and how clever I was. I was fully prepared to revise and re-write the whole play had I thought it necessary, but I did not think it necessary. I knew from the first morning's work that I was on the right track and that it would be difficult, with that situation and those characters, to go far wrong. I can see no particular virtue in writing quickly; on the contrary, I am well aware that too great a facility is often dangerous, and should be curbed where it shows signs of getting the bit too firmly between its teeth. No reputable writer should permit his talent to bolt with him. I am also aware though, from past experience, that when the right note is struck and the structure of a play is carefully built in advance, it is both wise and profitable to start at the beginning and write through to the end in as short a time as possible. On the occasions when I have followed this procedure with other plays, notably *Private Lives* (four days) and *Present Laughter* (six days), the results have, I believe, justified the method. *Blithe Spirit* was exceptional from these two that I have mentioned only because its conception was followed immediately by the actual writing of it. *Private Lives* lived in my mind several months before it emerged. *Present Laughter* had waited about, half formulated, for nearly three years before I finally wrote it. Somerset Maugham has laid down that a good short story should have a beginning, a middle and an end. To me this is unassailable common sense and applies even more sternly to playwriting. Before the first word of the first act is written, the last act should be clearly in the author's mind, if not actually written out in the form of a synopsis. Dialogue, for those who have a talent for it, is easy; but construction, with or without talent, is difficult and is of paramount importance. I know this sounds like heresy in this era of highly-praised, half-formulated moods, but no mood, however exquisite, is likely to hold the attention of an audience for two hours and a half unless it is based on a solid structure.

Between May the 9th, when *Blithe Spirit* was finished at Port Meirion, and June the 16th, when it opened its preliminary tour in Manchester, several things happened. Rudolf Hess arrived in Scotland, which affected me very little, although it flung the Press boys at the Savoy into a frenzy of excitement and wild surmise. The Metro-Goldwyn-Mayer epic film of *Bitter Sweet* in violent Technicolor arrived at the Empire, which affected me even less, for I had already seen it in a projection room in Hollywood and had decided, sensibly, to wipe it from my mind. It was directed with gusto by Mr Victor Saville and sung with even more gusto by Miss Jeanette Macdonald and Mr Nelson Eddy. It was vulgar, lacking in taste and bore little relation to my original story. What did affect me, however, was the news on May the 27th of the sinking of H.M.S. *Kelly*, although naturally I had no idea at the time how much more this was destined to affect me in the future.

Immediately the news broke I telephoned to Robert Neville at the Admiralty, and he told me that Mountbatten had survived and was coming home. This was a great relief, but knowing how much his ship meant to him, and remembering with what pride he had taken me over her only a short while ago, I felt miserable.

Blithe Spirit, after the usual casting troubles and complications, duly opened in Manchester and was an enormous success. The London opening night was on July the 2nd at the Piccadilly Theatre, and a very curious opening night it was. The audience, socially impeccable from the journalistic point of view and mostly in uniform, had to walk across planks laid over the rubble caused by a recent air raid to see a light comedy about death. They enjoyed it, I am glad to say, and it ran from that sunny summer evening through the remainder of the war and out the other side. A year later it transferred to the St James's Theatre for a while, and then finally went to the Duchess, where at last it closed on March the 9th, 1946.

Later on, the play was produced in New York by Jack Wilson, where it ran for eighteen months, and I am prepared to say, here and now, with the maximum of self-satisfaction that those six days in Port Meirion in May 1941 were not wasted.

A few days after the *Blithe Spirit* opening, a deputation of three gentlemen, Filippo del Giudice, Anthony Havelock-Allan and Charles Thorpe, called on me at the Savoy Hotel. I received them warily because I knew that the object of their visit was to persuade me to make a film, and I had no intention of making a film then or at any other time. I had generated in my mind a strong prejudice against the moving-picture business, a prejudice compounded of small personal experience and considerable intellectual snobbery. I had convinced myself, with easy sophistry, that it was a soul-destroying industry in which actors of mediocre talent were publicised and idolised beyond their deserts, and authors, talented or otherwise, were automatically massacred. Of all my plays only one, *Cavalcade*, had been filmed with taste and integrity. The rest, with the possible exception of *Private Lives*, which was passable, had been re-written by incompetent hacks, vulgarised by incompetent directors and reduced to common fatuity. My only experience as a film actor had been *The*

Scoundrel, which was made in New York, or rather at the Astoria Studios, Brooklyn, in 1935. It was written and directed by Ben Hecht and Charles MacArthur and I agreed to do it because I thought the idea was good and, most particularly, because I was promised that Helen Hayes, whom I love and admire, would play the young poetess. However, at the last minute she was unable to get out of some contract and the part had to be re-cast. Finally, after much trial and error, Julie Haydon walked into the office, read the part sensitively and was engaged. The picture was made quickly and fairly efficiently; most of its speed and efficiency being due to Lee Garmes, the cameraman. The direction of Charlie MacArthur and Ben Hecht was erratic, and I, who had never made a picture before, was confused and irritated from the beginning to the end. *The Scoundrel* was hailed with critical acclaim. I made a success in it and so did everyone concerned, but I still wish that it and they and I had been better.

It can be seen therefore, with this annoying episode strong in my memory, why I received Del Giudice and his confrères with a certain lack of enthusiasm. The interview passed off pleasantly enough. Del Giudice was flattering and persuasive, Tony Havelock-Allan equally persuasive and rather more articulate, while Thorpe, who represented Columbia Pictures – why I shall never know – remained watchful and uncommunicative. This non-committal attitude was explained later on when he and Columbia Pictures withdrew their support from the enterprise because they did not consider that my name had sufficient drawing power. When the three of them had filed out I had agreed to think the proposition over carefully and give them my answer in a week's time. The actual proposition they had put to me was that if I agreed to write and appear in a picture for them I should have complete control of cast, director, subject, cameraman, etc., and that all financial aspects would be, they assured me, settled to my satisfaction once I had consented. It would have been churlish not to appreciate that this was a very flattering offer indeed, and although all my instincts were against it, I was forced to admit to myself that, provided I could think of a suitable idea, there was a good deal to be said for it. The very next evening Fate obligingly intervened and rang a bell so loudly in my brain that I was unable to ignore it. I happened to dine in Chester Street with Dickie and Edwina Mountbatten. Dickie had only been home in England for a little over a week, and although I had seen him briefly at the first night of *Blithe Spirit* I had not had an opportunity to talk to him. After dinner, he told me the whole story of the sinking of the *Kelly* off the island of Crete. He told it without apparent emotion, but the emotion was there, poignantly behind every word he uttered. I was profoundly moved and impressed. The Royal Navy, as I have explained elsewhere in this book, means a great deal to me, and here, in this Odyssey of one destroyer, was the very essence of it. All the true sentiment, the comedy, the tragedy, the casual valiance, the unvaunted heroism, the sadness without tears and the pride without end. Later on that night, in my bed at the Savoy, I knew that this was a story to tell if only I could tell it without sentimentality but with simplicity and truth.

Within the next few weeks *In Which We Serve* was conceived, although it was not until much later, after passing through various metamorphoses, that it achieved its final script form. The first stumbling-block was that although Dickie was all for a film which would be good propaganda for the Navy, he was not unnaturally afraid of my basing my story too exactly on the *Kelly* lest the film should in any sense become a boost for himself. After I had reassured him on this point, and in particular had made it clear that I had no intention of copying his own particular character, he undertook that he and some of the survivors of the *Kelly* would give me that help without which it would have been very difficult to have produced a convincing film. First of all, the Royal Navy's permission was asked for and willingly given. Dickie's personal enthusiasm cut through many strings of red tape and set many wheels turning on my behalf. From the beginning he saw the idea as a tribute to the Service he loved, and he supported me through every difficulty and crisis until the picture was completed. But that happy moment was over a year away and, in the meantime, there were many tiresome obstacles to be surmounted. I could never have surmounted them without his constructive criticism, his gift for concentration, his confidence in the film and in me. This might so easily have been strained beyond bearing within the ensuing few months, for neither of us dreamed in those first days of enthusiasm what a variety of dim-witted ogres we should have to vanquish. To begin with, the Press, led exultantly by the section which had proved hostile to me before, proceeded to sabotage the project from the moment the news broke that I was going to do it. There were sneering articles, contemptuous little innuendoes in the gossip columns, letters of protest written, I suspect, editorially, and the suggestion that I was going to portray Lord Louis Mountbatten on the screen, a suggestion for which no possible evidence had been furnished, was reiterated *ad nauseam* until even the Admiralty became restive and, I believe although I am not certain, protested strongly to the Ministry of Information. I only know that after a few weeks the clamour died down. The fact that there had never been any question of my portraying Lord Louis Mountbatten on the screen was, of course, ignored. 'Captain (D)' in *In Which We Serve* was conceived, written and acted to the best of my ability as an average naval officer, whereas Mountbatten was then, and is now, very far from being an average naval officer. He is definitely one of the most outstanding men of our times and showed every sign of becoming so when I first knew him in the early 'twenties. My 'Captain (D)' was a simpler character altogether, far less gifted than he, far less complicated, but in no way, I hope, less gallant. The story of the film was certainly based on H.M.S. *Kelly*, for the simple reason that through Mountbatten himself, and his shipmates who survived, I was able to get first-hand information and accurate details, both technical and psychological. The story, however, could have applied to any other destroyer sunk in action during the war. In all of them were the same potentialities, the same bravery, the same humour and the same spirit.

It would be wearisome to recapitulate all the irritations, frustrations and tiresomeness which had to be coped with during those difficult weeks. It would also involve undignified recrimination and possibly several libel suits. One thing I cannot forbear to mention was a letter to the Lords of the Admiralty from the head of the film department in the Ministry of Information. This letter, written on receipt of the final script, stated unequivocally that in the Ministry's opinion the story was exceedingly bad propaganda for the Navy, as it showed one of

H.M.'s ships being sunk by enemy action, and that permission would never be granted for it to be shown outside this country. The contents of this letter were communicated to me over the telephone by the head of the Ministry of Information's film department himself and, I need hardly say, left me speechless with rage. It was also made known by some means or other to the Two Cities Film Company, which had already invested a great deal of money in the production. The information, naturally enough, terrified them, and if I had not acted quickly the whole project would probably have been abandoned, at considerable financial loss, a few weeks before the actual shooting was due to begin. Fortunately for me this serious setback occurred later on in the production of the picture, when Mountbatten was back in England again, having been recalled from his command of the *Illustrious* to take over Combined Operations. I telephoned him immediately and he asked me to have a script delivered to him right away, and that he would show it to the Member of the Board of Admiralty who would be most likely to be called upon to make a decision in this matter. This gallant Admiral, who was afterwards lost in action, took the view that the story was very good propaganda indeed, and that the fact that the film portrayed a destroyer being sunk in war-time was certainly not necessarily a reflection on the Navy, where so many gallant ships were fighting to the end in the defence of the country's vital sea-lines of communication.

So, upheld by this moral support, Dickie and I went to the Ministry of Information, where we were received by Brendan Bracken, who kindly sent for the writer of the letter. Dickie went off like a time bomb and it was one of the most startling and satisfactory scenes I have ever witnessed. I actually felt a pang of compassion for the wretched official, who wilted under the tirade like a tallow candle before a strong fire. The upshot of it all was that from that moment onwards I had to endure no more nonsense from the Ministry of Information. In the following September, when *In Which We Serve* opened at the Gaumont, I received a congratulatory letter from this very official saying that the film was as moving and impressive as he had always known it would be. A curious missive.

In the meantime the Two Cities Film Company's fluttering hearts were stilled and on we went with the production.

At the very beginning of the whole enterprise I had been warned that the British Film Industry was a jungle of intrigue, politics and treachery, and a breeding ground of desperate chicaneries. Actually I found it none of these things. What I did find was that it was extravagant to the point of lunacy and, on the whole, fairly inefficient. The people who worked with me on the picture, however, were hand-picked and, with one or two exceptions, one hundred per cent efficient. It would have been difficult to go far astray with David Lean as my co-director, Tony Havelock-Allan in charge of production and Ronald Neame as director of photography. From these three I had whole-hearted, intelligent, and affectionate co-operation from the beginning to the end, and we have been close friends ever since. I was sorry, later on, when the three of them split up to go their different ways. They were a formidable trio together, and I owe to them much of the success of *In Which We Serve*, *This Happy Breed*, and above all, *Brief Encounter*. I will draw a light, spangled veil over *Blithe Spirit*, which they made while I was away in South Africa. It wasn't entirely bad, but it was a great deal less good than it should have been.

Apart from these three, there was the over-exuberant and most lovable Filippo del Giudice. His English was appalling and his enthusiasm boundless. He was another who, in spite of all storms and stresses and difficulties, never allowed his faith in me and the picture to be shaken for a moment. I find, on looking back, that I entered the jungle of the movie business with exceedingly staunch native bearers. They knew every inch of the perilous terrain and, I am convinced, saved my life repeatedly.

There is a French word that has been appropriated to describe a necessary technical expedient in the making of a moving picture: the word is 'montage'. Montage is usually employed to convey a lapse of days, weeks or years by telescoping events into the shortest possible screen time. For instance, if the heroine has abandoned the static domesticity of her home life in Omaha, Nebraska, and decided to go to Europe and become an opera singer, and it is essential for a few months to elapse before we see her making her

1. As Captain (D) in *In Which We Serve*

2. With Judy Campbell in *Blithe Spirit*

3. With Judy Campbell in *Present Laughter*

4. As Frank Gibbons in *This Happy Breed*

5. With the R.A.F., Middle East, 1943

6. Irak, 1943

7. Alderley Street, Cape Town

8. With American troops, Assam

début at La Scala, montage is used to cover those pregnant months. There will be a series of quick shots dissolving into one another – the wheels of the train bearing her to New York; an Atlantic liner steaming past the Statue of Liberty; a lightning glimpse of her practising in a Montmartre attic; a panoramic flash of the city of Milan dissolving into an empty theatre where she is seen struggling to master a difficult aria; a few fleeting visions of her trudging wearily through empty, alien streets with her music case; being fitted for her dresses; staring with tear-filled eyes at a photograph of her mother; a shot of the orchestra tuning up; another of the Opera House itself, crammed to the roof with Hollywood extras in deep evening dress applauding wildly; then finally a long shot of her bowing to her ovation and preparing to get on with the story at a more leisurely pace. From this brief description it will be readily understood that montage is a most convenient trick and can be used as effectively in writing as on the screen.

On looking back on the seven months between the original conception of *In Which We Serve* and the day on which we actually began shooting, I find I can see them only in terms of montage – endless conferences; hours in Wardour Street projection-rooms looking at British films; casting discussions, technical discussions; days at sea in destroyers; drives to and from Denham Studios in winter weather; arguments about the budget of the picture; moving into a dank cottage so as to be near the studios; crises, triumphs, despairs, exultations; tests in the Gaumont British studios at Shepherds Bush; hours of staring at myself on the screen – heavy jowls, no eyes at all; lighting wrong, lighting better; visits to shipyards in Newcastle; to dockyards at Plymouth and Portsmouth; endless discussions with experts – naval experts, film experts, shipbuilding experts, gunnery experts; and last, but by no means least, the nerve-racking business of my court proceedings at Bow Street and the Mansion House, which I will deal with more fully later.

On February 5th, 1942, we had our first shooting day of *In Which We Serve*. David and Ronnie and I were quivering with nerves, but, as the day went on, they evaporated as they usually do under stress of intensive work, and in the evening we had a drink in my dressing-room to celebrate the fact that at last, at long last, our preliminary troubles were over and we were under way.

From then on for five months the world outside Denham Studios virtually ceased to exist for me. Gladys Calthrop, who was my personal art director for the picture, had rented a cottage next door to mine. The two crouched together in a grove of morose trees which dripped in the rain, moaned in the wind and, in the spring, robbed us of the daylight. In the winter this didn't matter so much, for except on Sundays we never saw the daylight; we left for the studios in the blackout at about 7.30 a.m. and usually got home in the evening in time to hear the nine o'clock news, have dinner and go to bed.

I made occasional trips to London on days when for some reason or other I was not wanted at the studios. It felt strange and almost alien and it was often a relief to get into the Tube at Piccadilly Circus, get out at Uxbridge, pick up my car from the hotel garage and drive back to the familiarity of that beastly little cottage. Later on I moved into a much nicer one near Fulmer, but in the dark days 'Pine Cottage' was my hearth and home and I couldn't have disliked it more.

Work on the picture proceeded slowly but steadily. There were good days and bad days, cheerful days and bad-tempered days. There were nine very uncomfortable days when John Mills, Bernard Miles and I, and twenty others, spent from 8.30 a.m. to 6.30 p.m. clinging to a Carley float in a tank of warm but increasingly filthy water; also we were smeared from head to foot with synthetic fuel oil, only a little of which we were able to scrape off for the lunch break.

At certain times we had two hundred and fifty cheerful British sailors, kindly supplied by the Royal Naval Barracks, Portsmouth. At others, serried ranks of Coldstream Guardsmen greeted us briskly when we arrived on the floor. Those 'Big Scene' days were enjoyable, and David and Ronnie, with their various assistants, handled them with calmness and efficiency. Other days were devoted to small dialogue scenes in cramped circumstances (in moving-pictures dialogue scenes are almost invariably played in cramped circumstances). These days were sometimes less happy. I was, and still am, prone to become irritable when forced to say the same few sentences over and over again in long shots, medium shots and finally close-ups, with the camera a couple of inches from my nose and the microphone dangling one inch above my forehead. I got more and more used to it after a while, but for the first few weeks I was fairly fractious. I still think that *In Which We Serve* was one of the best acted pictures I ever saw. The leading actors, Celia Johnson, Kay Walsh, Joyce Carey, Johnnie Mills, Bernard Miles and Kathleen Harrison were impeccable (modesty compels me to dissociate myself from this assessment), but all the, at that time, smaller-part actors, including Richard Attenborough, Michael Wilding, Philip Friend, James Donald, Hubert Gregg, Derek Elphinstone, Dora Barton, Walter Fitzgerald, Gerald Case and a number of others, played with the utmost integrity.

There were many heated discussions concerning naval procedure. My 'Wardroom and Bridge' adviser was an ex-Destroyer Commander, 'Bushy' Clarke. My 'Lower Deck' adviser, a diminutive young man called Terry Lawlor, had served with Mountbatten as his cabin hand and had been burnt practically to death when the *Kelly* was sunk. Later, he was returning home in a hospital ship when it was torpedoed and he was burnt all over again. The plastic surgeons had done a miraculous job for him, and unless you looked closely you would never have realised that the skin of his face was almost entirely grafted. He was altogether a remarkable character and invaluable to us. I realised from the outset that it was essential to the accuracy of the picture that the lower deck and fo'c'sle should be represented as accurately as the quarterdeck, the bridge and the ward-room. The arguments between Bushy Clarke and Lawlor were frequent and sometimes very funny. They each held on to their ends of the controversial point like bull-terriers with a bone. Occasionally I was even forced to telephone to Dickie Mountbatten for impartial arbitration. Half-way through the picture, to our dismay Bushy was called back to do a course. His successor was Charles Compton, an amiable young lieutenant who obliged with advice when wanted, but by that time most of the important advice-giving had been done by Bushy, so there was not really much for him to do. However, I think on the whole he enjoyed himself.

In the middle of August, before embarking on the actual

writing of the script, I decided to assist inspiration by absorbing some authentic naval atmosphere. Captain Brojah Brooking, my staunchest supporter at the Admiralty, arranged for me to visit the Home Fleet at Scapa Flow for a week or two. At the same time I was invited by another of my old friends, Admiral Philip Vian, to go for a short cruise with him in his flagship H.M.S. *Nigeria*. As the *Nigeria* happened to be at Scapa this fitted in conveniently, so I travelled to Edinburgh by night, arriving at 4 a.m., caught the five o'clock train for Inverkeithing, where I was met by a car in the pouring rain and driven to the naval air-base at Donnibristle. Here I shaved and washed and was given breakfast by a pretty W.R.E.N. In due course Vian arrived and we discovered to our irritation that the plane which was to fly us to Thurso could not take off owing to the weather. There was nothing for it but to scramble into a crowded train on which we had no reservations. Appointing myself as the Admiral's unofficial flag-lieutenant, I forced the guard to accommodate us in his van, where the Admiral sat in a baby's perambulator all the way to Inverness. In pre-war years I had often been to sea with Vian when he was Captain of H.M.S. *Arethusa*. Since then he had distinguished himself in many ways, notably in the episode of the *Altmark*. He is a man of charm, sardonic humour, occasional irascibility and immense kindness. He also, like so many of his colleagues, is a stranger to fear. This was exemplified only too clearly to me during our nightmare drive from Inverness to Thurso. The roads were like glass, the visibility almost nil owing to the deluge, and the driver obviously a homicidal maniac. Being temperamentally unable to share Vian's immunity from stark terror, I arrived shaking like a leaf and moaning for gin. Happily in H.M.'s ships this is usually procurable, and after an hour or so in the ward-room of H.M.S. *Lively*, which was at Thurso to meet us, my nerves were soothed. The *Lively* deposited me on board the *King George V*, where I was to be the guest of the C.-in-C., Admiral Tovey, and took Vian on to his own ship, in which I was to join him two days later. From then on the atmosphere which I had come to absorb proceeded as usual to absorb me, to the exclusion of all other considerations. Even the primary object of my being there, which was to gather as much technical information as possible for the film, was forgotten in the pleasure of being with the Navy again. I was entertained in various ships; I opened a new cinema for the troops in Thurso; I watched, through the scuffle of the Admiral's cabin, H.M.S. *Prince of Wales* come to anchor, bearing Winston Churchill home after the signing of the Atlantic Charter. In fact it wasn't until a week later, when I arrived in Iceland on board the *Nigeria*, that it occurred to me to ask Vian where we were going and how long we should be away. He replied cheerfully that our immediate destination was Murmansk and that we might be away anything from two weeks to two months. This startled me into a sudden realisation of my own self-indulgence and my own responsibilities. I had promised the film unit before leaving London that I would not be away for longer than three weeks at the outside, and here I was, heading for Russia, with no way of communicating with them, for it was obviously impossible, for security reasons, to send home reassuring radiograms from a cruiser at sea in war-time. Vian, I regret to say, showed little concern with my problem and said gaily that the film could wait and that the sea air would do me good. Fortunately at this moment we were sharing an Icelandic fjord with H.M.S. *Shropshire*, which was on her way home from South Africa. I managed, with some difficulty, to persuade Vian that it really was essential for me to get back, and so signals were exchanged and I was transferred to the charge of Captain Borrett. I hated leaving *Nigeria* just as I was beginning to know the ship and become part of the ward-room family, but it had to be done and I spent a dismal hour going round and saying good-bye to everyone. Later that evening after dinner with 'Jacko' Borrett, who had received me with the usual naval hospitality, we watched the *Nigeria* sail out of the fjord and into the dark night. It subsequently turned out that had I only been able to sail in her I should have been in an exciting action during which half her bows were shot away. I should also have been out of contact with the film boys for more than seven weeks.

The trip home in the *Shropshire* was uneventful except that we sailed blithely through a minefield regardless of the fact that our Asdic apparatus had packed up. Back in Scapa, I stayed on in the ship for a few days, laughed a lot, drank a lot, engaged in further naval junketings, and was finally flown in a seaplane to Inverness, where, after badgering the R.T.O. at the station, I managed to get into the train for London.

9

On Thursday, October 16th, when I was hard at work in my studio in Gerald Road on the second draft of *In Which We Serve*, I was interrupted by the arrival of two police inspectors with two summonses from the Finance Defence Department. They told me, politely enough, that I was to appear, on Friday the 24th, before a court and that I was liable to a fine of £22,000 for having broken certain rules, the very existence of which I knew nothing about. They also informed me that another summons was on the way. This, naturally, was a shattering blow and I was horrified and extremely angry. I realised that unless I could get the case postponed, pending further investigations, I should be landed with a Press scandal which not only would smear my personal reputation, but might quite conceivably damage my relations with the Admiralty, Mountbatten and the Navy, and place the whole film in serious jeopardy. As it subsequently transpired, I needn't have worried about the Admiralty, Mountbatten or the Navy because, I am proud to say, they held me in too much honour to pay any attention to such palpable celebrity-baiting. Nevertheless it was a black moment and had to be dealt with firmly and swiftly. I immediately telephoned Nicholas Lawford, Anthony Eden's secretary at the Foreign Office, and asked him for the name of a good lawyer. The one he suggested, although sympathetic, was unable to represent me, for he was representing the other side, i.e., the Bank of England and the Treasury, but he was kind enough to ring up another lawyer, Dingwall Bateson, who agreed to deal with my case. A few days later I was served with three further summonses. These dealt with currency. I was told for the first time – my accountants having maintained a stately silence on the point – that on August 26th, 1939, a law was passed decreeing that all English people with money in America must declare it and not spend it in any circumstances whatever. This was entirely news to me, and exceedingly unpleasant news, for it meant that by spending the money I had spent from my personal account in New York, principally on work for my Government, I had been committing a criminal offence.

Bateson, who was understanding and shrewd, took a gloomy view. I gathered from his manner that he suspected somebody high up was specifically gunning for me. He said, at all events, that the Treasury was out for well-known blood, but that he hoped at least to be able to get a temporary adjournment. This he succeeded in doing, and my case was ultimately tried at Bow Street Police Court on October 30th. In the meantime Geoffrey Roberts ('Khaki' Roberts) had been engaged to defend me. Four days before the case I was surprised and most touched to receive out of the blue the following letter from George Bernard Shaw:

4, Whitehall Court,
London, S.W.I.
26/10/1941

DEAR NOËL COWARD,

The other day George Arliss, being in trouble about his American securities, pleaded Guilty under the impression that he was only admitting the facts and saving the Lord Mayor useless trouble. There was nothing for it then but to fine him £300.

He should have admitted the facts and pleaded Not Guilty, being as innocent as an unborn lamb. Of course the facts have to be established before that question arises; but when they are admitted or proved they leave the question of innocence or guilt unsettled. There can be no guilt without intention. Arliss knew nothing about the Finance Clauses, and did not even know that he owned American securities. He was Not Guilty, and should have said so and thereby put his defence in order.

Therefore let nothing induce you to plead Guilty. If your lawyers advise you to do so, tell them that *I* advise you not to. You may know all this as well as I do; but after the Arliss case I think it safer to warn you.

G.B.S.

Armed with this I went straight to Roberts and declared my intention of pleading Not Guilty. He explained to me patiently and at length that legally, not morally, I was guilty and that, as the maximum fine on all the charges might conceivably be £61,000 and the minimum £5,000, it would be much wiser to plead Guilty and hope for the latter. With the phrase from Shaw's letter, 'There can be no guilt without intention', stuck firmly in my mind, I held to my decision. He warned me that I should have to endure cross-examination, to which I replied that if all the most brilliant K.C.s in England cross-examined me until they dropped in their tracks they would be unable to prove me guilty when I bloody well knew I was innocent. I added defiantly that I would rather go to prison than pay the smallest fine for an offence about which I knew nothing. He thought poorly of this idea and the argument went on for a long time until finally I won my point.

On the morning of that unpleasant day I arrived with Lorn and Bateson at Bow Street at ten o'clock. Gladys and Joyce were in the body of the court to give me moral support. The counsel for the prosecution led off with the statement that I was liable to a £61,000 fine. The Magistrate looked, I thought, both disgruntled and unyielding, and I was in no way comforted when someone hissed in my ear that he was one of the most dreaded magistrates on the bench. Actually, as far as I was concerned he proved to be neither disgruntled nor unyielding; on the contrary he was, after the first few minutes of my evidence, both courteous and considerate. Under cross-examination I kept my head and answered briefly and to the point. It was apparent to me early on that the prosecution was anxious to prove that I had not been sent to America by the Ministry of Information, but had wangled my way out of the country by some means or other, presumably to live in sophisticated luxury on my illicit American earnings, and as far away from the discomforts of war-time England as possible. The letter, or what purported to be the letter, I had taken to Lord Lothian was suddenly produced and I was asked if I recognised it.

I replied that it was a private communication between the Minister of Information and the British Ambassador, that naturally I hadn't read it and so, obviously, couldn't recognise it. The production of this letter in Court puzzled me at the time and has puzzled me ever since. It was not offered to me to look at closely, but, as far as I can recall, it was on one sheet of thin paper, whereas the letter I actually delivered to Lord Lothian was quite bulky. A reference to my courier's passport agitated me rather. I was determined not to mention Little Bill's name whatever happened to me, but I reasoned that, the passport having been officially issued by the British Embassy in Washington at his request, it was fairly certain that nothing would be said likely to compromise him in any way.

The hearing of the case was a dreary business and seemed to drag on interminably. Roberts made an excellent, if somewhat embarrassing, speech about my honour and integrity, and I felt myself assuming the kind of expression I wear when I am obliged to listen to a eulogistic mayoral address at a civic function. The upshot of the whole business was that the Magistrate, after some scathing but, I fear justified, comments on my financial vagueness, fined me £200 with £20 costs. Considering that the minimum fine was assessed at £5,000, this was more in the nature of an accolade than a penalty, and I left the court relieved beyond words and went back to my script.

A week later I was summoned at the Mansion House on the charges relating to my American securities. The difference between the conduct of the court at the Mansion House and the court at Bow Street was as marked as the difference between the production of a play by a first-rate West End management and a production of the same play by a suburban Amateur Dramatic Society. The same questions which had been put to me at Bow Street were reiterated *ad nauseam*, and the Bench, struggling in a welter of dates and figures, interjected comments from time to time of quite startling irrelevance. The one fact that struck like a burr in their minds was that I had failed, while in America, to discuss finance, lease-lend and international economics with the British Purchasing Commission which had happened to be there at the time. In spite of my repeated assurances that I had not the faintest knowledge of such matters, and that had I attempted to discuss them with anybody at all I should merely have made a cracking ass of myself, they returned valiantly to the charge until I gave up all attempts to convince them and confined my answers to weary 'Yes's' and 'Noes'.

Having adjourned my case once for an hour while they tried a minor one, adjourned it again for lunch, and still a third time whilst they retired to consider their verdict, they finally imposed on me a fine of £1,600, graciously adding that they would allow me a month in which to pay it.

It seemed to me then, and it seems to me now, a curious reflection on British justice that whereas a trained lawyer had fined me £200 when the country had lost, through my ignorance, £11,000, an unprofessional Bench fined me £1,600 when the country had lost absolutely nothing.

At all events, the whole nasty business was mercifully over; the Press had treated me with unexpected kindness throughout both cases, and I was now free to wipe the whole thing from my mind and get on with my work. I still wonder if the Lord Mayor ever received the £2,000 sent to his Relief Fund by the Mayor of Sydney after my farewell concert.

10

The miserable winter of 1941–2 dragged on with the war news getting worse and worse. Gladys and I, crouching over the radio in the smoky discomfort of Pine Cottage, listened every morning to the clipped, impartial voices of the B.B.C. announcers telling us of further defeats and further disasters. The *Prince of Wales* and the *Repulse* were lost, Singapore fell, the Japanese began their invasion of Sumatra and Burma and the Germans advanced again in Libya. Two other warships that I knew well were lost, the *Cornwall* and the *Dorsetshire*. I remembered a gay dance on *Cornwall's* quarterdeck with coloured lights, a marine band and a full moon shining over Hong Kong harbour. I remembered the warm friendliness of *Dorsetshire*'s ward-room. Most of those cheerful, kindly young men who had entertained me so hospitably were now drowned or burnt and lying at the bottom of the sea.

One day Gladys, who had been in London, arrived at the studio having heard the night before that her only son Hugo had been killed in Burma. Hugo was young, good-looking and finely intelligent, and on the day in July 1940 when I had sailed for America he was in one of the other ships in the convoy, bound for Egypt. That was the last Gladys had seen of him. She demanded no pity and got on with the job as usual, and I knew that there was nothing to be done but to play up to her own integrity; it was not until several weeks had passed that we talked of him.

The picture progressed. There were, inevitably, troubles and crises and arguments, and on one occasion, when the entire electrical staff had descended from their perches at ten-thirty in the morning to have tea, leaving me with two hundred sailors waiting for the lights, I lost my temper and let fly. The result of this fracas was greatly increased efficiency for the remainder of the picture.

On April the 8th, I note in my diary, we had a proud and pleasant day. The King and Queen arrived in the afternoon with Princess Elizabeth, Princess Margaret and Dickie and Edwina Mountbatten. I met them with Arthur Rank and the Directors. We took them first to Stage Five, the big set, to see H.M.S. *Torrin*, our magnificent life-sized replica of a destroyer. Bushy Clarke called the sailors to attention and His Majesty, in his uniform of Admiral of the Fleet, took the salute. The Royal party were then installed on a rostrum to watch me do the 'Dunkirk' speech. The ship rolled, the wind machine roared and everything went beautifully. After three short 'takes' I took them all over the ship, presenting various people to them on the way. Then they inspected the Pattern shop and Stage One and spent half an hour in the projection-room looking at some rough-cut sections of the picture. Throughout their whole visit they were charming and easy and interested in everything, and I was amused to observe the impact of their perfect manners on some of the 'pinker' members of the staff. Altogether their visit was an unqualified success, from every point of view, and I hoped that it impressed the studio as much as it should have. Not because of Royal grandeur, but because the King and Queen and the Princesses of England had put themselves out to make everyone they met happy and at ease.

To quote Mr Bernard Shaw, the most ardent Socialist of his day: 'The constitutional King of England stands for: "the future and the past, the posterity that has no vote, and the tradition that never had any . . . for the great abstractions, for conscience and virtue, for the eternal against the expedient, for the evolutionary appetite against the day's gluttony, for intellectual integrity, for humanity . . ."'

The truth of these words seemed to me to be very apparent on that 'proud and pleasant' day.

Spring gave way, rather grudgingly, I thought, to summer and in late June we were about to complete the last shot of the film. It was an uncomfortable shot that was almost lethal for me. A replica of the bridge of the destroyer had been made of light wood and real glass and placed on the edge of the large outside tank at Denham Studios. Above it, a few hundred yards away on a scaffolding, were perched two enormous tanks filled with thousands of gallons of water. On a given signal a lever would be pulled, whereupon the tanks would disgorge their load down a chute, and overturn and capsize the bridge with me on it. Shivering in the bitter summer weather, I looked at the flimsy structure on which I was to stand and then up at the vast tanks and said 'No'. David and Ronnie, whose nonchalant attitude to human endurance had been engendered by years of film-making, looked at me with rather contemptuous disappointment. If I was frightened, David said, a stand-in would do it first, although this would entail a three hours' wait while the tanks were filled up again. These words, obviously intended as a spur to my failing courage, fell on stony ground for the simple reason that I knew a great deal more about the weight of water than they did. I replied that in no circumstances would I either do it myself or allow any living creature to stand on the bridge until I saw what the impact of water would do to it. Finally, after some grumbling at the time waste, they gave in to my insistence and ordered the signal to be given. The whistle blew and we all stood back and watched. There was a loud roar as the released water came hurtling down the chute and, in a split second, there was nothing left of the bridge at all. It was immediately obvious to all concerned that anyone standing on it would have been killed instantly. David and Ronnie, pale and trembling, returned silently with me to my dressing-room, where we each of us downed a strong tot of brandy.

A few days later the bridge was rebuilt, breakwaters were installed and tested, and on June the 27th the shot was at last taken. I cannot say that I enjoyed it and the moment before the whistle blew I was terrified. From that moment on, all was chaos. I flattened myself against the Pelorus; the water struck me in the small of the back, knocking all the breath out of me; the structure slowly capsized as planned and after a few desperate moments I fought my way to the surface. Happily the cameras had been efficient, so the shot did not have to be repeated. On the screen the episode is over in a flash, but I have never looked at it without a retrospective shudder.

II

Earlier in the year, when the routine of the film studio was beginning to get me down, I had decided, after a conversation with Hugh Beaumont, the managing director of H.M. Tennent, to return to the stage. Hugh (Binkie) Beaumont, one of my closest friends and my business associate for many years, was delighted with the idea and it was arranged that I should do a twenty-eight weeks' provincial tour with a repertoire of three plays, *Present Laughter*, *This Happy Breed* and *Blithe Spirit*, opening in September. From July onwards therefore, I bade a relieved and respectful good-bye to Denham Studios, and, with the exception of a few days here and there of dubbing and post-synching, plunged back into the familiar, comforting business of planning, auditioning and casting.

On August 20th, having agreed to replace Cecil Parker in the London production of *Blithe Spirit* for two weeks, I appeared on the stage for the first time since 1937, when I had concluded the run of *Tonight at Eight-Thirty* in New York. I arrived at the St James's Theatre in the evening after a reasonably slick midday rehearsal feeling apprehensive and troubled with the thought that I might have lost the knack of being a light comedian. After I had been on the stage for a few minutes, however, the old-well-remembered magic began to happen and I felt myself beginning to time my lines and movements. After the initial strain had worn off, it was wonderful to be able once more to play consecutive scenes of more than a few sentences, and to get laughter and applause from actual audiences, after months of acting my heart out before a preoccupied production unit and the silent regard of disinterested property-men and electricians.

I was delighted to be back in the theatre and undaunted by the prospect of a long tour through the provincial cities in war-time, when the hotel amenities were likely to be austere and travelling accommodations erratic.

My life seemed to have fallen into place again in spite of the fact that all the fine schemes I had had at the beginning of the war for doing important work for the country had been temporarily frustrated. It had certainly not been my fault. I had done my best, or what I thought was my best. Perhaps that was where the trouble lay. My best might more certainly be achieved in my own job after all. Possibly I had been over-sanguine and even a trifle conceited to imagine that my abilities could be transferred immediately and successfully to such very different milieux. At least, on my own ground, I would not have to endure bureaucratic pomposity and attacks on my personal character. I think I realised, even in that mood of rosy introspect, that the time would come when I would be restless again, yearning to be up and away, to be doing a little more for the war effort than merely earning my living in slightly more uncomfortable circumstances than usual. But such rebellious urges were far in the future and I knew I should be much too occupied during the next eight months to allow them to disturb me.

During the two weeks that I was playing at the St James's, the Duke of Kent was killed in an air crash in Scotland. I had first met him during the run of *London Calling* in 1923, and we had been friends ever since. My cottage near Fulmer was only a couple of miles away from Coppins, the house of the Duke and Duchess of Kent, and I had dined with them there on an average of once a fortnight since the beginning of the film. I had actually talked to him on the telephone two days before he was killed, and made a date for him to come on the following Friday to see me in the play and have supper afterwards. The news was announced over the air on the evening of August 25th, but I was supping out and knew nothing of it until the following morning when I read the newspaper headlines. It was an appalling shock and, as often happens at such moments, my mind at first refused to believe it, which of course was foolish, because in those dark years we were all of us learning by bitter experience that it was only too easy to believe someone young and gay and kind was dead. They were dying all the time. My heart ached for the poor Duchess and I could think of no articulate words to write to her. I did my best, but on such occasions there is little to be said or written. Memories of her unfailing sweetness to me ever since I had first met her in London, just after her engagement was announced, flooded into my mind; memories of all the happy times the three of us had had together in the following years; the twinkle in the eye suddenly caught and registered on grand occasions; the absurd word games played on quiet evenings in the country; the irrelevant jokes, all the fun, now suddenly tragically over. It was a black and miserable day, and when I arrived at the theatre for the evening performance I was grateful to Fay Compton for warning me, just before I went on, to be on my guard against certain lines in the play which might surprise me, by their dreadful appositeness, into a betrayal of my feelings. She was right to warn me. *Blithe Spirit* certainly treats the subject of death lightly, and although I still maintain that Death in the abstract is not nearly so solemn and lachrymose as many people would have us believe, it is not always possible to treat it with the proper disdain when the personal heart is quivering with a sense of loss.

A few days later I drove down to Windsor for the funeral service in St George's Chapel. The service was impressive and supremely dignified. I tried hard not to cry, but it was useless. When the Duchess came in with the Queen and Queen Mary, and when the coffin passed with a simple bunch of flowers from the garden at Coppins and Prince George's R.A.F. cap on it, I was finished. At the end, when the King had sprinkled the earth and the Royalties had gone away, we all went up, one by one, to the vault and bowed and secretly said our good-byes to him. Then we filed out into the strong sunshine and, for me, a nineteen-year-old friendship was over for ever except in my memory.

12

On September the 20th my tour opened at Blackpool with *Present Laughter*. On the two subsequent evenings we opened *This Happy Breed* and *Blithe Spirit*. My cast was excellent: Joyce Carey, Judy Campbell, Beryl Measor, Jennifer Gray, Molly Johnson, Meg Titheradge, Gwendolyn Floyd, Dennis Price, Billy Thatcher, Gerald Case and James Donald. All three plays were successful, and my satisfaction was only slightly offset by a violent cold which I had started at the Monday morning word-rehearsal. The theatre was packed at every performance and the Blackpool audiences, although a trifle confused by the 'brittle sophistication' of *Present Laughter*, were, on the whole, receptive.

From then on our Odyssey continued until the following April. The routine was broken from time to time by week-end visits to London. The first of these came at the end of the first week because I had promised, and was indeed eager, to be in London for the first showing of *In Which We Serve*, which took place on Sunday evening, September the 17th. The Press showing, a few days previously, had resulted in ecstatic reviews in all the papers. The première was given in aid of Naval Charities and the pre-ponderance of naval uniforms and gold lace gave a considerable *cachet* to the occasion, and I was moved and proud to see the impact of the picture on that distinguished audience. Towards the end there was a great deal of gratifying nose-blowing and one stern-faced Admiral in the row behind me was unashamedly in tears. For me it was a wonderful experience. I had, of course, seen the film in all its phases, but I had never seen it entirely completed nor heard an audience react to it. I felt that it was a fine piece of work which more than justified all the troubles, heartburnings, disappointments and frustrations we had endured in the making of it. There it was, once and for all, well directed, well photographed and well played and, above all, as far as I was concerned, an accurate and sincere tribute to the Royal Navy.

When it was over there was a party at the Savoy, and David and Ronnie and I received happily most of the superlatives in the English language, several in French, Norwegian, Danish and American, and none in Russian or German.

The following morning, blown up with triumph, Joyce and I travelled to Bristol to carry on with the tour. I would not have missed those months of flogging through the provinces for anything in the world, for although there were many moments of bitter cold, discomforts, exhaustion and near-starvation, there were also many compensations and we were an exceedingly happy company. There were no scenes or squabbles or unpleasantnesses from the beginning of the tour to the end. My stage staff, Peggy Dear, Charles Russell and Lance Hamilton, achieved miracles by successfully getting the plays lit and set in time for each Monday evening performance on stages that varied in size and shape from the vastness of the Bristol Hippodrome to the tiny intimacy of the Theatre Royal, Exeter. In Inverness we opened *Blithe Spirit* in a small converted cinema which had been closed for two months and was like a frigidaire, which was not surprising as it was January and there was a blizzard raging. After the first act I complained to Joyce and Judy that I had been unable to hear myself speaking owing to the chattering of their teeth. In the second act, to our immense relief, the theatre caught on fire; clouds of acrid black smoke rose from the orchestra pit and we chokingly carried on with the play, longing for the flames. It turned out to be merely a stoppage in the wardrobe chimney and we were obliged to press on, to an audience coughing its lungs out.

I had agreed, at the request of the Director of Naval Intelligence, to give a five-minutes security speech at the end of each performance. This was a good idea in theory, but it is not actually easy, when you have been striving all the evening to make people laugh and enjoy themselves, suddenly to turn on them at the end and admonish them sternly with grim little anecdotes of death and betrayal resulting from their not keeping their traps shut. In addition to this, one speech was not enough, for I was playing three plays consecutively which were attended, as a general rule, by the same audiences. I had to invent three entirely different security speeches to save myself the embarrassment of seeing my public gathering up their hats and coats and programmes and walking out on me as I began to speak. The Admiralty promised to supply me with a series of true incidents concerning the losing of lives by careless talk. The incidents they produced were meagre from the dramatic point of view, so I was forced to invent myself a few hair-raising stories about ships being sunk, spies being landed from submarines and munition factories being sabotaged because some garrulous citizen in a pub or a shop had said something indiscreet. Fortunately the audiences took these little tirades in good part and, of course, the company adored them. Whether or not they did the slightest good I shall never know.

There was still in my mind a core of discontent because I was engaged on a pleasant and profitable acting job which contributed nothing actually to the war effort. This perhaps was silly, because at least I was amusing people who were having a dreary time and making them laugh and forget their problems for a few hours. But there it was, this nebulous dissatisfaction, and in order to quell it I rashly agreed to give an average of four to six concerts a week in munition factories and hospitals in each town we visited. Judy agreed to appear with me and I engaged an accompanist in London, Robb Stewart, to tour with us and be available when required. He was an excellent musician and played beautifully for me when he was in the mood, but owing to a certain inherent vagueness in his temperament he was not always in the mood. Those concerts, all in all, were shattering experiences. Usually we appeared in factories during the lunch hour and had to bellow desperately to make ourselves heard above the din of crockery and the clangour of metal plates. Our audiences were apathetic as a rule and were flung into a state of leaden bewilderment when Judy sang to them that Arthur Murray had taught her dancing in a hurry and that there was a nightingale singing incessantly in

Berkeley Square. I confused them still further with 'Don't Put Your Daughter on the Stage, Mrs Worthington' and 'Mad Dogs and Englishmen'. We fully realised that our songs were not entirely appropriate and tried to vary them with more popular favourites. These were received with much the same apathy, excepting 'If You were the Only Girl in the World' and 'There'll Always be an England', which they generally knew and were able to sing themselves. After a few weeks of these uninspired entertainments I was forced to the conclusion that I would rather sing to an audience of hostile aborigines than to a group of over-tired, and obviously ravenous, factory girls. The hospitals were a bit better, but somehow or other there was always something wrong with the organisation. Either the car didn't arrive to fetch us in time, or there was no microphone, or the microphone there was shrieked like a banshee and broke down. At all events my conscience, which, although perhaps over-sensitive, is not entirely an ass, finally persuaded me that if I continued to beat my brains out giving concerts four or five times a week as well as playing eight performances of three plays, I should probably crack up and have to cancel the tour, thereby throwing my company out of work and disappointing a large number of people. The common sense of this was obvious, and so bit by bit we cut out the dreadful concerts and by Christmas time we had dropped them entirely, although we later gave a few troop shows in Scotland.

We spent a happy Christmas in Aberdeen. On Christmas morning I gave a party for the company in my hotel sitting-room, and for days before it we were continually meeting each other in Union Street, furtively darting in and out of shops and buying each other identical presents. *George Bernard Shaw*, by Hesketh Pearson, and drinking-flasks were the most popular purchases. We all gave and received several of them. Mary Garden, as dynamic as ever, came to the plays and I saw to it that she was treated as Royalty. There were flowers in her box, and Hugh Kingston-Hardy, our business manager, received her with his usual charm. In my opinion she was one of the greatest operatic actresses in the world. The years had left no apparent mark on her and when I asked after her voice she said gaily she had given up singing for ever and preferred smoking and bridge.

The tour pursued its course through the dark winter months into the spring. Each town we visited had its surprises for us, some of which were agreeable and some very much the reverse. In Hull there was no heating in the hotel; although there were fires temptingly laid in our rooms we were not permitted to light them without a doctor's certificate to prove we were ill. The promptitude with which Joyce, Judy and I arrived at Death's Door between Sunday evening and Monday morning was remarkable. We all three arrived at the nearest doctor's consulting-room palpably on the verge of pneumonia and returned triumphantly to the hotel clutching our certificates.

In most towns our evening performance coincided with the hotel dinner hour and we seldom got a hot meal after the show, in fact in certain places it needed all our persuasions to get some cold spam and damp salad left out for us. Those of the company who were in digs were, on the whole, better off, although even they frequently suffered from conscientiously austere landladies who seized gleefully on war-time conditions to starve them to death. In Scotland the situation was happier and we were given sausages, bacon, kippers, eggs and even occasional steaks. Our luck still held in Carlisle owing to the kindness of our hotel proprietor, but as we progressed further down into the depressing English Midlands our treats became fewer and much further between. Our Sundays, of course, we spent in unheated trains, except on one occasion, when, bundled up like Eskimos in woollies and coats and fleece-lined boots, we found ourselves in a train so over-heated that we could scarcely breathe. There were seldom restaurant cars and, when there were, the food served in them was inedible. In many towns the transport problem was a serious trial. The few trams there were had usually stopped by the time we emerged from the stage-door, and as taxis were frequently unobtainable we had to foot it through pitch-black, unfamiliar streets, and stumble along with our electric torches, the bulbs of which had to be painted blue and therefore gave hardly any light at all. We generally managed to rise above these inconveniences with fortitude, but occasionally, when we had colds or headaches or were over-tired, they got us down. We played through a certain number of air raids, but neither the audiences nor ourselves were unduly agitated by them.

For me the tour fizzled out ignominiously. I had managed to keep reasonably well ever since my original cold in Blackpool. Some of the company fell by the wayside at different times and missed a performance or two, but most of us continued to keep on our feet until our opening performance in Exeter, when, to my dismay, I knew beyond a doubt that I was running a temperature. I got through to the end of the play, *This Happy Breed*, though my head was spinning and my voice sounded as though it belonged to somebody else. When I took my temperature it was 102, and had risen the next morning to 104. A doctor arrived at the hotel and told me there was no question of my playing. Dennis Price, who was my understudy, played *Blithe Spirit* that evening, after which, when it was realised that I was really ill with a bad attack of jaundice the rest of the tour was cancelled with the exception of a week in Bournemouth, where Dennis played for me very well. Jaundice is a depressing disease and I do not wish to dwell on it. I was wretched with it for several weeks and lay yellow and desolate in the Imperial Hotel, Torquay. Bert Lister, my dresser, nursed me with a fervour that Florence Nightingale would have envied. Lorn, Gladys, Binkie and others came down from London to visit me and did their best to cheer me, but it was not until I had spent a month convalescing at Tintagel on a rigid diet that I felt well enough to contemplate without dismay my forthcoming season at the Haymarket.

My room in the King Arthur's Castle Hotel at Tintagel looked out over stormy seas, cliffs, gorse and seagulls. Bert came with me for the first few days, then I sent him to London and gave myself up gratefully to solitude. I went for a brief walk every day, read numberless books and, for the only time in my life, listened consistently to the radio. It was a good radio and it tuned in easily to foreign stations. I listened to Spanish politicians, German sopranos and French collaborators. Occasionally I even listened to the B.B.C. entertainment programme. The war news was brighter but not bright enough to give any illusions of swift victory. The world was still suffering and fighting and dying, and the ordinary years that we had lived and enjoyed and taken for granted receded further and further into the limbo, until I began to feel they were figments of imagination that had never existed at all. It was difficult to realise that only three years ago the Germans had overrun Europe, that our Army had been driven back to the beaches of Dunkirk, and that France had fallen. I had the feeling that my life had retreated into a vacuum, comfortable enough, but without significance. I also realised, for not even jaundice had entirely submerged my common sense, that these bouts of melancholy introspection were the inevitable results of months of hard work followed by a depressing illness; nevertheless something at the back of my mind was nagging at me and after a little while, when the process of recuperation was almost completed, I was able to identify it. It was my old familiar urge to change my course and do something different and to go somewhere different. I had agreed with Binkie to play an eight-week season at the Haymarket with *This Happy Breed* and *Present Laughter*. I had also agreed to tack on an extra week in Plymouth to compensate for the one cancelled on account of my illness. After this, however, I was without commitments and free to go where I wanted, provided I was adroit enough to steer clear of officialdom and wriggle through a few bureaucratic fences. I am certain, on looking back over the war years, that much of the irritation and obstructiveness I aroused in official breasts was due to my determination to play a lone hand; to do what I considered the best thing to do in my own way and on my own responsibility. This resolute individualism is seldom a popular quality, but it happens to be an essential part of my character. I had no intention of offering my services to E.N.S.A., for I was suspicious of its efficiency and my instincts rebelled, as usual, against the idea of being subject to the whims of any Government department. I decided therefore to get myself to the Middle East by some means or other, entertain troops in places where I considered I would be most needed, and visit hospitals whenever and wherever I found them. I knew that, once out of England, I could rely on the Fighting Services for transport. I also knew that on my own I could get to certain obscure places where officially organised entertainments had not penetrated. The moment I had arrived at this decision my spirits lightened and I strode out on to the edge of the cliffs and recited Clemence Dane's 'Trafalgar Day' defiantly to the seagulls.

13

On April the 20th my mother celebrated with suitable rejoicing her eightieth birthday. Aunt Vida, with whom she shared a flat in Eaton Mansions, was a trifle supercilious over such a fuss being made, as she herself was several years older and spry as a grass-hopper. I gave Mother a silver fox cape, in which she swaggered up and down the room like a mannequin.

On Thursday, April the 29th, *Present Laughter* opened at the Haymarket Theatre, and on the following evening *This Happy Breed*. Both plays were successes and we played happily to capacity for the entire season. To me the Theatre Royal, Haymarket, is not only the nicest theatre in London but probably the nicest in the world. It is neither too large nor too small, its acoustics are perfect and it is rich in tradition.

During those weeks my days, excepting Wednesdays and Saturdays when we played matinées, were largely occupied by discussing with David, Ronnie and Tony at Denham the film script of *Blithe Spirit* and looking at the rushes and rough-cuts of *This Happy Breed*, which was in course of production.

I usually went down to my cottage near Fulmer after the evening performance, travelling by Tube to Uxbridge and by car from then onwards. It was pleasant to be concerned with the picture but not trapped by it. I could never quite prevent a sinking of the heart every time I drove through the gates of Denham Studios – they recalled so many leaden and difficult days; but at least in these circumstances, with David and Ronnie doing all the actual work, I could say what I had to say and get out again before the atmosphere really defeated me. The picture of *This Happy Breed* was on the whole very well done. Celia Johnson, Kay Walsh, Johnnie Mills and Stanley Holloway were first rate, and the tech-nicolour, after much discussion, was reduced to its minimum, delicately balanced and for once did not sear the eyeballs with oleographic oranges and reds and yellows.

The war, meanwhile, was becoming increasingly dramatic and increasingly hopeful. We were achieving staggering victories in the

Desert. The Russians were holding their own, Italy was dis-integrating. The papers were full of premature clamour for a Second Front and it looked, at long last, as though the tide really was turning in the Allies' favour.

Our Haymarket season closed on July the 3rd and we played our final week of all at Plymouth as promised. The audiences were wonderful and, casting aside my security speeches, I recited at the end of the play a poem by Clemence Dane called 'Plymouth Hoe'. She had been most impressed the year before when I had described to her the people of Plymouth dancing on the Hoe every evening at a time when the town was enduring intensive air raids every night. The poem she wrote was simple, touching and to the point, and needless to say it was a triumphant success. The idea of the people dancing had been conceived by Lady Astor, the Mayoress, in the summer of 1942. It was a fine idea and she fought with all her extraordinary vitality and determination to get it carried out. Much has been written and said about Lady Astor as a politician, she is renowned for throwing monkey wrenches into debates, attacking Winston Churchill and inveighing, occasionally tiresomely, about the evils of intemperance, but nobody who saw her, as I did, when Plymouth was being bombed almost out of existence could feel for her anything but profound and affectionate admiration. I remember in 1942 walking with her through the devastated streets of the town one morning after a bad blitz, and her effect on the weary people was electrifying. She indulged in no facile sentimentality; she was cheerful, friendly, aggressive, and at moments even a little governessy. She dashed here and there and everywhere, encouraging, scolding, making little jokes. In the sitting-room of one pathetic house, the roof and kitchen of which had been demolished, she ordered a pale young man to take the cigarette out of his mouth. With remarkable presence of mind he held out his hand in the Nazi salute and said with a giggle: 'Heil Hitler, my Lady!' My Lady, not in the least nonplussed, laughed, told him he would ruin his morals and his lungs with nicotine, slapped him on the back and on we went. Occasionally we encountered hopelessness and tears and deso-lation. At these moments Lady Astor discarded her morale-lifting cheerfulness and, from the depths of her genuine kindliness, found the right words to say. I have little reverence for the teachings of Christian Science; as a religion it has always seemed to me to induce a certain arid superiority in its devotees, as well as encouraging them to swish their skirts aside from many of life's unspiritual, but quite unquestionable, realities. But, like many other sects which are offshoots of Christianity, some of its tenets are based on solid ground. Lady Astor is, I know, an ardent Christian Scientist, but I feel that she would be equally kind, dynamic, gallant, intolerant and warm hearted had she been a Bhuddist, a Seventh Day Adventist or a Holy Roller.

During our week in Plymouth Judy and I did various concerts for the Navy, all of which were enjoyable. On the last night of our final performance of *Present Laughter*, in spite of a very dressy audience, the company was high and, I fear, rather badly behaved, but we were all feeling sad inside and so perhaps a little carrying on was permissible. At the end the company assembled on the stage for me to say 'Good-bye', and to present me with two very fine eighteenth-century cannon heads and a ship's lantern. Meg Titheradge, being the smallest member of the cast, had been chosen to make the presentation, which she did with tears running down her cheeks. The emotion of the moment was catching, and I found that I could only stammer out a strangulated 'Thank you', say how much I loved them all, and retire hurriedly to my dressing-room.

They were a dear company, we had worked happily together for many months and it was a suitably sentimental finale.

It had been arranged, through the kindness of Brendan Bracken, that I should fly to Gibraltar the following week under the aegis of the Ministry of Information. From then onwards, I was told, to my relief, that I could fend for myself. It was also arranged that I should carry traveller's cheques, duly approved by the Treasury, so that there could be no further questions asked about my betraying my country by the wild expenditure of my own hard-earned money in the middle of the Sahara desert.

A few days before I was due to leave, a message arrived from the Ministry of Information informing me that I was to submit for censorship the words of all the songs I intended to sing. Realising this meant that the songs would probably not be returned to me in time to take with me I telephoned the Ministry of Information censorship department and protested. The gentleman at the other end of the telephone, who I suspected was wearing bottle-green corduroy trousers and an oatmeal tie, assured me in thin, Bloomsbury tones that in the event of delay the songs would be sent on to me in Gibraltar. Aware that the mills of bureaucracy grind even more slowly than the mills of God, I thanked him graciously, selected at random from my files at least a hundred lyrics that I had not the slightest intention of singing and despatched them to the Ministry of Information by special messenger. I then telephoned the Commander-in-Chief at Plymouth, Admiral Forbes, told him that I was flying to Gibraltar at the end of the week, but would much prefer to go by sea. He replied that nothing could be easier and that if I could get myself to Plymouth on the night train I could leave the following evening.

The rest of that day was devoted to saying good-byes and packing a great deal more than I should have been allowed to take in a plane. My farewell scene with Mother passed off smoothly; she behaved beautifully and didn't shed a tear. My Aunt Vida enquired if I had to wear a special boating costume when travelling with the Navy, to which I replied that the usual formalities were relaxed in time of war, so I would be required to wear only a sword and a cocked hat in harbour, and only the hat at sea.

Gladys, Lorn, Joyce and Bert saw me off at Paddington after a gay dinner at The Ivy, and with a light heart I set off on my travels once more.

The next morning I breakfasted with the C.-in-C. and Lady Forbes. Several Admirals came to lunch, also Captain Voelcker, who had agreed to give me a passage in his ship, H.M.S. *Charybdis*. I warmed to him immediately and felt fairly certain, judging by his personality and the way he talked, that the ship would be a happy one. In the late afternoon he called for me in his boat, my bags were put inboard by two grinning ratings, I said good-bye to the C.-in-C. and Lady Forbes and we chugged across the Sound to where the *Charybdis* was lying, grey and purposeful, with steam up.

~ About an hour later, when I had been comfortably installed in the Captain's day cabin, introduced to the Commander, John Whitfeld, and the ward-room officers and, at my own firm request, been made an honorary member of the bar, we upped anchor and sailed. From the bridge I watched Plymouth fade into the distance and the cliffs of Cornwall pass by. It was the first time I had been on the bridge of a warship since H.M.S. *Torrin* in Denham Studios. I fell automatically into my 'Captain (D)' postures and it was only with a great effort that I restrained myself from pushing Captain Voelcker out of the way and shouting orders down the voice pipes.

14

The next three months of my life I have already dealt with in a small book called *Middle East Diary*, published in 1944. It achieved only a moderate success and I find on re-reading it that it is only moderately interesting. My original intention in writing it was to describe what, to me, was a memorable experience, and at the same time to pay a tribute to the fighting men I met in ships, camps, air-bases, and hospitals. Unfortunately it was done too hurriedly, with neither sufficient selectiveness nor sufficient perspective, and it relies too much on actual quotations from my day-to-day diary, many of which, though valid enough for a private record, emerge on the printed page as trite, sentimental and, at moments, trivial. Also it suffers from a rash of pompous footnotes which helped to damn the book in the eyes of the American critics. At all events, the book was never intended for American consumption and it was foolish of me to allow it to be published there. I have regretted this ever since because, apart from the damning notices it received, it involved me in an unpleasant and entirely unexpected fracas. On page 106 of this ill-starred little volume I made a careless mistake. In describing a visit to a large hospital in Tripoli, soon after the landings at Salerno, I explained at some length how impressed I was with the superb spirit and courage of the United States soldiers I talked to, most of whom had been grievously wounded and were in great pain. Gallantry in the face of suffering always moves me and it was only with difficulty that I prevented my feelings from showing on my face. On my way out of that crowded and agonised ward I stopped beside two beds near the door in which two young men were weeping bitterly. When I had talked to them for a few moments and done my best to cheer them up, I asked them where they came from and they replied, Brooklyn. I then discovered that one of them had had a bullet through his toe and the other a fractured arm. Both these wounds, although perhaps painful, seemed hardly to justify such abandonment of grief. My mind, although well conditioned by this time to tragedy, was still quivering from the gruesome horrors I had seen at the other end of the ward and, I must honestly admit, the commotion these two were making irritated me. I controlled my irritation, wished them well and left them, but the incident remained in my memory and was duly recorded in my diary. The offensive paragraph which ultimately caused such a storm read as follows: 'There was a mixed lot in this particular hospital, among them about a hundred Americans in from Salerno. I talked to some tough men from Texas and Arizona, they were magnificent specimens and in great heart, but I was less impressed by some of the mournful little Brooklyn boys lying there in tears amidst the alien corn with nothing less than a bullet wound in the leg or a fractured arm.' That the people of Brooklyn should have been bitterly offended by this was more than understandable, for it is careless and inaccurate: the word 'some' implies that all Brooklyn boys are craven, whereas in this case there were only two and although, unfortunately, they both happened to come from Brooklyn they might just as easily have come from anywhere else. Neither courage nor cowardice belong exclusively to the people of any city, state or country, and loose generalisation is a trap into which we all fall far too frequently. It still astonishes me, however, that this admittedly unwarranted phrase should have caused so violent a storm. It was of course exacerbated by newspaper columnists and also by the late Mayor La Guardia, who delivered a vituperative broadcast about me with, I suspect, the object of increasing his Brooklyn vote. The general hysteria finally reached such a pitch that a club was formed, I think by the Mayor of Brooklyn, for the 'Prevention of Noël Coward re-entering America'. I still have in my possession a card of membership kindly procured for me by Beatrice Lillie. It is not surprising that by this time my friends in America were seriously perturbed, although not any more than I was myself. I apologised publicly to Brooklyn with complete sincerity, which I am happy to say damped down the flames until at last they fizzled out. It was not until a long while later that Leonard Lyons and Edna Ferber both told me in London that the term 'Brooklyn Boys' had been generally understood to be a snarling reference on my part to the Jewish Race. This, although palpably idiotic, shocked me more than anything else, for I have always detested any form of racial discrimination and consider anti-Semitism to be silly, inconsistent, cruel and entirely beneath contempt. At all events, I have been to America many times since and passed through Brooklyn unmolested, which proves, I sincerely hope, that I have genuinely been forgiven.

Middle East Diary, in spite of its apparent triviality and occasional triteness, is not entirely without merit. There are certain descriptive passages and recorded observations that convey at least a little of what I was feeling and thinking at the time. Some of these I intend to incorporate into this book, for it would be a waste of time to attempt to paraphrase them. I will, however, refrain from placing any of these extracts in inverted commas, and if any of my readers should detect here and there a few paragraphs that they have already read, I must ask them to forgive me and press on.

15

I enjoyed every moment of my voyage to Gibraltar in H.M.S. *Charybdis*. I roamed the ship from stem to stern, talked to ordinary seamen, able seamen, leading seamen, stokers, torpedo-men, signal-men, gun ratings, engine-room artificers, petty officers and ward-room officers. I had cocoa and rum with them, shared jokes with them, sang songs to them and on the last day, when we had abandoned the convoy we were escorting and were only a few hours from land, I was asked formally if I would consent to be godfather to the ship. I accepted with pride and we sailed through the sunset into Gibraltar harbour with the Marine Band playing the *Bitter Sweet* waltz.

Gibraltar is an extraordinary place and I have always been fond of it, not only because of the happy times I have had there with the Navy in the past, but because of its own very definite personality. There is charm in its narrow streets and some of the old houses are lovely. It was enjoyable to climb again up to the Rock at sunset and look across the bay to Algeciras and the purple mountains behind, or across the narrows to the coast of Africa; to watch little ships, minute as toys from that height, making pencil marks across the darkening sea and to hear the distant bugles blowing and see the lights come up in the town.

Two days after I arrived the Governor received a signal from Lord Gort saying that he was expecting me in Malta as soon as possible, and so on August the 2nd I took off with H.E. in his private Hudson for Oran, where we touched down at about three o'clock. We drove through the town and out to a Battle School by the sea which H.E. was going to inspect. Here at last the real heat for which I had been pining for so long began to seep into my bones. Freezing memories of Hull in November, Inverness in January, and even London in June, melted away under the burning sun as we drove through the hot streets. The familiar French North African atmosphere was unchanged. Arabs were scurrying about in tarbooshes; camels wandered along the side of the road in the sparse shade of the dusty trees; faded, striped sunblinds shaded the windows of ornate French villas; and I noticed a waiter doing his accounts under the awning of a deserted café that might have been transplanted, lock, stock and barrel, from the Boulevard Raspail; there were French names over all the shops, and in the centre of the town, of course, stood that inevitable, imperishable monument to French provincialism, the Municipal Opera House. This one looked a bit decayed: its façade was battered, either by bombardment or climate, and a lot of its plaster work was cracking, but there was still a weary old playbill of *La Bohème* pasted on to one of its columns. There was a new note, however, in this dusty French Colonial symphony, and a pretty sharp note at that. This was struck by the American occupation. There were evidences of it on all sides. Over a 'Café-Tabac' was a sign with 'Doughnuts' printed on it; there were khaki-clad figures everywhere; and outside a canteen was a bill-board announcing 'To-Nite Bing Crosby and Dorothy Lamour'. I really felt quite sorry for the poor old Municipal Opera House.

The next day we flew to Algiers, where I said good-bye to Mason-Mac, who was going off for a series of conferences. It had been arranged for me to stay at A.F.H.Q., which, translated, means Allied Forces Headquarters.

I lunched in the mess, which had an air of cheerful informality about it. There were five resident American officers and five English, and if only the larger issues of Anglo-American relation-ships could be run as smoothly the future would offer few problems.

My three days in Algiers were fully occupied. I gave three troop concerts, comparatively small ones, to only five or six hundred men, at which I played for myself, there being no accompanist available, and got away with it reasonably well. I was taken to a couple of French cocktail-parties, one Giraudist and one de Gaullist, both chirrupy and rather tiresome.

I visited one of the larger military hospitals. This was not an unqualified success. The matron was nice, but the commanding officer received me with bored casualness, as though I had just come in to get out of the rain. After I had been through two wards he said, stifling a yawn, that we had better go and have tea. I explained, perhaps rather tartly, that I had not come to tea but to see the patients, and so we went on and I am delighted to say I ran him off his feet.

The day before I left I went to call on General Eisenhower, armed with a letter of introduction from Dickie Mountbatten. I waited a bit in a light, sunny ante-room, signed several autographs for members of the Staff, and was eventually shown in to the inner room where General Eisenhower was seated at his desk. I delivered my letter of introduction and he read it through quickly and offered me a cigarette. He had a tough manner and a warm, Middle Western voice, and after I had told him where I was going and what I proposed to do and asked him for a few facilities here and there, I got up to go, but he made me sit down again, offered me another cigarette, and proceeded to talk more horse-sense about Anglo-American relationships than I had heard for a long time. He seemed to me to have most of the points of this vexed, and at moments very vexing, question at his fingertips.

I sailed for Malta in H.M.S. *Haydon* a small 'Hunt' class destroyer, which, together with the *Kelpi*, and another destroyer whose name I forget, was escorting a large convoy of twenty-seven ships. They were of all shapes and sizes varying from liners and big freighters to small tankers and coaling vessels. Standing on the bridge that first evening I watched them streaming along under a cloudless sky, on a calm sea that only one short year ago had been the most dangerous route of all. They looked complacent and unflurried, as though submarines and torpedoes had never been invented and the Mediterranean had always been at peace.

At about four o'clock on the afternoon of our second day out, while I was having a cup of tea with the Captain, and he was apologising for the uneventfulness and dullness of the trip, the buzzer rang. I said gaily 'Enemy Submarines!' He lifted up the receiver and said 'Christ! Torpedo!' and rushed up on to the bridge. I went out on to the fo'c'sle and saw, only a little way off, one large old ship sinking. It was all over in three minutes. She seemed to kneel apologetically in the calm sea, linger for a few moments, and then, with desolate resignation, she disappeared utterly. The whole thing was unspectacular, and oddly silent, like a film without the sound track. There were a few bits of wreckage and a few heads bobbing about in the water, but that was all. The convoy streamed on as though nothing had happened; a couple of escort vessels stood off to pick up the survivors; the rest began dropping depth charges and we did too. The dazzling white columns of spray looked beautiful. I returned to the cabin, put on my Gieves waistcoat and most meticulously filled my cigarette-case, reflecting that a cigarette is at least an aid to outward nonchalance. There was tension on the bridge and a great deal of staccato conversation; signals flashed back and forth between the escort vessels; more depth charges were dropped, and presently our sister ship signalled that she had firm contact, which meant that there was a fifty-fifty chance that the depth charges had disabled the submarine. A couple of hours later we saw an immense column of smoke on the horizon.

On the third morning I looked out of the scuttle and saw Malta, like a child's complicated sand-castle, glowing in the sunshine. An Army captain, Jim Holland, came on board to fetch me off. The ship's motor had broken down and so we went ashore in a Dhaiser, got into a car and drove to Government House, a fifteenth-century castle perched on the top of a hill. Lord Gort received me and we had breakfast, after which we listened to the morning news and then marched, quite fast, up and down a cement tennis court for about twenty minutes. I had a suspicion that the object of this was to keep fit, so I tactfully evaded it for the rest of my stay.

A gentle austerity was the keynote of breakfast at Government House. There was a copy of the *Malta Times* for everyone present, but Lord Gort, rightly, was the only one who had a sort of lectern on which to prop it. Conversation was sporadic and consisted mostly of a brisk interchange of questions and answers. On the dot of eight-fifteen we adjourned to the large salon to listen to the news, which came to us very faintly by courtesy of the B.B.C. Regularly as clockwork at eight twenty-five Lord Gort said: 'Padding – turn it off' and marched out for his morning drill on the tennis court.

My activities usually began fairly early with a rehearsal and a visit to a hospital. I gave an average of three shows a day. The hospitals in Malta were well run and, for me, walking through those endless wards was a salutary experience. Right up until the end of the war, by which time I had visited hundreds of hospitals and become accustomed to the sight of sickness and suffering, I never ceased to be impressed by the endurance of those soldiers, sailors and airmen; and by their capacity for overcoming, or at least appearing to overcome, desolation, boredom, homesickness, pain and discomfort. They lay, day after day, week after week and sometimes month after month, with nothing to do but swat flies if they happened to have an uninjured hand to do it with, and I seldom heard them complain. Many of them had snapshots of their wives or mothers or girlfriends or children always close at hand so that they could look at them whenever they could bear to. Many of them hadn't been home for two or three years; some of them would never go home again. It was only after I had left them that any sadness came into my mind. In their presence their own good manners made any display of sympathy impossible. I could only hope that by just chatting to them for a few minutes I had at least temporarily mitigated their boredom and given them something to talk about in their letters home.

My flight from Malta to Cairo was uneventful and at about seven in the evening we sighted the Nile Delta in the distance, a spread of dark, rich green lying like a carpet across the desert. The Pyramids showed up clearly in the setting sun, but they looked minute, like models in some Luna Park panorama; behind them, in the further distance, were palm trees and the tiny, clustered doll's-houses of Cairo. We circled round the desert aerodrome and slowly came down; the air became hotter and hotter; we landed smoothly, and by the time we had taxied along to the reception hut the sun had gone and it was dark. I was met by a gentleman from E.N.S.A. and a Major Pennington, who was a Welfare Officer.

It felt strange to be driving along that familiar straight road from the Pyramids to Cairo again. It seemed to be comparatively unchanged except for the addition of a glittering new open-air night-club, called the Auberge des Pyramides, which was conforming very little to the blackout regulations. The air was soft and hot, expensive cars whizzed by and as we crossed the bridge over the Nile I could see the feluccas with their curved white sails gleaming in the moonlight. The crowded pavements of the city were ablaze with light and there was the usual cacophony of street noises: shouts and yells, motor horns, klaxons and a thudding in the background as though a lot of people were banging invisible trays.

Sitting on the terrace at Shépheard's, the next morning before lunch, I observed that restrictions of war-time were unknown; people sat there sipping gin slings and cocktails, and chatting and gossiping, while waiters glided about wearing fezzes and inscrutable Egyptian expressions. Almost everyone was wearing uniform of some sort or other, including Constance Carpenter, who was in a natty sharkskin two-piece with E.N.S.A. on her epaulettes. These uniforms indicated that perhaps somewhere in the vague outside world there might be a war going on. But here, obviously one of the last refuges of the *soi-disant* 'International Set', all the fripperies of pre-war luxury living were still in existence. Rich people, idle people, cocktail parties, dinner-parties, jewels and evening dress; Rolls Royces came purring up to the terrace steps; the same age-old Arabs sold the same age-old carpets and junk; scruffy little boys darted in between the tables shouting '*Bourse! Bourse!*', which when translated means the Egyptian *Times*. There was the usual undercurrent of social and political feuds and, excepting for a brief period when the 'flap' was on and the Germans were expected to march in at any moment, here these people had stayed, floating about lazily in their humid backwater, for four long years. It was odd to see it all going on again; enjoyable for a brief, a very brief, visit, but it seemed old-fashioned and rather lacking in taste. I spent the rest of the day interviewing various military welfare High-ups. They were all called by complicated initials and I became very confused. *H.Q.*, an over-crowded hive of questionable efficiency, was heavily fortified. Myriads of people were working away in their offices secure in the knowledge that they were surrounded by barbed wire, guns, pill-boxes, and sentries and were still further protected by a bureaucratic system of regulations and passes, which had to be signed and counter-signed. I had a feeling that had I arrived with a smoking bomb in my hands I should have been immediately allowed in with it provided I had filled in the correct forms. There is no doubt that, as a nation, we have a passion for needless formalities. As far as I was concerned everything was comparatively easy, for I was led up and down stairs, along passages and in and out of rooms by Major Pennington. The officers I talked to were pleasant to me, and General Lindsell asked me to go to Iraq and visit 'Paiforce'. He warned me that it was the worst possible time of the year, that the climate was hell, that there was a lot of sand-fly and malaria, and that the whole trip would be the acme of arid discomfort – but, he added, the troops there had

had practically nothing in the way of entertainment and needed it desperately. I said I'd go, of course, and that was settled.

I idled about for a few days while H.Q. was working on itineraries, transport forms, signals and other paraphernalia to facilitate my journeys to Syria, Iraq and Iran. Cairo was stuffy, so I went briefly to Alexandria, where I gave several improvised concerts in hospitals and convalescent camps. These were mostly short and only of routine interest, but they were good practice for poor George Worthington, an accompanist procured for me by Major Pennington; he, being unable to play by ear, had to read everything at sight and at the same time become acquainted with some of my vagaries as a performer. I know that I am not easy to play for and it was much to his credit that he did as well as he did. The open-air shows were, of course, an added nightmare for him, because malignant little gusts of wind were liable to blow the music away in the middle of a number. On these occasions I carried on, disregarding the sudden silences and scufflings behind me, and hoping that in God's own time he would catch up with me, which, in fairness to him, he usually did.

On August the 23rd I flew from Cairo to Beirut, where my hosts were General and Lady Spears (Mary Borden). In the summer their 'Spears Mission' house in Beirut was too hot, so they lived at Aley in the mountains. It was only half an hour's drive, but the change of climate was violent. There were strange rock formations surrounding the terrace where we dined which gave it a Wagnerian air. Louis Spears said it always gave him the feeling that he was sitting inside a hollow tooth.

I stayed with them for three days, during which I gave two concerts and made a broadcast. Also I was taken by Mary to a leave camp, which was on the edge of the sea, which had a perfect bathing beach. Here the troops came from all over the country to have a week's rest and do exactly what they liked. There were no restrictions or discipline of any kind and, if they wanted to, they could even go into the town and get happily sozzled, for which the only penalty was imposed by nature in the form of a hangover, and even this could be swiftly mitigated by a plunge into the sea. They were looked after and waited on and allowed to have morning tea brought to them in bed. The atmosphere of genuine cheerfulness and relaxation about the place was impressive; I talked to several of the men. They were homesick, of course, and plied me with questions, many of which I should have been unable to answer if I had not done that twenty-eight-weeks tour. As it was, I could talk to men from Hull, Nottingham, Inverness, Glasgow, Cardiff, etc., with the added authority of having recently been to these towns. Some of their questions were quite routine: 'How's Sauchiehall Street?', 'Is it still raining in the Oxford Road?' or 'Is the Tower still open in Blackpool?', but some were more personal and touching and betrayed a certain unexpressed worry in their minds. I often came across the same uneasiness among the men I talked to in the Middle East. Most of them treated it gaily, of course, and made a joke of it, but I could see it was there, gnawing at them behind their gaiety and light words. This half-formulated unhappiness was concerned with the presence in England of American and Dominion troops. I imagined that a good deal of it had been deliberately fostered by enemy propaganda and also by careless and irresponsible letters from home. The Press too had contributed to it by headlining localised scandals, thereby implying that these incidents were the rule rather than the exception of it. Men in desert camps with nothing much to contend with in the way of enemy action, but a good deal to contend with in the way of loneliness and boredom, had a lot of time in which to think and jump to conclusions. The conclusions they jumped to were fairly obvious and generally wrong, but it was not their fault. They read in the papers that England was overrun by Canadians and Americans, who were flinging money about and striking up friendships with their sisters and sweethearts and wives, and, perfectly naturally, jealousy and doubt began to torment them. I explained to a number of them that they were building up delusions in their minds. During the last nine months I had had many opportunities of seeing, at first hand, conditions in London and in all the principal provincial towns, and I could honestly say that at least ninety per cent of the American and Dominion troops I encountered in pubs, trains, Tubes and so on were behaving with perfect courtesy.

Mary, doubtless feeling that sharp contrast gives a spur to the imagination, also took me to a Lebanese dinner party. This was given on a roof hung with coloured lights and overlooking a ravine. The Arab food was highly spiced, delicious and very rich. The host and hostess and their other guests were even richer. The Lebanese ladies were *mondaine*, ornately dressed, and they wore a great deal of baroque jewellery which I am afraid was real. I enjoyed the evening on the whole, but it had a quality of fantasy about it. I felt as though I were appearing in a novel by Pierre Loti.

From Beirut I flew to Bagdad, which looked fascinating from the air: minarets, mosques, date palms, camels and the Tigris winding through the town, its banks lined with opulent oriental palaces. But the short drive to General Pownall's house was long enough to convince me that, however fascinating and fraught with Eastern glamour it might look from above, close to, Bagdad was stifling, dirty and without charm. General Pownall, however, was friendly, clean and had great charm. We dined on a terrace looking across at the winking lights on the other side of the river; the air, although not cool, was at least cooler and the wail of Arab music came to us intermittently from the town. For a little while, aided by the tactful darkness, the city looked almost as romantic as I had expected it to be.

I gave two concerts on the following evening, the first one at seven-thirty and the second at ten, in a pleasant garden overlooking the river.

The next day we flew to Shaibah. The flight took three hours and was immeasurably boring; just sand, interminable, everlasting and stretching to the farthest horizon. However, at last it was over, and the heat rose up from the ground and enveloped us and pressed down from the airless sky on to our heads, and shimmered visibly all around us like fumes from a burning brazier. Shaibah consisted of Nissen huts, hangars and sand. There was nothing else except, of course, aeroplanes to go in the hangars and several thousand men to gasp the hours away both inside and outside the Nissen huts. Upon arrival I gave a concert to several thousand men in a large hangar, after which I was shepherded into a car and driven over a bumpy desert road to Basra. Here, more dead than alive, I gave, almost immediately, my second concert in a garden next to a railway siding. I cannot say that this performance was one of my best. I am capable, if necessary, of handling difficult audiences, of rising above minor production difficulties such as bad acoustics, insecure stages and eccentric lighting, but I had never before had to compete with engine whistles and goods trucks being shunted back and forth only a few yards away from me. I bawled through the microphone and tried frantically to get my points over in the pauses between puffings and whistlings and clankings. I gave such an abandoned display of facial expressions that the audience must have thought me either dotty or blind drunk. I looked occasionally at poor George pounding away on an execrable piano and was rewarded by a pitying smile.

The next morning we flew back to Habbaniya and on to Beirut for three days, because I had promised Mary Spears to give a concert at the Kit Kat Club for about two thousand men, and also to give a show in the hospital at Sidon. The first of these concerts was distinguished by the presence of Alice Delysia and her fiancé a Commandant in the French Navy. For two years she had been back and forth across the desert, tirelessly entertaining the troops, frequently under conditions that would have driven artistes of less stamina into nervous breakdowns. She had bounced about in lorries and trucks, been under fire and lost in sandstorms, and here she was, chic and cool in a pink linen *tailleur*, looking younger and more vital than I had ever seen her. It gave an added impetus to my performance to know she was there.

The evening before I left Beirut, Gyles Isham, who had been all through the desert war and was now doing an Intelligence job, drove me up to Sofar in the mountains to dine in cooler air.

While we were at dinner in the somewhat baroque hotel dining-room at Sofar, an impressive figure appeared, accompanied by a gravely subservient retinue. Gyles rose to his feet, bowed politely and sat down again. The man, who was in the late thirties, handsome and with the ivory skin of the Bedouin, acknowledged the bow with a slight smile, and I asked who he was. Gyles told me that his name was Fawwaz Ibn Shaalan, and that he was the grandson of Nuri Shaalan, who had been a great friend of Lawrence of Arabia. Fawwaz Ibn Shaalan, the head of the Runwalla tribe, was exceedingly pro-British, and after dinner he invited us to have coffee with him. He spoke French well, but no

English. I said that I had known Lawrence during the last few years of his life, whereupon his aloof, almost expressionless face lit up, his eyes ceased to be sleepy and veiled and became alive. It was touching to see how deeply Lawrence was loved in this part of the world, and to know that his name was still so potent a talisman.

Aircraftsman T. E. Shaw 338171. I remembered writing to him early on in our acquaintance and beginning the letter 'Dear 338171, may I call you 338?' He had been delighted with this little gibe at his passion for anonymity, and had sent me by return the typescript of his Air Force Diary, a most curious, self-revelatory, and beautifully written document. He was, to my mind, a great writer of English and in that alone his death was a bitter loss to our world. As a man I found him strange and elusive. He neither drank nor smoked and, as far as I could see, very seldom ate. He was painfully shy at moments, so much so that he seemed to withdraw himself completely from his surroundings and almost achieve invisibility. At other moments, when he was in a good mood, he was gay and loquacious and often didactic. There was, I think, twisted up in his character a certain inverted exhibitionism. I remember one occasion when he arrived at my house in Kent on his motor-cycle, wearing his aircraftsman's uniform. He was on his way to spend the week-end at Lympne with Phillip Sassoon, who at that time was Minister for Air, and visit 601 Squadron at Lympne aerodrome. When the news got around that Lawrence was coming to visit them, there was considerable excitement and preparations were made for a carefully chosen lunch-party in the officers' mess. It was therefore disconcerting for them when he appeared resolutely wearing his aircraftsman's uniform, because it created a ticklish ethical situation. Had he worn an ordinary lounge suite he could be received by the officers as an honoured civilian, whereas 338171 Aircraftsman T. E. Shaw should by rights be entertained in the airmen's mess, which was totally unprepared for the privilege. None of this really was of the least importance and, apart from some whispered consultations and a certain preliminary strain, everything went smoothly, but knowing how he shrank from any form of limelight and how he loathed any attention being called to himself, it was surprising that he should choose the one sure way of getting them. I asked him later about this and he laughed, rather self-consciously, I thought, and changed the subject. What I am trying to analyse in my memory of him is the genuineness of his desire for self-effacement, and whether, by so rigidly disciplining his own definite ego, he was not really gratifying some deep-rooted, subconscious masochism. In most of his writing, particularly *The Seven Pillars of Wisdom*, and the Air Force diary, one can discern a certain bitterness directed against himself, a contempt for his smallness of stature. There was in him, I am sure, a terrible area of discontent. Others who knew him far better than I have ascribed it all to his heartbreak and disillusionment over the Damascus problem, but I am not so sure. I believe that there must always have been, deep down in that strange, mystic, dynamic mind, the seeds of despair and an impulse towards self-martyrdom. To me it is infinitely tragic that all he might have given us in the forthcoming dangerous years, his genius, courage, strength of purpose and vision, should have been snuffed out in one blinding, noisy moment on that idiotic motor-cycle.

Back in Cairo I did a week's tour of the canal zone, the usual routine of hospitals and concerts.

The desert hospitals were remarkable, all things considered. Most of the wards were merely tents and the ingenuity of the staffs was extraordinary; they had thought of so many little ways of making the men as comfortable as possible. The nursing sisters all contrived to look as though they had spent at least two hours on their toilettes; their uniforms were always spotless and looked cool and pleasant. They achieved this in circumstances that would drive ordinary women dotty: the sanitation was usually primitive, the heat terrific and the glare and sand and flies appalling. If I had seen nothing else on that trip, those desert hospitals would have made it worthwhile.

After this dusty excursion I had a day off, most of which I passed reading in the Caseys' garden at Mena. That evening at dinner a South African General, Frank Theron, appeared. He was tall, distinguished and persuasive. The persuasiveness particularly struck me, for he spent an hour on the terrace when we were having coffee coaxing me to do a tour of South Africa. Dick Casey backed him up, and finally I agreed, with the proviso that I could do it early in the New Year and have two or three months in England first.

The effects of that quiet evening in the suburbs of Cairo were, for me, far-reaching and sent me a good deal further on my travels than I intended to go. At the time, of course, the momentousness of the occasion was not apparent, and I let Theron and Dick Casey draft out cables to Field-Marshal Smuts and Lord Harlech without further protest. I was tired and the thought of an organised tour of the camps and hospitals of South Africa was alarming, but I knew that after a couple of months at home I should probably be straining at the leash again.

During the next week I gave an average of three concerts a day in and around Cairo and Alexandria and flew on to Tripoli, where the hospitals were crammed because the Salerno casualties had been heavy. Only one incident haunts my memory and, I suspect, will always do so. In one of the wards was a young man who had, that morning, had a serious operation. He was still unconscious and was having a blood transfusion. His eyes were closed and he was the colour of wax, so I didn't disturb him and passed on. About an hour later, when I was at the other end of the hospital, a sister came with a message that he was asking to see me. I hurried back at once. He was hardly able to speak, but I held his hand and told him that he would soon be better. He smiled at this and said he was feeling better already, and then he died.

There was a certain air of pathos about the town of Tripoli, the foolish pathos of an expensive tart who has allowed herself to go to seed and forgotten to do her nails. The city had been well laid out; there were gardens and terraces and grandiose buildings, but it all had the impermanence of some over-modern World's Fair exhibit. The coloured plaster was already peeling from the angular, self-conscious architecture and the streets were dusty and woebegone. The whole place was obviously never intended to withstand bombardment and conquest. There could never have been either in its conception or its achievement any real spirit. What pride it ever had, had wilted immediately in adversity; like the Italian Army, it could only have been impressive in peace and fair weather. Now, with truckloads of bronzed, tough British and American soldiers whooping up and down its once immaculate boulevards, it seemed cringing and submissive and utterly lacking in even the dignity of decay.

On September the 27th I landed at Algiers. It was bitterly cold and pouring with rain and I felt shaken and bad-tempered. My tour, so far as work was concerned, was over. I had bidden goodbye to George at Tripoli and presented him with a wrist-watch as a token of my very sincere gratitude for all he had done. Never in all the weeks he had played for me, in all the differences of climate and all the difficult circumstances, had he once complained or even looked disconcerted. He had always been there when I wanted him and faded away with the most unobtrusive tact when I didn't. Now I was alone again, on my way home, and the adventure was nearly over.

The next day I took off in a battered D.C.3 which had just been through a storm and smelt of sick.

The flight was beautiful, for the weather had cleared. I sat in the cockpit with the pilot, a most engaging young tough from Indiana; he switched on the radio and we listened to Judy Garland far away in California crooning faintly through waves of crackling 'static'. The Mediterranean was calm and highly coloured and we flew up the middle of it with Europe on our right and Africa on our left; it was so clear that Gibraltar became visible a hundred and forty miles away.

John Perry, who was A.D.C. to the Governor, met me and told me that Mason-Mac was away and so, with the exception of a few transients, we should have Government House to ourselves. I was actually rather relieved to hear this, for I was dead tired and starting a cold, the inevitable effect of the sudden change of climate between Tripoli and Algiers, and felt more than ready for a few days of relaxation.

One evening John and I went to have a drink in a house halfway up the rock and overlooking the harbour. We sat on a terrace listening to the noises of the town drifting up from below and watching the sunset. H.M.S. *Charybdis*, my 'godship', which I had hoped was going to take me home to England, had received a change of orders at the last minute and was sailing off on another assignment. From that terrace on that lovely gentle evening I watched her putting out to sea, I thought gratefully and affectionately of all my friends on board as she moved smoothly and with dignity out over the darkening water. That was the last time I saw her, or ever shall see her, for she was sunk in action off the coast of France in the early hours of the morning of October the 23rd. There were very few survivors.

A few nights later I got into a plane for England.

The shades were taken off the windows at about six o'clock a.m. and I woke up and looked out. We flew low over the Bristol Channel and the green hills of Somerset; the sun began to dispel the morning mist and mark the long shadows of trees across the fields. I looked back in my mind over the last crowded three months: the seas and mountains and deserts I had crossed; the moving sights I had seen; the different faces, voices and hand-shakes. I thought of all the thousand men who had talked to me in camps, ships, canteens, airfields and hospitals, and realised how much it would mean to any one of them to be looking at what I was looking at now, the familiar, gentle English countryside, still, after four years of war, waking peacefully to an autumn day.

PART FIVE

I

The weeks I spent in England between October the 10th, when I returned with a cold from the Middle East, and December the 2nd, when, with the same cold, I set off on my travels again, are recorded in my day-to-day diary with even more niggardliness than usual. It gives reluctantly a few staccato reminders of whom I saw, where I went, and what I did, but withholds both comment and explanation and is frequently illegible. I gather from it, however, after much memory-straining and concentration, that my days were fully and variously occupied. There were film conferences with David and Ronnie regarding present activities (*Blithe Spirit*) and future possibilities (undecided); interviews with Brendan Bracken at the Ministry of Information and with officials at South Africa House concerning my forthcoming tour; an interview with Field Marshal Smuts himself at the Hyde Park Hotel, where he made me welcome in advance to South Africa and assured me that my visit was being eagerly looked forward to; and a week-end at Chequers, when the Prime Minister told me, in strictest secrecy, of the loss of the *Charybdis*. This last was a painful shock and robbed the day of all pleasure. The bar of secrecy lay heavily on me until the following Tuesday, when I received a considerate message from 10 Downing Street saying that I was now free to make any enquiries I wished. I telephoned immediately to Commander Whitfield, who fortunately had left the ship a week before the action. He told me that only fifteen ratings and four officers had survived. This saddened me for a long time; even now, after ten years have passed, my heart is heavy when I think of it.

I managed, during those few weeks, to do a few troop concerts here and there, just to keep my hand in. Two were in London, at the Wings Club and the Nuffield Centre, and the rest at airfields in the country. On December the 1st I said all my good-byes again and got into the night train for Glasgow. I had arranged, with Brendan Bracken's consent, to go to New York by sea, do a couple of broadcasts there for Henry Morgenthau, who had specially asked me to, and fly to South Africa on the first of January. I had also arranged for Bert Lister to come with me on the South African tour as a personal representative-cum-secretary. Cole was unavailable, having been in the R.A.F. since 1940, and I felt unequal to facing the stresses of another Dominion tour without someone I knew and who knew me. Bert was to travel by sea to Suez and meet me in Khartoum on January the 5th. Norman Hackforth, who had agreed in Cairo to come with me as my accompanist, was to meet me in Pretoria. So with these essential comforts taken care of, I set off, snuffling but with an easy mind. The name of the ship in which I was sailing had been withheld for security reasons, but I knew, I suspect in common with any enemy agents still at large, that it would be either the *Queen Elizabeth* or the *Queen Mary*, for one or other of these ships sailed regularly once a week from Greenock. It turned out to be the former. I was fetched from the Central Hotel, Glasgow, in the early morning by an M.O.I. representative and we drove out of the city and along by the Clyde. The *Queen Elizabeth* was unmistakable from miles away, towering grey and impressive over the surrounding country-side. I mentioned to my escort that I was glad it was the *Q.E.* because I knew her well. He placed his finger to his lips, said 'Hush' and nodded warningly towards the driver. I looked suitably apologetic and, reflecting that security-mindedness could at no time be carried too far, said loudly: 'Look at that pretty little private yacht with steam up, I expect she is in for repairs.' I do not think that my friend was amused.

The *Queen Elizabeth* was crammed with American troops and was consequently 'dry'. Having been warned of this beforehand I had packed a few bottles of whisky and gin in one of my suitcases. Anthony Biddle, who was also travelling, had done the same, only with more lavishness, and so between us we had enough liquor to keep several people in a drunken coma for five days had we wished to. In our anxiety to forestall the possibility of enforced sobriety we had left out of consideration the ships' officers, who, from the Captain downwards, gave a series of high-powered cocktail parties, sherry parties, egg-nog parties and beer parties in the seclusion of their cabins to the transient V.I.P.s. I seldom remember a more cheerful voyage and we finally landed in New York with our personal 'caches' untouched. Cabins were allotted according to rank, and as Biddle and I were the only civilians on board I asked the purser how it was that we had been given such comfortable accommodation, whereupon he showed me his private passenger list in which both our names appeared with the honorary rank of Admiral tacked on to them. From then on we saluted each other elaborately several times a day. The ship sailed on a zig-zag course, unescorted, and it was hoped that her speed and agility would frustrate any attempt by enemy submarines to torpedo her. Inevitably I was pressed into service to entertain the troops, and I performed in the main lounge, the smoking-room, the cabin class and in the tourist class, in which a section had been transformed into a sort of mental hospital for men suffering from war neuroses. Incidentally they turned out to be the brightest audience of the lot.

Thanks to Anthony Biddle's ex-ambassadorial status he was given the courtesy of the port on arrival, and swept me off the ship and through the Customs with him, in an aura of polite officialdom, in less time than it usually takes to get one's baggage on to the dock, after which we saluted one another breathlessly and drove off to our separate destinations. Mine was in Jack's flat in East 55th Street, where he and Natasha were just on the point of leaving to come and meet me.

I had not been in New York since March 1941, nine months before the tragedy of Pearl Harbour blasted America's neutrality to smithereens. The United States had now been in the war for two years, but New York betrayed no outward signs of conflict. Theatres, restaurants and night-clubs were flourishing; the lights of Broadway were as bright as, if not brighter than, they had ever been. All the comforts and amenities of urban life were easily procurable and it was, of course, a relief to be able to stroll home from a theatre through light streets after the fumbling gloom of the London blackout; to be able to eat steaks, drink orange juice and order omelettes; to be able to hail a taxi when you wanted one, and to sleep at night without an air-raid siren dragging you awake; but my relief, I fear, was tinged with irritation, an unmannerly, irrational resentment. I wished New York no ill fortune, I had no desire to see its hard beauty chipped by bombs and made shabby by paneless windows and dust and rubble. It was only that it seemed almost intolerably shiny, secure and well dressed, as though it was continually going to gay parties while London had to stay at home and do the housework.

My own friends were as dear as ever, but some of the conversations at dinner and lunches seemed unreal. There seemed already to be an assumption in the champagne American air that Britain had muddled through for the last time, that her former greatness together with her die-hard Imperialistic pretensions were flaking off her as dried old paint flakes off a decrepit building. Economically we were done for, and in the general, and particularly the American, view to be economically done for was the end, or at least the beginning of the end. I do not subscribe to this view now any more than I did then in 1943. If, in the next fifty years of wars and revolutions, Great Britain should sink wearily into being economically a third-rate power, so much the worse, but I cannot believe that the quality of its people nor the curious tenacity of its traditions will change.

The fourth day after my arrival in America I was struck down with 'flu and retired to bed with aching limbs and a temperature. This only lasted a day or two, but it left me weak and listless.

I did two broadcasts, and an extra one on Christmas Day to Paris, organised by the Free French.

On Christmas night I dined with Bill Stephenson (Little Bill) and Mary his wife. It was a small party and Bill asked me to stay behind when the other guests left as he had something of importance to say to me. What he had to say turned out to be a firm and uncompromising lecture on my health. He said that I looked awful, that I had obviously been doing far too much far too quickly, and that to contemplate a strenuous tour of South Africa in my present exhausted and almost voiceless condition was foolhardy to the point of imbecility, and could only end in disaster.

He then said, more gently, that he had arranged for me to go to a house in Jamaica for two weeks, where I should see nobody and give myself a thorough rest. I protested that Bert and Norman were waiting for me, that my South African itinerary was probably already set and that to cancel it would cause many troublesome complications, to which he replied, with truth, that the complications would be far more troublesome for everyone concerned if I had a breakdown when I got there and was unable to continue. At all events, he said, two weeks couldn't make all that difference one way or another, that the arrangements for my journey to Jamaica were already made and that he would send the necessary explanatory cables to South Africa; he added that all I had to do was to shut up and obey orders.

On Sunday, January 2nd, Neysa gave a farewell cocktail-party, after which I was escorted to La Guardia Airport and placed on the night plane for Miami. In due course the plane thundered along the runway and zoomed up through the clouds of 1944; the vivid lights of New York flickered out in the mist and rain below and I was once again, in every sense of the word, up and away.

2

My first view of Jamaica was from an altitude of about eight thousand feet. The morning was cloudless and the island was discernible from many miles away. Now, remembering that moment nine years ago, my mind becomes choked with clichés. 'Had I but known then . . .' 'Little did I dream,' 'If only I could have foreseen,' but of course I didn't know or dream or foresee how familiar that particular sight would become, how many times in the future I was destined to see these green hills and blue mountains rising out of the sea. Today, sitting on my Jamaican veranda and looking out across the bay at Port Maria, it is difficult to imagine that I ever saw the island for the first time, for it has become so much a part of my life, and given me such pleasure and peace of mind, that I feel that I have known it always. Leaving aside the lush beauty of its scenery, its lovely climate and the pleasantness of its people, it has given me the most valuable benison of all: Time to read and write and think and get my mind in order; time to be utilised and, above all, time to be wasted without regret. I have always been a staunch upholder of 'early to bed, early to rise', as a theory, although in practice I have only rarely been able to carry it out. In Jamaica it is not only possible but automatic; there is nothing to do in the evenings and the morning hours are the loveliest of the day. To have eight or nine hours of sleep and still to be able to see the sun come up is, to me, a happily recurring miracle, and for at least three months of every year I intend to enjoy it to the end of my days.

My first arrival in 1944 was accomplished, thanks to the efficiency of Little Bill's organisation, with impeccable secrecy. I was met at the plane by a naval officer, who whisked me out of a side entrance at the airport and deposited me in a waiting car. Within a few moments my baggage appeared and we drove through the outer fringes of Kingston and up into the mountains. The N.O., acting on orders from above, suspected, I am sure, that I was engaged on nefarious work of the direst significance, and I forbore from disappointing him by explaining that the whole operation had been set in motion merely to give me a nice lie-down.

'Bellevue' is about thirteen hundred feet above sea-level and looks over the whole valley and town of Kingston to the peninsula of Port Royal in the distance, crawling out like a green snake into the sea. In the old days the house had been the property of the resident Admiral, and at one time Nelson, shivering and racked with fever, was conveyed to it on a litter to regain his health in the cooler air and fresher breezes. Although I was not, like Nelson, shivering and racked with fever, I was certainly over-tired and stuffed with catarrh and I hoped that the cooler air and fresher breezes would do as good a job on me as they had on him. I was received by a smiling, dusky major-domo called Montgomery, and several other equally smiling and equally dusky characters, and when I had explored the house and garden, I settled myself in a hammock slung between an orange tree and a coco-palm and felt peace already beginning.

Later in the day a brisk young woman called Florence Reed appeared with a piano. She was private secretary to Robert Kirkwood, to whom I had a letter of introduction, and it was she who had corralled the staff and put the house in order to receive me. She also had been sworn to secrecy and assured me that although it was already known by the grapevine intelligence that a mysterious gentleman had arrived at Bellevue, no one had the slightest idea who it was. From then on, apart from Florence, two American soldier friends of hers and Sybil and Bobby Kirkwood, I met no one in Jamaica until a day or two before I left. It was a perfect holiday. The house was comfortable, the garden lovely and there were masses of books to read. I sat each evening on the terrace watching the sun set and the lights come up in the town. On the third night the moon was full and fireflies flickered among the silvered trees, in fact no magic was omitted. The spell was cast and held, and I knew I should come back.

By the end of the first week my catarrh had gone, my voice had come back and I was satisfactorily sun-tanned and feeling better than I had felt for ages. The creative urge, seldom long in abeyance, reared its sprightly head again and I wrote a song called 'Uncle Harry'. It was a gay song and I hammered it out interminably on Florence's piano until it was so firmly stamped on my memory that I knew I couldn't forget it. I don't suppose that Montgomery and the staff have forgotten it either.

A few days before I was due to leave, Florence procured some petrol coupons and I went for a tour of the island. The chauffeur was a mine of information, but at that time I had not become used to Jamaican inflections and only understood about a quarter of what he told me. We drove through Kingston and on through Port Antonio by the coast road. From there we followed the North Shore road, through Robin's Bay, Anotto Bay and Port Maria, past the strip of coast which one day was to belong to me – no bell rang, no angel voices warned me, no prescient instinct took the trouble to point it out – and on to Oracabessa, Ocho Rios, St Ann's and the long stretch of Falmouth and Montego Bay. The sun shone, the sea sparkled, the coco trees swayed gently in the light trade-wind and it was altogether enchanting. At the Casablanca Hotel in Montego I met, for the first time, my old friend Carmen Pringle. We sat under the stars and listened to native singers and the noise of the surf on the reef. The next morning I drove back via the south coast to Bellevue, and girded myself for my last day in Jamaica, which included a Press reception in Kingston and lunch at King's House.

The following day I was called at four a.m. and drove through the still darkness to the airport. The plane took off just as dawn was breaking and, pressing my forehead against the glass of the window, I murmured a silent *au revoir* to the island that had done much for me even in two short weeks.

At Barranquilla another of Bill's representatives met me and took me to the Hotel del Prado, where a reception and dinner-party had been arranged in my honour. I had to make a speech at the reception, half in English and half in Spanish. I cannot for the life of me remember what I spoke about, but it seemed to go down all right. The dinner-party was large, impressive and bilingual and it went on for a long time.

In Trinidad I was weatherbound for three days and stayed with Sir Bede Clifford at Government House. I utilised one of those days by making a tour of the Naval Base and giving two concerts in the evening.

On January the 21st I drove out to the airport at midnight in a tropical deluge, climbed into a Liberator which was occupied only by four other bodies, and flew off into the storm. The other bodies were cheerful American Air Force technicians and, after a fairly bumpy night, we made ourselves hot egg sandwiches and coffee. We came down briefly at Belem in Brazil, where we had a larger breakfast and drove for half an hour through the haunted tumble-down streets that once, when the town was originally reclaimed from the jungle, had been prosperous and well cared for. Now wealth had wandered away from Belem and the jungle was most decidedly getting its own back.

We got to Natal at six-thirty in the evening. Here I was met by still another of Bill's men, Lieutenant Dick, who took me to an officers' mess. By this time I had become devoted to the Liberator; it was friendly although it certainly couldn't be described as the last word in smooth luxury. It was carrying, in addition to the Americans and me, a heavy load of technical equipment, and although we had managed to make ourselves comfortable enough by twining ourselves round pieces of machinery and sleeping on mailbags, when we emerged from the plane we were all fairly grubby. The 'wash and brush up' I had in that officers' mess was bliss; after dinner in the mess there was a soldiers' dance, at which the commanding officer asked me to make a brief appearance. There was only time for one number, so I obliged breathlessly with 'I'll See You Again', accompanied by the dance band in the wrong key, and got back into the plane. At seven-thirty next morning we came down for an hour on Ascension Island, where we were given breakfast in a large mess-room while the refuelling was going on. Ascension Island seemed strange and desolate, with two sharply pointed hills, one deep red and the other purple. The sea looked wonderful, curling in over orange sands, and, excepting for a clump of trees on top of a low hill where I was told the Resident lived, the whole landscape might have been painted by Vlaminck or Matisse at the peak of their 'Fauve' period.

In Accra I had a twenty-four-hours breather. Lord Swinton's A.D.C. met me and I stayed in the mess. The next morning the A.D.C. drove me to a dusty beach where we bathed in coffee-coloured surf. The coast was flat and sinister and a shrill, warm wind blew the sand into our eyes. After a lunch-party at Government House with several pukka sahibs, a few drained-looking ladies in flowered chiffon and, surprisingly enough, Walter Elliot, who was passing through on some unspecified mission, I flew off in a D.C.3 to Lagos. Here the lush, tropical, 'white man's grave' atmosphere was very strong. I stayed the night in the house of the Acting Secretary, a dim cool house with punkahs creaking over the dining-table and black lizards coughing on the veranda like old bishops in the Athenaeum Club.

Having dragged myself awake at six a.m. and driven out to the airport, I was told that my plane would not take off until midday, if then, for the weather was very bad. Although well accustomed to the capriciousness of air travel, this depressed me. I was already late on my schedule and South Africa was still a long way away. I sat in the B.O.A.C. Club for an hour, drinking coffee and gloomily visualising several days of maddening inactivity, when a message came to say that a large Ensign was about to take off and that they were holding it for me. Within five minutes I was back at the airport and in the plane. I fastened my seat belt tightly and looked out at the appalling weather: thick rain drove horizontally across the airfield, the visibility was practically nil and although my relief at leaving was considerable it was offset by several minutes of stark terror. The Ensign was enormous and carrying a heavy load, and as it lumbered along the sodden runway preparatory to taking off into the full force of the storm my heart sank and, like the wife of a famous statesman on her wedding night, I closed my eyes and thought of England.

That evening we came down at Maiduguri, a town of mud huts in the northwest corner of Nigeria. The day's flight had been uneventful except for a hair-raising landing and take-off at Kano. The weather was clear at Maiduguri, and the Resident, an agreeable man called Thompstone, came to meet me and drive me back to his house. On the way we stopped off for a drink at the club, which as an example of the 'Outpost of Empire' tradition was accurate to the last detail. There were bead curtains, faded chintz covers and a rack full of months-old English newspapers and magazines. There was a mixed tennis foursome going on which might have been lifted bodily, court and players, from Cheltenham and set down in one piece in this savage, alien land. 'Well played,' 'Yours, partner,' 'Love-fifteen'. Clear English voices echoed across the dusty grass separating the veranda from the edge of the court, while from the village near-by came the thud of native drums and the thin wail of reed instruments. The natives of Maiduguri move beautifully and wear robes of the most lovely shades of blue which they dye themselves. The resident British moved perhaps less beautifully and their apparel was nondescript, but their quality was unmistakable. That small club, so very far away from home, was touching and curiously impressive.

At four a.m. I flew off again and, as the long hours of the day passed, the land beneath us changed shape and colour until there was nothing but desert sand. In the early evening we had arrived in Khartoum.

Bert Lister, after various vicissitudes, had got himself and my heavier baggage to Khartoum two weeks before. When I arrived I found him thrashing about in the hotel bedroom with tonsilitis and a high temperature. He was in a suicidal rage, having been perfectly well until the preceding morning. This of course was a maddening setback. I couldn't very well go on and leave him alone and ill, so I was forced to postpone our flight to Pretoria for three days. By this time I was getting panic-stricken. In addition to my pre-arranged two weeks' holiday in Jamaica, I had been delayed three days in Trinidad, another night and day in Accra and here was a still further hold up. I sent an explanatory cable to Norman Hackforth, who had already arrived in South Africa, and fortunately received a reassuring one back. Happily the three days were enough to bring Bert's temperature down and get him up and about, and on January the 30th I set off on the last lap of my journey. Our plane was crowded with gay homeward-bound South Africans and our first night stop was at a strange place called Mallakel, where we were put up at a rest-house. Before dinner we went for a stroll along a river bank, hoping to encounter some of the Dinkas whose terrain it was. The Dinkas' claim to fame is that they are very tall, have the longest penises in the world and dye their hair with urine; doubtless cause and effect. We only saw two standing listlessly on the opposite side of the river and, as far as we could judge from that distance, they were right up to standard.

Part of the next day we flew low over animal country: the wings of our plane made swift shadows on the land, which startled herds of static elephants into sudden activity and sent hippos and crocodiles slithering hurriedly from sandbanks into the gleaming rivers. We dropped down at Juba in the Congo for refuelling, and in the evening got to Totara, Tanganyika. Here a young Station-Commander took Bert and me for a drive and to dinner in the mess, thereby annoying the local Resident, who had apparently come down to the rest-house to look me over but had neither met me nor invited me to anything. I was told later that there had been a fine shindy over this and that our friend had got into trouble. I certainly hope that it wasn't true, because we were much in his debt for welcoming us so enthusiastically and giving us such a good time.

Finally, on Feburary the 1st, after a long day of very rough flying, we arrived at Bulawayo. The hotel was modern and comfortable and I was able to telephone to Myles Bourke, who was to be my host in Pretoria and was also in charge of my itinerary. He sounded charming on the telephone, and assured me that I needn't worry about being late, and that everything was under control. This was comforting and I was able, with a light heart, to put myself down and relax. Unhappily the light-heartedness and relaxation didn't last, for we spent the next three days driving to the airport, getting into planes, getting out again and driving back to the hotel. The weather reports from Pretoria were bad on the first day and so we didn't take off, on the second and third days the weather had cleared in Pretoria, but was vile in Bulawayo and so we didn't take off. At last, when I was practically a nervous wreck with frustration, a Captain von Roon arrived in a Lodestar and told us that he had two vacant seats and would take us on the following day. This was too good to believe, but sure enough on that next afternoon off we went at three-forty-five and at long last arrived in Pretoria at seven o'clock in the evening. Myles Bourke was at the airport to greet us, with Norman and several others, including the Quartermaster-General with a welcoming message from Field-Marshal Smuts. A horde of Pressmen rushed at me, flash-bulbs seared my eyeballs, I mumbled a few words into a microphone and drove off with Myles and Norman, leaving Bert to follow in another car with the luggage.

3

A chronological, day-by-day, account of my three months in South Africa, although fraught with personal interest to me who lived through them, would, I fear, be fraught with impersonal tedium for any reader who had not. I will try therefore to be as concise as possible and fish out of the welter of routine, troop concerts, Rotarian lunches, rehearsals, public performances, bazaar openings, arrivals, departures and civic receptions a few outstanding incidents, agreeable or otherwise, a few hurried but very definite impressions of that remarkable country and the people who live in it. It was inevitable, I suppose, that at first I should compare it in my mind with Australia, but after a while I realised that such a facile comparison was neither valid nor intelligent. The Union of South Africa is comparable to other Dominions of the British Commonwealth only in its most superficial aspects; beneath these seethes a ferment of racial problems and political unrest. Between die Afrikaans and the British there is distrust, and between the blacks and the whites a deadly fear. This underlying, perilous discontent soon becomes apparent even to the most casual visitor. The air is deceptively clear and the country beautiful, but even in its beauty there is a quality of potential danger as though the land itself was beginning to lose patience with its fractious tenants and might at any moment heave itself up and send the whole lot tumbling into the sea. As soon as my instincts recognised this fundamental disharmony I resolved to guard my tongue, watch my step and strain every nerve to be as tactful as possible. I was the guest of Smuts and the Government, and therefore an obvious target for the Opposition Press, so it would be wise to steel myself against some inevitable slings and arrows; aware also that my strong contempt for any sort of racial discrimination might if expressed, however casually, imperil the success of my tour, I decided to sidetrack the subject whenever possible and, when not possible, to keep my mouth firmly shut. In this I succeeded on the whole, although there was a bad moment when I unthinkingly suggested in my farewell broadcast that the 'Cape Coloureds' should be encouraged to start a repertory company of their own. Fortunately an official of the South African Consolidated Theatres spotted this heresy in the nick of time and it was hurriedly deleted from the script. Heavens knows I would be the last to upset dear African Consolidated Theatres, for without their co-operation and efficiency my tour might have been a dire flop. On my first morning in Pretoria, when, with Norman and Bert and Myles Bourke, I went through my proposed itinerary, I saw clearly that it would have to be entirely reorganised. Myles, who was officially in control of entertainments for the Forces, had either not understood or been misinformed about my requirements. He had arranged for me to open in Durban at a time when the Government and everyone of importance was in Cape Town. He had also engaged an Air Force dance band to accompany me wherever I went. This band, complete with a crooner, was to precede my own appearance at every concert. Even for troop shows this would have been unsatisfactory, because much of my performance depended on a microphone, and to have someone else moaning into it, possibly more effectively, immediately before I came on, would be redundant to say the least, but for my big public concerts which I was to give in every big city in aid of Mrs Smuts' Comforts Fund, an Air Force band of twelve pieces would be ineffective from the point of view of balance and inadequate for the size of the theatres. My own intention, needless to say, was to make my first public appearance in Cape Town at the height of the season with a symphony orchestra or nothing. Poor Myles, who took my fairly acrid criticisms of his itinerary charmingly, was shocked at such an exhibition of brash showmanship, and when I added that Field-Marshal Smuts, Mrs Smuts and the entire Cabinet should attend my opening performance his eyes glazed, he muttered: 'True, O King,' in a strangulated voice and retired from the arena.

Marguerite Bourke, Myles's wife, received the news of this preliminary skirmish with a twinkle in her eyes. She was a small, grey-haired woman, humorous, intelligent, always impeccably dressed and, to me, a unique and enchanting character. She also ran her house so well, and provided us with such perfectly cooked food, that wherever we stayed afterwards seemed an anti-climax. I expect she will laugh when she reads this glowing description of herself, but it will, I know, be a laugh of deep affection. At all events, I had pangs of conscience about the itinerary. Myles had taken so much trouble, and, with my usual ruthlessness where my own professional interests are concerned, I had virtually torn it up and flung it in his teeth. Marguerite, understanding swiftly that right or wrong I intended to get my own way, proceeded with exquisite tact to dispel all traces of friction and, unlike the Union of South Africa as a whole, the atmosphere of that house vibrated with dulcet harmony until the day we regretfully said good-bye to it.

Realising that if everything had to be reorganised from scratch there was no time to be wasted, I set out with Bert immediately to beard the South African Consolidated Theatres in their den in Johannesburg. Dick Harmel, a shrewd and kindly man, received us, and when I had explained my dilemma, agreed to take control of all my public appearances, rearrange my whole tour so that I could make the maximum amount of money for the Fund, provide through his organisation the requisite publicity and draft and have printed an expensive and attractive souvenir programme.

The next ten days hurried by, panting and breathless, as though they were running to catch a train, which in a sense they were, the train to be caught being February the 21st, the date set for my opening in Cape Town. Fortunately we were staying in the Bourkes' peaceful house and we were able to get to bed early, for there was no time during the day to relax for a moment. There was a great deal of driving back and forth between Pretoria and Johannesburg, an endless series of conferences – planning conferences, Press conferences, souvenir programme conferences – and Norman and I spent several hours in a dilapidated film studio being photographed, informally rehearsing, for the newsreels. Our actual rehearsals also took up a lot of time. It was many years since Norman had played for me and although, to me, he is the best and most sensitive accompanist in the world, he has to know each number thoroughly before either he or I can feel really secure. The Cape Town Symphony Orchestra had agreed by telegram to take over the first part of each of my three public concerts at the Alhambra. The arrangement was that the orchestra should play a forty-five-minutes programme of discreetly classical music, there would then be a ten minute *entr'acte*, and then Norman and me for an hour and a half. That ominous hour and a half haunted our waking hours and troubled our dreams. We knew, having seen the seating plan, that the theatre was enormous, and to hope to keep a vast, and presumably fashionable, audience happy and amused for such a long time seemed rashly optimistic. However, Dick Harmel had assured me that all would be well, though why he was so certain I shall never know, as he had never heard me in his life, and so we overrode our quaking fears and rehearsed feverishly. I decided to break the monotony of my adroit but thin singing by reciting these verses in the middle of my programme: 'Trafalgar Day' and 'Plymouth Hoe' by Clemence

Dane and a short piece of my own called 'Lie in the Dark and Listen'. During this brief patriotic interlude Norman was to leave the stage for a breather and return refreshed to play a five-minute medley of my tunes. This medley, known affectionately as 'Scrambled Father', would allow me to retire to my dressing-room and decide whether or not to shoot myself. Then, provided the audience was still present, I would come back and round off the evening with the strongest comedy numbers in my repertoire. Bert, throughout all these anguished plannings, struck and maintained a note of breezy confidence. He pooh-poohed the least suggestion that I could be anything but a triumphant success and swirled away our misgivings in a spate of Cockney invective. Bert's phraseology was rich and varied, and although in public an acquired sense of propriety stemmed its flow, in private his command of the more idiomatic ebulliences of the English language was truly remarkable. Abetted by a slight stammer and deep-rooted indestructible Cockney humour he could charm a bird off a tree, provided the bird was familiar with race-track jargon, rhyming slang and the more trenchant four-letter words of our native tongue. Besides this enviable talent he had other gifts, among them tact and understanding. He was also entirely undisciplined, an inveterate gambler, and, in spite of his determined efforts to appear tough, an incurable sentimentalist. Throughout the whole arduous South African tour he was invaluable to me. He upbraided me when I was over-nervous, laughed me out of tantrums, upheld me staunchly when there was a battle to be fought and very seldom irritated me at all. An extraordinary achievement.

As the time drew near for our departure for the Cape I thought it wise, both for Norman's sake and my own, to try out our programme in military camps in and around Pretoria. We did five shows in three days, all of which were hearteningly successful except the first one. This went down all right on the whole, but I was nervous and put off by a glum-faced Padre in the front row who so obviously disapproved of my performances that I became fascinated by him like a rabbit with a python. I heard afterwards that he complained that my songs were suggestive and lowering to the morale of the troops. Bert's summing up of this gentleman was hilarious and would have sent the morale of those troops soaring.

At last, on the evening of February the 17th, we drove over to Johannesburg and got into the evening train for Cape Town. The Government had provided me with a private coach, which was just as well, for my entourage had swollen. In addition to Norman and Bert and myself there were Frank Rogali, my troops entertainment organiser appointed by Myles Bourke, his assistant and a Press representative. Through the whole of the next day we traversed the flat plains known as the Karoo. Small humpy hills, kopjes, broke the monotony, and the light was extraordinary. At eight-thirty a.m. on the morning of the second day we arrived at Paarl, a town apparently a hundred per cent Afrikaans and notorious for its anti-British feeling. However, for some reason or other, possibly the efficient advance publicity of African Consolidated Theatres, it decided to rise above all nationalistic prejudice and come and meet me. As the train drew in to the station I looked out of the window and saw a small boy scout holding a banner twice as big as himself with on it a Victory V and 'Welcome to Noël Coward' in scarlet letters. I stepped out of the train, was presented with a bouquet by a little girl in a pink dress and received by the Mayor in full regalia. The Mayor read me a letter of welcome in halting English, to which I replied with a few even more halting phrases of Afrikaans which I had been practising with Frank Rogali during the journey. After this polite exchange we stood, rather uneasily, and stared at one another. A small but interested crowd watched the proceedings from a roped off section of the platform, and out of the corner of my eye I caught a glimpse of Bert's face, convulsed with laughter, at a lavatory window. Having exhausted my meagre stock of Afrikaans and realising that the Mayor couldn't understand English, I became slightly panic-stricken and fought down an impulse to laugh madly in his face. Fortunately at this moment I noticed some large crates being loaded into my coach. I pointed to them and enquired in exaggerated sign language what they were. He responded gravely by pouring imaginary wine from a bottle and drinking it, with every sign of enjoyment, from an imaginary glass. This endeared him to me and, remembering suddenly that Frank had told me that Paarl was celebrated for its wine, I clapped my hands with pleasure, capered about and gave an overdone display of simulated drunkenness, which went with such a swing that the Mayor's gravity melted, the crowd applauded and cheered and I climbed back into the train flushed with triumph.

My reception at Cape Town lacked the cosy intimacy of my welcome in Paarl. The train arrived at eleven-thirty instead of nine-thirty and consequently the crowds had been waiting in the streets for over two hours. I was received at the station by the Mayor and a group of local dignitaries, including a representative of Field-Marshal Smuts, several officers, a lot of Press and, curiously enough, Marie Ney, who had greeted me on my arrival in Melbourne. She looked charming in a shantung suit and a large white hat, and I had the feeling that whatever Dominions I was destined to visit in future, however far away and inaccessible, there would be Marie Ney, smiling and friendly, ready to help and advise and warn me against local pitfalls.

When we had all shaken hands and the cameras had clicked, we walked sedately through lines of onlookers to the exit. The station yard was packed with people who cheered and waved flags and handkerchiefs. The Mayor ushered me into an open car, and at this moment unfortunately a hitch occurred. Norman, who should have been with me, had completely disappeared. I didn't want to leave without him, and Bert, frantic with irritation and hissing obscenities out of the corner of his mouth, flew off to look for him. Meanwhile the Mayor and I sat in the car conversing nervously. The plaudits of the crowd, naturally enough, dwindled into silence and I have seldom felt so acutely uncomfortable. After a few minutes Norman appeared, looking sheepish, having been snatched from the embraces of an ex-Principal Boy who had waylaid him by the bookstall. The outriders revved up their motor-cycles, the crowd kindly lashed itself to a final outburst of enthusiasm, and the procession moved off. We drove at a snail's pace through the town until we arrived at Adderley Street, which was so densely packed that I could only assume African Consolidated Theatres had threatened any Cape Town citizens who showed unwillingness to greet me with mass execution.

The Mayor asked me to stand up in the car as we drove along and so I complied, steadying myself with my left hand on the windscreen, waving graciously with my right hand and feeling fairly silly. The houses and shops were hung with welcoming flags and banners and the crowd cheered like mad. I was told afterwards that it numbered thirty thousand people, but at the time these appeared, to my startled eyes, to be at least thirty million. At a given moment the procession halted and I was led through a shop, up some stairs and out on to a flower and flag-bedecked balcony; the Mayor made a speech of welcome, handed the microphone to me, and I embarked, with outward urbanity but inward panic, on a short string of clichés, dragging in my Afrikaans phrases whenever I could. After this the crowds melted away with almost disconcerting swiftness and I was driven to the Mount Nelson Hotel.

When the dignitaries had departed, the last Pressman gone and Norman, Bert and I were left alone in my suite, we had a large horse's neck each and laughed. This was not, I hasten to say, lack of appreciation of the warmth of my welcome. I hope and believe that amid all that organised hullabaloo there was a lot of genuine interest and kindliness, but I could not help feeling that the scale of the demonstration had been slightly out of proportion. But having asked African Consolidated Theatres to see to it that my tour was efficiently publicised, it would have been ungrateful to complain, so I resigned myself then and there to accept my place on the band-wagon with as good grace as possible. In this I was wise, because a similar ballyhoo took place, in varying degrees, in every town I visited, though never quite to the same extent as in Cape Town. Perhaps by the time I reached the other cities the word had gone round that although my performances were pleasant and entertaining they hardly merited a public holiday.

The following day I lunched with Field-Marshal Smuts in the House of Assembly and enjoyed it enormously. Only having met him, briefly, once before in London, I had no idea of the true quality of that extraordinary man. His memory was fantastic and the range of his general knowledge remarkable. We discussed books, painting, politics and even the Boer War. His mind was as swift and agile as that of a dynamic young man of thirty. He exuded physical health, and apparently walked up to the top of Table Mountain and down again several times a week for the sheer pleasure of it. I was told afterwards that his house-guests were warned, on arrival, never to accept an invitation from him to go for a little stroll before lunch. Fortunately he was too busy to suggest going for a walk with me.

My opening performance at the Alhambra was nerve-racking but, I am more than thankful to say, a triumphant success. To have failed after that majestic parade through the streets would have been too humiliating. The theatre was packed to the doors, which, considering that over half of the tickets were five guineas each, was gratifying, not only to me, but to Mrs Smuts' Comfort Fund. Both Field-Marshal and Mrs Smuts were present, together with the entire Cabinet, the Crown Princess of Greece and all the bigwigs of Cape Town. Such an array of social *crème de la crème* usually makes for a bad audience, but this occasion was certainly an exception. They were a very good audience indeed and saved me, in the first ten minutes, from ruining my performance by my own nervousness. I have never been so miserably nervous in my life and I hope and pray I will never be so again. The hour I spent with Norman and Bert sitting in my dressing-room while the Symphony Orchestra was on is branded for ever on my memory. Then came the *entr'acte*, which seemed an eternity, then the lights went down, Norman banged out the opening chords of 'I'll See You Again', the curtain rose and on I went. They gave me a wonderful reception and I finally started to sing, shakily and with neither precision nor taste. I got through my opening waltz medley somehow, with the sweat running off the back of my head and down my back, and my hands trembled so much when I held them out that I had to keep them to my sides. I knew I was doing badly and seriously contemplated pretending to be ill and having the curtain rung down. Happily, 'Don't Put Your Daughter on the Stage, Mrs Worthington' was my second number, a fairly solid standby. Before I was half through it the audience's obvious enjoyment began to relax me and from then on all was well. I sang ten songs in the first half, did my three recitations reasonably well, Norman played 'Scrambled Father' better than he had ever played it before, and then I came on again, sang eight more songs, finishing with Cole Porter's 'Let's Do It', which brought the house down. The applause was terrific, I made a brief 'Thank you' speech and went to my dressing-room, where Bert was waiting for me with a large whisky and soda and hopping up and down with excitement, but he wasn't so carried away that he didn't say what he had steeled himself to say. When the crowd of visitors had left and I was taking off my make up he told me, stammering a bit but with great firmness, that I had buggered up my first number completely, only just managed to put 'Worthington' over, and that if I ever allowed nerves to take such a hold on me again he would look on me not as a professional but as a— amateur. Curiously enough the virulence of this attack, which had a great deal more to it than I have quoted, had a lasting effect on me. I have never been so nervous again. I have suffered, as we all do, on opening nights, but never since that agonising experience in Cape Town have I permitted my nerves to jeopardise my performance.

After the concert there was a supper-party given in the theatre restaurant upstairs. This was my first meeting with Mrs Smuts ('Ouma') and I loved her at once. She had curly grey hair, twinkling eyes, a dress that conceded little to any specified mode, and a downright, entirely beguiling manner. During supper the crowd was still yelling outside and the Field-Marshal and 'Ouma' tried to push me out on to the balcony by myself, but I wasn't having any of that nonsense and dragged them with me. It was a happy moment, and if blood and sweat and tears are any guarantee of an accolade I had certainly earned it.

I spent nineteen days in Cape Town, during which I gave three consecutive public performances at the Alhambra, and about thirty-five camp and hospital shows within a radius of fifty miles or so. This was hard going for Norman and I changed the programme constantly to avoid getting stale, but the results were rewarding. At several of the earlier troop shows I was surprised to see the same civilian sitting in the audience, a nice-looking man in a navy-blue suit. Puzzled by his recurrent presence I sent Bert to find out who he was and ask him round for a drink at the hotel. In due course he arrived and we talked pleasantly of this and that. I found the conversation a bit of an effort because there seemed to be something withdrawn, almost taciturn, in his manner. Presently when the whisky had mellowed him and he had begun to suspect that I was not quite the clipped, ultra-sophisticated, affected type that he had expected me to be, he broke down and confessed that he was the local representative of a prominent London newspaper and had been ordered to attend all my troop concerts until he was lucky enough to see me booed off the stage. I received this fascinating information with the correct smile and warned him that judging by results hitherto his assignment looked like being a long and tough one. I then chided him gently for being so conscientious. 'Why not,' I said, 'use a little imagination and invent a nice degrading incident in which I am howled down by enraged Service men and pelted with ripe tomatoes?' His paper would be quite satisfied, never having been exactly renowned for its veracity, and he himself would be saved a great deal of boredom and frustration. He laughed, a trifle shamefacedly, at this and we had another drink. He was really quite an agreeable character. A day or two later he was rewarded for his conscientiousness, though perhaps not quite in the way he had hoped, for a member of the Government Opposition rose up in the House and asked why a 'Music Hall crooner' (me) should be accorded a private car on the train. The gentleman's name was Sauer and his question was headlined immediately in the Press. It was also answered immediately, by Smuts himself, who explained that I was a distinguished guest of the Government, that I had, on his request, agreed to entertain troops all over the Union in addition to giving my services in aid of the Comforts Fund, and that in the circumstances it was the Government's duty to facilitate my efforts with every possible courtesy. This, I need hardly say, was never reported in the London Press, although Mr Sauer's unmannerly question was given considerable space. As a matter of fact I believe it was the only time that my South African tour was ever referred to in the English newspapers.

Before I arrived in the Union someone concerned with my proposed itinerary – I never discovered who – suggested to several prominent hostesses that they invite me to stay in their houses during my visits to the different cities. With typical South African hospitality they agreed, and at once proceeded to make plans for my social entertainment. This was one of the earlier dilemmas with which I had to grapple. I was touched by the kindness, but appalled at the idea of staying in a series of strange houses with people, who, however friendly and charming they might be, could not be expected to understand that any free time I had would have to be devoted to resting and conserving my energies. I am naturally gregarious and would have enjoyed being their guest and meeting their friends had I been on a casual holiday, but this was far from being a casual holiday. I had come to South Africa to do a job and, with memories of Australia and New Zealand fresh in my mind, I knew in advance that it would be strenuous. It is always difficult to convince people outside the world of the theatre that performing in public is a dedicated and arduous business. To act a long part in a relaxed manner, to sing a few songs, bow to applause, make gracious little speeches of thanks, all this looks, or should look, so effortless, so easy, but actually it isn't. The conscience of a true artist always stands like an implacable barrier between him and peace of mind. The process is very, very rarely as gay and enjoyable as it appears to be. Out of all the hundreds of troop concerts I gave during the war I can only remember a half a dozen that were, to me, entirely satisfactory. There was always a strain, always a lurking fear, not of failure exactly, but of inadequacy, of not being absolutely at my best. The amount of vitality expended in playing even to a quick and receptive audience is considerable, but when, as is the case nine times out of ten, you are faced with a dull audience, an audience that has to be coaxed, cajoled and won over, it is not to be wondered at that all sensible performers dread and evade any wastage of their nervous energy.

It was for this reason that I was forced to forgo the pleasure of staying with those kindly hostesses, and I am afraid that some of them were rather put out, but it couldn't be helped and I hope that by now they have forgiven me. One of them, a vivacious and attractive social leader in Cape Town, evinced such bitter disappointment that I should prefer the Mount Nelson hotel to her very lovely house that she finally prevailed on me to spend a restful week-end in it. 'Restful' was the operative word as far as I was concerned, and like an ass I fell for it and accepted her invitation. I arrived, fairly worn out, on Saturday, in time for lunch, which was an intimate affair for twenty people. This was followed by a bathing-party at somebody's pool, a tea-party, a cocktail-party and a large dinner-party. The house was delightful, but it contained, apart from the family and the other guests, four cats, three large dogs, a six-months-old baby and apparently no servants. I spent a troubled night in a glorious early Dutch four-poster on what I can only conclude was an early Dutch mattress. At ten-thirty the next morning there was a tea-party in the garden for about twenty ladies, which went on until some anxious-looking Kaffir servants miraculously appeared and served a buffet lunch at one-thirty. In the afternoon we piled into cars and went visiting returning at six o'clock for a cocktail-party for thirty souls. Dinner was the *bonne bouche* of the whole gay adventure. My hostess had corralled six socially prominent young women of various degrees of attractiveness and placed them at six small tables. It was my privilege and pleasure to eat one course of the meal *tête-à-tête* with each of them. My convulsive progress from table to table occasioned considerable merriment, and the whole thing was regarded by everyone but me as a delightful social innovation. Very shortly after this I managed to slip away and telephone Bert at the hotel. Fortunately he was in and a half-hour later he arrived in a car with some garbled tale about an important telephone call from London. Evincing the most poignant regret at having to leave so suddenly, I bade my hostess and the assembled company a fond adieu and was out of the house like a flash.

This, over and above a few pleasant semi-official lunch-parties and a quiet week-end with Lord Harlech, the High Commissioner, was the peak of my social activities in Cape Town. Norman, Bert and I did contrive, however, to spend some gentle evenings with the Cameron McClures, Kiki and Mac, whose house was always open to us and with whom we could put ourselves down after a hard day's work. Gwen ffrangcon-Davies and Marda Vanne had introduced us into this less demanding milieu, and the hours I passed in that pleasant unpretentious little house are among my happiest memories of South Africa.

Our next date after Cape Town was Durban, and Field-Marshal Smuts urged me, as there were a few days to spare, to go by train along the coast route and enjoy some spectacular scenery. This sounded restful and would give me time to prepare myself for any further excesses the A.C.T. publicity department might have in store for me, and so in due course Bert and I left, waved away by a group of new and old friends including the McClures, Gwen, Marda and Norman, who was going to Durban via Johannesburg. This time, possibly out of deference to Mr Sauer, the private car was not quite so spacious, but it was comfortable and the journey was fascinating. The Field-Marshal had been right about the scenery. The train crept along for the whole of the first day between the bright sea on one side and sinister Wagnerian mountains on the other. It rained for a great part of the time, but this gave an added quality of mystery to that fantastic landscape. Bert and I slept, read and played rummy, occasionally getting out at isolated stations to stretch our legs. At one of these a woman appeared with her ten-year-old son. They had driven eighteen miles in a farm cart so that the little boy could get my autograph. Bert rooted about among the suitcases and produced the largest photograph he could find; happily the train stopped at that particular station for nearly half an hour and so we had time to talk to them. The boy's father was a farmer and they lived in a lonely valley in the interior. There were no neighbours nearer than eleven miles, where there was a small Kaffir village with a general store. The mother asked a number of questions about England, and once or twice I thought I detected a tear of homesickness glistening in her eye. The little boy, with his brown face and sun-bleached hair, was startlingly English. I asked him if he could speak Afrikaans, whereupon his mother said 'No' almost sharply and changed the subject. When the train bore us away I leant out of the window and waved. They waved back violently until they looked like two little fair dolls in the distance. Bert, whose emotions were never far below the surface, was moved to tears. 'Christ!' he said, sitting down at the table and shuffling the cards with unnecessary vigour, 'the poor sods, the poor lonely sods. Living in this — place, — year in and — year out.'

The journey took four days and five nights. We had a few hours in Port Elizabeth, where we visited a snake farm, in a deluge of rain, and watched the attendant twining deadly cobras and mambas round his neck as though they were knitted scarves; an evening in Bloemfontein, very European in atmosphere, where we sat and had a drink in a tree-fringed public square with an illuminated fountain in the middle; and three hours in Ladysmith, where we drove out and bathed in a very cold river. We arrived at Durban at seven-fifteen on a Sunday morning and as my official entry was planned for the next day our car was shunted on to a siding. This depressed us, but presently a Major Leon arrived and banished melancholy by driving us to Umdoni Park, fifty miles away. Here we stayed in a rest house for officers on the edge of the sea. There was an enormous bathing pool blasted out of the rock which was refilled daily by the tide, and there was no one in the house except two pleasant naval officers and Mr and Mrs Reynolds who ran the place. It was lovely to be in the tropics again. Monkeys chattered in the trees; a large iguana, looking like a toy dragon, ambled across the drive as we arrived; and after the bracing but sharp air of Cape Town the heat was wonderfully soothing.

The next morning we rose at dawn and drove back to Durban, where we slipped unobtrusively into the King Edward Hotel by the back way.

In due course the inevitable open car arrived, accompanied by outriders, and off we went. The streets were fairly crowded, but not as densely as they had been in Cape Town. The Mayor was away in Johannesburg and so I was received on the red-carpeted steps of the Town Hall by the Deputy Mayor, who was trembling. A Ladies' Orchestra was sawing away at *Bitter Sweet* under a striped awning and the square facing the Town Hall was crammed. The whole thing passed off without a hitch. The Deputy Mayor delivered his welcoming address, I thanked him and everyone within sight, the Ladies' Orchestra attacked 'Someday I'll Find You' with unparalleled fervour, and we all retired into the Mayor's parlour for iced coffee. My public concerts in Durban took place at Ye Playhouse, a large cinema, the interior of which had been got up, surprisingly, to represent a medieval castle. It was full of battlements and turrets and false stone work, and the ceiling was a deep blue sky studded with stars, some of which fused from time to time, but the acoustics were good and the concerts successful. From then on, our tour proceeded at an increasing tempo. My diary records a jumble of Rotarian luncheons, civic receptions, rehearsals, journeys in trains, journeys in planes, journeys in cars, performances in camps, hospitals, cinemas, Town Halls, Institutes and hangars. I also opened bazaars, flower shows, photographic exhibitions, art exhibitions, boys' clubs and girls' clubs. I inspected sea cadets, air cadets, land cadets, nurses and voluntary workers, and on one occasion, owing to my royal determination not to miss anything, I inspected a ladies' lavatory in a Victoria League hostel before anyone could stop me.

We appeared in Pietermaritzburg, Bloemfontein, Kimberley, Pretoria and, finally, Johannesburg. From all these places we drove out daily to outlying camps and air-bases.

On the night journey from Bloemfontein to Pretoria I was suddenly aware of a rather tiresome South American rhythm thumping in my head. This went on intermittently all night and emerged next morning as 'Nina'. Both Norman and I were delighted with it and, gaily ignoring the fact that both the lyric and the accompaniment were complicated, we decided to put it into the second half of our programme the following evening. Unfortunately during the day I had to make a long speech at a public luncheon, open something or other in the afternoon and attend a reception in my honour at the Country Club, and so, apart from an hour or two in the morning, I had had no time to rehearse it. Experience should have warned me that to attempt to sing a new song when it was still hot from the oven was dangerous, but the voice of experience was silenced by over-confidence and it was only when I heard myself announcing to a packed audience that black fear descended on me. I shot Norman a hunted look while he was bashing out the introductory chords, started on the first verse and dried up dead. Norman, with misguided presence of mind, prompted me loudly with what I knew to be a phrase from the second verse. There was a dreadful moment of silence during which my heart pounded and my brain searched vainly for the right words, then, realising that the game was up, I laughed with agonised nonchalance, asked the audience to forgive me, and started again from the beginning, praying that when I came to the forgotten phrase it would drop automatically into my mind. This was a desperate risk, but it worked; I scampered through the whole number without a further hitch and the audience were delighted with it. I, on the other hand, was furious with myself and ashamed at my casual non-professionalism, and before I attempted 'Nina' again it had been rehearsed two hours a day for a week.

Johannesburg was our last date. We made our usual official entrance with open cars, outriders, crowds and speeches. By this time it was generally known that the whole tour had been a success, and our reception was tremendous. The two weeks we spent there were more crowded and hectic than anything we had experienced hitherto. We had one Sunday off, which we spent in Mrs Baillie-Southwell's house. Erica Baillie-Southwell was one of the hostesses who had originally been asked to entertain me. She was elegant and charming and understood completely my reasons for preferring to stay in the Carlton Hotel rather than with her. We had a quiet, restful day with her and her family, picnicked in the garden and returned to our tasks and occupations greatly refreshed. Apart from this oasis the going was heavy; heavy from the point of view of actual work, but highly satisfactory on all other counts. Barragwanath Hospital alone took the best part of three days. It was a fine hospital but enormous, and we did four shows in different sections of it, besides visiting all the wards. We flew to Kimberley for a day and a night; reception and speech outside City Hall – visit to diamond mines – early morning tea-party in somebody's garden – civic lunch with speech – concert at aerodrome – cocktail-party – public concert in local cinema – further speeches – after-concert reception – five hours' sleep in the local club – up at dawn and back to Johannesburg.

Our two farewell public concerts took place in the Empire Theatre, which was vast and packed to the roof. These two performances netted six thousand pounds for the Fund. Combined symphony orchestras played for an hour, after which Norman and I took over. They were, I think, the best performances we gave; the piano was good and the lighting excellent. I was not nervous and consequently sang with authority and enjoyed myself. The audience apparently enjoyed themselves too and it was with very real regret that I bade them good-bye.

On my last day of all in South Africa I went over to Pretoria in the morning to say good-bye to the Field-Marshal and Mrs Smuts, and returned to Johannesburg to make my farewell broadcast in the evening. That interlude with the Smuts stays pleasantly in my memory. They lived in complete simplicity in a ramshackle old house which had been, ironically enough, a British barracks during the Boer War. The Field-Marshal was wearing faded shorts and an open-necked shirt; 'Ouma' was shuffling about happily in carpet slippers and a sort of overall. The inside of the house was cosily untidy; books were piled up indiscriminately all over the furniture and I observed, sticking out from under the sofa, a heavily embossed but dusty piece of paper which stated that General Smuts had been given the freedom of somewhere or other. I refrained from asking which city because it might have been London, which would have been faintly embarrassing: only faintly however, because no embarrassment could exist for long in the presence of Ouma Smuts, her kindness and humour would whisk it away and up the chimney before you had time to think. We sat round a wooden table on an enclosed 'stoep' and had coffee and biscuits. They questioned me about my tour and laughed appropriately at some of the funnier episodes, the conversation was gay, irrelevant and, I fear, without significance. They made me feel as though I were one of the family and that anything of importance could be said later. When I rose to go 'Ouma' kissed me lightly and thanked me for helping her Fund; the Field-Marshal rummaged in a desk stacked with papers and produced a photograph of himself which he signed and gave me. As the car bore me away those two most remarkable characters came on to the front steps and waved. That was the last I saw of them.

4

After a two-days holiday with Bert at Victoria Falls, which, as a wonder of nature, resolutely defy description, we returned to Bulawayo, where Norman was waiting for us, and started off on our tour of Rhodesia. This, after the strenuousness of South Africa, was a rest cure. We only gave nine shows in the whole eleven days we were there, and these included our two public performances in Bulawayo and Salisbury. There were, of course, the usual civic receptions and lunches and a few social functions, but the sense of urgency had gone; the power of the African Consolidated Theatres publicity department did not extend to the uplands of Rhodesia, the air was gentle, the streets clear of crowds and outriders, the whole atmosphere so English and parochial that I felt no one would have been surprised had I arrived at my first civic reception on a bicycle. There was no uneasy awareness at the back of my mind that sinister forces were at work below the surface. There was certainly no lurking fear of an anti-British demonstration, for all the people we met were British from the tops of their heads to the soles of their boots and, as audiences, cheerful and appreciative.

It had been arranged for us to fly to Bulawayo to Nairobi, give a few shows there and in Mombasa, then to fly on to Cairo and straight home to England. The last part of this plan was drastically changed by the arrival of a cable from Dickie Mountbatten in Ceylon, asking us to come out and entertain the Fourteenth Army in Assam and Burma. This cable was a bombshell. I had been out of England for five months and was longing to get home. Also I was very tired and felt that I needed at least a month's rest. On the other hand Mountbatten's cable stressed very strongly the need of entertainment in the Burma area, and I knew he would not have asked me to go unless he considered it really important. Norman, Bert and I sat up in the hotel in Bulawayo until three in the morning discussing the pros and cons, but I knew, and I think they did too, that there was no question of refusing. Admittedly we had done a good job in South Africa. The Comforts Fund had made twenty-two thousand pounds from our twelve public performances; the Flag had been shown with reasonable dignity all over the Union, and the Fighting Services and hospitals had, I hoped, benefited by my visit. But the fact remained that the troops we had entertained and the hospitals we had visited were in South Africa, many miles away from the war, and surrounded by far more creature comforts than England had enjoyed since 1939, whereas the troops and hospitals Mountbatten had invited us to visit were virtually in the front line. We drafted a cable to be sent first thing in the morning saying that we would come immediately we had finished with Nairobi and Mombasa, and would let him know as soon as possible how we proposed to accomplish the journey. I remember, before I went to sleep that night, envisaging Mother's and Lorn's disappointment when they heard I was not coming home after all, wondering which was the swiftest and least complicated way I could get Norman, Bert and myself across the Indian Ocean to Ceylon, and hoping against hope that by agreeing to Dickie's request I was not, in my present state of tiredness, taking on an assignment that I was not physically capable of carrying through.

5

Ten days later, on the evening of May the 16th, I sailed from Mombasa in one of H.M.'s destroyers, the *Rapid*, for Ceylon. Norman and Bert were flying direct to Cairo, where they were to wait until I sent for them. After three performances in Nairobi we had flown to Mombasa, where a kindly man called Granville Roberts lent us his beach house for four days. It was a small wooden bungalow looking out over a coral reef, and although far from luxurious it had, for me, the greatest luxury of all, absolute quiet except for the sound of the surf on the reef. The sea was almost too warm in the heat of the day, but in the early morning and in the evening before sundown it was delicious. I re-read Lytton Strachey's *Queen Victoria* and *Bleak House,* and slept twelve hours a night.

On the evening I sailed we gave a performance in Mombasa. The theatre was stuffy, the microphone bad and the piano vile, but realising that it was the last time we should have to rise above such horrors for at least three weeks, we pressed on cheerfully, and the audience, although a bit sticky at first, cheered at the end, stamped its feet and gave every indication of being a great deal more satisfied than we were.

The voyage in the *Rapid* took twelve days. The ship was not belying her name and could easily have done it in five, but we had to escort a convoy for part of the way. For me, at any rate, the time was all too short; after the first three days, when the sea was so rough that I had to lash myself into my bunk at night, we slid out on to the bosom of the Indian Ocean into halcyon weather. I lunched *tête-à-tête* every day with the Captain, and spent the rest of the time lying on the fo'c'sle in the sun, or wandering about the ship and talking to whoever was interested. As is usually the case in small ships the atmosphere was friendly and informal. There were terrific arguments in the ward-room after dinner on various subjects; the problems of the tortured world, the colour question, the Indian question, Communism, Toryism, Socialism, sex, music, literature and, when I was allowed my head, the Theatre were all analysed and discussed with passionate zeal. Sometimes, after one of these intellectual free-for-alls, I felt disinclined for sleep and went up to the bridge to chat with the Officer of the Watch and have some ship's cocoa under the vivid stars.

I also managed during these twelve days to write a short story called 'Mr and Mrs Edgehill'. To have time, even so little time, after the overcrowded, hectic scramble of the last few months, was a great pleasure to me. I had begun to think that I should never be able to write again, and that, even were I to try, the gift would have atrophied and no words come. However, the words did come and I scribbled and typed for hours daily in the Captain's cabin until, two days before we were due to arrive at Colombo, the story was finished. It was an imaginary tale based loosely on Mr and Mrs Fleming at Canton Island. The story was ultimately published with five others in my book *Star Quality*, which can be bought for the modest price of five shillings, by anyone who has been careless enough to overlook it.

At last the voyage was over and the island of Ceylon appeared on the horizon, its mountains blue and purple in the morning light. The day before, I had given two improvised shows for the ship's company and been given a farewell party in the ward-room, and now the moment had come for another regretful good-bye. Mike Umfreville, one of Mountbatten's A.D.C.s, came on board to fetch me; we had a cup of coffee with the Captain and went ashore. Umfreville told me, in the course of our drive up to

Kandy, that he had been accredited to me for the whole tour of Assam, India and Burma, and as he was friendly and appeared to be pleased at the prospect, I was pleased too and we had a nip out of his flask to cement the deal.

On my first evening in the King's Pavilion in Kandy, which Dickie Mountbatten had made his G.H.Q., he and I dined quietly. He outlined to me all the arrangements he had made for my tour and briefed me about the different units I was to visit, warning me at the same time that in certain sections I should find conditions fairly tough, for I should be in Assam and Burma at the peak of the monsoon period, and must be prepared to be wet and muddy and uncomfortable for days on end. The valley of Imphal, for instance, had been under siege for three months, and he had arranged for us to be flown in over the Japanese lines in one of the transport planes that delivered supplies to the beleaguered troops. This sounded dashing enough to erase from my conscience all memories of private cars and social junketings in South Africa. He talked as usual with utter concentration and high-powered enthusiasm, but although he looked sunburnt and outwardly fit I detected a strain in his eyes. He was on a difficult wicket in his position as Supreme Commander. Portions of the American Press were gunning for him, his administrative problems were considerable, and a large percentage of the war equipment he had been promised had failed to materialise owing to the preparations in England for the launching of the Second Front. In addition to this, as is now well known, the American General Stilwell (Vinegar Joe), who was in command of the United States and Chinese troops in North-Eastern Burma, must have been an added problem for Mountbatten – although Mountbatten was far too tactful even to hint that there was any sort of trouble. I myself experienced one of the reasons why Stilwell was called Vinegar Joe, because although Mountbatten had persuaded him to allow me to visit his troops on the Ledo Road, he personally refused to allow me to go on up to the front line. I lay awake for a long time that night under my mosquito-net looking back over the years I had known Dickie Mountbatten, and reflecting on our enduring and curiously unlikely friendship. Temperamentally we were diametrically opposed; practically all our interests and pleasures and ambitions were so divergent that it was difficult to imagine how, over such a long period of time, we could have found one another such good company. We had, I knew, a mutual respect for one another, admiration too for our respective achievements, but although respect and admiration may form a basis for affection they do not explain it. I respect and admire many people with whom I have no personal contact whatever. Dickie is exactly six months younger than I. I met him and Edwina in the early 'twenties, when he had just returned from a world tour with the Prince of Wales. For several years our acquaintanceship was only casual; he was fully occupied in being an up-and-coming sailor, and I was equally concentrated on being an up-and-coming playwright. How and when we really began to know one another I cannot remember, perhaps suddenly at some forgotten dinner-party a conversation started up that rang a bell; there was certainly no mutually endured crisis to strike the spark, so it must have been something light, a song or a well-timed witticism, possibly a betrayal of my hero-worship for the Royal Navy, but most certainly not a betrayal of Dickie's hidden passion for the theatre, for he has little more than a cursory interest in it. However, in due course and much to my surprise I found myself in the summer of 1932 traipsing across Greece during a series of earthquakes to join him in the *Queen Elizabeth* at Mudros. From then on, our relationship stabilised itself, and whenever I wanted a holiday I went to wherever his ship happened to be. I spent one of the gayest months I have ever spent with him and Edwina in Malta. It was the first time he had ever had command of a ship and *Daring*, one of the new 'D' class destroyers, was the first nautical apple of his eye. There have been many progressively larger, apples since. In the late 'thirties he asked me to work with him in forming the Royal Naval Film Corporation, which was to equip all the ships of the Navy, excepting sloops and submarines, with film-projectors and films. This, owing to Mountbatten's drive and determination, was a *fait accompli* by the end of 1938. My own contributions to the carrying out of the whole scheme were, I am afraid, fairly negligible, and consisted mainly in visiting all the ships of the Mediterranean and Home Fleets and questioning the sailors about what sort of films they preferred. This assignment although it took quite a time, came under the heading of enjoyment rather than hard work. In after years, when the showing of movies on board H.M. ships had become an accepted routine, I have felt proud, I must admit, to have been even lightly associated with such a wise and important innovation.

Now, after all the storms and stresses of *In Which We Serve* in 1941, here I was in Ceylon, of all places, in the fourth year of the war, swirling once more in the orbit of Mountbatten's unpredictable star, and viewing the immediate future with excitement tinged with dismay. More troop concerts, more rows and rows of amiable but sometimes bewildered faces, more hospitals, more bad pianos and defective microphones, more commanding officers making speeches of thanks, more jolly parties in messes when we were worn out and longing for sleep. Only this time, of course, there would be the added fillip of monsoons, mosquitoes and mud.

On the fifth day after my arrival in Ceylon I took to the air again. Mike Umfreville was with me, looking angular and distinguished in a khaki bush jacket. Dickie Mountbatten waved us away into the morning sky and returned to more austere responsibilities, and thus began my most arduous and certainly most interesting adventure of the war.

For anyone who wishes to experience an authentic foretaste of hell and damnation, I heartily recommend the city of Calcutta in the weeks immediately preceding the breaking of the monsoons. The heat was more appalling, more inescapable, more utterly disintegrating than any I had known in my life. It burned all oxygen from the air and left us limp, drained of vitality and gasping for breath. The nights were as hot as, if not hotter than, the days. The large old-fashioned punkah in my hotel room revolved very slowly like an aged ballerina and, far from cooling the room, seemed to make it even more stifling.

Norman arrived from Cairo having left poor Bert behind in a hospital in Alexandria with a bad attack of malaria. This, we agreed sadly, was not to be surprised at, because in spite of our remonstrances he had contemptuously refused to take any of the necessary precautions. The little bungalow we had been lent outside Mombasa was near a mangrove swamp and every evening at sundown, while Norman and I sensibly sweltered in mosquito boots, long-sleeved shirts and scarves, Bert had laughed at us for being fussy. Sundown was the time for his evening swim, after which he liked to sit naked on the veranda rail and enjoy a cigarette. We warned him repeatedly that by so doing he was presenting a fascinating area for the Anopholes to explore, but with his inherent gambler's belief that everything would be all right he had persisted. Now, to his own and our bitter disappointment, he was separated from us and would have to return sadly to England when he was strong enough. In the meantime we had much to do and only three days in which to do it. To begin with, we had to find a portable piano, no easy task in Calcutta. Norman was gloomily prepared to make do with a miniature piano if there was nothing else procurable, but fortunately a kind lady agreed to lend us her small upright which was not too ungainly and in excellent condition. I fear, however, that by the time she got it back its condition was fairly critical. It went with us everywhere, in aeroplanes, trains and trucks, and once it made an eighty-mile journey in a jeep. It was known as the Little Treasure and Norman tuned it lovingly every day. We also managed to find a travelling microphone that in no circumstances ever merited the name of Little Treasure. It was from first to last a malign, temperamental little monster.

Our tour began at Chittagong with two highly successful shows, one at five and the second at eight, and from then on, life was real, life was earnest, and although the grave was not actually the goal it seemed at moments as though it quite possibly might be. The monsoons broke and we drove, usually in a jeep, through sheets of heavy warm rain, along the jungle roads of the Arakan. We slept at nights in 'Bashas', which are bamboo huts, generally open at one side. Our camp beds and mosquito-nets travelled in a lorry with the Little Treasure. As a rule they left before us, but occasionally we would get to some isolated camp and discover that they hadn't arrived, which, of course, meant hours of feverish agitation as the time for the show drew nearer and nearer. Only once did we have to do a performance without a piano at all. This fortunately was at a small gun emplacement on a rain-sodden hilltop. There were only about sixty men, so I rendered a few comedy numbers unaccompanied, talked, told archaic funny stories and finally started them off on community singing. Throughout this curious entertainment Norman sat on an ammunition box and applauded politely.

The Arakan place names fascinated us: Dozahri, Deuchapalong, Tambru Gat and, most surprisingly, Cox's Bazaar. The latter was by the sea, a turgid dun-coloured sea, and was one of the most squalid places I have ever been to. In Tambru Gat I was having half an hour's rest in my 'Basha' before the evening show when I heard a sinister rustling sound and watched, without enthusiasm, a long green snake, wriggle from under my bed and disappear outside. After a moment or two, when I was about to go out and see where it had gone, I heard some shots, and by the time I had emerged on to the little bamboo veranda I had the pleasure of seeing it borne away draped over a pole like a bright ribbon.

After about ten days in the Arakan we returned to Chittagong and thence to Comilla, where we were to wait until circumstances were favourable enough for us to be flown over the mountains into the valley of Imphal. Comilla, after the jungle and the 'Bashas', was luxurious. There was an actual theatre to play in; the microphone (not ours) was perfect and the audiences at the two shows we gave them really wonderful. It was suffocatingly hot, of course, and I sweated through three shirts, but it was well worth it. By this time Mike Umfreville had gathered two batmen for us. They were B.O.R.s – British Other Ranks; one was tall, the other short, and both were lugubrious. Neither of them betrayed the faintest sign of emotion in any of the adventures they shared with us; we might be bogged down in mud, cowering in trenches during a Jap air raid, or strapped to our seats in a bucketing plane during an electric storm, but they remained silent and solid as the cliffs of their native Yorkshire. They looked after us with routine efficiency but little initiative; they listened to our, at times unconventional, dialogue with never the slightest twitch of the ear or gleam in the eye. I think they liked us all right, because when we finally parted from them they presented each of us solemnly with a photograph of themselves in lurid colour. They were known privately by Norman and me as The Ball of Fire and The Spirit of Jazz. I don't think they ever knew this, but even if they did they would undoubtedly have ignored the irony as stolidly as they ignored the wayward circumstances in which they found themselves.

In Comilla I lunched with General Slim and he talked, unsentimentally but with moving sincerity, of the Fourteenth Army. He referred with sudden bitterness to the phrase 'Forgotten Army' which had been coined by some zealous newspaper man who was evidently more interested in *mots justes* than *noblesse oblige*. The General explained that, although the morale of the troops had remained astonishingly high throughout all the vicissitudes of their repeated advances and retreats, this label 'Forgotten Army' had really stuck in their minds like a prickly burr and hurt them out of all proportion to its actual significance. The trouble was that there was a germ of truth in it. They realised, when papers were sent them from home, that, as far as news value was concerned, the war they were grimly fighting year in year out was apparently not important. Columns were devoted to raids on European strongholds, to air battles and sea battles, but their exploits, if mentioned at all, were usually relegated to the back page. General Slim asked me if I could do anything to remedy this situation when I got back to England and I promised to do a broadcast at the earliest opportunity.

A day or two later, after several false starts entailing early morning drives to the airstrip, hours of waiting about and ignominious retreats back to the officers' club, we finally took off for Imphal in very bad weather indeed. Our plane was a D.C.3 transport and carried, in addition to ourselves and the Little Treasure, a large consignment of food supplies and, I believe, ammunition. We bumped through a bad electric storm, cleared an eleven-thousand-foot mountain range, flew over the Japanese lines and bounced down on the flooded Imphal airstrip with an impressive splash. General Scoones's headquarters, where we were billeted, consisted of a series of wooden huts and 'Bashas' scrambling down a steep hillside. The actual mess-room was on the top and was reached by a stairway of wooden slats embedded in the mud. It was impossible to negotiate these without a stick because the mud was not only thick but very slippery. General Scoones, a gentle and intelligent man, was just saying how do you do to us when a Jap air raid started and he ushered us firmly into a deep trench, where we continued our mutual politenesses until a bugle played a very flat D Flat to announce that the skies were clear again.

I think I am right in saying that the valley of Imphal is an area of approximately fifty square miles. Mountains rise all round it, and on and behind those mountains were the Japs. The siege had lasted for three months, but there were signs that the enemy was retreating and everyone seemed fairly certain that it would not last much longer. During those three months our troops, vulnerable to air attack and continually repelling enemy sorties, had lived on supplies dropped by the R.A.F. air-lift from Comilla. These planes were sometimes shot down, indeed the one immediately preceding ours had been, and I must admit that when they told me this my heart missed a couple of beats.

Our daily routine varied very little. At 6.30 a.m. we were called; we shaved and washed in a tin basin on a tripod and then clambered up to the mess-room for breakfast, after which we slithered down again, and Norman went off in a lorry with the Little Treasure to wherever we were to give our first show of the day. I meanwhile was driven, either in a car or in a jeep to different hospitals. Some of them were comparatively large, consisting of a group of 'Bashas' or wooden huts connected by covered ways; others were small advance clearing stations. There were no matrons or nurses; the men were cared for by surgeons, doctors and orderlies. In many of them there was no flooring and one had to squelch from bed to bed through the pervasive mud. The men lay under mosquito-nets reading magazines if they were well enough, and, if not, just staring up at the roof and listening to the drumming of the rain. There was a preponderance of malaria and other jungle fevers, and the nursing, as far as I could see, was as expert as conditions permitted. Most of the badly wounded were flown to Comilla and thence to better equipped hospitals in India, but the chest cases could not be flown out because it was necessary for the planes to fly at an altitude of fourteen thousand feet to clear the mountain range. These men, left behind in the steamy, oppressive, perpetually moist heat of the valley, were the most pathetic. They were resigned to their fate, few of them complained and all of them made a valiant effort to be cheerful when I talked to them. Even the worst cases, who were too weak and grievously injured to speak above a whisper, managed to smile or wink or give some sign that they were still undefeated.

The advance clearing stations were inevitably gruesome, but the gentleness and efficiency of the Field Surgeons impressed me deeply. Under appallingly difficult conditions I watched emergency operations performed with the same unflurried skill and precision that I have seen in the most lavishly equipped modern operating theatres. It is not my intention to harrow my readers with descriptions of physical horrors – I saw enough of these during the war to last me for a lifetime – but I cannot withhold comment on the routine heroism of those whose interminable job it was to mitigate the horrors and alleviate the suffering. It might be a small comfort to the mothers and wives and friends of those wounded men to know that everything that could be done for them in the circumstances was done and done well.

I usually managed to get through a couple of hospitals each morning, after which I was driven to wherever our first afternoon concert was to take place. The organisation of all this was well handled and there were only a few hitches. We appeared on shaky wooden platforms, tank transports and sometimes on the bare ground. If we were lucky we had a tarpaulin rigged over us, if not we shared the rain with our audience. We gave one show a thousand yards from the Jap lines. This was an uneven performance because the intermittent gunfire made timing very complicated. The men, having been withdrawn from the line for two hours, an hour and a quarter for the entertainment and the remaining forty-five minutes for tea, sat cross-legged in the mud at our feet with their rifles across their knees. At one alfresco show we gave, the sun made a brief and disconcerting appearance, which brought forth dense clouds of Burmese midges which rushed up my nose and into my mouth and settled on the microphone like caraway seeds on a bun. With the capricious sun came a sharp change of wind, and with the change of wind a most horrible, nauseating stink, which emanated from several hundred rotting Japanese bodies stacked in a clearing a quarter of a mile distant. After the concert I was discreetly sick in a bucket before going on to the next show some miles away. Norman remained unmoved and captain of his soul.

Only one unhappy incident occurred during our ten days in Imphal, and as this redounds little to my credit I will recount it with the utmost brevity. On a certain evening, when I had done two hospitals in the morning, two shows in the afternoon and a small extra one on a gun emplacement, Norman and I were invited to drink and dine in a mess hut with about a dozen officers. The C.O. was florrid and affable and we accepted two large drinks gratefully, our day's work being done. At the end of dinner, which was convivial, the C.O. told us that our piano had been placed in the ante-room (an adjoining hut) and that he and his officers would be bitterly disappointed if we did not give them a show. Although we had had a heavy day we knew we couldn't refuse, and so, with a sinking heart, I agreed, signalled to Norman, who stared at me in horror from the other end of the table, and together with our, by this time, vociferous audience we adjourned to the ante-room. The officers, amid much badinage and merriment, settled themselves to their satisfaction and I began to sing. They remained fairly quiet, but their attention was, I felt, divided. There was a good deal of whispering and scuffling and one officer, to everyone s amusement, made a stately but insecure exit through the door at the other end of the hut. Realising that sentimental songs would be out of place in such a cheerful atmosphere I hissed 'Stately Homes' to Norman and we began it. Before I had completed the first refrain I noticed an officer immediately in front of me hand the C.O. a packet of snapshots. The C.O. scrutinised the first one, gave a guffaw, and passed it to his righthand neighbour, who also greeted it with the amusement I have no doubt it merited. From then on no one present paid the faintest attention to me. Faced with this curious display of bad manners I made the mistake of losing my temper. It is one of my ingrained professional principles never to allow myself to betray irritation with an audience however badly behaved it may be. But on this occasion my control snapped, I stopped singing, signalled to Norman to follow me and walked out of the hut. The C.O. after a minute or two came after us and, still convulsed with uninhibited laughter, tried to show me one of the snapshots. I slapped it out of his hand, told him that I considered his manners intolerable, climbed into the waiting jeep with Norman and away we went. I fumed with rage all the way back to our headquarters and went to bed exhausted, depressed and ashamed. In the clearer light of the next morning I told General Scoones the whole episode and endeavoured to remedy my own lack of manners by sending the C.O. a letter of apology. In due course he replied correctly but without warmth, and afterwards, when my acids had simmered down, I realised that my apology had not been to him but to myself. I also realised that such an outburst was a bad sign, a warning indication that my nerves were becoming over-strained and that I had better watch my step. There is no place for artistic temperament in battle areas.

We left Imphal on the day the long siege was raised. The Japs had been finally beaten back and there was great jubilation. From then on, our tour was devoted to the Americans along and about the Ledo Road. We reverted to our Arakan travelling routine: jeeps, trucks and planes. I changed my programme drastically, inserting numbers which were not aggressively British and were likely to be recognised and appreciated by the G.I.s, who were as a general rule excellent audiences. There was one disastrous occasion when I bounced on unannounced to sing to about two thousand coloured troops who had never heard of me in their lives and couldn't have cared less. As a matter of fact they couldn't even hear me then, for the show took place on a small, dimly lit, wooden stage only twenty-five yards from the main Ledo Road along which lorries and tanks rumbled continually. I tried grimly to keep them quiet, but when they began to shout and give catcalls I realised, all too clearly, that I was getting the bird, and so Norman and I beat a dignified retreat. To offset this there was an exhilarating performance in the compound of a convalescent hospital. The stage was under cover, but the men and nurses sat on wooden benches in the mud. About halfway through my performance the skies opened and down came a deluge of rain, which made such a deafening noise on the tin roof of the stage that it was impossible to go on. I stopped and asked them all to get under cover, promising them to finish the show another day, but they roared and shouted, covered their heads with mackintosh capes and refused to budge. For the next hour we all sang songs together, soaked to the skin and happy as mudlarks.

During this phase of our travels I developed a mild fever of some sort. No one ever discovered what it was; I had a check-up in one of the hospitals, but no sinister germs were found, my stool was as fresh as a daisy and my urine cloudless as a summer day. This unspecified malaise lasted for about five days and broke the smooth-flowing rhythm of our performances somewhat, for I was unable to get through more than four or five numbers without rushing off the stage and being sick. Fortunately the act of being sick does not prostrate me as it does some people, and I was able to pop back and get on with the programme until the next bout. Norman's presence of mind rose to the occasion and he dreamed up some charming little musical interludes to cover up my spasmodic disappearances. At a place called Digboi we stayed in the house of a Scottish planter and his wife, Bill and Jean Fleming, who accepted the invasion of Norman, Mike, me and the two batmen without even wincing. Their house was cool, comfortable, and stood on a hill overlooking a lush valley. To sleep in a proper bed again with a bathroom adjoining and a lulu that worked; to be brought ambrosial breakfasts of crisp bacon, fruit, Cooper's marmalade and china tea; to be valeted and looked after by well trained servants was so unexpected and so deeply enjoyable that with ruthless determination I persuaded the dear Flemings to let us stay a week instead of two nights. The shows we had to give in that sector were all within an area of about eighty miles and, however hard the roads and however turbulent the weather, the thought of bumping home every night to that lovely haven on the hill shone like a star in our minds. At last we had to bid those kind, hospitable people good-bye and press on for our last lap of jungle before flying back to India. Nothing spectacular happened except one nightmare moment when we were sitting at midnight in a Liberator on an airstrip waiting to take off, and the plane in front of ours crashed in flames. It was an ammunition transport carrying twelve men, all of whom were killed. Our take-off was delayed for a couple of hours and we sat wretchedly in a canteen, drinking Coca-Cola and waiting for the wreckage to be cleared away.

The last few days we spent with the American Army in that beautiful but oppressive jungle country were no more strenuous than the others had been, but they seemed so. The fever had left me a bit drained and it was an effort to pump enough vitality to get through the shows. Norman, as usual, was unflagging. He tuned the piano whenever it needed it, which was practically every day; he kept his temper, his sense of humour and his health, which was the most surprising of all, for his looks as resolutely belied his constitution then as they do today. His face is always wan and set in deceptively morose lines, and no burning sun, no stinging wind has ever succeeded in tinting lightly its waxen pallor. Sometimes in these later years, when I am singing in the luxurious intimacy of the Café de Paris, I glance at him sitting impeccably at the grand piano, and my mind flashes back to those rickety wooden stages, to the steaming heat, the wind, the rain, and the insects, and I see him with sudden vivid clarity divested of dinner-jacket, red carnation and brilliantine, and wearing instead an open-neck, sweat-stained khaki shirt, with a lock of damp hair hanging over one eye, and hammering away at the Little Treasure as though he was at his last gasp and this was the last conscious action of his life.

When we had waded through the dozen or so rain-sodden, mud-caked villages with unpronounceable names that remained on our itinerary, we got wearily into a Dakota at a place called Panitola and flew back to Calcutta. It was an uncomfortable and terrifying journey; the plane was crammed with G.I.s going on leave and the electric storms were so violent that we had to be strapped together like trussed fowls throughout the entire flight. At last, only about ten minutes before we were due to land, the weather cleared and we were able to unstrap ourselves, stamp our feet, stretch our legs and ease our aching buttocks from the dreadful grip of the bucket seats. The plane touched down on the wide runway of the Calcutta airfield in a blaze of late afternoon sunlight and, after baking for an interminable quarter of an hour while a bright green official sprayed us with insecticide, we were allowed to clamber out on to the sizzling tarmac.

6

A great deal has been written about the vast sub-continent of India and it is not my intention to add more than a few words to it. I was only there for a month all told and I have no particular desire to go there again. I was too tired to be interested in its problems and had no time to appreciate or even take in the beauty of its scenery or the quality of its people. All my energies were concentrated on the performances I had undertaken to give and the camps and hospitals I had promised to visit. My itinerary was fairly formidable but not alarmingly so. My public performances in each city were to be in aid of war charities and, as in South Africa, troop shows were to be given whenever and wherever possible. I knew that both Norman and I needed a rest, and I also knew that there was little likelihood of our getting one beyond a day or two here and there. On the morning of our arrival at Government House, where we were staying with Richard and Male Casey, we started rehearsing and reorganising our programme for the first two public performances we were to give a few evenings later in the New Empire Theatre. After the rugged discomforts of the Arakan, Burma and Assam the luxury of Government House was soothing, but I was aware, naturally enough, of a sensation of anti-climax. During those weeks with the advanced Forces we had been upheld by the very fact of having to overcome stresses and strains and difficulties, and also by the knowledge that, however untidy and haphazard our performances might be, we were at least giving them to men who had had no sort of entertainment at all for months and possibly years. There was a deep satisfaction in this, and the enforced 'roughing it', which as a rule I detest, added to rather than detracted from it. India would inevitably be a reversion to more familiar and less stimulating routines. Microphones breaking down, lights fusing and such-like hazards could be laughed away in the presence of entertainment-starved men who were just out of the front line and grateful even for the hour's rest, but we couldn't expect dressy pukka sahibs and memsahibs who had paid heavily for their seats to tolerate such nonchalant improvisation. We should have to be slick and professional once more, reorganise our values as well as our programmes, and see to it that the 'mike' was faultless, the lighting perfect and the veneer smeared on again and polished until it shone. The prospect of this necessary transition dismayed us, because without Bert to handle the technical problems for us we knew that we should have to deal with them ourselves, thus becoming embroiled in arguments with inefficient stage staffs, further arguments with well-meaning but inexperienced charity organisers, and probable hand-to-hand fights with ubiquitous Welfare Officers. These, we had learnt to our cost, had, as a rule, little knowledge of the professional theatre and were more prone to hurt feelings, umbrage-taking and hot flushes than the most temperamental opera singers. Our forebodings were fairly well justified; the irritations occurred, the arguments and frustrations also. The Welfare Officers appeared as predicted, faffed about, used either too much initiative or too little, and retired in due course licking their wounds. Their chief was apparently an old General who sat majestically in Simla, from which cool eminence he controlled a vast network of inefficiency. It is a matter of lasting regret to me that I never met him, for by the end of our Indian tour I could have supplied him with some fascinating information. We appeared in and around Calcutta, Delhi, Bombay, Bangalore and Madras. In Delhi we stayed in the Viceroy's house with Lord and Lady Wavell, who attended our public performance and several of our troop concerts. I had heard that Lord Wavell was taciturn and difficult to talk to and that Lady Wavell was inclined to be remote and unapproachable. Personally I found them both exactly the contrary. Lord Wavell's passion for poetry alone would have been enough to endear him to me; his memory was remarkable and his own anthology, *Other Men's Flowers*, was selected with taste and imagination except, in my opinion, for a preponderance of Macaulay. I remonstrated with him about this, and, far from being taciturn, he merely laughed and said that he found Macaulay the most satisfactory of all for reciting out loud in a noisy aeroplane. I shall always cherish a mental picture of him flying back and forth across the Sahara during the Egyptian Campaign shouting, 'Oh Tiber! Father Tiber! to whom the

Romans pray' at the top of his lungs. Lady Wavell was a dear and allowed me to inaugurate High Tea at five o'clock every day, so that we could get away to do our shows. Not only did she allow it but took to the idea herself with enthusiasm, which, I was told later by an irate A.D.C., disrupted the smooth running of the house and caused a considerable lash-up in the kitchen.

From Delhi we flew to Bombay, where I stayed for three days with an old friend, Eric Dunstan, in a small villa by the sea. We gave our public performance on a Sunday evening, and the next morning I escaped a violent death by a few inches. We were bowling along at about forty-five miles an hour in a sleek limousine belonging to Aly Khan when a naval lorry in front of us turned, without warning, off the parkway. I knew in that split second that we were bound to hit it and shut my eyes. There was a shattering crash, our car ricocheted off the lorry, skidded for ninety yards, crashed into a palm tree, the impact of which wrenched off the back wheels, careered across a patch of grass and crashed finally against the sea wall. If the palm tree had not broken our impetus we should undoubtedly have jumped the sea wall, which was only a few feet high, and hurtled into the sea.

I was knocked out for a few seconds and was brought to by Eric, miraculously unhurt, shaking my shoulder and saying in an anxious voice: 'Are you all right? For Christ's sake say you are all right!' I answered obligingly that I was quite all right, which was not quite true, for I was badly bruised and felt shattered. A crowd collected and we were helped out of the overturned car. The Indian driver, although not seriously hurt, was bleeding profusely. I sat on the ground with my back against a tree and tried to light a cigarette, but my hands were shaking so that somebody had to light it for me. I must still have been concussed, because I don't remember anything more until a half-hour later when we got back to the villa in another car and I had a stiff brandy. I had a shock when I looked at myself in the glass, for Fate, emphasising the comic rather than the tragic aspects of the situation, had arranged for a two-pound packet of freshly-ground coffee to burst on my head during the crash. My hair was full of it and it had streaked down my face in brown stripes, giving me a family resemblance to Pocahontas. I laughed, perhaps too hysterically, at this and was led away to lie down. Later a doctor appeared, examined me and told me it would be wiser to cancel my flight to Bangalore for a few days. I discussed this with Eric and Norman and finally decided against it. I was not injured in any way apart from a few bruises, we only had two more weeks to do and cancellations and post-ponements would cause a lot of complications, besides putting us behind on our schedule. This decision I afterwards regretted, for the shock to my whole system had been more serious than I realised. However, I forced myself up at six o'clock the next morning and off we went. On arrival at Bangalore I was in considerable pain and so I went to a hospital to be X-rayed, but no bones were broken and the pain would obviously have to be borne until the bruises went down and the stiffness wore off. We gave a concert to fifteen hundred men that evening which must have looked rather stilted, for I was unable to move my right arm at all.

Our last town in India was Madras, where we stayed in Government House with Lady Hope and went through our usual routines: rehearsals, mike tests, two public performances, several troop shows and finally, after an affectionate farewell to Bill Erskine, who had been with us since Calcutta in the capacity of assistant bottle-washer to Mike Umfreville, we flew back to Ceylon.

We gave a show in Kandy to Dickie Mountbatten's personnel, three or four more in various camps which entailed some long drives, and then what I had been dreading for a long time happened. I collapsed finally and knew that I had come to the end of my rope. The collapse was unspectacular and devoid of drama. It began during a long drive home after a show at a newly built R.A.F. base. I had got through the performance drearily, but without mishap, and been mildly sick afterwards. The C.O. gave me a stomach powder, but the effect of it wore off after a little while and I was seized with agonising indigestion, and felt myself inflating as though I were being blown up by a bicycle pump. The drive took two hours and a half and when I got out of the car I could hardly stand. Norman helped me to bed, which was a slow process because I could neither sit nor lie down without excruciating pain. I remained in this state all through the night and the following day, when a doctor was summoned and administered several remedies, none of which had any effect. On that evening Nature intervened with prodigal generosity, and at last the 'great winds shoreward blew', leaving me weak, uninterested and in deep melancholy. I lay on the edge of sleep, for I dared not take even a Secconal for fear of bringing on another bout of indigestion, and whenever I did manage to drop off for a little I was torn awake by nightmares, most of which were reversions to the car smash in Bombay. I realised in my wakeful moments that I was obviously suffering from delayed reaction, but I also knew that delayed reaction, however unpleasant, could not have brought me so low if I hadn't already been nervously exhausted. I am physically pretty strong; my height is six foot and my average weight eleven stone. At the time of that breakdown I had been working at high pressure for eight months in addition to travelling, not always in the most comfortable circumstances, half round the world, and I weighed exactly nine stone one. This left very little margin for resistance to unexpected shocks, my vitality had been expended to the last drop and I knew beyond any question that the moment had come to pack up. This meant cancelling about a dozen shows I had promised to give for Dickie in Ceylon; I hated doing this and compromised by giving three, a week later, in the Naval Base in Trincomalee, but they were forced and not very good.

I stayed for a few days in the Galle Face Hotel in Colombo, waiting for a plane to take me home. Norman had got off, through the kindness of Air Marshal Garrod, the morning after our return from Trincomalee. I hated to see him go, but comforted myself with the thought that without him I had an excellent excuse for refusing to do any more concerts. The few days at the Galle Face were peaceful and without incident. I spent most of the time lying by the swimming pool and reading. Eventually I took off at dawn, a very overdone tropical dawn with scarlet clouds piled against a lemon and blue sky, and flew home to England in a succession of different planes via Karachi, Shasah, Bahrein, Cairo, Tripoli, Rabat and Casablanca.

7

The remainder of 1944, although eventful for the world, was not particularly eventful for me beyond the fact that I adapted *Still Life*, one of my *Tonight* at *Eight-Thirty* plays, into a film script, rechristened it *Brief Encounter* and persuaded David Lean and Ronnie Neame to put it into production. This, after some argument, they agreed to do, which was lucky from all points of view, for it turned out to be a very good picture.

After the strenuousness of South Africa and the rigours of the Far East it was pleasant to have nothing to do but read the increasingly heartening war news, make plans for the future, and dodge doodlebugs. My plans for the future were vague and fluid and only one or two of them materialised. I recovered my health and put on weight. I attended Peter Glenville's production of *Point Valaine*, played by the Liverpool Old Vic Company. Mary Ellis and Frederick Valk played very well the parts created in America by Lynn Fontanne and Alfred Lunt, and the production was good; in spite of which I saw more clearly than ever the fundamental weakness of the play was its basic theme. It was neither big enough for tragedy nor light enough for comedy; the characters were well drawn, but not one of them was either interesting or kind. The young man, the only one with any claims to sympathy from the audience, although played well in both productions, struck me on closer analysis as silly, over-idealistic and a prig. The play had opened originally in Boston on Christmas night, 1934, with an excellent cast: Osgood Perkins, a subtle and fine actor, and Louis Hayward, whom I had imported from England to play the young man, in addition to Lynn and Alfred. Somehow everything seemed to go wrong from the beginning. Alfred and Lynn and I were irritable with each other, which we had never been before and seldom have since; Gladys Calthrop's sets were too heavy for the quick changes and had to be cut down at the last minute. There was a disastrous rain machine which flooded the whole stage at the dress-rehearsal and had to be scrapped. We all pressed on with 'Old Trouper' determination, but none of us was happy, and none of us quite knew why until sometime afterwards, and the revelation burst on us that what was really wrong was the play. The New York critics gleefully encouraged us in this belief after one of those doomed opening nights that occur, I think, more in New York than anywhere else. The first-nighters were soggy and comatose if not actually hostile. Lynn and Alfred received only a spatter of applause when they came on, and Gladys, Jack Wilson and I sat at the back of the theatre and watched the play march with unfaltering tread down the drain. It was not surprising that seeing it again, however well done, should give me a few pangs of rather embittered nostalgia.

On November the 1st another, less poignant, revival of my work opened at the Apollo Theatre. This was John Clements' and Kay Hammond's production of *Private Lives*, and it was, as it usually is, a great success. They both played it wittily and well for a very long time. I am deeply attached to *Private Lives*, for although it has always been patronised by the American and English critics, it has also been enthusiastically and profitably patronised by the public wherever and in whatever language it has been played.

In addition to enjoying these reminders of the past, I fulfilled my promise to General Slim, by writing and delivering a broadcast on the subject of the Fourteenth Army. The response to this was varied. I was congratulated by the King and Queen, received over two thousand letters of thanks in one week from relatives of the men in the Forgotten Army, and a full page of unqualified abuse from Mr John Gordon in the *Sunday Express*.

In November I dismounted graciously from my high horse and agreed to appear in Paris and Brussels for E.N.S.A. It was, on the whole, a tiresome experience and almost entirely uninteresting. The company included, as well as myself, Geraldo and his band, Bobby Howes, Nervo and Knox (for one performance only), Frances Day and, later, Josephine Baker. We played at the Marigny Theatre in Paris, in a rococo eighteenth-century frigidaire in Versailles and an Olympian Music Hall in Brussels. The organisation was slap-dash and the audiences, as a rule, slow but appreciative. Field-Marshal Montgomery came to our last performance in Brussels, and there was a moving incident when

Frances Day sang 'Thanks for All You've Done' at him and roguishly presented him with a pair of her drawers. He received both the sentiment and the drawers with dignified restraint.

To return to Paris after its four years' humiliation was a curious and sad experience. Not entirely sad, of course, because the city itself was unharmed and as beautiful as ever, but there was, to me at any rate, a feeling of malaise in the atmosphere, a malaise compounded of recrimination, shame and bitterness. Outwardly all was bright, perhaps a trifle over-bright, but I couldn't help being aware of much cynicism and distrust below the surface. I soon gave up enquiring from my French friends as to who had been collaborators and who had not, for, with a few notable exceptions, they all seemed to be accusing each other. In any event it was none of my business, although it confirmed my belief that worse things than bombardment can happen to civilians in war-time.

Back in England, on Christmas Day I drove up from the country, where I was staying with Larry and Vivien Olivier, and appeared at the Stage Door Canteen. Although it was annoying, having to leave my friends and crawl into London through a yellow fog, virtue for once was rewarded because the Canteen was packed with troops who had nowhere else to go and greeted all of us who appeared with boisterous enthusiasm. There was a lightness in the air, a tacit awareness that this might conceivably be the last Christmas of the war. The show started at eight and continued until one-thirty, by which time a great deal of beer had been drunk and so many cigarettes smoked that the atmosphere inside was almost as thick as the pea-soup fog outside. The combination of fog and the blackout in London was awe-inspiring. I don't know how the audience or my fellow artists managed to get home that night, but it took me an hour and a half to grope my way from Piccadilly to Gerald Road through familiar streets that had been entirely obliterated. Occasionally the concrete blackness was broken by the gleam of somebody's electric torch, or the dim blue light of a car, but only very occasionally, for there was very little traffic about. The rest was silence; silence and darkness so profound that I felt that the world had come to an end, quietly and without fuss, while we were singing our songs in the stuffy, brightly-lit Canteen, and that I was now stumbling away into eternity.

The first few weeks of the New Year, 1945, Victory Year, were punctuated by rocket bombs as well as doodlebugs. Of the two I favoured the latter because at least you could hear them coming and lie down briskly in the gutter when they cut out immediately over your head, whereas the V.2s dropped without warning and seemed to shake the universe.

In February I went to Tintagel for a week by myself, remembering gratefully how it had comforted me and restored me to health in 1943 when I was convalescing after jaundice. This time I required no comforting and my health was perfect, but it was good nevertheless to be completely idle for a few days, to read books, to go for walks along the cliffs and look at the sea and the sky and the gulls wheeling in the winter sunshine. It also gave me time to assemble some ideas for a revue I was planning for the summer. The planning was then only tentative, because although it was generally presumed that the war would end within a few months, this was by no means certain, and if it didn't end I knew that I should have to be up and away again. At all events I had thought of a good title, *Sigh No More*, which later, I regret to say, turned out to be the best part of the revue. However, that was all in the indefinite future and in the meantime there were other chores to do. One of them was the opening of a Stage Door Canteen in Paris in March. Marlene Dietrich, Maurice Chevalier and I inaugurated the three opening performances, and it was a tough assignment for me particularly, because a cold I had been warding off for several days finally caught up with me and crouched, with gleeful malignity, on my vocal chords three hours before I was to appear. Fortunately, with the aid of Dr Leme, a famous throat specialist, I managed to get through all three shows without utterly disgracing myself, but I loathed every minute of them.

On April the 14th came the tragic news of Roosevelt's death, which was a personal sadness to me, because although I did not know him really well he had been friendly, kind and unpompous and had treated me with respect at a moment when I most needed it. On April the 29th came the less tragic but macabre news that

Mussolini had been tried, shot and hung upside down in the streets to be spat at.

On May the 3rd, when the complete surrender of Germany was imminent, I dined quietly with Juliet Duff in her flat in Belgrave Place. There were only the four of us: Juliet, Venetia Montagu, Winston Churchill and myself. The Prime Minister was at his most benign, and suddenly, towards the end of dinner, looking across the table at the man who had carried England through her dark years, I felt an upsurge of gratitude that melted into hero worship. This was a profoundly significant moment in the history of our country; the long, long hoped-for victory was so very near, and the fact that we were in the presence of the man who had contributed so much foresight, courage and genius to winning it struck Juliet and Venetia at the same instant that it struck me. Emotion submerged us and without exchanging a word, as simultaneously as though we had carefully rehearsed it, the three of us rose to our feet and drank Mr Churchill's health.

8

On the morning of Victory Day I visited my mother and then wandered about the London streets in the hot sunshine. The crowds were gay and good-humoured, the bells clanged and the flags fluttered. In the evening I went along to have a drink with the *Blithe Spirit* company and then to Clemence Dane's flat, where we had cold food and drinks and listened to the King's broadcast, followed by speeches by Eisenhower, Tovey, Montgomery and Alexander. Various people came and went: Joyce, Lilian Braithwaite, Lynn and Alfred, Dick Addinsell, Lorn, Gladys, etc. The room looked as comforting and relaxed in victory as it had in disaster. Winnie and Olwen bustled about, looking after everybody as they had always done. In the later evening some of us went out into the streets again and wandered down the Mall through the orderly London crowds to Buckingham Palace, the whole façade of which was illuminated. The people sang and cheered, and presently the King and Queen came out on to the balcony and we cheered still more. There was, as in all celebrations of victory, an inevitable undertow of sadness. Parades generate only a superficial gaiety because we all know that they cannot last, and although this was the end of the war it was far from being the end of the world's troubles. Japan was still unconquered and even when she was vanquished there was still the future to be fought.

Past Conditional

PAST CONDITIONAL: 1931–1933

WRITTEN: 1965–67
FIRST PUBLISHED: 1986

I

Having already written two autobiographies *Present Indicative* and *Future Indefinite* I feel that the moment has come for me to write a third, and possibly, later on, a fourth. To pretend that my life has not been varied, interesting and extremely successful would be both affected and unconvincing. It has brought me in contact with a number of diverse and fascinating people and carried me to many strange and far off places. It has taught me several lessons from which I hope I have profited and also inculcated in me an insatiable and profound interest in the behaviour of my fellow creatures. The impulse to put on record the events and encounters, the achievements and failures and some of the unlikely adventures that have befallen me in the course of my sixty-five years is a fairly reasonable one, also, taking into account the amount that has already been written about me by other people, it is not I think arrogant to suppose that when I have gone far away into the silent land, there will be a great deal more. If only for the sake of anyone who in future years feels that I might be a suitable subject for a 'revealing' biography, a statement of the facts of my career might at least give them something to go on. I am aware of course that these facts might conceivably be disregarded or misinterpreted or even wilfully distorted, but that contingency is obviously beyond my control. I am not now and never have been very preoccupied with the verdict of posterity. It would be agreeable of course to feel that some of my work might be remembered with pleasure, but if on the other hand it fades swiftly into oblivion, there will be nothing then that I can do about it.

In any case the urge to write this particular book has been growing in my mind for some time, ever since, in fact, I realised that eight vital years of my earlier life have never been recorded at all. *Present Indicative* began with my birth and ended in November 1931, while *Future Indefinite* only covered my experiences during the war years beginning in 1939 and ending in 1945. Therefore there are two gaps to be filled. The eight years from late 1931 to mid-1939 and all the years from 1945 onwards. These I feel will have to wait until I have dealt with the 'Thirties'. I cannot any longer allow those, for me, most important years, to slip further and further into the limbo, even as it is I am bound to find some details of them elusive for although I am gifted with good memory, I never begin to keep any sort of diary or 'journal' until 1940. Lorn Loraine, my beloved secretary, managed to keep a sort of office diary which dealt with dates of opening nights and times and places of Actor's Orphanage meetings and the names of the committee members etc. Beyond these stark and only temporarily relevant facts, her entries are far from stimulating. It is tantalizing, when racking the memory for details, to find; 'Feb. 27th Noël went abroad,' and, several pages later; 'May 17th Noël came back. Met him at Southampton.' Perhaps Lorn's ingrained and stubborn insularity made even the scribbling down of foreign places obnoxious to her, at any rate Feb. 27th until May 17th have to be gouged out of the past somehow or other. Where did I go on that fateful day Feb. 27th? Was I alone? Had I a planned itinerary? Did I go to America, China or Heligoland? And if so for what reason? These sort of questions have teased my mind considerably throughout the months that I have been compiling the notes for this book. Some of the riddles I have finally managed to solve and others I have just had to guess at and pray that some unexpected spur to memory will suddenly arrive out of the blue. A quarter of a century has passed since I wove my hectic course through the Thirties, and a fairly turbulent quarter of a century at that, however I hope and suspect that the perspective provided by those twenty-five years will aid me in selecting events that were really important to me and save me from encumbering my narrative with too many casual and insignificant details.

2

In November 1931 Jeffery Amhurst and I embarked on the second of our long journeys together. The first had begun in 1929 and finished in 1930 and had covered Japan, Korea, Northern Manchuria, Southern China, Siam, Malaya, Indo-China and Ceylon. This time we were headed for South America. We intended to start at Rio de Janeiro, get into the interior of Brazil and work our way down one of the tributaries of the Amazon until we reached the Argentine, then go on from there either South, East or West as the spirit moved us.

On a grey day we set off from Folkestone on the ordinary boat and arrived at Boulogne in time to get on board the *Antonio Delfino*, a fair to middling little ship belonging to the Hamburg-Süd-Amerikanische line. Its personnel was mainly German; its passenger list also. Our cabins were clean and comfortable and the food was good. The weather, after the first few days, became steadily warmer and gentler until soon we were lying about on deck in shorts and sunglasses watching flying fish and feeling the damp of England drying out of our bones. It was an agreeable, uneventful voyage. We fraternized to a certain degree with our fellow passengers, but no lasting friendships were formed. We played 'Russian Bank' endlessly, a game which when played in its double form, can be one of the most irritating in the world. We read books. I remember trudging manfully through H. G. Wells' *History of the World*, Green's *History of England*, several light novels and a number of execrably written travel books about Latin America. I also had a portable gramophone and a set of Linguaphone records in Spanish which I listened to assiduously for an hour every day and even now there is little about La Familia Fernandez that I could not tell you straight off the bat. As things turned out it was lucky that I forced upon myself this burden of self-education, because with the aid of those reports, plus a brief course at the Berlitz School some years before, I managed to acquire a reasonably fluent vocabulary and an excellent accent which rapidly became debauched when I reached the Argentine.

The Argentine accent in Spanish is soft and alluring and very confusing if you have already happened to learn the more guttural intonations of 'Castiliano Puro', lisp and all.

Meanwhile behind us in England God seemed to be, politically at least, firmly ensconced in his Conservative heaven and all was right with the world. There was a feeling of hope in the air and a sort of rebirth of honest, homely patriotism. *Cavalcade* was playing to capacity at the Theatre Royal Drury Lane and I had been assured on all sides that I had done a great service for England by writing it and producing it at such a timely moment. I suppose I believed all this? Looking back so far from now to then it is difficult to believe that I did. But perhaps the laurels rested comfortably enough on my head and I accepted the tributes without irony. I can realise even now that it gave to those who saw it, or to the majority of them at least, a nostalgia for the more dignified past, a sense of English pride. I know that it made many people cry and gave to some of them a feeling of hope for England's future, so perhaps I did do them a service after all, for it is better to hope than to despair. In any event either emotion may turn out to be illusory and a waste of time. I remember clearly however that it gave me personally a tremendous and most gratifying sense of achievement. It was a vast production and I was proud of it. There were certain specific scenes in the play of which I was proud also. The Queen Victoria Funeral scene dialogue, and the outbreak of the 1914–1918 War particularly. It was written with sincerity and as much truth as I knew. I couldn't have been expected to have known then what I know now thirty-four years later when I am thirty-four years older.

Curiously enough with all the violent changes that have taken place in our world since 1931, my basic feelings about my country, those that inspired me to write *Cavalcade* have not altered and are still, to me, valid. *Cavalcade* was hailed as a patriotic fanfare, an expert bit of Jingoist flag-waving, cunningly put on the stage at exactly the right political moment. In point of actual fact, it was a great deal more than that. I had no idea about the accuracy of the political moment because I was far too busy in the theatre, nor had I any conscious intention of Jingoistic flag-waving. It merely occurred to me, as an Englishman of thirty-one years old, who was observant, fairly well-read and more travelled than the average, that I belonged to a most remarkable race. In later years I have seen no reason to revise this opinion. I am quite aware of our shortcomings, perhaps even more so than more impartial observers because I have suffered from them personally. I despise our national docility, the silliness of some of our laws, our meek acquiescence to circumstances which, with a little extra work on our part, could be twisted to our favour rather than allowed, through our mental and physical laziness, to dominate us. I also detest the climate except for sudden, unforgettable days of magic which, alas, are all too rare. However so much as I may loathe this and that and the other, it is what I love that really counts, and what I love about my country is really quite simple. I love its basic integrity, an integrity formed over hundreds of years by indigenous humour, courage and common-sense.

Love of country, of our own territory, is more deeply ingrained in the human animal than the shrill anti-nationalist, anti-patriotic, citizen-of-the-world pamphleteers and orators would have us believe. It is useless to try to dismiss this inherent pride in the land of our roots as facile patriotism, as nothing more than a convenient banner to be waved by unscrupulous politicians and newspaper Barons when a commercial trade agreement is at stake or a war is in the offing. For the human animal as for the primates from whom he descended millions of years ago, there is nearly always a war in the offing. And, as scientists have incontrovertibly proved, the instinct for protection of territory in millions of varieties of mammals, reptiles, birds, insects and fish, is far stronger than the urge for food, sex or self-preservation.

In the year 1956 when I decided, for carefully considered financial reasons, to give up my English residence and become domiciled abroad, I was reviled and execrated by the majority of the British Press for being unpatriotic and failing in my duties as an Englishman. The force of these accusations is liable to fade a little under a modicum of intelligent scrutiny. In the first place, patriotism is an emotional instinct compounded of love of country and pride in that country's achievements and inherited characteristics. In my own case at any rate it most emphatically does not embrace the various Governments under which I have laboured, nor many of the laws that they have seen fit to pass. In the second place, I feel it to be the primary duty of a creative and talented Englishman, or indeed a creative and talented Chinaman for the matter of that, to continue with his work wherever he sees fit and, by doing so, contribute perhaps a little to the sum total of his country's proud artistic record. I cannot feel that my obdurate refusal to pay taxes which I consider to be both exorbitant and unjust, need in any way prevent me being of value to my country whether I decide to live in Switzerland, the Galapagos Islands or Kathmandu. It does not seem to have occurred to my self-righteous, journalistic attackers, in whose attitude may I say I detect a tiny streak of envy, that I may prefer to live out of England, taxes or no taxes. As a matter of fact, however, that happens to be the truth. I do. And for further information on this point it may be of interest to note that I have not *lived* in England for more than two or three months a year since 1948 when I built my house in Jamaica. My course has wobbled variously across the world mainly between America, France, England and Jamaica, with a number of other foreign countries thrown in. I happen to have an insatiable wanderlust, a personal eccentricity which I should think should by now be fairly widely recognized. In any event, in those far off days when I was rolling serenely across the South Atlantic in search of new adventures, my patriotic reputation in my damp but lovable homeland had reached dizzy heights. I was the hero of the hour, a fairly brief hour I may add in the stately progress of recorded time, but at the moment, a little startling and entirely gratifying. The gentlemen of the Press outdid themselves in praise of my skill and talent and, above all, my political acumen. There were a few faintly dissentient voices heard chirping reprovingly in some of the more intellectual weeklies, and one very loud voice indeed, emanating from none other than the late Sean O'Casey, who was seeking refuge from Irish discomforts in the Devonshire dales. For some reason, best known to himself, he decided that *Cavalcade* was beneath contempt. So violent were his diatribes that the late James Agate sprang articulately to my defence either in the *Sunday Times* or the *New Statesman*, I forget which, and the controversy raged for some weeks. As I had never met Mr Sean O'Casey and had never to my knowledge, done anything to rouse his ire, I can only conclude that his loathing of me, which continued briskly until his death, must have been inspired by some curious mental obsession. On the other hand of course he may merely have seen a photograph of me in the papers. In any case I am bound to admit that the disagreeable old *embusqué* wrote at least a couple of very good plays.

3

Our first view of the harbour of Rio de Janeiro was as sensational as we had expected it to be. The Sugar-Loaf mountain climbed up into the sky and the other mountains behind it emerged from the morning mist, shedding their clouds gracefully and looking a little self-conscious as though they had been caught washing their hair. After an hour or so in a suffocatingly hot customs house we drove off, bag and baggage, to the luxurious Copacabana Hotel where we had reserved a suite.

It is not my intention, even were my memory capable of it, to stun my readers with a blow by blow account of every incident that occurred, of every person we met and every scenic marvel we gazed at during those long-ago, erratic wanderings across the sub-continent of Latin America. It is inevitable in the course of my narrative that a scenic marvel or two will pop up now and again and that a few outstanding characters will emerge, but they will be severely rationed for, as the Genie succinctly remarked at the end of the first act of *Where The Rainbow Ends*, 'Time is short and we have far to travel'.

The first outstanding character to appear in Rio was Mr Edwin Morgan, the American Ambassador, who called on us the afternoon of the day we arrived and invited us to a sumptuous party which was to be given that evening. After fourteen days spent in the company of our relentlessly Teutonic fellow-passengers, the idea of a slap-up Brazilian social soirée appealed to us immediately, and we accepted with enthusiasm. The party fulfilled our highest expectations. It was indeed sumptuous and glittering and gay and, thanks to dear Edwin Morgan for taking us to it, we were able to meet all the crème de la crème of Rio society at one fell swoop. From then onwards we never looked back. There were bathing parties, barbecues, formal ambassadorial receptions and informal moonlight picnics to say nothing of fancy dress balls and a couple of treasure hunts. An English Major with a black patch over one eye took us riding up a perpendicular mountain on sturdy but resentful Brazilian ponies. Later on, this kind and most hearty man, took me aside and, flushed with manly embarrassment, handed me a bundle of poems that he had been working on secretly for years. He stood over me anxiously while I read them. I can still remember the last two lines of the first one. 'Oh simple shepherd praise thy God – That thou art nothing but a sod.'

Two life-long friends emerged from those dizzy three weeks in Rio. One was 'Baby' Guinle (now Mrs Richard Pendar) a strikingly beautiful Argentine who reappeared in my life in Paris during the first weeks of World War Two and managed, with glamorous efficiency, to find me a charming flat in the Place Vendome. The other was Daan Hubrecht, the son of the Dutch Ambassador. He was twenty-one, tall, handsome and dashing, he spoke several languages perfectly, and he only needed side-whiskers and a moustache to have been a credit to Ouida. He was, at the moment, embroiled in a rather perilous love affair with an Englishwoman married to a Brazilian and so when, a little later on, Jeff and I asked his parents if they would allow him to come with us on our expedition into the interior, they agreed with ill-concealed alacrity.

The Maté Langeiras Company, for some obscure reason that I have never been able to fathom, most generously invited us to make our projected journey to the Iguassú Falls via the Paraná river, as their guests, even going so far as to provide us with a private coach on the train, cook and all, for the three days journey from Sao Paulo to the railhead at a place called Presidente Epistacio. From here we were transported, still as privileged guests, down the river to La Guaira on a curious contraption consisting of three boats lashed together. Jeff and Daan and I occupied the middle one while the two on either side carried the captain and crew respectively. It was a mysterious and enchanting experience floating endlessly downstream on that wide, beige-coloured river in the middle of the Brazilian jungle. Occasionally we would tie up alongside a rickety wooden pier and go ashore for a while to stretch our legs in some primitive little Indian fishing village. I remember that I celebrated my thirty-second birthday on the Rio Paraná. The birthday feast consisted of two small tins of caviar and a great deal of luke warm Vodka on which we all three got hilariously drunk. In the evenings we sometimes asked the Captain to shut off the engine for an hour or so and we would drift along silently through the brief tropical twilight, watching strange animals come down to the waterside to drink and listening to the eerie sounds of the jungle preparing for the night. As the light swiftly faded from the sky it seemed to be caught and held for a few extra moments on the surface of the water so that the whole stretch of the river before and behind us looked like luminous glass. It was romantically awe-inspiring to reflect that the dense, matted jungle on the right bank extended for two thousand miles across the vast continent to the mountains of Bolivia and Peru; two thousand miles of mainly unexplored virgin forest in which one could become hopelessly lost only a few hundred yards inland from the shore. Those remote, still evenings on the Rio Paraná, even now in 1965, stay clearly in my mind. It is such moments that explain my wanderlust and justify my eternal restlessness. They are rare of course, extensive travel does not automatically provide an inexhaustible supply of glowing memories, very often it can be arduous, uncomfortable and disillusioning, but when all the discomforts and setbacks and irritations can suddenly add up to an hour or so of untarnished enchantment, then, to me, they are all more than worthwhile. I have never yet, in all my years, outgrown the childish and perhaps egocentric pleasure of being able to say: This is I, myself, sitting on top of this alien mountain; in this ferry boat chugging across Hong Kong harbour; staring out through coco-palms at this coral sea. I, myself, who in my earlier days knew the grey drabness of provincial lodging-houses, the oppressive gentility of English suburbia, who so often trod hot, unyielding London pavements between various theatrical agents' offices in my midsummer search for an autumn engagement. Look at me now! My spirit crows, lying on the deck of a swaying ship gazing up at the crowded, tropical stars. Look at me now! I cry, even at this very moment, sitting on my high-up Jamaican verandah, watching the changing shadows on the sea, my full grown, scarlet tulip trees which I planted only eight years ago, glowing in the hot sunlight, and, over and beyond the diminishing headlands, the jagged range of Blue Mountain peaks standing against the sky.

I trust that the reader will not be too embarrassed at this sudden outburst of self-congratulatory enthusiasm. It is only that whenever I reflect with what alarming rapidity I am trundling towards old age and the dusty grave, I find it comforting to count my blessings. And although the future, like the late Mrs Fiske, is heavily veiled, my blessings, up to date, have certainly been considerable.

4

Guaira, where we finally disembarked from our three-fold river craft, was a settlement inhabited by three hundred thousand Indians and one white Resident and his wife. He was a husky-looking Argentine attired in 'bombachos', elaborately ornamented leather boots and a rather skittish beige hat. He spoke no English but greeted us politely and led us to a guest house on a spick and span and faintly irrelevant boulevard lined with trees. Beyond the boulevard, in fact all round the township, the jungle was waiting to pounce and it took a good deal more than seven maids with seven mops daily to keep it at bay. The town itself was clean as a whistle and even boasted a railway station for a train which ran exactly two hundred and fifty kilometres and came to an abrupt stop in a jungle clearing. The guest house was also as clean as a whistle which was more than we were. On the boat we had emptied buckets of water over each other at stated intervals but we had none of us had a bath or a shower for several days. We drew lots as to who should have the first go at the bath and I won and within a few minutes I was lying blissfully in tepid fresh water gazing up at the wooden ceiling.

Here I must digress for a moment to explain that before we left Sao Paulo we had paid a visit to the snake farm in order to become acquainted with some of the perilous reptiles and insects we might possibly encounter on our expedition. A delightful man called Doctor Almeira took us round and cheerfully showed us a number of the more deadly hazards in store for us. He also presented me at parting with a tiny and exquisitely coloured coral snake (harmless) which lived happily in my breast pocket for several days until Jeff, unbeknownst to me, gave it a few sips of his dry martini which killed it instantly. Among the various lethal creatures Doctor Almeira introduced us to was a peculiar deadly type of tarantula which, apart from its instantaneous death-dealing capacities, was so repellent to look at that we shuddered and turned away. Its body was about the size and shape of a small bun the colour of red lacquer and covered with bright ginger hairs. It had a beastly little beak and a multitude of long legs also hairy. The memory of this hideous example of nature's tastelessness haunted me for some days. It was while I was lying in that longed-for ecstatic bath in the guest house at Guaira that my memories of it were revived with ghastly suddenness. I noticed, on the wooden ceiling above my head, a slight movement, after a second look I was out of that bath and screaming down the passage in a split second. Eventually the house-boy appeared with an O-Cedar mop and killed it in the bath where it had dropped, presumably a moment after I had vacated it. Both Jeffery and Daan rallied me with warm gin and, when their turns came, approached the bathroom with the utmost caution. I do not know the exact genus of this unattractive insect but I do know that if it bites you you are dead within ten minutes and that if it only sees fit to crawl across any area of your exposed flesh, that area is liable to be paralysed for ten days. I retailed my gruesome little adventure to Señora and Señor Rhode after dinner in halting Spanish, and they rocked with laughter.

The scenic marvels of Guaira being limited to a sedentary ride in the train and a tiring walk through the jungle to look at some sparse remains of a derelict seventeenth-century Jesuit village, we left after two days and pressed on towards the main object of our trip which was to see the famous Iguassú falls. This necessitated going on down the river in whatever steamers were available until we reached a disembarkation point near to Iguassú which was some way inland. I think the place we finally got to was Encarnación, or it might have been Piray or Posados. Whichever it was there was nowhere to spend the night except on board an ancient, long discarded pleasure steamer which had a sinister, 'Outward Bound' atmosphere and contained a few cockroach infested cabins, a vast, dark dining-saloon and a mad steward dressed in a greyish-white bum-freezer, ominously stained blue trousers and multi-coloured carpet slippers. He had two complete rows of brilliantly gold teeth and, as it was his habit to go into gales of high-pitched laughter whenever we asked him for anything, we were almost blinded. Apart from him and us and the cockroaches, the only other living creature on board that macabre vessel was an incredibly old mongrel which had no teeth at all, gold or otherwise. Its name was Peppo. The food, needless to say, was disgusting, but fortunately we happened to carry our own liquor with us and managed to make ourselves a nauseating but potent brew of gin, boiled water, lemon-juice and brown sugar. After our nasty meal we sat out on the deck in the pitch dark listening to the river muttering by and chain-smoking cigarettes to discourage the insects. Later on in the evening Peppo made a determined effort to get into bed with me but I succeeded in repelling his advances and he finally retired wheezing down the dark corridor.

I would like to be able to describe the magnificence of the Iguassú falls. I am sure that they were as vast, impressive and awe-inspiring as they were claimed to be. Unhappily however we were unable to see them very clearly. Owing possibly to the time of the year or to some freak of Nature, the entire area was densely clouded with large black mosquitoes. We wore grubby cotton gloves, hastily borrowed from the waiter at the dilapidated rest-house where we lunched, and straw hats from which hung thick green veils which we were obliged to tuck into our shirts. Luckily our ankles were protected because we were all three wearing jodhpurs and boots. We were ushered into a curious squarish-shaped boat by a loquacious, half-naked young man whose *désinvolte* attitude towards the mosquitoes fascinated us. He chattered away merrily while they settled on his brown sweating body in swarms making his skin look like some new and outlandish material designed by Schiaparelli. What fascinated us less was the fact that, still talking, he steered us practically to the lip of the main falls, nonchalantly arresting our progress from time to time by leaning over the side and seizing hold of passing weeds. The roar of the waters hurtling into the abyss was deafening, and the heat, under our hats and veils, intolerable. When finally, in what seemed to be the nick of time, we turned back, soaked to the skin with sweat and spray and dry-mouthed with terror, he helped us ashore and led us, at a stumbling trot through a 'rain forest' which ultimately led to a narrow, slippery ledge on which he forced us to crouch and peer down through large ferns and our green veils, at a churning tumult of waters several hundred feet below us. Admittedly there were a couple of rainbows scintillating in the humid air, and a few harebrained birds whizzing about, but we were too exhausted and uncomfortable to do more than acknowledge them briefly and stagger back to the rest-house as quickly as possible.

With this dramatic but agitating adventure behind us we made our way back to the main river again and proceeded in a leisurely manner downstream in a small trading steamer until we arrived at Corrientes. Here we embarked on a pseudo-de-luxe passenger boat for the last lap of our journey to Buenos Aires. There are few things more agreeable than a bout of luxury after a prolonged period of roughing it and we were looking forward eagerly to soft beds, clean sheets, hot baths and all the other amenities of expensively civilized travel. A greater power than we could contradict however, thwarted our intentions, the greater power being invested in the Captain and personnel of that pseudo-de-luxe floating monstrosity. We went on board in the later afternoon, and having washed and showered and tidied ourselves in our genuinely luxurious cabins we made our way to the bar to have a drink before dinner. The first blow fell when the barman refused contemptuously to serve us. We then sent for the Chief Steward who informed us, not over politely, that we were not suitably dressed to be served in either the bar or the dining-saloon, nor would we be permitted to enjoy any of the privileges of the first class accommodation unless we wore coats and ties. Considering that (a) we were all three tired from having travelled fairly ruggedly for a long time; (b) we were spotlessly clean in our khaki open-necked shirts and jodhpurs and (c) that we had paid the maximum for our first class tickets, it was not surprising that we all three lost our tempers immediately, and the row was on. It was really quite a good row as rows go and attracted a gratifyingly large crowd of our more correctly attired fellow passengers. The Purser was sent for and finally, the Captain himself. He was a tubby, red-faced little man with a slight squint. He was also pompous, obdurate and entirely bloody-minded. By that time of course it had occurred to all of us that we *had* got coats and ties packed away in our suit-cases and it would perhaps have been both time- and trouble-saving to have given in. But our blood was up. It had by then become a question of principle and the idea of surrendering to their pettifogging little rules and regulations could not be entertained for a moment. The steamer had already sailed so it was impossible for the Captain to order us ashore. Finally, after the battle had been raging for some time, I raised my hand, and my voice, to silence the general hubbub and announced icily that, having seen the first class accommodation and the type of people that occupied it, I felt that we should be more comfortable if we spent our three days' voyage with the crew. With this we all stalked majestically away to our cabins where we broke into giggles and drank our own gin from tooth mugs. The net result of the whole absurd fracas was, that after sending a radiogram to the British Consul in Buenos Aires protesting against our treatment, we removed ourselves, with the help of the Purser in whose eye we detected a sympathetic gleam, to three cabins below the water-line. The cabins were hot and stuffy, but three electric fans were produced. Meals were served to us on a trestle table set up in the wide passage outside our cabins and we appropriated a minute space on the after deck where we reclined, on mattresses during the daylight hours, with no clothes on at all. News of the imbroglio had spread through the ship and the stewards and the members of the crew we happened to encounter, were all on our side. We organized little community singing groups in the evenings and, on the whole, enjoyed ourselves very much.

Upon arrival at Buenos Aires three days later we were met by the British Consul, a friendly man called Gudgeon. Needless to say we emerged, at a carefully chosen moment when all the first class passengers were milling about preparatory to going ashore, impeccably turned out in white tropical suits and ties which the stewards had gleefully pressed for us the evening before. Mr Gudgeon made a formal complaint to the Captain and forced him to apologize to us, which he did with obvious reluctance. We accepted his apology with stately dignity and I, as spokesman, delivered a short homily in which I suggested that the next time an Ambassador's son, an eminent English writer and a British Peer of the Realm set foot on board his ship, they should be treated with the courtesy due to them no matter if they happened to be clad in nothing but jockstraps. I forget now what word I used in Spanish for jockstrap but I remember that I had looked it up in the dictionary and managed to arrive at some sort of approximation. I don't think however that it could have been a very accurate approximation because the Captain stared at me in blank astonishment.

Mr Gudgeon, who had evidently enjoyed the whole situation, drove us into the city and deposited us at the Plaza Hotel where we were received most affably by the manager who ushered us into the bridal suite. Jeffery and Daan got on with the unpacking while I gave a few press interviews in a mixture of Spanish, French and English. After this we ordered a bottle of pink champagne, drank it, and went happily down to lunch.

5

Our social career in the Argentine was launched initially by the British Ambassador and Ambassadress, Sir Ronald and Lady MacCleay. They were tremendously hospitable and kind and, under their aegis we sailed through three weeks of almost continual entertaining. In my own country I only rarely attend large-scale receptions and dinner parties and dances, mainly I suppose because I am usually working too hard to have the time to enjoy them. In a strange foreign city however it is different and in any case it provided a marked contrast to our wanderings through the jungle. Sir Ronald MacCleay's reception of us was also a marked contrast to our encounter with our Ambassador (or Minister, I forget which) in Rio, who, ten days after we had dutifully signed our names in the book had invited us to tea. He greeted us vaguely and with conspicuous lack of enthusiasm. At tea, we sat, in comparative silence, watching him devour, with the utmost concentration, two boiled eggs, after which we went away.

Shortly after our arrival in Buenos Aires Sir Ronald took me aside and asked me tentatively whether or not I would mind being 'used' as a celebrity every now and again during my visit. He explained that the only Britisher of any eminence who had come out during the last few years was Philip Guardella, who had given some brilliant lectures and gone away. Since then the Prince of Wales and Prince George had paused there for a while during their South American tour and had been an enormous success with the Argentines to whom the Prince of Wales talked Spanish with immense brio and considerable personal satisfaction. The Royal visitors, according to Sir Ronald, had not apparently paid quite enough attention to the English residents thereby causing a certain feeling of resentment. In fairness to the Princes I had to admit that I rather saw their point. It is obviously more important during an official tour to devote yourself to your foreign hosts rather than to any of your own countrymen who happen to be about. However be that as it may I was naturally flattered to be told that by opening an art exhibition, a flower show and making speeches at one or two clubs, I could in any way enhance the prestige of my country, so I agreed. My official appearances were brief and quite painless and as a matter of fact I rather enjoyed them.

A few days before the end of our stay in the Argentine Daan left us to return to Rio. We missed him sadly because he had been gay and charming company. Shortly after this we made a series of good-bye visits to all our newly found friends, and departed ourselves, in a very hot train, for Patagonia. I cannot honestly recommend to any travel-lover, however enthusiastic, a three days' and two nights' railway journey across the Argentine Pampas in a midsummer dust storm. However we emerged from it gritty but unscathed and spent an enchanting week with Carlos and Leonora Basualdo at a place called Nahuel Huapi. Leonora was an old friend and we had first met when she had been the Leonora Hughes, dancing partner of the famous 'Maurice'. She looked as lovely as ever and Carlos, her husband, and the whole Basualdo family entertained us so sweetly that I shall never forget them. It was a strange and fascinating house, 'rough luxury' at its best, glorious beds, marble bathrooms and every conceivable modern convenience set in the middle of wild, untamed country verging on the Chilean lakes. We bathed and sailed and explored the lakes in a speed-boat. We also rode for miles on well-mannered horses equipped with Mexican saddles which I had never tried before and found extremely comfortable. Somebody once wrote a book called *The Horse as Comrade and Friend*, a title which has tantalized me for years, perhaps because I have never had neither the time or the opportunity to cultivate such a relationship. Being an inveterate animal-lover I am quite fond of horses although, unlike many of my countrymen, I do not idolize them. I have ridden a certain amount in the earlier years of my life but with neither style, grace nor technique. Curiously enough, although I have frequently been bolted with, I have never either fallen off or been thrown which, in one way, stamps me as a bad rider I suppose. All experienced horsemen are constantly flung from their steeds as a matter of course. The horse, to me, has always been an unpredictable and slightly hysterical animal. I have encountered placid ones, spirited ones, fiendish ones and even sentimental ones but none of them has ever quite qualified for the status of Comrade and Friend. I think perhaps that the only thing that has saved me from being rolled on and trampled to death years ago is the fact that I am not afraid of them. Fear, I am told, exudes a certain unmistakable odour which is immediately recognizable by our four-footed Comrades and Friends. I can only conclude therefore that in this respect I am odourless.

In Nahuel Huapi the horses were models of good behaviour and there was one, called Carmencita, with whom I achieved, as near as no matter, a true homo-equine affinity. Lolling on her broad back in my comfortable Mexican saddle and encouraging her occasionally with a friendly pat or a honeyed word, I cantered about the countryside for hours at a time and, apart from feeling a little stiff in the evenings, was all the better for it. Eventually we bade good-bye to our delightful hosts and all the horses and set forth across a series of lakes to reach the Chilean frontier. Carlos Basualdo had organized the first part of our trip in advance, for which we had good reason to be grateful to him because it turned out to be a fairly complicated procedure. A series of lakes had to be crossed in various ramshackle little steamers and over the frequently mountainous tracts or territory separating them we were conveyed, with all our luggage, on even more ramshackle little mules. This experience precluded once and for all any possibility of my writing a book called *The Mule as Comrade and Friend*. We were assured by our Indian guides that these disagreeable animals were instinctively intelligent and sure-footed but I am bound to confess that those that I bestrode betrayed no signs of either of these excellent qualities. In fact the last one I hoisted myself onto seemed to have only one idea in its horrid little mind which was to 'un-mule' me as soon as it possibly could. It lurched and stumbled and frequently lay down without warning, preferably on the edge of a ravine and I was constantly having to yell to Jeffery and the Indians who turned back perilously down the jagged path and with oaths and blows forced it to stagger to its feet again. When, at long last, we came down to the shore of the final lake, I tried, magnanimously, to pat it good-bye, but it merely bared its hideous yellow teeth and plunged at me. Happily, being more sure-footed than it was, I managed to dodge aside, kick it as it passed, and retire hurriedly to the boat.

Our journey from then on to the railhead where we were to entrain for Valparaiso, was relatively uneventful. All I can remember of it is a gloomy rest-house at a place called Tronador in which we ate a greasy and unpalatable dinner and were later subjected to a plague of large white flying ants which successfully kept us awake until dawn.

We spent the early hours of that morning sitting in the station waiting-room waiting for our train which was late, sleepily playing 'Russian Bank' on the top of a suit-case and glancing occasionally at our fellow-passengers who sounded as if they were conducting a full-scale revolutionary meeting, but were actually merely discussing the weather and the crops. They were a picturesque group consisting of one enormously fat old Priest who mopped his face continually; several dusty looking nuns; a young man and a girl, possibly a honeymoon couple, dressed to the nines and sweating profusely; a few working types; two hirsute and tiny sailors; and a florid lady with a basket in which were three hens and a baby. Every now and then the baby shrieked whereupon she disentangled it from the hens and jammed its face irritably against a vast yellowish gas globe which she produced from inside her bodice.

When the train finally arrived we managed to get a first class compartment to ourselves, stretch ourselves out and go to sleep. The journey was interminable and hot and monotonous, a monotony which was rudely shattered by a sudden grinding of brakes and a dreadful scream. I looked out of the window and saw, before I had time to turn away, the bleeding torso and head of a young man who had been cut completely in half by the wheels. Even now, after all these years, that ghastly sight is imprinted indelibly on my memory. The train was halted for an hour or so in the blazing midday heat, a crowd of officials appeared and some of the poor boy's relatives who were apparently travelling in the train. One of them, presumably his mother, flung herself on to his remains and had to be dragged away shrieking. The general clamour was so excruciating that finally Jeff and I retired to the lavatory where we sat, sickened and shuddering, until the train started again.

We arrived late in the evening at Valparaiso, installed ourselves in a comfortable modern hotel and, after a delicious dinner for which we had little appetite, we retired to bed and slept for twelve hours.

6

The few days we spent in Valparaiso were enlivened for us by the Royal Navy. There was a light cruiser accompanied by two destroyers in the harbour and it wasn't long before we met some of the officers either in the bar of the hotel or at somebody or other's cocktail party. From then on we were swiftly whirled through a number of enjoyable Naval occasions including a whole day of gunnery practice some fifty miles out to sea; a couple of fairly libidinous 'guest nights' and various other marine junketings.

This was one of the very early stages of my long and proud association with the inaccurately termed 'Silent Service' and consolidated the opinion I had formed a few years before when Jeff and I had travelled from Shanghai to Hong Kong in H.M.S. *Suffolk*, which was that the officers and men of the Royal Navy, apart from being gay and delightful company, have the best manners in the world. In those early days of the Thirties, halfway between World War One and World War Two when the illusion of Peace in our Time was firmly imbedded in the ostrich minds of our Western Governments, the activities of our fleets, both at home and abroad, were little more than perfunctory. The disciplinary morale was of course upheld by a series of battle exercises, target practices, occasional mock invasions and various other prescient operations, while, behind the scenes, the backroom boys were secretly preparing future scientific miracles. The outward aspects however were fair and untroubled and the international seas appeared to be as calm as millponds. One of the principal functions of His Majesty's ships at that time was merely to 'show the flag' which meant sailing the smiling oceans in 'Battle's magnificently stern array' with no ulterior motive beyond the perhaps naive assumption that 'To impress the Natives' was 'A Good Thing'. In my experience, which is considerable, the Royal Navy invariably executed this task with triumphant style and dignity. In my time I have visited a great many foreign ports as a guest in our warships and I have never once known the performance to fail. I would like to add however that these successes were by no means so casually achieved as they appeared to be. Nonchalant 'panache', like expert high comedy acting, can only be acquired after meticulous rehearsal. The luncheon and dinner parties on board for local dignitaries, the receptions, both formal and informal, the cocktail parties and the inevitable dances on the Quarter Deck englamoured by flags, bunting, coloured lights and the cynical radiance of alien stars, were all organised down to the minutest detail. Even over the lighter entertainments unobtrusive tradition presided, benign but watchful, like an insular English 'Nanny' at a possibly unpredictable children's party.

I am glad to say that even in this grubbier era the disciplined grace of Naval manners still persists. Only a short while ago when I was passing through Hong Kong I was telephoned by a Flag Lieutenant and invited to lunch on board the flagship with an Admiral Scatchard. I naturally accepted with pleasure and, during my voyage across the harbour in the Admiral's barge which had been sent for me, I racked my brains to remember where in the past, in what circumstances and in which ship I had met Admiral Scatchard before. It was only when he greeted me on deck that I recognized, through the lines that years and the weather had lightly etched on his face, the cherubic countenance of a young midshipman I had known over a quarter of a century before, who had brought me cups of ship's cocoa up to the bridge and called me 'sir' with such relentless persistence that I had felt like clouting him. It was now my turn to call him 'sir' and, after we had lunched in his comfortable cabin and I had been taken to the ward-room to be introduced to the rest of the ship's officers, he saw me over the side. As I bounced across the glittering water of the harbour, sitting in the stern of the barge, I looked back at the grey ship set against the multi-coloured panorama of the island peak, and happily reflected that I had been infected all over again by the Navy's, to me imperishable magic.

In Valparaiso, our principal host was a Captain Vivian, who, many years later, I encountered during the war when he was Admiral-in-Charge of The King Alfred Training Establishment in Hove. He invited me to a guest night to witness a number of young cadets 'pass out', not, I hasten to add, in the alcoholic sense. Their 'passing out' was a joyful ritual, a longed for milestone in their young careers, a celebration of the fact that their months of shore training had been successfully accomplished and they could now look forward to the very near future, when they would go to sea for the first time. I remember being driven back to London by Admiral Vivian through the rainy, blacked-out countryside and wondering, in the intervals of pleasant reminiscence about our long-ago days in Valparaiso, how many of those eager, cheerful young men would survive the dark years ahead.

7

In Santiago we spent a halcyon week with the British Ambassador, Sir Henry Chilton, his wife and their two daughters. I must apologize to the reader if the pages of this narrative up to date seem to have been overloaded with Ambassadors, but he must realise that in those days Englishmen of the mildest repute travelling abroad gravitated automatically to their country's nearest and highest representatives. Not invariably of course. There has always been a percentage of the more hard-bitten, before-the-mast, work-your-own-passage, types of travellers who, for various reasons, deliberately eschew all social contacts above a certain level and ardently pursue discomforts even when they are not strictly necessary. I am naturally not referring to those whose means preclude them from luxuries and whose true spirit of adventure impels them to travel on the cheap rather than not travel at all. For these I have nothing but admiration. But I have, in my day, run across certain characters who, although they could perfectly well afford comfortable hotels wherever they were available, deliberately, and perhaps a trifle self-consciously, head for the nearest waterside doss house. It is unnecessary to state that I do not belong in this category. I am prepared to accept cheerfully any hardships that happen to come my way when I am travelling, providing that they are unavoidable, but I see little sense in seeking them out.

Nor need it be assumed from the above that I make a habit of staying in Embassies, Residences and Government Houses on my journeys. On the contrary, as a general rule, I avoid them. To my mind there is a good deal more to be said against official hospitality than there is for it. In the first place, unless your particular host and hostess happen to be old friends with whom you can kick off your shoes and giggle after the last more transient guest has departed, the strain of continual 'best behaviour' is apt to become intolerable. It has fortunately not often been my lot to find myself, for some reason or other, an official guest of a Governor and Governor's lady whom I have never met before and who are pompous and stiff-necked into the bargain, and even on these rare occasions I have usually managed, with a calculated performance of modest, unspoiled-by-my-great-success simplicity to puncture, after a little while, their pro-consular reserve. These tactics I find tiring and frankly not worth the trouble, and I would infinitely rather exert my winning ways to charm hotel managers, floor-waiters and chambermaids from whom I can hope to get more appreciable rewards.

In any case I find, as a general rule, that I would rather stay at an hotel than in other people's houses, official or otherwise, unless of course they happen to belong to close friends with whom I can relax. I do not care for the obligation of having to be considerate to other people's servants, nor do I care to experiment with other people's ideas of comfort which are so often widely dissimilar from my own. In an hotel I can ring the bell or raise the telephone and protest if there aren't enough pillows or the bedside lamp doesn't function properly. In a private house I cannot. In an hotel room I can put a 'Don't Disturb' sign on the door and sleep for as long as I like and capriciously demand a poached egg and a cup of tea at three o'clock in the afternoon, if I feel so disposed, without feeling that I am shattering an established routine and possibly causing my hostess's cook to give notice. To me the very idea of a round of country-house visits is anathema, although many of my more social-minded friends take this curious practice as a matter of course. Whenever I hear one of them announce with every sign of pleasurable enthusiasm; 'I am spending from Tuesday until Friday with darling Ronnie and May at Cratchley, then the week-end with poor Walter and his ghastly new wife, then for the whole of the following week I shall be in Dumfries with the MacRattigans before going to Michael at Snurbdridge for Easter' I shudder with dismay. I am also given to wonder whether darling Ronnie and May, Walter, the MacRattigans and Michael are equally enraptured at the prospect. Possibly they are, but I am fairly certain that I wouldn't be. I am apt to find professional guests almost as tedious as professional hosts.

To the dear Chiltons in Santiago, Chile, however, none of the above strictures apply. They were un-ambassadorial to a degree and the word pomposity was not in their vocabulary. While we were staying with them a large package of long delayed English mail caught up with us, and I remember sitting in the garden with Jeff in the shade of some unpronounceable tree reading the news from home. There was a good deal of it one way and another; long letters from Lorn, Gladys and Joyce and Binkie (see footnotes, if any) explaining who was doing what and with whom. There was a lot of enjoyable theatrical gossip but nothing of any special significance. What was of considerable significance however was a cable from Alfred Lunt and Lynn Fontanne in New York saying tersely; 'Darling, our contract with the Theatre Guild up in June, what about it?' This shocked me into the sudden realisation that floating down strange rivers, clambering up far away mountains on mules and basking in tropical sunshine was all very well in its way, but that life was real, life was earnest and that the world was too much with me late and soon. Indeed the theatre world to which the major part of my life had been dedicated had almost vanished from my consciousness. 'What about it?' was the operative phrase in the cable and I knew what it meant only too well. I also knew that although the call of the wild might charm my ears for a brief while, the call of the Lunts had a stronger resonance. There was no rush, no urgency, no immediate necessity to plunge back into the hurly-burly, but from that moment onwards, my South American wanderings, although they were to continue for some months longer, lost a little of their initially carefree abandon.

In the summer of 1921 when Lynn, Alfred and I were all in New York together, they in lodgings on West 73rd Street and I in a small, lent apartment on Washington Square, we had made a mutual pact that when we had all three achieved individual stardom in our own rights, I should write a play and that the three of us would play it together. In those suffocatingly hot days eleven years away from the shady coolness of the Chilton's garden, the idea had seemed to be little more than a far-fetched and over-ambitious pipe-dream. But a lot can happen in eleven years and, to Lynn, Alfred and me, a lot had. For one thing we had achieved the first part of the pipe-dream, we were all three established stars in our own rights. The first move towards fulfilling the second part of the dream was now obviously over to me. The play had to be written and, what was more, written before June. I couldn't expect the Lunts, much as they loved me, to wait about indefinitely once their rather irksome Theatre Guild contract came to an end. Also, once it became known that they were at long last available and free to pick and choose, every management and playwright in America would be deluging them with scripts. I remember going to bed that night in a fairly pensive state of mind.

I would like to explain here and now that to sit down and write an effective vehicle for one talented personality in the theatre is none too easy, to attempt to write one for three, particularly three of such equal status as Lynn, Alfred and me, seemed to me then, as indeed it seems to me now, an exceedingly tricky assignment. It was also of course one of the most stimulating challenges I have ever faced in my life. In any event from the moment that cable arrived my casual 'Traveller's Joy' was abandoned; not with gloom but with a sense of restlessness and urgency. We still had a long way to go before our self-imposed itinerary was completed; there were still many experiences and adventures to enjoy and still many wonders to see but for me there was a slight withdrawal of concentration. I was not unduly haunted or worried because I knew from experience that once I could snatch out of the air the right idea for a play, the actual writing of it would not take long. Once the basic theme of a play has been worked out in my mind, I have always written quickly. It's getting the basic theme that takes the time. And of course as I was so intent on getting a plot for the three of us, my own eagerness defeated itself.

We battled our way through jungles and over mountains; we

met diverse characters and had a number of bizarre travelling adventures, some enjoyable, some maddening and all of them, with a few rare exceptions, interesting. We visited Cuzco high up in the Andes and Alleantitambo, the source of the Amazon where the great river gurgles out from under some small stones. We encountered strange birds and beasts including a herd of carpinchos which are of the guinea pig family and the size of Shetland ponies. They are also riddled with lice and extremely friendly. We travelled for hundreds of miles in an auto-carrill, a small Ford car attached to the railway tracks which, whenever there was the danger of meeting an express train head-on, was shunted into a siding.

It was an extraordinary journey, as clear in my memory as if it had happened only last week. I recall a moment of particular enchantment when we stopped in bright moonlight to stretch our legs and eat some sandwiches. An enormous valley spread all around us encircled by snow-capped mountains under a sky blazing with myriads of stars. The silence was awe-inspiring and broken only by an occasional raucous cough from a herd of llamas grazing nearby. We felt that we were on the roof of the world and it was with the utmost reluctance that we finally climbed back into our bizarre vehicle and continued our journey to Arequipa where we arrived at two in the morning and drew up before the Quinta Bates.

The Quinta Bates was a hotel and rest-house, and we were greeted by Tia Bates, the redoubtable lady who ran it, who was waiting for us in a red merino dressing gown. She was an eccentric and delightful character, long since dead, with wild grey hair, a humorous glint in her eye and an air of ineffable distinction. A mixture of cosy landlady and Grand Duchess, whom we loved immediately. I had the luck to see her once again in later years when she suddenly appeared in my dressing room after a matinée of *Design for Living* in New York. We stayed with her gratefully for ten days before going on to La Paz and Lima where, all in one day, there was a revolution and an earthquake. The former left us unmoved but the latter knocked us off our stools in the bar where we were having a drink before lunch and caused me to crack my head against a heavy brass spittoon.

After this, having mutually agreed that Peru was a trifle restless, we flew to Panama where we relaxed for a few days in lovely tropical heat. It was in Panama, or rather Colon, which is the Atlantic end of the Canal, that our journey ended. Jeff had to go back to England and I discovered a Norwegian freight-boat called – why, I shall never know – the *Toronto*, in which I was able to reserve the Owner's Suite for myself. It was a small ship and I was the only passenger. I took my meals with the Captain who was a Joseph Conrad character; clear-eyed, humorous and a militant atheist. Occasionally in the evenings after dinner which was served at six o'clock sharp, I used to join the crew in the fo'c'sle for drinks and a sing-song. The drinks were potent and the sing-songs remarkable for their complete lack of musical talent. I should like to be able to state nostalgically that rich tenor and baritone voices echoed out into the darkness and mingled with the eternal murmur of the sea and the sighing of the wind through the rigging, creating an atmosphere of sublime nautical magic, but to do so would be, alas, sadly inaccurate. Their voices echoed out into the darkness all right but with such violence that only a cyclone sighing through the rigging could have been heard above them. Those raucous evenings however were sufficiently charged with maritime romanticism to remain for ever in my memory. One of the crew members, a strapping bearded young Viking clad in the briefest pair of shorts I have ever seen, not only played a guitar but actually wore a single gold earring. I remember reflecting at the time how much better it would have been if he had been content to allow his spectacular appearance to strike the romantic note and left his guitar at home.

The ten days I spent in that small cargo ship creeping slowly up the Pacific coast of America were among the most enjoyable I have ever known. I was only slightly weary after the ardours and adventures of Latin America. I had no fellow passengers to fascinate, bore or repel me. There was nothing to do from dawn until dawn. As a concession to the Captain I wore shorts and a shirt for meals, for the rest of the time until the night closed down I wore nothing at all. I had, as always, a suitcase full of books. I also had my typewriter on which, with no urgency, no consciousness of Time's winged chariot at my back, I began and completed *Design for Living*. The idea slipped into my mind, with neither prayer nor supplication, on the first evening out of Panama. I wrote it morning after morning almost effortlessly, with none of the routine moments of unbalanced exultance or black despair. It was a painless confinement and no instruments were required to ease the birth beyond an extra typewriter ribbon, which I happened to have with me. I finished it tidily two days before we were due to dock in Los Angeles and celebrated the occasion by having a royal piss-up with the crew, in which even the Captain, briefly shedding a little of his Nordic austerity, joined with enthusiasm. The ship, curious to relate, remained on an even keel and in due course, about twenty-eight hours later, deposited me in a blaze of early morning sunshine on to the dockside of Los Angeles harbour where Jack, in a state of controlled hysteria, met me. What had caused his hysteria was that none of the port officials had ever heard of the *Toronto*, and he had spent a frantic hour rushing from shipping office to shipping office trying to locate it. Jack of course was unaccustomed to meet any craft of lesser tonnage than the *Queen Mary* and when he finally appeared, breathless in my cabin, had to be soothed by gin in a toothglass.

8

The next ten days were in direct contrast to those I had passed on board that tranquil little ship. I have been assured by many of my friends that life in Hollywood can be as calm and uneventful as in an English Cathedral town. This may be so for those who live there but for those who visit it as I did, for a brief spell, it is hectic in the extreme. When ultimately I fell into my bed on the Super Chief at Pasadena I was so exhausted that I slept almost continually until the train got to Chicago. I had enjoyed myself immensely but the pace had been killing. Dinner parties, supper parties, brunches, hours spent in driving over mountains and through valleys to get to and from the various houses of hospitable friends. I had forgotten the vast distance it is necessary to travel to get from one gracious home to another. I had also forgotten how curiously similar they seem to be once you have arrived in them. All luxuriously comfortable, all with swimming pools and every one of them the pride and joy of its owner. The food I ate in them seemed to have been cooked by the same expert chef. True the cocktail canapés or 'Appetizers' varied a bit in different houses; in some the little rounds of toast with meltingly succulent cheese might be discarded in favour of little rounds of toast with little rounds of bacon wrapped round little hot prunes but the main gastronomic delights were, or seemed to have been, identical. I had downed so many endless slices of rare roast beef, so many thousand perfectly roasted potatoes and fields of tender green broccoli submerged under yellow seas of sauce Hollandaise that when in the dining car of the Super Chief I was faced with a tough railway steak and some pressure-cooked tasteless vegetables, I fell on them with a sigh of relief.

Then of course I realised, as the train gathered speed, that for the next three days I would also not have to keep awake until the small hours staring at a movie screen. In those days in Hollywood no private dinner party was complete without a full length epic beginning before you had gulped down your coffee. It was all done with the greatest style and comfort. The guests settled themselves in vast arm-chairs with drinks on small tables at their elbows. A screen either rose noiselessly from the floor or came down from the ceiling or swung into view on hinged bookshelves and there you were luxuriously stuck for a minimum of two hours. If you happened to have seen that particular movie before it was just too bad, but in fairness it must be admitted that this contingency seldom arose. The film exhibited was invariably brand new and usually starred your hostess which was all very well if you enjoyed it but embarrassing if you didn't. Happily for me the majority of my hostesses were good actresses and most of the movies excellent but there is no denying that those sybaritic evenings were conversationally arid. In addition to these nocturnal distractions there was the daily dose of celluloid to be digested. I never set foot in a studio without being led almost immediately to a projection room where I was installed in the usual vast arm-chair with a drink at my elbow and shown whole films, half films, rough-cuts and rushes. It was in one of these projection rooms that I first saw Norma Shearer and Robert Montgomery in *Private Lives.* I remember that just as the lights went out Bob, who was sitting next to me, slipped into my hand an expensive watch with my initials on it. 'This,' he hissed, 'is to prevent you from saying what you really think of my performance!' It didn't, because I thought his and Norma's performance charming and was not required to dissemble. At all events it was a beguiling and typical gesture.

So much has been written about Hollywood both in praise and dispraise that I feel it would be redundant to add my own view to the swollen flood; however I cannot resist making a few comments, not on the basis of the brief ten days described above but because since then I have revisited it several times and on one occasion actually worked there. Not in a movie, but in a television 'Spectacular' of *Blithe Spirit* with Claudette Colbert, Lauren Bacall, Mildred Natwick and myself in the four leading parts. I rented a small attractive house on the side of a hill and for six weeks lived a regular Hollywood life. Regular is the operative word, for anyone who works professionally, even for a short time, in that curious environment realises very quickly that discipline, and fairly rigid discipline at that, is the keynote of existence. For those readers of movie magazines who imagine that life in that unique Never Never Land is an endless round of glamorous parties and star-spangled orgies, the truth would be sadly disillusioning. Perhaps in its earlier years when fascinating silent stars galloped about on mettlesome horses, indulged in over-publicised marriages and divorces and flung themselves in and out of each other's swimming pools life was less real and less earnest. Now, at any rate, it is so controlled and ordered as to be almost humdrum. True, on Saturday nights with a work-free Sabbath just ahead, there are occasional social and even sexual junketings, but on the other six evenings of the week most of the big box-office stars are usually in bed by ten with Ovaltine rather than champagne and scripts rather than lovers. Film-making, contrary to much popular belief, is a demanding and exhausting business. The working hours alone preclude many opportunities for casual dalliance. During the shooting period of any movie not only the floor crews and the studio operators but the directors and extras and actors have to be ready and on the set by eight o'clock in the morning. For those performers who happen to be playing characters necessitating an elaborate make-up, the call is still earlier. This, taking into account the time getting to the studio from wherever you happen to be living, means being torn from sleep at about five-thirty a.m. When I was making my first picture *The Scoundrel* in 1936 at the Paramount Astoria Studios in Brooklyn, I remember driving over the 59th Street Bridge every morning for weeks and watching the dawn come up. In Hollywood of course, owing to the climate for one thing, conditions are more agreeable than in New York in mid-winter. To watch the sun rise over majestic mountains and the Pacific Ocean is pleasanter than watching it rise over skyscrapers and blocks of dirty ice drifting down the East River.

Another dismaying facet of 'Movie' life in Hollywood – and alas elsewhere – is the soul-destroying tradition of 'conferences'. I don't know when this ghastly innovation first came into being but I do know from personal experience that it is the most monumental, ego-strutting time-waster in the business. A film conference, ideally speaking, should be a brief discussion between the director and heads of departments concerning ways and means, general procedure and time schedules. What it usually is is nothing of the sort. A large group of people, many of them redundant, sits around a table in somebody's office with pads and pencils and sometimes a jug of water and a few glasses in front of them, and talk a great deal.

I must here state parenthetically that I am temperamentally allergic to conferences or committee meetings of any kind. During my twenty years tenure of office as President of the Actor's Orphanage I incurred much criticism for cutting them down to the minimum. We are all aware that the egos of most human beings are frustrated in some way for some reason or other, and, so far as I have observed, committee meetings of any sort provide baleful opportunities for these egos to puff themselves up and waste their own time and everybody else's. I am convinced that the frequent recurrence of Board Meetings in all big businesses can mostly be accounted for by the fact that the majority of the members present welcome a chance to show off which their wives deny them at home. When a committee is formed by actors and actresses whose egos are overdeveloped anyhow, the result is more often than not, chaotic.

I remember once, at one of the first Orphanage meetings at which I presided, a famous actor who shall be nameless, stood up and delivered an impassioned speech in defence of a former administrator of the funds whom I had sacked for gross incompetence. The actor, with blazing eyes, fulminated against me for dismissing this saintly character who had lovingly devoted thirty years of his life to the dear children. (The actor was unaware that the saintly character had not only been more than adequately paid for his lifelong devotion but was rumoured to have handled the funds of the charity a trifle whimsically.) When he had finished his tirade and sat down, deeply moved by his own eloquence, I asked him civilly whether he had ever been to the Orphanage and if he knew where it was. He was forced to admit, as I suspected, that he hadn't and didn't. My lawyer, whom I had wisely invited to be present, then produced documents proving conclusively that the financial affairs of the Orphanage had been consistently mismanaged for many years; that many important decisions had been made in committee lacking the adequate quorum and that the administration had been so lax for so many years that many of the committee members present might be liable to criminal prosecution. This, not unnaturally, caused a profound sensation and I was feverishly elected President for five years.

The first film conference I ever attended took place in Hollywood three days after I had landed from my South American travels, in an office on the Fox lot. As I entered the room my heart sank at the familiar spectacle. There was the shiny table, there were the pads and pencils and the jugs of water. On this occasion however it was not Child Welfare that was to be discussed but the movie version of *Cavalcade*. Also present was a collection of people, many of whom I had never seen before and have never seen since. What their particular functions were and why they were present I had as little idea then as I have now. In due course, after various introductions had been made, we all sat down. I was placed on the right of the Chairman whose name unfortunately eludes me. He was exceedingly courteous and had one of those affable grey faces that one immediately forgets. An anonymous script writer – not Reginald Berkely, who ultimately did a fine script – was invited by the Chairman to start the ball rolling by giving us his ideas. There was a slight pause while he put on his glasses and assembled a sheaf of typewritten sheets of paper before him. He then cleared his throat and began, with admirable assurance, to speak.

'The opening of the picture as I see it should be as follows.' He paused, consulted his notes for a moment and then went on. 'After the credits, which should rise slowly up the screen from the bottom to the top against a panorama of moving clouds, we see the branch of a tree in winter. The branch is flecked with snow, and on it is perched a little bird, just one little bird, looking lonely and forlorn. As we look at the little bird the background music swells and it is suddenly Spring. The tree is covered with tender young leaves and the original bird has been joined by hundreds of other birds, fluttering and chirruping and building their nests.' He sat back in his chair and regarded us with a complacent smile. Whether he expected us to give a round of applause or cry in unison that we did believe in fairies I shall never know because, seized with a violent inward fury, I rose to my feet. I think it was that smile as much as anything else that exasperated me. I looked around the table at all those vacuous faces waiting so attentively for further treacly symbolism and realised with dreadful clarity that all the worst stories I had heard about the Hollywood mentality must have been, if anything, understated. I also knew that if I stayed at that table one minute longer I should probably lose my temper and be very rude indeed and that to make an ugly scene at such an early stage of the proceedings would do more harm than good. So, forcing my lips into an apologetic smile, I said that I had completely forgotten an appointment of pressing urgency at the Beverly Wilshire Hotel and left the conference room never to return.

The sale of the *Cavalcade* movie rights had occurred long after the play opened, actually only a few weeks before it closed. I thought, in common with everyone else connected with the production, that of all the plays I had ever written *Cavalcade* was the most likely to be snapped up immediately by the movie boys. It had a stirring story, good parts, lots of opportunity for spectacle and as it had originally been written in a series of short scenes it could, with the minimum of effort, have been adapted for the screen practically as it was. The cinema Moguls however thought otherwise. *Cavalcade* was relentlessly turned down by all the major studios in Hollywood and in England. It was ultimately bought by the flimsiest of coincidences.

A certain Mrs Tinker, to whom I have every reason to be grateful – as indeed have numberless other people – happened to be in London during the last weeks of the run of *Cavalcade* and went with a friend to Drury Lane Theatre. She was so impressed by the play that, on returning to her hotel, she immediately sent a cable to Mr Tinker, urging him to acquire the film rights at all costs. Mr Tinker had recently been elected as one of the Directors of the Fox Studios and, obviously aware that he had married a remarkably intelligent woman, put her suggestion before the Board. Not having been present I cannot vouch for the accuracy of what I have been told took place. Apparently Mr Tinker was swiftly snubbed for his pains and the suggestion arbitrarily dismissed. However dear Mr Tinker, whom sad to say I never met, was obviously not the type of man who cares to have his opinions summarily ignored; in addition to which he was very rich, and it was thanks to his financial intervention that Fox Studios had evaded bankruptcy by the skin of their perfectly capped teeth. I like to imagine that there was a strong dramatic Galsworthian scene in course of which Mr Tinker, purple in the face, delivered a blistering tirade, hammered the desk with his clenched fist and finally by sheer force of Right over Might won his point and sank down in his chair mopping his face with a bandana handkerchief, but I fear that the reality was more prosaic.

At all events he did win his point and, bitterly against its will, Fox Films capitulated. A week or so later, evidently having decided that they might as well be hung for a sheep as for a lamb, they sent over to London a posse of cameramen and cameras and assistant directors and production managers and, possibly, clapper boys to film the play as it was presented on stage. (Actually a very sensible procedure and I could only wish that other Hollywood studios would adopt it.) This resulted in three days intensive work and my beloved company earning a lot of extra money. Having gone this far Fox considered that it had done enough, Tinkers or no Tinkers, and beyond engaging an English director called Frank Lloyd, who I believe had been wandering unemployed through the Hollywood limbo for some time, they washed their hands of the whole affair and turned their dangerous attention to more important matters.

This of course was the greatest luck of all. Had they been enthusiastic about *Cavalcade* it would inevitably have been ruined. Millions would have been spent; scads of script-writers would have been engaged to change the play beyond all recognition; stars of grotesque unsuitability would have been asked to play the leading parts; Ace directors would have been hired and fired left and right and the result would have been an epic Hollywood shambles. As it was, their sulky withdrawal from the situation enabled Frank Lloyd, who was a brilliant director, to carry on with his job without indeed much encouragement but also without interference. He proceeded to engage an excellent cast headed by Diana Wynyard, Clive Brook, Frank Lawton, Ursula Jeans, Una O'Connor and Irene Browne (the latter two actresses having played in the London production), none of whom could be described as top-flight Hollywood stars and all of whom were first rate actors. The picture was shot within a reasonable time and I believe stayed more or less within its financial budget. It was also shot in almost cloistered seclusion. Few if any top executives' wives and sweethearts and friends were invited on to the set to stand about and gape and get in everyone's way, although it would delight me to think that Mr and Mrs Tinker had been granted full access at all times and been provided with canvas chairs with their names emblazoned on them in gold.

It was only I believe when the picture was in its last days of shooting that word got around that it was liable to be fairly sensational and all the little Foxes scurried out of their embossed leather holes and began to sniff around and clamber on to the bandwagon. When at last it had been titled and dubbed and shown secretly in Foxy projection rooms, the jig was up. Rumour has it that a very bright young man who had ardently supported the film at one of the initial conferences and been immediately fired was hurriedly re-engaged with an astronomical rise in salary. I devoutly hope that this is true but fear it is apocryphal.

As far as I can remember *Cavalcade* opened more or less simultaneously in Hollywood and New York and was acclaimed on all sides as one of the greatest pictures ever made which, at that time, I honestly think it was. A little later it repeated its triumph in London and throughout the world. All of which was highly gratifying for the authors, actors, the director and all concerned, and absolutely lovely for Mr and Mrs Tinker.

9

Upon arrival in New York I read *Design for Living* to Lynn and Alfred who were even more enthusiastic than I had hoped they would be. Like many people, myself included, neither of them really enjoy being read to. They much prefer to have the script to themselves and concentrate on it without the distraction of having to listen to someone else's voice and intonations. I, however, while agreeing with them entirely, have my own ego to think about. Much as I dislike being read aloud to, I very much enjoy reading aloud, and the Lunts with loving indulgence resigned themselves to the inevitable. They sat like beautifully behaved mice, nobody sighed or yawned or coughed and Alfred mixed stimulating little drinks between each act. It was a very happy occasion. So often in our profession, as indeed in many others, dreams are dreamed which are never realised and hopeful plans made which ultimately come to dust. This was a long established dream for all three of us and that first reading was the moment when it actually came true. Fortunately later on it didn't let us down, the play was an enormous success and all was well, but that was the moment of magic. I am aware that my worst friends could not accuse me of diffidence. I am and always have been self-assured, on the surface at any rate, but no good writer, even when exultant at having finished a new work, is ever quite quite sure, just as no actors, or at least very few, can step on the stage on an opening night without being nervous. A few pretend to be immune to this occupational disease and a few are strong willed enough to convince themselves that this immunity is genuine but I for one find it hard to believe. Admittedly when I was a child in the theatre I bounced on without a qualm and thoroughly enjoyed myself, but a child – even a child star which I was not – is too young to feel the weight of responsibility which comes when a certain status has been achieved. It is only natural I think that established stars should become more and more prone to stage fright as the years stack up behind them. They have gradually, in course of their careers, unconsciously set their own standards, and it is not fear of the audience or terror that they might forget their lines that makes them tremble; it is the dread that those self-imposed standards may not, for once, be upheld. I do not believe this to be a conscious thought process but I do believe that it is the fundamental reason underlying our first-night miseries. I have little patience however with those who indulge their nervousness to the extent of spoiling their performances. I have seen this happen on occasion and been aware of irritation rather than professional sympathy. If an actor is undisciplined enough to allow his own self-consciousness to intervene between himself and his talent he should leave the theatrical profession and devote himself to some less agitating occupation.

First-night nerves are inevitable and have to be taken into consideration as one of the hazards of the game. It is no use hoping to banish them entirely so therefore the obvious thing is to utilise them. To be able to do this successfully requires humour, technique and a strong will. Fortunately very few first rate actors lack these requirements. On they go with trembling hands and dry mouths, longing to be anywhere else but where they are and praying for the stage to open and pitch them into oblivion. Then, when the applause which greets their first entrance dies away like a volley of musket fire on a battlefield and they discover, astonishingly, that they are still alive, the stage music begins. They hear their voices saying the lines and identify gratefully (sometimes) the misty faces of their fellow actors and suddenly, sometimes gradually, they begin almost to enjoy themselves. The sooner they do this the better it is for the audience and the author and certainly for themselves.

The Lunts were so pleased with the play and we were all three in such a state of happy excitement that we longed to cast it and go into rehearsal right away, but circumstances and common sense restrained us. It would be the height of folly to open a new play in New York at the beginning of summer when all but the biggest hits are about to fold up. Also I had a contract with C. B. Cochran to do a revue at the Adelphi Theatre in London, so we agreed, reluctantly, to postpone the production of *Design for Living* until early in the following year.

Before I left for London however a few important decisions had to be made. The first and most important of these was which management to select to present the play. On the face of it this statement appears to be insufferably smug, but it must be remembered that in 1931 Lynn and Alfred and I were individually ace-high box office attractions. (To pursue smugness still further, we still are in 1967, although we may be getting a little brown at the edges.) Had any of us decided to star in any given play we could have been pretty certain of success, always provided that the given play was a reasonable one. Few stars, however popular, can triumph over a bad script. The combination of the three of us therefore, in the eyes of all the commercial managements, was 'a consummation devoutly to be wished', even though we had stipulated a limited run. I found myself in a very enviable situation, and it would be hypocritical to pretend that I didn't enjoy it very much indeed. I was overwhelmed by vast bouquets of flowers and cases of champagne, whisky, gin and brandy from most of the leading New York managements. On the cards accompanying these gifts no mention of my new play was made, they were apparently just friendly, motiveless gestures of welcome. I enjoyed receiving them immensely although my hotel room became as stuffy and overcrowded as the Orchid House in Kew Gardens.

The only manager extant who didn't send so much as a box of chocolate peppermints was Max Gordon, possibly because at that particular moment of his career he couldn't afford to. Instead he appeared a few days after my arrival and announced dramatically that if I didn't allow him to present *Design for Living* he would cut his throat then and there. I cherished then and still do a warm affection for Max Gordon. His passionate love of the Theatre illuminates his whole personality like a travelling spotlight. No dedicated crusader, no valiant knight of King Arthur's Court could have pursued the Holy Grail with a quarter of the ecstatic adoration that Max pursues the Drama. When, in response to his threat of immediate suicide, I replied nonchalantly that of course he could present the play, he went into such convulsions of gibbering ecstasy that I had to give him some water in the tooth mug from my bathroom. It was a highly gratifying moment for both of us. For Max, because he had, during the last few seasons, fallen from grace as a successful producer by putting on a series of flops, for me because it enabled me to pay off a debt that I had owed him for a long time. It was not a financial debt but a moral one.

In 1930 when Gertie and I were playing *Private Lives* at the Phoenix (Adrianne Allen and a young actor called Laurence Olivier were also in the cast), Max Gordon had come to see the play and burst into my dressing-room after the performance like a fire-cracker. Never have I been drenched by such a flood of articulate praise. He ranted and roared and bounced up and down and the air glittered with superlatives. It was not until he had exhausted himself (not me) that his theatrical integrity over-rode his professional tact and he blurted out, almost shockingly in the golden glow he had created, a home truth which endeared him to me for ever. 'Why the hell did you ruin the effect of your whole performance by mugging and overplaying the breakfast scene in the last act?' The smile of delighted but modest deprecation that I always assume when receiving extravagant praise was wiped away as abruptly as if he had suddenly emptied a jug of iced water over my head. I was, for a split second, completely flabbergasted. Disregarding my pained astonishment and carried away by his own conviction, he proceeded to press his point home with deadly determination. To see an actor of my quality and experience descend to the depths of cheap vaudeville hamming in the last act of a play after playing the first two with unparalleled taste and brilliance (better) was one of the most miserable experiences he had ever had in the theatre. It was not only an insult to the audience but to my own talent and, he continued, so outraged was he that if he had not happened to be sitting in the middle of a row he would have got up and left the theatre. He went on in this vein for several minutes until suddenly seized by the suspicion that he might be going too far, he struck his forehead a resounding blow and faltered to a stop.

Dear Max, I can clearly remember his expression of guilty dismay until this day. There was, so far as I can recall, a moment or two of fraught silence, which I shattered by bursting out laughing. It was quite genuine laughter although I must admit that quite a lot of it was on the wrong side of my face. Sometime later when the success of *Design For Living* had rocketed him back to his rightful place as a leading New York producer he came, rather coyly, to visit me. I received him sitting up in bed in my hotel bedroom. I don't remember that I was ill, merely sitting up in bed. Max bumbled about the room for a while until he finally sat down and looking almost sheepish, he made me a proposition. The proposition was that from that moment onwards he wished me to have first refusal of the English rights of every play he produced. Not unnaturally I was touched by this most generous gesture and accepted it with alacrity. We shook hands solemnly on the deal and that was that.

He was of course true to his word, and, as a result of this sentimental little episode, I received, wherever I happened to be, every new script that was bought by the Gordon Office. For one reason or other I was compelled to turn them all down until one day there arrived the script of *Born Yesterday*. The play, which I had not seen, was a smash hit in New York, and when I read it I clearly understood why. Written by Garson Kanin, an old friend of mine, it was witty and well constructed and obviously a pretty sound commercial proposition for London or anywhere else. Delighted that I could at last avail myself of Max's initial gesture, I cabled to him immediately and said I was prepared to direct the play myself under the Tennent Management in London within the next few months. Shortly afterwards, when I had discussed it with Hugh Beaumont and we were tentatively casting it in our minds, a further cable arrived from Max, and a very agonised cable it was, explaining that after all I couldn't have the English rights because, unbeknown to him, Garson had already promised them to Larry Olivier who was then in management at the St James's Theatre. This naturally was a disappointment but as all concerned were personal friends of mine, my only course was to bow myself gracefully out of the picture, so I cabled Max at once renouncing my promised rights and wishing everybody good luck. When the play was ultimately produced in London it ran for a year, and a few weeks after it had finally closed, I received a cheque from Max Gordon for all his personal royalties. It was a fairly large cheque, and certainly a very large gesture.

10

In the spring of 1932 I sailed from New York to England in the *Bremen* or the *Europa*, I forget which, because the Germans with their usual low cunning had designed both their principal Atlantic liners to look exactly the same. I presume that there must have been some minor difference but to the casual eye they were identical. The same ornate decor in the main saloons and private cabins; the same expensive but rather sickly colour scheme in curtains and upholstery; and the same, faintly guilty obsequiousness of the personnel. I may of course have imagined this because of my own suppressed guilt in travelling in a German ship. The 1914–18 war was long over and done with, but it had cast a heavy shadow over my adolescence and although in the nineteen-thirties the international skies were apparently cloudless and Europe was just one big cosy happy family, I was perceptive enough to realize that none of it quite rang true. Later, as the decade progressed towards the holocaust of 1939, my sense of inward insecurity proved to have been dismally prophetic. With a few individual exceptions the German people have always been antipathetic to me. There is something about the Teutonic mentality that grates on my nerves and although in the twenties and thirties I had been received by them with the utmost courtesy and hospitality and although their appreciation of me as a writer has been unstintingly generous there remains in the depth of my mind an area of resistance, an inherent feeling of distrust. On the surface this can easily be accounted for by the two World Wars, but actually I think it is something more, possibly their fundamental lack of humour. No nation with a grain of genuine humour could have accepted seriously the grotesque rantings and roarings of Adolf Hitler. His physical appearance alone should have been sufficient for a belly laugh. I find it almost impossible to believe now as I found it impossible to believe at the time that a man with those stumpy female little legs, those rounded hips and that comedic moustache could subjugate a nation of several millions. I remember that even during the gloomiest days of the war I was unable to look at him on a cinema screen without giggling. Mussolini with his vast head and pop eyes was admittedly fairly silly-looking but at least he had a certain masculine virility and compared with the Führer he was an Adonis.

In the summer of 1938 I happened to be in Rome on my way either to or from Capri. I lingered for a few days because Rome has for me much charm, particularly in the summer. I have spent many happy hours sitting at a café table on the Via Veneto and watching the crowds stroll by. I find this an enjoyable occupation in whatever city I happen to be in, except London of course where one can't do it at all, but Rome is my favourite. That long sloping promenade from the gates of the Farnese gardens to the Excelsior Hotel, and the slow-moving, ceaseless procession of summer-clad individuals of all shapes and sizes and nationalities, fascinates me for hours on end. When in 1938 I decided one sunny afternoon to renounce the pleasures of the Via Veneto and go to a rally in the Stadium in order to see Mussolini in the all too solid flesh, it was with considerable reluctance. However my curiosity to see The Duce at close quarters overcame my midsummer lassitude and, having procured an aisle seat on the third row from the hotel concierge, I drove off through the parched terracotta streets to have a look at Italy's saviour.

It was a long time before he appeared and I sat sweating on a skittish little wooden chair that wobbled dangerously if I made the slightest movement, while hundreds and hundreds of Fascist youths marched up and down and back and forth shining with zeal and drilling themselves to a lather. They were on the whole a handsome lot but the expression of dedicated fanaticism on their moist young faces was fairly irritating. A few weeks previously I had spent a week-end in Kent with Anthony and Beatrice Eden. Anthony, just returned from summit conference or other, had given me a blow by blow description of Mussolini at an official lunch party given in Anthony's honour. Apparently the harmony of the occasion had been unwittingly shattered by Anthony himself at the very outset. The guests, I think about twenty of them, were standing about sipping their cocktails and making polite conversation when the large double doors were flung open and luncheon was announced. The Duce, with an imperial gesture motioned Anthony to come with him into the dining-room but Anthony, with his customary good manners, hung back and said, 'What about the gals?' This apparently so infuriated Mussolini that he marched angrily into the dining-room himself leaving Anthony and the rest of the party to follow as best they might. I don't know why but I have always treasured this little vignette; I suppose it is the conflict between dictatorial flamboyance and unyielding British public school rectitude that makes it so funny. Anthony had also told me that The Duce, at close quarters, had a trick of whirling his tiny brown eyes round and round like catherine wheels. I suspected at the time that Anthony had invented this fascinating accomplishment, but I learned later from other impeccably reliable sources that it was absolutely true.

So it was not without pleasurable anticipation that I wriggled on my uncomfortable little chair on that blazing summer afternoon in 1938. At long, long last the interminable drilling came to an end and after a pause during which the vast audience chanted 'Duce-Duce-Duce' at the top of its lungs, he, himself, the cocky little big-shot strutted into the arena. Prepared as I was to be discreetly amused, as I always am when faced with blatantly organised rabble-rousing, I was not prepared for the actual close-up of the hero when he appeared. He had, most unwisely, squeezed his squat little figure into a dazzling white uniform; his face, bursting out of the top of it looked like an enormous, purple-red Victoria plum surmounted by a black and gold tasselled forage-cap several sizes too small. In addition to all this his expression, as he stood acknowledging the shrieks of the crowd and shooting his right arm out and back like a clockwork doll, was so ludicrously pompous and self-important that I burst into uncontrollable laughter. Realising that in the circumstances this was not only tactless but downright dangerous, I tried, not entirely successfully, to disguise it as a coughing fit and, with my handkerchief pressed against my face I stumbled up the steep wooden steps and out of the Stadium, hailed a taxi and collapsed on the back seat of it. This was the only time in my life I have experienced a full, hundred per cent, knockout *fou rire* all by myself. I have endured many a bout of hysteria in the company of sympathetic friends and have had to be led, sobbing convulsively, from theatres, churches and opera houses, but never before entirely alone in alien surroundings. I can remember now the bewildered expression of the taxi driver as he watched me in his driving mirror writhing and groaning in the back of his cab. On reflection I can only thank God that I never attended one of Hitler's free-for-alls in Munich or Berlin. I have a feeling that the Germans might have been quicker on the draw than the volatile Italians and that I should have found myself in very serious trouble indeed.

II

During the run of *Design For Living* there had been much cable communication between Cochran and me regarding the revue I had undertaken to write for him. This revue, after various titles had been suggested and discarded, was ultimately called *Words and Music* and was presented by C. B. Cochran at the Opera House Manchester on August 25th 1932. On September 16th it opened at the Adelphi in London where it ran for several months, not, as I had hoped, for two years. It was a good revue on the whole and received excellent notices but what it lacked was a big star, or better still, two big stars. The cast included Ivy St Helier, Joyce Barbour, John Mills, Romney Brent and Doris Hare, all of whom were expert performers but none of whom at this time had that indisputable star quality which commands queues at the box office. Later it was produced in New York under the title *Set To Music* with Beatrice Lillie and Richard haydn. Nobody could question the 'star' status of Beatrice Lillie but even with her name over the marquee the show, after three months capacity business, lingered on for a further month or so and then closed. All of which, I am reluctantly forced to admit, proves that the revue itself wasn't quite as good as it should have been. It had some good songs in it, notably 'Mad Dogs and Englishmen' and 'Mad About the Boy' and a hilarious first act finale, 'The Midnight Matinée', in which Beatrice was inimitably funny as the amateur lady organizer, but it didn't hit the jackpot and that was that.

When I was a very little boy my beloved housemaid-cum-nurse, Emma, used to admonish me by saying, 'Don't be too sharp or you'll cut yourself!' This I think, on looking back, was what was wrong with *Words and Music*. It was too clever by half. It contained too much satire and too little glamour to attract the masses. However as it didn't exactly flop humiliatingly in either London or New York I can quite happily chalk it up as a near miss and remember it with affection. I am also grateful to it for giving me one of the most fascinating experiences of my life.

During the Manchester try-out the Musical Director was suddenly taken ill and I, at two hours' notice, decided to conduct the orchestra myself. This, considering that I could neither read nor write music, was a fairly impertinent decision. I have never been embarrassed by my technical ignorance. Many of the most successful composers of light music are unable to transcribe a note of it. Being gifted with an impeccable ear I can distinguish a wrong note in a symphony orchestra providing that the symphony orchestra happens to be playing one of my own compositions. This 'Musical Ear' is far from being unique and I am proud to share it with Irving Berlin and the late Jerome D. Kern to name only two. Even George Gershwin before he devoted four years of intensive study to counter-point and harmony was unable to write down his music unaided, although he had already been responsible for several Broadway musicals loaded with song hits. Irving Berlin, who I suppose has composed more lilting popular melodies than any man alive, cannot even play his own tunes effectively on the piano. He hammers them out, without brio, in the key of C Major which (for the benefit of the uninitiated) is the only key on the piano that has none of those tiresome black notes in it. Many years ago another haphazard composer, George M. Cohan, was generous enough to send me a specially designed upright on which the key could be changed by turning a handle. It was a fearsome instrument and the tone was ghastly but I was able to strum away on it in my own favourite key – E Flat – with no danger of imperilling my vocal range. Later, impelled by a guilty feeling that I was somehow cheating, I discarded it and forced my reluctant fingers into dreadful keys bristling with unsympathetic sharps but I soon gave up the struggle and reverted to my own true love. Over the years my untutored piano playing has improved considerably but still today when I have heard a tune in some musical or other that I wish to recapture, E Flat is my first instinctive choice. Later, with blood and sweat, I may succeed in transposing it but the effort involved is seldom worth the trouble.

Although a composer of popular music can afford to be as key-bound as he likes, a conductor of an orchestra most certainly can't. He must be able to recognise accurately every confusing little squiggle on the manuscript and issue instructions to his instrumentalists in the complicated jargon that they alone can understand. As I was abysmally incapable of any of this it was with considerable trepidation that I walked into the band-room of the Opera House Manchester a quarter of an hour before the overture and announced to the startled gentlemen of the orchestra that I was going to conduct that evening's performance. I had taken the precaution of rehearsing for two hours in my suite at the Midland Hotel during which Elsie April, my staunch musical adviser, patiently explained to me the changes of rhythm I should be required to beat out in course of the evening. When finally I arrived, more dead than alive, in the orchestra pit itself, I placed

326

her on the ground at my feet just below the podium where she crouched like a gnome with the open score on her knees. When I appeared, the front of the house limelight operator, whom I could willingly have garrotted, flung a dazzling pink and amber spotlight on to me and I was forced to acknowledge a cheerful round of applause. Then, a trifle theatrically I fear, I held out my arms commandingly, whereupon there was a loud roll on the drums. I jumped as if I'd been shot and hissed to Elsie out of the corner of my mouth. 'What the hell's that? It isn't in the score.' 'Don't be silly dear,' she replied calmly. 'It's the National Anthem. Just a straight four-four all through. Take it nice and slowly.' There was nothing to do but obey her instructions, so I chopped my right arm in a firm down-beat and a wave of deafening sound enveloped me through which I could hear the scuffling noise of the audience rising to its feet behind me. Then, after a short pause out went my arms again and I began to beat out the first number of the overture which incidentally I had never heard before owing to being occupied with the company back-stage while it was being rehearsed. I went on doggedly while Elsie, at my feet, kept up a running commentary. 'That's right dear – just go on like that for thirty-two bars – look out here comes a modulation into three-four – that's right you're doing fine, nothing to worry about now until you get to the six-eight, just two in a bar dear nice and steady.' By the end of the overture I had begun to feel my oats and managed to beat my way more or less successfully through the whole show. For the rather complicated ballet music I surrendered the baton to Spike Hughes who had orchestrated it.

Taken all in all those were two of the most alarming and enjoyable hours I have ever spent. The next morning I was unable to move my right arm but after having it massaged several times during the day I was able to conduct the show again in the evening. I conducted every performance for two weeks, and it wasn't until Hyam Greenbaum, whom Cockie had himself engaged in London, arrived in Manchester that I was forced to relinquish that lovely little white stick with the knob on the end. Only three more times in later years was I able to enjoy the exacting, ego-boosting experience. Once was during the run of

Operette in Manchester, when more or less the same sort of crisis occurred. This time the cast was headed by Peggy Wood and Fritzi Massary. Fritzi Massary, who had been the greatest operatic star in Germany for many years until the advent of the Nazis in 1933 forced her to leave the country, had been, during her resplendent and glamorous career, accustomed to the best conductors and composers in Europe including Leo Fall and Franz Lehár, several of whose operettas she had created in Berlin. I fully expected an ugly but justified display of temperament when she found herself on the stage faced by an amateur who couldn't even read a page of sheet music, let alone an orchestral score. But I needn't have worried. She was too great an artiste and too wise a woman to waste time in an emergency. She gave me such professional, whole-hearted co-operation that, when it came to her big *Wiener Valse* number in the last act, the applause was overwhelming and held up the show for several minutes. Later on when *Operette* had opened in London at His Majesty's Theatre and she had scored a personal triumph, it became an understood thing between us that, on gala occasions when visiting celebrities or members of the Royal Family were present, I would slip into the orchestra pit to conduct that particular number especially for her. I am bound to admit however that she tore the place up with it at every performance whether I was there or not, but I can also assert, without undue modesty, that a little extra magic occurred when she looked down and saw me poised, with my arms out, red carnation and all. Fritzi Massary was one of the most important artists I have ever been privileged to work with and I shall never cease to be grateful to her.

The third and last time I waved a baton was on the quarterdeck of H.M.S. *Arethusa*. The ship, in which I was the guest of Admiral Wells and Captain (then) Philip Vian, was lying in a tranquil bay off one of the Greek Islands. On a Sunday evening the ship's band gave a concert and I was invited by the Bandmaster to conduct a selection of *Bitter Sweet*. After a moment of panic I agreed and managed to get through it all right, principally because the bandsmen knew it by heart and were wise enough to pay scant attention to me. Naval good manners, as usual, saved the occasion and I received a tumultuous but ill-merited ovation. The setting was perfect to begin with. There was a full moon and a sky blazing with stars. The quarterdeck was illuminated by festoons of little coloured lights, and the sea, flat calm and almost motionless, glimmered with streaks of phosphorous. The officers sat in a wide semi-circle with the rest of the ship's company behind them, some clinging to the rigging and all in their tropical 'whites', which seemed to gleam in the darkness. That evening remains in my mind as one of the most visually romantic memories of my life.

12

The end of the three-weeks' try-out of *Words and Music* in Manchester coincided with the return of my brother Eric from Ceylon, where he had been a tea planter on the hills of Naralia. A year or two previously Jeffery and I had visited him on his plantation, and he had, with inordinate pride, taken us over every acre of it. I think my relationship with Eric requires a little explanation, principally because he played such a small part in my life that many people would have been surprised to know that I had a brother at all. He was five years my junior, having been born in Sutton, Surrey, in 1905. I was reasonably fond of him but I cannot honestly say that we were ever very close until perhaps the last sad months of his life. Perhaps this five year difference in our ages was either too long or too short. At all events I have to admit, a trifle guiltily perhaps, that I never found him very interesting. It is possible that I might have been subconsciously jealous of him and resented his intrusion into the cosseted 'only son' pattern of my life, but in fairness to myself I don't think that this was so. I tolerated him, was occasionally irritated by him and, engrossed as I was by my crowded and exciting career as a boy actor, paid very little attention to him. He was there, an accepted member of my immediate family circle, but no real intimacy between us was ever established.

When in the autumn of 1932 he was sent home to England on

sick leave my first sight of him was a profound shock. He seemed to have shrunk to half his normal size, his face was gaunt and drawn and it was obvious that he was very seriously ill. I immediately appealed to that remarkable woman Almina Carnarvon, whose well-known efficiency was only equalled by her kindness, and he was installed in her nursing home in Portland Place the very next day. After Lord Moynihan had made a thorough examination he sent for me and told me that Eric was suffering from a lethal form of cancer and could not be expected to live more than six months. Realising that Eric was anxiously waiting for a medical verdict and that he was also desperately frightened I asked Almina to think up quickly some ultimately curable disease that I could convince him he was suffering from, something preferably that he could verify in a medical dictionary if he had a mind to. After some thought and hurried research we decided on 'Hyperplasia of the Abdominal Glands' and armed with this dubious but necessary fabrication I returned, with a sinking heart, to his room. He accepted my explanation suspiciously at first but after a while I managed to convince him. I told him, truly enough, that there was no necessity for him to stay in the nursing home longer than a few more days and that I would arrange for him to go down to Goldenhurst, my home in Kent, where he could slowly convalesce with a nurse. I also, in a moment of inspiration, told him that he could repay me by making an accurate and detailed index of all my gramophone records. He perked up considerably at this and I left him and drove back to Gerald Road for a couple of hours' rest before attacking my next miserable assignment which was the breaking of the news to my father and mother. This ghastly interview, organised with consummate tact and sympathy by Lady Carnarvon, took place in her private sitting-room in the nursing home at four-thirty on the same afternoon. I do not wish to enlarge on it because even after so many years I find the memory of it intolerable.

13

Lynn, Alfred and I opened in *Design For Living* on January 2nd at the Hanna Theatre in Cleveland, after which we played Pittsburgh and Washington. On January 22nd, two days before we were due to open at the Ethel Barrymore Theatre in New York I received a cable from mother saying that Eric had died peacefully in his sleep at Goldenhurst. I immediately telephoned her and arranged for her and Aunt Vida to come out to New York, and ten days later they arrived. I was living in a rented apartment, 1 Beekman Place, and I managed to get reservations for them in the Beekman Tower which was just around the corner from me. Although *Design For Living* was a smash hit, which was of course immensely comforting from the professional point of view, achieving, as it did, an ambition which we had all three cherished for years, it was an unhappy and difficult period of my private life. Alfred and Lynn, I need hardly say, were marvellous to me and continued, with loving shrewdness, to be consoling and sympathetic, without overdoing it. I remember Alfred coming into my flat one morning and saying, with rather obviously simulated anger, 'Noëlie – you've been crying again!' A few days after Mother arrived, the strain of the whole dismal business went to my throat and I lost my voice on a Saturday morning. I telephoned to the Lunts and huskily explained that I couldn't possibly play the matinée. Alfred was round in a flash. 'You've *got* to play,' he said. 'If you don't we shall close the theatre.' This seemed to me to be over-dramatic, as I had a competent understudy engaged on his special recommendation. I argued vainly that if I could stay off just for that day, I could rest through Sunday and be perfectly all right by Monday but he would have none of it. 'Neither Lynnie nor I would dream of playing a single performance of this play without you,' he said, 'and that's final.' He then added, more gently, that if I would only make the effort and appear he would say as many of my lines as he could. Irritated by his stubbornness, I gave in and dragged myself to the theatre, feeling really dreadful and unable to make a sound. When I came on, shaking, for my first entrance Alfred confronted me with a blank stare and dried up dead. This so enraged me that I prompted him in a stentorian voice that Chaliapin would have envied and played through both performances without so much as a croak. All of which goes to prove that the Theatre is a remarkable profession, and Mrs Baker Eddy definitely had a point when she opined that Actors are very curious animals.

In the nineteen twenties, when I had played *The Vortex* in England and America for two years and finished up with a nervous breakdown, I made a decision that I have never regretted. The decision was that I would never henceforth play a play, however successful it might be, for more than three months. This was not quite so arrogant as it appears. If I were simply an actor, I would be grateful for the opportunity of playing a long run, but I am primarily a writer and I have found from experience that it is too much of a strain to be creative while playing eight performances a week. Acting a long part night after night requires maximum vitality and there is none left over for any other kind of work. It can be done of course in an emergency but as a steady routine it is impossible. Because of the special circumstances of *Design For Living* and Alfred and Lynn, I gladly broke my rule to the extent of two extra months. I rented a little cottage in the woods at Sneden's Landing on the banks of the Hudson. It was remote, utterly peaceful and only a thirty-five minutes' drive from the stage door. I had always loved Sneden's and had stayed there on and off for years with Kit Cornell and Guthrie McClintic. My cottage was small and primitive but well heated, the view through the trees to the river was enchanting and I was looked after by a round coloured servant called Henry who, in earlier days of glory, had played a Eunuch in *Aida*. His voice was, understandably, very high indeed and he fussed over me, cooked for me, cosseted me and, only very occasionally, sang.

My mother and aunt returned to England in May, and at the beginning of June we closed *Design for Living* in a blaze of triumph; in fact so great were the crowds during the last week that extra police had to be called to control them. During the run of the play a kidnapping scare swept America, touched off by the unspeakably horrible abduction and murder of the Lindbergh

Baby. There were other abductions and hold-ups as well and, having received several threatening anonymous letters, I engaged, on the advice of my local Chief of Police, a private detective called Tommy Webber, who accompanied me back and forth between Sneden's and New York and sat at the side of the stage nightly bulging with armaments. He was a delightful character and shadowed me faithfully right up to the moment when I stepped on board the ship for Bermuda. He was present in fact at the farewell cocktail party I gave in my cabin and poked me cheerfully in the ribs with a gun before vanishing down the gangway.

14

The vessel that took me to Bermuda was a cruise-ship crammed to the gunwales with Mid-Western tourists who throughout three whole days and nights drank themselves silly, although I suspect the majority of them were fairly silly to start with, and made such a hideous noise that I was forced to spend most of the time locked in my stateroom. The locking of the door was a necessary precaution because it was frequently banged on in the middle of the night by groups of drunken ladies wearing paper caps. I think those dreadful three days were responsible for my later satirical musical *Sail Away*. In course of my extensive wandering across the world I have formed a strong aversion to tourists *en masse*. I am aware that this attitude could be criticised as being selfish and perhaps snobbish. I know that, ideally speaking, it is a 'good' thing that people who have never before set foot outside their own back yards should be able to enjoy the wonders of the world and I chide myself with fanciful visions of sad little old ladies receiving unexpected legacies and gallantly spending them on adventurous travel. Unfortunately however very few of the old ladies I have encountered on cruise ships have been either sad or little. On the contrary, most of them have been aggressive, full-bosomed, strident and altogether intolerable. My fellow passengers on board the ship to Bermuda were no exception. They drank and shrieked and made such noisy vulgar beasts of themselves that if I hadn't had the forethought to provide myself with earplugs I should either have run amok and kicked them in the teeth or thrown myself overboard.

I have always detested crowds. The very idea of a vast number of human beings herded together fills me with dismay, except of course when I happen to be separated from them by a row of footlights. This personal antipathy to crowds has prevented me from enjoying all street processions and public parades of any sort. Even in England where the tradition of pageantry is more decorously organised than anywhere else in the world I shut myself indoors or flee to the country rather than become involved. Nowadays of course since the invention of television the problem for me has ceased to exist. If any famous personage is being hailed or crowned or buried I can sit cosily at home and watch the proceedings without being either pushed or buffeted or frozen or suffocated. In the United States unfortunately the mania for public parades has reached almost lunatic proportions, what with the Shriners, the Rotarians, the Kiwanis and countless other esoteric organisations, not to mention the Irish, whose frenetic celebration of St Patrick's Day annually reduces the city of New York to chaos. The ordinary citizen whose principal concern is to get on with his job and earn his living is reduced to a state of gibbering frustration. Many a time when I have been driving from my apartment on the East Side to play a matinée on Broadway I have had to hop out of the taxi and fight my way on foot across town, arriving at the theatre breathless a few minutes before curtain time looking and feeling as if I had been involved in a lynching, and all because a number of frisky old gentlemen wish to make figures of fun of themselves by staggering along Fifth Avenue in funny hats. I am sure that this irritable outburst will bring down on my head an avalanche of furious letters saying 'Who do you think you are?' and 'Go home Limey', in which case I will merely stick them into my 'N. C. Abuse Scrapbook', which is growing ominously thicker as the years roll by, and read them over on long winter evenings with a comfortable retrospective snarl.

The object of my voyage to Bermuda was to join a British light cruiser, H.M.S. *Dragon*, in which I had been invited to make a cruise of the Caribbean. My host on this occasion was the Ship's 'Number One' Lieutenant John Temple. My other hosts were Admiral Wells, whose flagship it was, Captain Philip Vian and the ship itself. Philip, or to me 'Joe', Vian was tall with piercing blue eyes and extremely aggressive eyebrows. Soon after World War Two broke out six years later, he achieved fame (which he detested) as the Hero of the *Altmark*. It was he in fact who spoke the now legendary phrase, 'The Navy's Here'. Having delivered this warning statement he proceeded first to rescue a number of British sailors who were imprisoned below decks, and then blow the hell out of the *Altmark*. On my first introduction to him on the quarterdeck he wagged his eyebrows ferociously and said 'What the hell are you doing on board this ship?' I replied cringingly that I was exhausted, over-worked and on the verge of a nervous breakdown and had joined the ship in order to be nursed back to health and strength and waited on hand and foot. Whereupon he gave me some gin in his cabin and sent me back, a trifle unsteadily, to the ward-room. Since that day I have been his guest in many different ships from Scapa Flow to the China Seas, and at the risk of infuriating him by my theatrical sentimentality I must flatly admit that I am very fond of him indeed.

That particular cruise in H.M.S. *Dragon*, of all my cheerful gallivantings with the Royal Navy, was one of the happiest. I actually was fairly exhausted after the run of *Design For Living* and to be at sea again, with nothing to do but lie about and enjoy myself in the best possible company, was the most reviving tonic I could have wished for. I insisted at the outset on being made an honorary member of the Ward-room, which meant that I could sign for loads of drinks myself instead of monotonously letting others do it. Naval hospitality being what it is I had to fight tooth and claw for this privilege but I won the battle and was able to relax.

I was supposed to leave the ship at Colon, but I dumped my luggage overboard on to a motor launch and sailed in her through the Canal. Unfortunately no-one had informed me that she was heading straight out into the Pacific without stopping at Panama, and I finally had to clamber down a rope ladder onto the pilot boat. It was a perilous exit because as I got to the end of the ladder the pilot boat, unheeding, hooted and turned to go back to shore. Frantic signals were made to the Captain while I dangled over the waves to the delight of the ship's company which was lining the rails. They were still more delighted when the boat finally came back and I flung myself onto the deck in a heap. They cheered vociferously and my heart was heavy as I watched the water widening between us.

After a few days of sitting about in the shady garden of the hotel in Colon watching the ships slide in and out of the Canal and feeling a little flat after my naval engagements, I sailed in the *Colombie* for Trinidad. The *Colombie* was one of the latest Messageries Maritime ships, and the local representative of the line who accompanied me on board and lavished on me the full V.I.P. treatment was as volubly proud of her as if he had laid her keel with his own chubby hands. He insisted on showing me over every inch of the ship including the engine-rooms after which we retired to the Captain's Cabin and had sweet champagne and chocolate biscuits. The three days' voyage was pleasant and uneventful and I passed most of it undisturbed in my cabin reading and sleeping. On the very early morning of the third day the mountains of Trinidad appeared on the horizon, and as we drew nearer to shore over a pale mauve motionless sea they seemed to change their positions as though they were gracefully moving themselves into the correct formations for greeting us. They also, as the sun climbed higher in the sky, began to glow with brilliant colour; every conceivable variety of green picked out with splashes of scarlet and pink and mauve when the Flamboyants, Flame-in-the-Forest and Jacarandas caught the early light. I have never, in all my travels, lost the thrill of arriving at a foreign port. From the moment that land is first sighted until the ship ties up alongside the dock I am aware of an inner excitement, a sense of new adventure. Even the long-familiar sight of the New York sky scrapers rising out of the morning mist enchants me as much to-day as on that summer morning in 1921 when I first saw it.

Of course there have been setbacks; my habitual delight at arriving at strange places has invariably been dampened from time to time: Shanghai in a thick wet fog; Liverpool in a driving blizzard; and the forbidding approach to San Pedro, Los Angeles with its forest of oil derricks and cranes depresses my spirit either in rain or shine. Now that I come to think of it our own dear Newcastle-upon-Tyne, even on a radiant summer day, is hardly likely to quicken the pulses of the most romantic-minded traveller. The glamour-seeker however must be prepared to take the rough with the smooth, and if, like me, he happens to be a genuine addict, the very fact of arrival provides enough of it.

Just off the coast of Trinidad there is a small island called Point Baleine. Having heard it enthusiastically described by various Trinidadians, I decided to have a look at it, so I hired a motor launch and on a cloudless shining morning set out over a flat sea accompanied for most of the way by a Homeric escort of dolphins, who plunged and curvetted round the bows occasionally flinging themselves bodily out of the water, as though unable to control their exuberant joy of living. I hope and believe that dolphins have as good a time as they appear to. To me they are the most beguiling and enchanting creatures, and I am ready to swear that this group that accompanied me to Point Baleine were in continual fits of laughter. It has been explained to me that all that uninhibited diving and leaping merely means that they are hungry and in grim pursuit of flying fish and other prey that saunter near the surface. I prefer however to hold on to the illusion that their laughter is genuine and that if only they were able to speak they would prove to be the gayest and wittiest company in the world.

The hotel on Point Baleine was owned and run by an ex-sailor and his wife to both of whom I took an immediate liking. The hotel was primitive according to Hilton standards but perfectly comfortable. It was, as far as I can remember a two-storied wooden building surrounded by a few single-room bungalows, one of which I inhabited. The food, mostly fish, was well-cooked and abundant and the whole atmosphere of the place enchanted me. Meals were eaten in the main house but my breakfast was brought to my private verandah, the mainland was only a very short way away and a little motor launch chugged back and forth several times a day. In later years I tried, not entirely successfully, to reconstruct the atmosphere of the place in my play, *Point Valaine*. It was a peaceful and lovely spot and only at weekends, when groups of visitors came over from the mainland, was its charm temporarily diminished.

From Trinidad I sailed back to England in another Messageries Maritime ship, the *Flandre*. It lacked the spit and polish of the *Colombie* but the food, as usual in French ships, was excellent and the passengers unobtrusive. The *Flandre* was far from being a Blue Ribbon record breaker but she had the same kind of peculiar, for me, nostalgic charm of a fat comfortable old concierge who sits day after day in a stuffy ground floor room with a bell on the door. I had a feeling that if I dived over the side I should find, instead of a keel, a pair of thick black stockings and faded red bedroom slippers. She chugged unhurriedly across the Atlantic, no capricious storms impeded her dogged progress and her bow wave was practically non-existent. Other ships of all shapes and kinds, including a fishing boat under sail, overtook and passed her effortlessly. In some of these the crews lined the decks and encouragingly cheered her on.

By the time she had arrived complacently in Plymouth Sound I had completed the libretto of *Conversation Piece*. The idea of it had come to me when we were two days out of New York and I had happened to read a delightful book by Dormer Creston called *The Regent and His Daughter*. Up until then the Regency as a period had never attracted me. The dramatic appeal of the late eighteenth century and the gas-lit glamour of the latter decades of the nineteenth had established prior claims on my imagination. In spite of Jane Austen, whose sly wit I am sure would have been equally enchanting in any period from the Ancient Britons to the present day, the years from the end of the French Revolution until the crinolines and chandeliers of the Second Empire, were for me undiscovered territory. Napoleon to me seemed to be the antithesis of glamour. His short legs and strutting didactism aroused in me no ardour. In later years I need hardly say I have revised this superficial opinion, but I still feel that a few extra inches would have enhanced his legend considerably. I remember when I was a child a very short verger in St Alban's Church Teddington for some reason or other roused my father's ire. He disposed of him in one terse phrase. 'His brains are too near his bottom.' It must not be imagined, being five feet eleven and a half inches tall myself, that I automatically deprecate those of lesser stature, indeed several of my most delightful friends barely reach my ear-lobes, but world-conquering demagogues and leaders of men should be, ideally speaking, taller than their fellow men. Alas, they seldom are. Few of the world's heroes have exceeded five feet eleven.

INDEX